77341330   2√

7/81

Toward a New
Strategy for Development

Pergamon Titles of Related Interest

Toward a New
Strategy for Development

A Rothko Chapel Colloquium

Contributors

Albert O. Hirschman
Dudley Seers
Paul Streeten
Fernando H. Cardoso
Bagicha S. Minhas
Harold Brookfield

Goran Ohlin
Bill Warren
Nurul Islam
Fawzy Mansour
Richard N. Cooper
Reginald H. Green

Pergamon Press
NEW YORK • OXFORD • TORONTO • SYDNEY • FRANKFURT • PARIS

Pergamon Press Offices:

U.S.A.   Pergamon Press Inc., Maxwell House, Fairview Park, Elmsford, New York 10523, U.S.A.

U.K.   Pergamon Press Ltd., Headington Hill Hall, Oxford OX3 0BW, England

CANADA   Pergamon of Canada, Ltd., 150 Consumers Road, Willowdale, Ontario M2J, 1P9, Canada

AUSTRALIA   Pergamon Press (Aust) Pty. Ltd., P O Box 544, Potts Point, NSW 2011, Australia

FRANCE   Pergamon Press SARL, 24 rue des Ecoles, 75240 Paris, Cedex 05, France

FEDERAL REPUBLIC OF GERMANY   Pergamon Press GmbH, 6242 Kronberg/Taunus, Pferdstrasse 1, Federal Republic of Germany

Copyright © 1979 Rothko Chapel

Library of Congress Cataloging in Publication Data

Main entry under title:

Toward a new strategy for development.

"Papers commissioned by the Rothko Chapel and presented at a colloquium held in Houston, Texas on February 3-5, 1977."
   Includes index.
   1. Underdeveloped areas–Congresses. 2. Economic development–Congresses. I. Rothko Chapel.
II. Hirschman, Albert O.
HC59.7.T7383 1979   330.9'172'4   79-9861
ISBN 0-08-023913-7
ISBN 0-08-023912-9 pbk.

Cover illustration: Ink drawing of olive tree by Le Chénier, 1975.

Printed in the United States of America

Toward a New Strategy for Development

A set of papers commissioned by the Rothko Chapel
and presented at a Colloquium held in Houston,
Texas, on February 3-5, 1977.

Members of the Colloquium Advisory Committee
Albert Hirschman
Dudley Seers
Samir Amin
Stephen Graubard
Herbert Holloman

Coordinator of Colloquium
James W. Land

Editor of the papers for the Rothko Chapel
Kim Q. Hill

To Dom Hélder Câmara

CONTENTS

ACKNOWLEDGMENTS

Our greatest debt is to the authors, all of whom interrupted busy schedules to make time for the preparation of these papers and to attend the Houston discussions. Moreover, each of them graciously cooperated in making the necessary reductions in the lengths of the papers to meet the space limitations for this publication.

We are greatly indebted as well to the members of the Advisory Committee, who had several formal meetings during the planning stages and who participated most valuably in the meeting itself. The three economist members of the Advisory Committee are: Samir Amin, now Director of the African Institute for Economic Planning and Development, Dakar, Senegal; Albert O. Hirschman, presently at the School of Social Sciences of the Institute for Advanced Study, Princeton, New Jersey; and Dudley Seers, a principal founder of the Institute of Development Studies at the University of Sussex, England. The two remaining members are from other fields: Herbert Holloman, originally educated as a metallurgist, is now Director of the Center for Policy Alternatives at Massachusetts Institute of Technology, and Stephen Graubard, a historian, is the editor of *Daedalus* magazine.

There are a number of people who contributed information, suggestions and advice. These include the late Roberto Rossellini, Leo Alting von Gesau, Fr. Cosmao, Anne de Lattre de Tassigny, George de Menil and Jerome Wiesner. Guillermo O'Donnell and Andreas Bianchi, international economists—then at Woodrow Wilson School of Foreign Affairs—participated also in formulating ideas at the first meeting of the Advisory Committee. The efforts of Claude Gruson, Louis P. Blanc, G. Ancian, and Charles Prou, all French economists who commented on ideas and sharpened the focus at an early stage of the planning, are acknowledged here. Ignacy Sachs, an international economist who proved most helpful in recommending and providing introductions to some of the best minds in the developing countries, is particularly thanked. Nor can we forget sociologist Peter Berger, whose participation in the colloquium brought to it his special and valuable perspective.

Colloquium III was jointly sponsored by the Rothko Chapel and the Program of Development Studies at Rice University, an interdisciplinary research institute looking into problems of developing countries. Particularly helpful have been its director, Ronald Soligo, who contributed his time generously at every stage; Gaston Rimlinger, Chairman of the Department of Economics; Don Huddle, an economist with extensive experience in Latin America; and Fred von der Mehden, Chairman of the Department of Political Science.

The Rothko Chapel board is particularly grateful to James W. Land, founder and former director of the Program of Development Studies at Rice University. He accepted the responsibility of planning and organizing the colloquium and had the difficult task of selecting and approaching the participants. Not only his persistence but the genuineness of his intentions, we believe, persuaded many of them to join this undertaking.

The board is also grateful to Kim Q. Hill, Professor of Public Affairs at the University of Houston at Clear Lake City, for his expert and informed editing of the papers.

The Board of the Rothko Chapel

PREFACE

The ten invited papers comprising this volume were first presented in outline at the Rothko Chapel, Houston, in February 1977. Unlike previous Rothko Chapel colloquia, this, the third, was held privately in a quiet setting in which the authors might freely consult with the Advisory Committee and among themselves.

The subject of the colloquium, "Toward a New Strategy for Development," had been chosen two and a half years earlier, when plans were first formulated. Actually its roots go back even further—to the second Rothko Chapel colloquium in December, 1973, which marked the twenty-fifth anniversary of the United Nations Universal Declaration of Human Rights. Colloquium II, inspired by Dom Hélder Câmara, voiced aspirations and articulated programs intended to deal with the growing gap in a great part of the world between the rich and the poor, political polarization and repression of human rights, and the failure to attain genuinely adaptive modes of social behavior. It was hoped that Colloquium III would begin where Colloquium II had ended, that it would deal more concretely with the issues of human freedom, economic and social development, and cultural values.

The ten papers were each a response to one of the five questions chosen by the Advisory Committee, each question having been addressed to two of the writers. In some cases, a question is addressed both to an author whose views are representative of developed countries and to another representative of developing countries. In other cases the authors are specialists in different fields, for example economics and sociology. The intention of such a plan was to focus on the intense debate over needs and programs from the standpoints of the developed countries at the center of the world's economic system and of the developing countries at its periphery, and from the standpoint of different disciplines.

James W. Land

FOREWORD

"Mankind always takes up only such problems as it can solve." This confident assertion was made by Karl Marx in his famous thumbnail sketch of historical materialism. A full generation has now elapsed since "mankind" took up the problem of development of the less developed countries; but its "solution," in any meaningful sense of that term, still eludes us, as basic human needs remain unfulfilled for large masses of people in the Third World and while elementary human rights are often disregarded or totally suppressed. Is Marx proven wrong then? It is difficult to say; for, like all successful prophets, he was prudent. He did not tell us how much time must reasonably be allowed for the solution to be found, and for the truth of his statement to be thus tested.

Without referring to his eminent predecessor, Anthony Downs has recently grappled with the manner in which problems are taken up and disposed of by society. The proposition he has come up with is considerably less optimistic than that of Marx; it is also more detailed and therefore more falsifiable. Restricting his generalization to one country, the United States, Downs asserted that here problems pass through an "attention cycle" consisting of the following five stages:

1. The "preproblem stage" during which the problem exists all right, but not much public attention is paid to it.
2. Then comes "alarmed discovery and euphoric enthusiasm." The problem is considered a priori fully solvable "if only we devote sufficient effort to it."

3. In the next phase, it is realized that solving the problem may be costly and goes against the immediate interests of large and influential groups of people.

4. As a result of this realization, there is then a gradual decline of intense public interest, which is helped by the providential appearance of another problem that will move into the limelight.

5. Finally, there is the "postproblem stage" which differs from the preproblem stage in that a number of agencies that have been set up to "solve" the problem in stage 2 continue to exist and may actually make some quiet progress. Also, once the problem has passed through the cycle it will continue to receive a modicum of public attention.*

No doubt the Downs sequence does capture something about the changing attention to the development problem over the past 30 years. The early excitement over it and the great doctrinal debates over alternative solutions or strategies have considerably abated; and both work on the problem and thought about it have become more subdued, diffident, perhaps lackluster, yet also more steady. Nevertheless, Downs' proposition misses an essential aspect of the particular problem with which we are concerned. To a considerable extent his cycle is premised on the technocratic assumption that it is up to the policy makers to take up a problem that has long been neglected, that they will focus on it, perhaps after a certain amount of public clamor, but that they are also quite free to reneglect it if a solution cannot be found speedily or is judged to be too costly. This is surely not so in the case of the less developed countries, for these particular problem victims have now been roused to insist that attention be paid to their plight on a continuing basis. Here lies the significance of the North-South debate. Even though some of the northern countries which were at one point so "excited" about the possibility of solving the problem of underdevelopment may by now be in a very different nonactivist mood, concern over the problem and activist grappling with it depend no longer on their *bon plaisir*.

Returning to the time of the original "excitement" over the problem of economic development, that is, to the first decade after World War II: it has often been remarked how unfortunate it was that the problem was taken up in the wake of the successful effort at postwar reconstruc-

---

*"Up and Down with Ecology—the 'Issue-Attention Cycle'," *The Public Interest*, no. 28 (Summer 1972), pp. 38-50.

tion in western Europe. The remarkable ease and speed with which that task was mastered, with the help of foreign aid and of some economic planning and cooperation in Europe, engendered wholly unfounded optimism with respect to the much more complex and necessarily far more protracted task of economic development in Latin America, Asia and Africa. Many of the later disappointments, with their often serious social and political consequences, can be traced, so it is said, to this early optimism.

Without denying the validity of this argument I would like to look at another aspect of the situation. True, the success of the Marshall Plan deceived economists, policy makers and enlightened opinion in the West into believing that the problem of underdevelopment was roughly of the same nature as that of postwar reconstruction, that an infusion of capital helped along by the right kind of investment planning would grind out growth and welfare all over the globe. In other words, the West took up the problem of underdevelopment not because it *could* solve it (à la Marx) but because it was tricked into the *mistaken belief* that it could solve it. But was that not perhaps a good thing? Had the size and toughness of the problem been correctly visualized from the outset, the considerable intellectual and political mobilization around it would most likely not have occurred and we would be even farther away from an acceptable world. As a result of the intensive wrestling with the problem over the past 30 years, we can look back on a series of experiences, some successful, others failures, and many where success and failure are oddly intertwined.

Several essays in this book undertake to appraise these matters. And indeed one of the advantages of writing at this comparatively late and therefore "unexciting" stage of the development effort is the ability to look back and to learn from past mistakes, of which there have been many. Nevertheless, there are pitfalls here also. As is well known, it is only too easy to learn the wrong lesson from history. In the case of development, wrongheaded learning of this sort is already in evidence and takes typically the following form. A particular kind and phase of development—say, an industrialization in which the production of consumer durables plays an important role—occurred in country A. This form of industrial push coincided more or less (1) with the establishment of an authoritarian regime, and (2) with some movement toward a more unequal income distribution. A connection is then established between that sort of industrialization and the two other, clearly undesirable phenomena, and before long that connection is viewed as a necessary and inevitable causal chain. Take now country B which finds itself at a less advanced stage of development than A and which considers its own development strategy: it will surely be apprised of the dire results that are *bound* to follow if it were to promote a consumer-durables industry even though that industry may have some excellent market prospects and would be the source of considerable employment. "Learning from experience" would thus result in obstructing a perfectly feasible path because of its allegedly inevitable unfortunate consequences and side effects. Actually, of course, those consequences and side effects are not nearly as certain as they are made out to be; for even though there may have been a connection in the original case, there need not be a repetition under different and, moreover, *forewarned* circumstances.

There is a real danger then that scrutiny of past development experiences will turn up all manner of "roads not to be taken" and will constrict and paralyze policy makers anxious to learn from other countries' mistakes. There once was a flourishing literature on the institutional and cultural obstacles to development. As evidence accumulated that what is an obstacle in one country is often a stimulus to development in another, writing on this theme has fortunately gone into eclipse. It is much to be hoped that the lessons from past development experiences will not be allowed to turn into a new and tougher generation of obstacles.

Albert O. Hirschman
New Delhi, India
March 1978

Introduction

THE CONGRUENCE OF MARXISM AND OTHER NEOCLASSICAL DOCTRINES[1]

Dudley Seers

Half a century ago, a famous collection of ideological statements, "The Modern Symposium" edited by Lowes Dickinson,[2] covered the views of British intellectuals over a wide political range, from an anarchist on the extreme Left to a high Tory on the extreme Right. In 1977, a number of social scientists, also of widely differing viewpoints, came together at Houston to discuss the central issues of *our* time, now those of the world as a whole, not just of an advanced industrial society. Moreover—and this is the point on which I want to focus—the old "Left-Right" spectrum no longer seemed adequate to classify the views which were expressed.

One of the participants was Bill Warren, who revised his chapter for this volume shortly before he died. This death was a great loss, not merely because of Warren's personality and intelligence, but because he was a very unusual Marxist, one who found postwar trends in the capitalist world on the whole satisfactory, and thus forced others to consider more carefully their own positions.

Warren reminded us—as practitioners of the "dismal science" sometimes need to be reminded—that widespread acceleration since the war
in the growth of per capita incomes was unprecedented and had benefited the great majority of the world's population.[3] Warren saw many
of the Third World nations, such as Brazil (a favorite example of his),
going through a youthful, progressive phase of capitalism, much as
Western Europe had in the nineteenth century. Marx himself of course
had recognized that capitalism could play a constructive role in breaking down the remnants of feudalism—indeed the well-known eulogy of
capitalism in the *Communist Manifesto* itself might seem more appropriate to the pages of *Fortune*.

Warren built on this particular strand in Marx's work and we are
much in his debt for working out the implications of perceiving world
capitalism as still having considerable vigor and expectation of life.
Its dynamism should not, he held, be impeded by egalitarian policies
("liberal-populist"), such as high direct taxes or insistence on labor-
intensive technology. These appeared to be benevolent, but were in
reality objectively reactionary and even likely to aggravate poverty.
The way to relieve poverty in the Third World was quite different, to
incorporate into the world capitalist system as fully as possible and let
capitalist development have its head.

His conclusions are breathtaking in their didactic, apparently perverse, logic—e.g., "the pursuit of income equality per se is both unjust
and undemocratic." At places, his arguments might be considered
tendentious,[4] and some would probe more deeply than he does the
factual basis of many of his generalizations. But the point I want to
stress is that on policy he is in complete agreement with writers such as
Peter Bauer, whom in fact he quotes with approval in a number of
places. Bauer is normally put in a very different category—the neoclassical or (in its purest form) Chicago School.

The similarity shows up in this book. There are two basically neoclassical authors, Ohlin and Cooper. They too do not view the postwar
record as basically negative: Ohlin echoes Warren's stress on progress.
The defects, in their view also, have been primarily due to failings within the developing countries—e.g., fast population growth and excessive
armaments, familiar targets of neoclassicals. Cooper questions the moral
basis of any claim to be compensated for past injustice. "That economic poverty exists, directly or indirectly, because of past colonial rule is
highly doubtful."[5] Warren goes further and opposes international aid
and the cancellation of debts of poor countries.

If one picked a page at random from Warren's paper, one could not be sure at first glance whether it had been written by Cooper and vice versa.

BASIC ELEMENTS COMMON TO MARXISM AND THE CHICAGO SCHOOL

Very few other Marxists share Bill Warren's assumption about the life expectancy of the capitalist era. Still, in other respects, much of his work falls squarely within the Marxist canon, as he claims. It raised for me, therefore, a fundamental question: Can the difference between Marxists and members of the Chicago School be as immense as is generally supposed?[6]

When one thinks about it, they each take perfect competition as a working hypothesis (the Marxist "law of value"), imperfections being considered not severe enough to deprive prices of meaning,[7] or of their functions in organizing the economy on a national or world scale and stimulating change. More basically, human beings are assumed to be driven—at least in their capacities as producers and consumers—by only economic motives. Consequently, material incentives are assumed to be the only ones that matter. Important economic areas where other influences are important, such as the distribution of income and organization of work within the household, have been almost completely ignored.

Indeed, Marxists and neoclassical liberals share many more articles of faith. They are both profoundly optimistic. History is seen essentially as a record of progress. Progress has occurred, is still taking place, and will moreover continue in the future: Warren was particularly insistent on this. The "invisible hand" in Adam Smith's graphic metaphor is, on the whole and in the long run, benevolent. Somewhere in the future, justifying sacrifices by the present generation (and many political crimes), lies a utopia, an integrated world of prosperity and peace (capitalist or socialist as the case may be) to be achieved if not in the next generation, then two or three later. They differ profoundly about the mechanisms by which it will be achieved but not about its likelihood or even in outlining its material conditions. (The visions of Herman Kahn and those of the Soviet futurologists are essentially identical.)

Though it seems provocative to say so, and always annoys both parties considerably, Marxism can be described as a neoclassical doctrine with precise accuracy.[8] There is no dispute that, like the Chicago School, its origins can be found in the work of Adam Smith and Ricardo, early in the industrial revolution. After the mainstream of classical thought split into two subsidiaries, they both continued to be developed in the same buoyant atmosphere of the nineteenth century, a time when the possibilities opened up by industrialization still seemed limitless.

Place was also important. Both these derivative schools, like their ancestors, were developed in Western Europe, more specifically Britain. Marx's *Das Capital* drew nearly all its illustrative material from this part of the world. While less was known then of the history of other continents, sources on them *were* available (e.g., Spanish documents on Latin America, already being used by Prescott), certainly enough for the colonial systems to be analyzed more exhaustively and more critically,[9] and for the embarrassing concept of the "Asiatic mode of production" to be avoided.

The temporal and geographical matrices of both neoclassical schools explain a further common element typical of nineteenth century Europe—"economism"; that is, progress is seen as essentially material, the necessary and, in the end, sufficient condition for advance on the political, social and cultural fronts (the "superstructure").[10]

They also explain the attitude of this type of economist toward science. An uncritical faith in scientists was another characteristic of Europe in the nineteenth century. The latest technology is still considered by most neoclassical economists as prima facie desirable (even if it has been devised for a completely different socioeconomic environment). Oil and other natural resources are tacitly assumed adequate to sustain any rate and pattern of economic growth, with scientists inventing gadgets to relieve scarcities as they arise. Even environmental constraints are only being studied belatedly and as a professional sideline (Pigou's suggestive treatment of this area not being followed up up at all comprehensively for nearly half a century), and the same could be said about the appropriateness of capital-intensive techniques of production.

There is another aspect to neoclassical technophilia, also rooted in the nineteenth century. Neoclassical economists like to consider *themselves* "scientific," able to emulate in their own field the accelerating progress in the physical sciences that was made possible by the work of Galton, Maxwell, etc. Such an approach has stimulated the systematic elaboration of models which reduce complex social phenomena to simple causal relationships, linking a few variables in a priori models, for which confirmatory material is then obtained. But this is "scientific" in a highly restricted sense, closer to the metaphysical sciences of the Middle Ages.[11] The resulting propositions are inherently difficult to verify or refute, and since they are often about matters of great social importance, carrying major policy implications, it is not surprising if neoclassical economists tend to show much greater dogmatism and emotional involvement than is customary even among real scientists. More modern scientific traditions would have suggested the patient collection of comparable material for the observation of the static and dynamic patterns of large numbers of economies over long periods, and their classification, before great theories were built. (A few economists such as Simon Kuznets and Colin Clark have in fact tried to do just this.)

Naturally, all neoclassical economists vehemently deny the specificity of their doctrines. It is characteristic, one must admit, of European social theorists[12] to believe that generalizations derived from their local experience in a particular period can have worldwide and permanent application.[13] (Unfortunately, because of the prestige of the European academic, those in other continents often accept this.) Even today, neoclassical textbooks of all kinds illustrate with purely local material what are put forward without qualification as general propositions.

Anyone who draws attention to some feature of neoclassical economics such as its "economism," must expect to be charged with oversimplification. As in a fairground shooting gallery, the target disappears from view as soon as it is hit. In Marxist company, what one is criticizing turns out to be "vulgar" Marxism, not the true faith. Indeed, since the war, the publication of early manuscripts of Marx has provided further evidence for believing that he was himself not always "economistic." Still, this is not an unfair characterization of the body of Marxist literature as a whole, especially the textbooks (e.g., *Political Economy*, published in the Soviet Union). Other types of neoclassical economists might well argue that *they* are not "economistic" either; they are only talking about economic phenomena, not about the social or political aspects, which might or might not be dominant. But, especially when they draw policy conclusions, they are mostly by implication "economistic" too, since they do not state, let alone assess, their political and social assumptions.

On the other hand, several economists (not merely Marxists), especially some Keynesians, would resent being called "neoclassical."

One cannot, however, necessarily accept the opinion of the objects of any classification on whether a class is being correctly described and whether they belong to it. A whale might well object to a zoological classification that puts him in the same broad category ("mammal") as a guinea pig. Although it is difficult for non-Christians to understand, many Catholics and many Protestants insist they belong to quite different faiths. (Not merely Buddhists, indeed, have difficulty in understanding the troubles in Northern Ireland.)

The criterion is surely one of utility. Is it not useful to look at the common origins of different dogmas within the classical tradition (including Keynesian), now that, as we shall see, there are many economists, especially in other continents, who do not in fact share them?

In the twentieth century, the economism of the neoclassical schools (Marxist or otherwise) has implied treating development as a largely, even purely, economic phenomenon. They all also take some conventional definition of national income as its measure.[14] The important test of a country's economy is the growth of its "productive forces," in Marxist terms. By one route or another this benefits the poor in the end. It is of course the emphasis on economic growth which largely explains the touching neoclassical faith in progress. In this area, there is some evidence of an improvement in the human condition in the last few decades, at least if one takes a measure which does not allow for depletion of nonrenewable resources, or the despoliation of the environment, or social "overheads," or the declining quality of goods and services, etc.,[15] and yet includes the output of weapons of human destruction. (Nearly all neoclassical economists even believe the collections of guesses and hypotheses—together with a few facts—called "growth rates" in Africa, Asia and Latin America, though that raises issues which would take us too far afield.)[16]

There is yet another simple belief central to the whole tradition that increases its logical attraction, namely that capital investment ("accumulation" in Marxist jargon) is overwhelmingly the most important determinant of economic growth—often the *sole* determinant (e.g., in the Harrod-Domar model and its derivatives and in the Marxist scheme of "reproduction"). Consequently—and this appealed to Victorian puritanism—the generation and allocation of savings are seen as the mainsprings of development. Education, by contrast, is treated in both types of national income accounts as a form of "consumption." Another corollary is that capital is generally assumed to be the most important form of property and determinant of inequality—educational qualifications, lifelong appointments, bureaucratic positions, etc., hardly being considered.

Because of this emphasis on capital, geographical influences on growth are also virtually ignored, even the size of a country's population, area, location, climate, soil, mineral resources, and so on. Indeed, an economics student can attend lectures for several years without ever hearing the word "oil," let alone being taught about the functioning of an oil-exporting economy, or the basic differences between, say, Kuwait and Venezuela.

Yet another corollary is a general disinterest in the ethnic, religious and linguistic composition of nations,[17] and thus in their cultural patterns (unitary or diverse), even though these largely explain important categories in schemes of economic analysis, such as consumption habits and savings propensities—both assumed in neoclassical economics to be functions of income[18] and of attitudes to work. If referred to at all, cultural influences fall under the heading "obstacles to growth."

Implicit in all neoclassical schools is a belief in modernization, the overwhelming and civilizing role of economic growth in obliterating archaic superstitions, rural customs and ethnic loyalties ("false consciousness" in Marxist terms). Urbanization and industrialization are inevitable and progressive (for some, such as Warren, apparently part of the definition of progress).

Naturally, there is no great interest in institutional change—at least, in the Marxist case, between the major institutional changes called revolutions.[19] While individual neoclassical scholars may study, for example, the organization, content and effects of education, these do not have nearly as central a place in any general theory as capital accumulation. Even the distribution of income according to the level of income has not been greatly studied by either school.

One could continue for many pages listing common beliefs, but there is one that cannot be ignored. Marxist economists, like the Chicago School, treat the quantity of money as a highly important policy variable. This is common ground between neoclassical economists in, for example, the governments of the Soviet Union and the United States.

Yet I do not want to exaggerate this common ground. There are very important differences as well. To mention just a few very briefly, Chicago School economists are characterized by a belief in the applica-

bility of quantitative techniques—much greater than held by Marxists—
and thus tend to select variables which are quantifiable. (They are particularly inclined to treat statistics as if they were facts.) And for them
a central concept is "equilibrium," which is normative. Marxists, on the
other hand, focus attention on social crises, due to class relations, study
the "internal contradictions" in capitalism and other neosocialist "modes
of production," and stress how "uneven development" is linked to
"imperialism."[20] Marxists, therefore, also tend to emphasise the historical origins of problems, and their long-term dynamics.

But the common points listed above are numerous and fundamental.
It can scarcely be denied that Moscow and Chicago (and Cambridge) do
share a common and important core of basic doctrine, and one which
would not be acceptable to other economists.[21]

EUROPEAN IDEOLOGIES IN THE 1920s

The reason why it appears shocking to group Marxists with other
neoclassical economists—especially to devout members of either
school—is that we are accustomed to the old European spectrum of politics running from Left to Right. Up to the 1920s, as was shown by the
"Modern Symposium," and later, one could place the political philosophy of an individual or movement or government in Europe somewhere on a straight line:

Ideological Map—Europe in the 1920s

	Social			
Communists	Democrats	Liberals	Conservatives	Fascists

◀——————————————————————————————————————▶

(E) EGALITARIAN   ANTI-EGALITARIAN (AE)

Those on the Left accepted (even if unconsciously) Marxism—the more
so the further Left they were, except for an extremist fringe. Those on
the Left accepted a package of attitudes that included not only favoring
more or less fundamental social change, but also a belief in pacifism,
disarmament, international solidarity, atheism, planning, progressive
taxation, high wages, state welfare benefits, civil liberties, birth control
and abortion, women's rights, easy divorce, penal reform, rights of
blacks, colonial liberation, etc., etc. Anyone on the Left might well be

shocked if a friend failed to support any of these, and one could mean-ingfully talk about some person (or group) being "further Left" or "more progressive" than another person (or group), meaning more enthusiastic about the whole package, and/or more convinced that social revolution was a necessary and even sufficient condition for achieving it.

Neoclassical economics (this time in the conventional sense of "neo-classical") did not cover nearly such a wide range of social questions, but it legitimated property income and when added to less rational beliefs in natural inequality and original sin, etc., provided arguments against egalitarian policies that seemed likely to impair thrift or incen-tives. It also justified freedom of trade, which is barely compatible with central planning. It therefore lay at the core of right-wing ideologies (except those on the extreme Right).

Countries, big ones especially, were also put on the same spectrum according to their official ideologies, ranging, in the 1920s, from the Soviet Union[22] to, say, Britain, each of which attracted the ideologi-cal loyalty of those in other countries.[23]

This way of looking at politics is also fundamentally European. Outside Europe and perhaps North America, such a spectrum has been far less relevant. How is one to classify Juan Peron for example? His fiscal policy was "progressive" and he espoused industrialization and "planning," but his foreign policy was nationalistic, and one can hardly see him as an upholder of civil liberties. While he certainly helped ad-vance the careers of two women, he made little attempt to reduce Argentinian *machismo*. A similar question could be asked about many non-European political leaders.

POSTWAR SHIFTS IN IDEOLOGY

In fact, despite efforts by the United States and the Soviet govern-ments to spread their respective forms of neoclassical ideology[24] in Africa, Asia or Latin America, neither has been very successful. It is true that in the postwar period, neoclassical economics has been widely used as a basis for growth models, which proved a convenient diversion from distributional issues—economic growth, not political action, would achieve social goals. Since growth was also a goal acceptable to Marxists, this provided the basis for political convergence covering a broad range.

Yet, as the chapters by Harold Brookfield, Bagicha Minhas and Paul

Streeten bring out, there has been mounting disillusion with national income targetry. The world of deteriorating social conditions depicted in these three chapters seems quite a different one from Warren's. Certainly, growth has accelerated since the war in the great majority of countries, but in many of them this has apparently been accompanied by rising waste of labor, in the form of, if not open unemployment, then of its disguised forms (such as makework schemes, and involuntary jobs on submarginal plots of land or in petty trading). There seems to have been increasing inequality. Although the process of growth has benefited sections of the urban proletariat and bureaucracy, it has passed by much of the population, especially in rural areas, often destroying forms of production, reducing employment and rendering capital idle (e.g., in handloom weaving).

Fast economic growth has, moreover, not been accompanied by greater democracy, as might have been expected. On the contrary, the combination of technological advance in surveillance, crowd control, etc., with the concentration of the benefits of growth has meant increasing repression. Those who believed that socialism would achieve the traditional left-wing aims have had to face the fact that equality and human rights have been flouted in the now numerous socialist countries, and it is unclear how powerful bureaucracies can ever be forced to relax their grip.

In addition, the widening international differences in wage levels and welfare benefits have undermined proletarian solidarity (leading to the neo-Marxist theory of "unequal exchange," mentioned by Mansour). It has become increasingly clear, especially since the sharp increase in the price of oil in 1973-74, that the welfare of a working class depends to a considerable extent on the bargaining capacity of its government. Meanwhile, as the transnational corporations and transnational culture have penetrated one country after another, nationalist resistance to them has increased.

Bagicha Minhas traces the way some of the multiple sources of disillusion have affected thinking about development problems. He sees them as necessarily leading to doctrines of "self-reliance" embodied, for example, in the Arusha Declaration. Fernando Henrique Cardoso examines the emergence of "dependency" theory in Latin America out of the criticism of the neoclassical school implicit (occasionally explicit) in the work of Prebisch and the Economic Commission for Latin America (ECLA).

In fact, the main touchstone of economics is now not so much egalitarianism as nationalism. This is where the real rift has opened between neoclassical economists and the rest of the profession.

Nationalism is in theory anathema to both the Chicago School[25] and conventional Marxists, as indeed it was (in the form of mercantilism) to the fathers of classical economics. So is separatism. These are incompatible with their assumptions of the overwhelming importance of material motives and therefore a form of "false consciousness." In Marxist demonology, nationalism is often prefaced by pejorative terms such as "petit bourgeois." To the Chicago eye, protectionism is even more evil than an unbalanced budget, and the transnational corporation is an agent of progress, as it was for Warren.

Yet perhaps the main political lesson of the twentieth century is the strength of nationalism, starting with the successful mobilization of European working classes in 1914 to shoot at each other for four years. In a tight corner—for example in Russia in 1942—even Marxist governments appeal directly to patriotism. To neglect nationalism may lead a government into serious policy mistakes (e.g., those made by both the Soviet and United States governments vis-à-vis China, especially in the 1950s).[26] Indeed, "social incentives" can be interpreted as largely "national incentives," especially in the non-European countries with Marxist governments, where they are heavily emphasized. And neo-Marxists, such as Fawzy Mansour, appreciate the potential role of nationalism in containing the penetration of a country by the international capitalist economy and culture, i.e., by "imperialism," mentioning—which is noteworthy—the importance of the country's size.

Yet the concept of "imperialism" is sufficiently elastic to mobilize not merely all exploited classes everywhere against "monopoly capitalism" (Lenin's original intention), but also country against country. This is particularly clear in the Chinese use of the term "imperialist" to designate the Soviet government, which by implication restores to the word an older, pre-Leninist connotation of national territorial ambitions. It has been similarly used in recent frontier wars between governments calling themselves "Marxist" (Cambodia and Vietnam, Ethiopia and Somalia). The only international wars in 1977 were between "Marxist" governments.

The old packages of "progressive" and of "reactionary" objectives have burst open and the contents have been reassembled in new packages. Nationalism is articulated in ("leftist") doctrines of planning and anti-imperialism, but draws on patriotic, often religious, traditions previously considered "right-wing," and uses them to supplement or even replace material incentives.

At the other extreme are not merely East European Marxist officials, but also the spokesmen of the transnational corporations (TNCs). Both of these apparently irreconcilable groups are increasingly co-operating economically (through "joint ventures") and politically in, for example, opposition to plans for far-reaching changes in the inter-national division of labor.[27] Both stress material incentives and show traditionally "right-wing" indifference to civil liberties, and dislike of spontaneous working-class action. (Indeed, to put neoclassical doctrines into full practice wherever workers have been accustomed to freedom of organization, requires fierce repression—e.g., in Chile or Czechoslo-vakia). Both demonstrate highly bourgeois lifestyles (including a pref-erence for large saloon cars and lounge suits). Both of them find the youth culture, with its tolerance of drugs, offensive, and they are particularly horrified by violent threats to any establishment, especially kidnapping.

They also both espouse the historically leftist slogans of internation-alism and modernization, barely tolerating religion. They share a similar technocratic culture (expressed for example in "brutal modern" archi-tecture). Neither of them sees much point in research to adapt tech-nology to local needs or has great patience with ecologists. Both await impatiently the age of nuclear power. They do, however, see the poten-tial threat of fast population growth to the status quo and use the arguments of Malthus (another European classical economist) to favor and facilitate the expansion of birth control and abortion services: their own managers and political leaders tend to have small families. Their collective ideology embraces feminism, which is demonstrated by at least token appointments to senior positions of women—and of what-ever are the racial minorities in the country concerned.

The missionary fervor of communist bureaucrats burned out long ago. On the other hand, the managers of big corporations do not find government planners or even leaders of organized labor nearly as objec-tionable as did their more individualistic forbears. Indeed, in some countries, including Britain, the at least tacit support of unions is essen-tial.[28] And nationalization of a subsidiary does not have to be very out-rageous to the TNCs provided they are left in control of marketing.

The fundamental ideological difference now is not so much whether mankind can be perfected by creating idyllic social conditions, as whether we can be homogenized. Are the specific cultural characteristics of nation, race and gender merely transient obstacles to the modern world that technological advance and economic growth have brought almost within our grasp? Or are they to be seen as the basic sources of personal identity under increasing attack by the modernizing transnational culture and its political and corporate agents?

IDEOLOGIES IN TODAY'S WORLD

The old Left-Right axis is not much use to us in handling such questions. We all need some ideological map, however, if only to help us assess political information and theoretical developments, and tell friend from foe (e.g., among the authors of this book). If we superimpose a vertical axis, showing the degree of nationalism, on the conventional "Left-Right" one,[29] we get the following new map.[30]

Ideological Map—Today

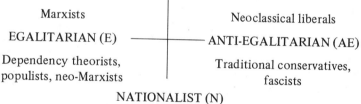

ANTINATIONALIST (AN)

Marxists

Neoclassical liberals

EGALITARIAN (E) ——————— ANTI-EGALITARIAN (AE)

Dependency theorists, populists, neo-Marxists

Traditional conservatives, fascists

NATIONALIST (N)

The old question: "Is X further Left than Y?" is shown as largely irrelevant, and to decide who is "more progressive" is even more difficult. But the problem of where to place Warren on the political spectrum, insoluble when using the simplistic Left-Right axis, now becomes easy. He was high on the vertical axis characterized by strong antinationalism—and also by the associated economism and beliefs in modernization, urbanization, etc. (Arguably, he could be put slightly to the left on this axis, though that depends upon whether one's view is long- or short-term.) Peron can also be handled, by putting him at the opposite end of the same axis. With this perspective, we can also see how to relate Warren's chapter to those of Cooper and Ohlin, who would usually be put at the opposite pole from him. The diagram makes this easy to grasp: in basic theory, as on practical issues, the three of them are really not far apart.

It is arguable whether Marxism has converged with other neoclassical doctrines in the sense that they have actually moved closer together. Certainly the ground between has been cultivated, especially by neo-Ricardians at Cambridge (such as Sraffa and Bliss) and by Lipton at the Institute of Development Studies (IDS). But the convergence is really relative; all neoclassical doctrines have been made to seem somewhat similar by the growing importance of nationalism and other non-economic factors, which are especially important in other continents,[31] where profoundly different approaches are being developed, as this volume brings out.

The ideology in the top right-hand quadrant (AN, AE) is broadly compatible with the interests of the TNCs. It also suits local capitalists who are associated with them, and certain other classes such as part of the armed forces and a small "labor aristocracy" which is provided with relatively high wages and fringe benefits by capital-intensive technology. These classes usually look to the United States or Western Europe for military support and technological and cultural inspiration, including higher education. Economic liberalism is one of the European cultural influences they imbibe. They mostly speak English.

In Eastern Europe, Marxism legitimizes bureaucratic rule. It is still the only fully worked out doctrine available in Western European countries for the bulk of the organized working class and for intellectuals who need a consistent intellectual framework basically critical of capitalism. Paradoxically, however, in the relatively contented and tolerant atmospheres of these very countries, milder versions, near the center of the circle, such as Fabianism, remain politically stronger. In other continents, Marxism provides for some classes an ideology of protest, sanctioned by the great prestige of European theorists.

Other intellectuals, however, especially in artistic circles, are, like peasant movements, better suited by something that is not only egalitarian but draws on national roots, like dependency and (other?) forms of populism. To call Mansour a Marxist would probably be misleading. Although he borrows from Marx, his departures from the central doctrine are significant. He not only emphasizes the economic pressures operating internationally, but also the autonomy of cultural forces. His position is not far from that of Cardoso, and they clearly belong in the quadrant (E, N), as do Minhas and Islam, and indeed most of the authors.

Landowners and indigenous capitalists naturally also prefer an anti-egalitarian ideology, but not one that is international. Significant parts of the bureaucracy and the armed forces also support ideologies in the bottom right-hand corner, together with some extremist religious groups, such as the Moslem Brotherhood. Fascist ideologies may have egalitarian elements, but basically they are hierarchical. This segment is not represented in the book.

This diagram helps us understand how a wide and continuous ideological and social spectrum can be spanned within nationalist parties such as the Indian Congress or separatist ones like Scots and the Basques (until independence poses serious policy issues). From this point of view, it is not surprising that—to take a few topical examples—"leftist" sections of the British Labor Party have cooperated with Enoch Powell and other "right-wing" Conservatives in opposing membership in the European Economic Community (EEC). Nor is it strange that "Arab socialism" and "African socialism" are vague ideologies as Mansour emphasizes. On the other hand, the map also explains tactical alliances in the upper half of the circle; for example, consider the alliance in the Republic of South Africa between what is now the Progressive Federal Party (backed by Oppenheimer mining fortunes) and Marxist groups, under the banner of multiracialism, against both Afrikaaner and black nationalism.[32]

Indeed, political movements as a whole are now much less monolithic. One consequence of the emergence of the nationalist dimension is greater instability. Any party may look not only horizontally but also vertically—or even diagonally in the case of moderates—for tactical allies, depending on what happen to be the dominant issues of the day.[33] There is now much more scope for individual leadership than in the days when a politician could only cooperate with either those on the immediate "right" or those immediately to the "left."

The map also provides an ideological grouping of countries according to their dominant ideology. Each quadrant in fact contains a major power—going clockwise from sector AE: the United States, Russia, Japan and China. (To justify this classification would take more space than would be warranted here. I shall take it up again in future work.)

Nearly all the other non-European governments, especially those of the larger countries, are best placed in the two lower quadrants because of their open reliance on nationalism. Many fall in the quadrant (AE,N). Whatever their rhetoric a government may in fact not bother much in its day-to-day business with the aim of reducing inequality.

Severe instability is chronic in international relations too. At any

one time, some governments are "delinking" from the transnational
system or the Soviet sphere of influence, while others, in response to
financial or military aid or other inducements, are moving closer to
the United States or the Soviet Union. It is true that they combine in
demanding a "New International Economic Order" and pay nodding
respect to "collective self-reliance." But their only common bond
(apart from historic resentments) is the need to use their bargaining
weapons (assessed by Islam) to reduce dependence on imports of
technology, equipments and arms, or to obtain these more cheaply:
and nationalism is by definition a weak basis for an international alliance. The "Group of 77" tends to fall apart as soon as issues become
concrete (e.g., whether to cover particular commodities in the proposed "common fund"). Mansour and Islam bring out the variety within this group in political systems, social strategies and economic levels.

This is also reflected in attempts by Organization for Economic
Cooperation and Development (OECD) governments to "differentiate"
in their policies towards different parts of the Third World, a line of
which Cooper approves. But like Reginald Green (whose chapter is
a very concrete program for negotiation), he notes the range of the
responses of OECD members to the "New International Economic
Order." The hard-line governments are led by the United States, where,
as in the Soviet Union, there has been a turning inward, to deal with
intractable internal problems. The "like-minded" governments of the
small nations of Europe, however, are seeking—with varying degrees of
enthusiasm—some accommodation with the South. Those in southern
Europe, especially, are under pressure from the transnational corporations and doubtless anxious about the supply of energy and other
basic inputs, like most governments in the Third World.

If anyone came to the Houston Colloquium expecting a single new
strategy of development, universally applicable, especially from such
a diversity of theorists, he was inevitably disappointed. The emphasis,
as has been indicated above, was on diversity. As Mansour says, "Any
attempt to put Third World countries in the straitjacket of a single,
predetermined path of development is bound to fail." Neoclassicals of
all types please note! Minhas and Brookfield are similarly careful to
stress the dangers of simplistic goals, unrelated to specific national
experience, a theme widely heard among "development" experts today.

One main conclusion is rather, as Paul Streeten argues, the unexciting
one of the virtues of pragmatism, dealing with each problem as it arises
out of the solution of others. Dogmatists, whether in theory (especially

some form of neoclassical) or policy, who ignore national realities, are likely, in this increasingly complex and fluid world, to be surprised, humiliated and frustrated. They will find that governments or parties or people who seem "leftist" on some issues turn out to be "rightist" on others. Today's enemies may very well prove tomorrow's allies, and vice versa, in national politics or international fora—even in academic controversy.

Because of cultural lags, the old Left-Right dichotomy will still be widely used when discussing parties or governments, and people will continue to categorize each other as Left or Right, progressive or reactionary. There are now strong vested interests (not only material) in these perceptions, which few will abandon readily. It would be like leaving a nursery, where one is told fairy tales in which one can identify with good characters and hate the bad.

The importance of the nationalist axis seems likely, however, to grow. A transnational culture, based on neoclassicism, may become more clearly defined; and, at its other end, the implications of planning self-reliance will no doubt be more fully worked out, reconciling traditionalist and revolutionary nationalism in new strategies of development.

The question which was raised by Bill Warren's paper has opened up some interesting issues, which could be considered part of his legacy, and I feel deeply indebted to him.

Part I
The Literature of Development

Chapter 1

DEVELOPMENT IDEAS IN HISTORICAL PERSPECTIVE[1]

Paul Streeten

THE NEW INTEREST IN DEVELOPMENT

Development Economics is a new branch of economics. There was little that went under this name before World War II, though many of the same problems were dealt with by members of the colonial services, anthropologists, and others. Since much of economics is a response to current political and social problems, it is pertinent to ask what new conditions gave rise to the new and rapidly growing interest in development.

First, there was a new awareness that poverty is not the inevitable fate of the majority of mankind. This new awareness was itself the result of the achievement of affluence for the masses in the West; the high economic growth rates of countries in Western Europe, of North America, of the Soviet Union, and of Japan; and the improvement in mass communications which brought events in the rich North to the consciousness of the poor South, and more specifically to the consciousness of the new elites there. As a result of the propaganda of politicians and economists, aided by the transistor radio, television, and jet planes, economic growth came to be regarded as a human right.

A second source was the cold war, in which East and West, the Second and the First World, competed in attracting the attention of the Third World. Both the capitalist, mixed economies of the West, and especially the United States, and the planned economy of the Soviet Union attempted to win friends and influence people by showing that their economic performance was superior, by holding up their respective regimes as ideals to be imitated and by giving development aid. It is interesting to note that with the thawing of the cold war (if this is the right metaphor) and with the relatively reduced significance of military expenditure, the expectations of those who thought that this would make more resources available for international aid were disappointed: the flow of aid leveled off and shrank as a proportion of national income. It not only shows up the limits of economics but illustrates the principle of the irrelevant alternative, according to which a boy comes home and tells his father proudly that he has saved tenpence by walking and not taking a bus. To this the father replies contemptuously: "You fool; why did you not save £1.00 by not taking a taxi?"

A third factor was the population explosion. When population was kept at a fairly constant level as a result of high mortality rates, poverty was bearable. There was no growing pressure on scarce resources, son followed father in his occupation and traditional ways continued. But a growing population requires production increases simply in order to maintain the level of living. The maintenance of traditional ways and freedom from the pollution and rapaciousness of modern civilization presents an attractive, romantic picture, but it is unrealistic. Admittedly, it was the introduction of modern medical and other scientific technology that spectacularly reduced mortality rates, while no equally cheap and effective method to reduce traditionally high birth rates was available. But it remains true that, without development and the disruption it brings, societies could not continue to enjoy the happy existence presented by some romantic anthropologists, but would be faced with growing misery.

The fourth source is the large number of countries that attained independence after World War II. Decolonization is the most important effect of the last war. One hundred and two countries achieved independence in the last 30 years. Membership in the United Nations increased from 51 to 147 (and the total number of countries to 153).

Development and planning for development were written on the banners of the governments of these countries.

An understanding of the reasons for the rapid growth of interest in development economics is both interesting in itself, and helpful in identifying possible biases and omissions in our work. Gunnar Myrdal, who has consistently tried to remain aware of these influences, wrote:

> For social scientists it is a sobering and useful exercise in self-understanding to attempt to see clearly how the direction of our scientific exertions, particularly in economics, is conditioned by the society in which we live, and most directly by the political climate (which, in turn, is related to all other changes in society). Rarely, if ever, has the development of economics by its own force blazed the way to new perspectives. The cue to the continual re-orientation of our work has normally come from the sphere of politics; responding to that cue, students are launched, data collected, and the literature on the "new" problems expands. By its cumulative results, this research activity, which mirrors the political strivings of the time, may eventually contribute to a rationalization of these strivings and even give them a different turn.
>
> So it has always been. The major recastings of economic thought that we connect with the names of Adam Smith, Malthus, Ricardo, List, Marx, John Stuart Mill, Jevons and Walras, Wicksell and Keynes, were all responses to changing political conditions and opportunities.[2]

It is not easy to convey, in the present atmosphere of gloom, boredom and indifference surrounding discussions of development problems, what an exciting time of ferment these early years were.

The excitement arose both from the challenge and the vision of eradicating poverty and opening up new lives and opportunities for hundreds of millions of people, and from the new ideas to which this challenge gave rise. These ideas were a revolt against the traditional, conventional views of the profession.

Albert Hirschman recently pointed to the importance, in the history of development economics, of Samuelson's proof of factor price equalization in 1948-49.[3] The articles proved that, on certain assumptions conventionally accepted in the theory of international trade, free trade would equalize wages throughout the world, so that a United

States worker and an Indian worker would be paid the same, and trade could therefore perform precisely the same function as free international movement of factors. In a world in which people became increasingly aware of wide and widening international income gaps, this was a brilliant and startling conclusion. As Albert Hirschman says, here the neoclassical paradigm was not undermined by the accumulation of contradictory evidence, as Thomas Kuhn's scientific revolutionary sequence would lead us to expect, but "the theory contributed to the contradiction by resolutely walking away from the facts."[4]

Raúl Prebisch, Hans Singer and Gunnar Myrdal, less elegantly but more realistically, challenged not only Samuelson's findings but the more general view that equilibrating forces meant that the fruits of economic progress would be widely and, after a time lag, evenly shared.

At the same time, the Harrod-Domar model, according to which the rate of growth of output equals the capital/output ratio divided by the ratio of savings to income, though formulated for different conditions than those of underdevelopment, added output-generation to the Keynesian income-generation of investment, and thereby provided the principal pillar for the analysis of development and for many development plans.[5] Capital accumulation became, if not the necessary and sufficient condition for development, at any rate the main strategic variable, and the propensity to save and the capital/output ratio became the basic equipment of development analysts, planners and aid officials. The notion that capital was scarce and savings difficult to raise in poor countries was qualified by pointing to the opportunities of attracting it from abroad, from the capital-rich countries, which would find new profitable investment opportunities in the countries to be developed. Notions like those of balanced growth (Ragnar Nurkse), the "critical minimum effort," and the big push (Paul Rosenstein-Rodan) threw new light on the role of market forces and planning.

From the beginning there were critics. Paul Baran argued that the political power structure in the poor countries prevented adequate and productive investment and that foreign investment and aid reinforced social and political systems hostile to development.[6] And between the position that development was ensured by adequate amounts of capital accumulation, and the conviction that the political power structure made development impossible, there were many intermediate positions. It soon became evident that some development was taking place in some places, but that it was not always simply a matter of capital.

The analysis was refined, qualified, criticized. Albert Hirschman emphasized entrepreneurial incentives, appropriate sequences of motivational pressures and linkages. Other writers attempted to introduce, in addition to total income, the distribution of this income as an important force determining subsequent investment. A more equal distribution was thought to be necessary in order to generate the mass markets which could exploit economies of scale; a less equal income distribution was thought to be conducive to higher savings. The choice of techniques was discussed in both its productive and distributional aspects.[7] What is remarkable about these early discussions is the proliferation of ideas, criticisms, and qualifications which contrasts sharply with the monolithic view that a single paradigm existed. This view is an optical illusion created by looking back from later vantage points. In subsequent sections, I may be guilty of such simplifications, but it should always be borne in mind that the early days of development economics were a time of intellectual pioneering, of considerable excitement, of the opening of new geographical and intellectual frontiers, of optimism and confidence.

> Bliss was it in that dawn to be alive,
> But to be young was very heaven!

CONTRASTING PERCEPTIONS OF DEVELOPMENT

Somewhat oversimplifying, we can identify five recent changes in the perception of the development process. "Perception" is intended to convey modesty and lack of pretension. Others might prefer terms like models, frameworks, or paradigms. Dudley Seers has suggested a hybrid between perceptions and perspectives: "perspections." Whatever name we give them, they certainly color the way in which questions are asked, empirical evidence is collected, selected and used, and solutions are presented.

Although the shift in perceptions has been described as "recent," some of these changes go back a considerable time. Indeed, hardly any of the features of the "old" perception were generally accepted at any stage, and qualifications, criticisms and alternative perceptions were put forward almost as soon as the "orthodox" perception had been formulated.

1. The first change between our perception of development until about 1970 and after can be traced to differences of view between the First World and the Third World, and the Right and the Left, although

there are all kinds of cross-alignments. The more popular (though not the academic) thinking of the Fifties and Sixties, codified in the Pearson Commission Report, was dominated by W. W. Rostow's doctrine of the stages of growth.[8] This perspective was, partly, superseded in the early 1970s by what has sometimes been called a "dependencia" interpretation of international economic relationships. To illuminate the shift in perceptions from the first of these views to the second, let us review briefly each in turn.

According to Rostow's doctrine, development is a linear path along which all countries travel. The advanced countries had, at various times, passed the stage of "take-off," and the developing countries are now following them. Development "was seen primarily as a matter of 'economic growth,' and secondarily as a problem of securing social changes necessarily associated with growth. It was taken for granted that organizing the march along the development path was the prime concern of government. . . ."[9]

The linear view begged a host of questions about the nature, causes and objectives of development. It tended to focus on constraints or obstacles (particularly lack of capital), the removal of which would set free the "natural" forces making for the steady move toward ever higher incomes.

Applied to the area of international relations, this view calls on the rich countries to supply the "missing components" to the developing countries and thereby to help them break bottlenecks or remove obstacles. These missing components may be capital, foreign exchange, skills or management. The doctrine provides a rationale for international capital aid, technical assistance, trade, private foreign investment. By breaking bottlenecks, rich countries can contribute to development efforts a multiple of what it costs them and thus speed up the development process in underdeveloped countries. Models pointing to gaps between required and available savings or foreign exchange are a rationalization of foreign assistance. The ultimate purpose of aid is to be rid of aid.

This linear or stages-of-growth view has come under heavy fire. It was criticized on logical, moral, political, historical and economic grounds. Logically, it should have been clear that the coexistence of more- and less-advanced countries is bound to make a difference (for better or worse) to the development efforts and prospects of the less advanced, compared with a situation where no other country was ahead or the distance was not very large. The larger the gap and the more interdependent the components of the international system, the less relevant are the lessons to be learned from the early starters. Morally and politically, the linear view ruled out options of different styles of development. Inexorably, we were all bound to pass through the Rostovian stages, in the words of the famous limerick, like a tram, not a bus. Historically, the view can be criticized as excessively determinist. Economically, it is deficient because it ignores the fact that the propagation of impulses from the rich to the poor countries alters the nature of the development process; that late-comers face problems essentially different from the early starters, and that "late late-comers" again find themselves in a world with a range of demonstration effects and other impulses, both from the advanced countries and from other late-comers, which present opportunities and obstacles quite different from those that England or even Germany, France and Russia, faced in their pre-industrialization phase.

Summarized briefly, it may be thought that too much weight is given to Rostow and to the linear view of the development. The "stages of growth" were criticized from the beginning by Kuznets, Gerschenkron and others. The heavy concentration on physical capital was criticized by Cairncross, Hirschman, and the human capital school of T. W. Schultz. There were many nonlinear theorists, from Schumpeter to Rosenstein-Rodan and Nurkse. The whole debate on balanced versus unbalanced growth does not fit into the linear perception. But it remains true that, though not in academic circles, the Rostow model had a powerful grip on the imagination of policy makers, planners and aid officials and that it was this view that gave rise to a reaction.

Succeeding the linear development perspective in popularity in the early 1970s was a second view, according to which the international system of rich-poor relationships produces and maintains the underdevelopment of the poor countries (the rich "underdevelop" the poor, in André Gunder Frank's phrase).[10] In various ways, malignly exploitative or benignly neglectful or simply as a result of the unintended impact of events and policies in rich countries, the coexistence of rich and poor societies renders the efforts of the poor societies to choose their style of development more difficult or impossible. Certain groups in the developing countries—entrepreneurs, salaried officials, employees—enjoy high incomes, wealth and status and, constituting the ruling class, they perpetuate the international system of inequality and conformity. Not only Marxists but also a growing number of non-Marxists have come to attribute a large part of underdevelopment and of the obstacles encountered in the process of development to the existence and the policies of the industrial countries of the West, including Japan and the Soviet Union.

This new perception is succinctly expressed in President Nyerere's address to the Royal Commonwealth Society in November 1975.

> In one world, as in one state, when I am rich because you are poor, and I am poor because you are rich, the transfer of wealth from the rich to the poor is a matter of right: it is not an appropriate matter for charity. . . . If the rich nations go on getting richer and richer at the expense of the poor, the poor of the world must demand a change, in the same way as the proletariat demanded change in the past. And we do demand change. As far as we are concerned, the only question at issue is whether the change comes by dialogue or confrontation.

According to one line of this second view, aid is not a transitional phenomenon to be ended after "take-off," but a permanent feature, like an international income tax. According to a more radical line, aid is itself part of the international system of exploitation, and self-reliant, independent development has to get rid of it.

The conclusion drawn from this perception is that the developing countries should put up barriers between themselves and the destructive intrusions of trade, technology, transnational corporations, and educational and ideological influences, and should aim at "delinking" or "decoupling," at pulling down a bamboo or poverty curtain, at insulating and isolating themselves from the international system.[11]

W. W. Rostow, for the first kind of perception, and André Gunder Frank, for the second, are the popular rather than the academic models. Prebisch, Singer, Myrdal,[12] Hirschman,[13] and Perroux, not to say anything of Marx and List, had long ago developed approaches to development that separated "spread" or "trickle-down" effects from "polarization," "backwash" or "dominance" effects. And many had raised doubts as to whether everything would be fine if all countries only pursued free trade policies and established competitive markets. But probably because of their more careful formulations, the impact of their thinking, important though it was, remained regional—"peripheral," not "mainstream"—and sales of their books did not reach the figures of A. G. Frank's.

Irrespective of whether the "new" perception is true, what matters is that many developing countries see their place in the international system in this way and their perception is a political fact to be reckoned with. This clearly does not mean that the perception should not be subjected to a critical analysis.

The transition between the two perceptions has been overdrawn. Perceptions alternate, points emphasized change and there is no rapid, large-scale conversion. At about the same time that the critics of the international economic order became more vocal, and advocated "delinking," there took place a rebirth of orthodox thinking. The work on effective protection by Johnson, Corden and Balassa, the Organization of Economic Cooperation and Development (OECD) studies of industrialization and trade centering on the work by Little, Scitovsky and Scott, research by the Brookings Institution and the World Bank, and the doctrines of the Chicago School that influenced many Latin American policy makers reflected a recoil against inefficient protectionism and "inward-looking" planning. The conclusions pointed to more "outward-looking" policies. These changing analyses and perceptions alternate and interact.[14]

A reconciliation between the two perceptions (viz., that development can be speeded up by the international "system" and underdevelopment is caused by it) is possible along the following lines.[15] The advanced industrial countries emit a large number of impulses of two kinds: those that present opportunities for faster and better development than would otherwise have been possible, and those that present obstacles to development, those that stunt growth. Arthur Lewis invited us in 1974 to imagine that the developed countries were to sink under the sea in 1984. (He gave us ten years in order to allow time for adjustments. He felt it necessary to add that this was not a recommendation.) He then posed the question: Are the developing countries better off, worse off, or would it make little difference?

The answer to the question neatly separates the adherents of different "paradigms." The upholders of the first "paradigm" would say "worse" (pointing to Korea, Singapore, and Hong Kong as beneficiaries from the international system and Burma and Uganda as losers from "closing themselves off"), those of the second "better," and Sir Arthur thought it would make little difference. But I submit that, whichever answer one is inclined to give, this is not a helpful way of presenting the problem, however useful it is in sorting out ideologies. The developed countries propagate a large number of impulses to the developing countries. Reasonable men may differ about the net balance of these impulses, e.g., whether the exploitation by ruthless transnational companies offsets the availability of a stock of scientific, technological and organizational knowledge, or whether the harm done by the brain drain is greater or less than the benefits from foreign technical assistance, or whether the inflow of grants and loans at concessionary interest rates is counterbalanced by aid-tying and capital flight, etc.[16] The interesting question then is not "Do the developing countries benefit or lose from their coexistence with developed countries?" but, "How can they pursue selective policies that permit them to derive the benefits of the positive forces, without simultaneously exposing themselves to the harm of the detrimental forces?" Looked at in this way, the question becomes one of designing selective policies for aid, trade, foreign investment, transnational companies, technology,[17] foreign education, movements of people, etc.

2. The shift from a linear theory of missing components to some version of a theory of neocolonialism and dependence was accompanied by another change. It amounted to a change in emphasis of what constitutes the meaning and measure of development.

Early thinking and policy making was dominated by economic growth as the principal performance criterion of development, not so much because growth was regarded as an appropriate objective in itself, but because it was thought either that its fruits would rapidly trickle down to the poor, or that corrective government action could be relied upon to redistribute them, or that inequality and poverty are essential for growth (which, through accumulation by the rich, would first have to create the productive base from which to launch the attack on poverty). But it was soon evident that none of these three assumptions was valid. It became clear that growth in many countries remained concentrated on a narrow enclave of modern, organized, urban industry; that governments often were unwilling or incapable of using taxes and services to offset growing inequalities; and that the concentration of income in the hands of the rich was not a necessary condition of development. (E.g., research has disclosed that small farmers with access to improved agricultural technologies save as high a proportion of their incomes as large farmers and are often more efficient in terms of yield per acre.)

The expected absorption of the rapidly growing labor force from the subsistence sector into the modern, industrial sector was considerably slower than expected. Dualism in many countries was marked and prolonged. The golden age of growth with greater equality, ushered in after a period of growing inequality, or by the full absorption of labor from the subsistence sector into the modern sector, seemed, with a few important exceptions, to move into the distant future. This awareness led to a new emphasis on rural development and "employment." It was soon seen, however, that the problem was not "unemployment," which is a Western concept that presupposes modern sector wage employment, labor markets, labor exchanges and social security payments in the form of unemployment benefits. (It has been said that only those relatively well-off can afford to be unemployed.) The problem was rather unremunerative, unproductive work of the poor, particularly of the rural poor. The International Labor Office (ILO) Kenya mission suggested the "informal sector" as not just another name for disguised unemployment but as a potentially productive labor force. The new emphasis on the "working poor" led to a concern for redistribution of productive assets as a path to reduced inequality. The relation between the increased concern for equity and conventionally measured economic growth presented a dilemma. On the one hand, it was accepted that in poor societies poverty can be eradicated only through increased production. On the other hand, the growth experience in some countries (though not in all) has shown that growth had reinforced inequalities in income, asset and power distribution which made it more difficult or impossible, both economically and politically, for its benefits to be spread widely. Attention, therefore, shifted to the conditions under which "redistribution with growth" is possible and desirable. According to one simulation exercise,[18] an annual transfer of two percent of GNP over 25 years into public investment to build up the stock of capital available to the poor, which appeared as a quite radical policy, shows very modest results. After 40 years, the rise in the consumption of the poor is accelerated by only 23 percent. The favored redistribution with growth strategy shows an acceleration of the rate of growth of consumption of the bottom 40 percent of the population of only half of one percent a year, or $1 for a $200 level.

The next step was to realize that what was needed was a more direct and speedier attack on deprivation. Reductions in inequality do not necessarily reduce poverty. It was not just inequality as such that was offensive, but also the fate of the destitute, whether working or incapable of working, whether unemployed, underemployed or unemployable. The objective narrowed down to "meeting basic human needs,"[19] which covers not only adequate earning opportunities to purchase the necessities of life, but also access to the provision of public services for education, health and safe water. The progress was from highly aggregated magnitudes like "national income" and "growth rates" to increasingly disaggregated objectives, like different types of employment (e.g., for the young, for recent migrants) and reduced inequality, to meeting highly specific human needs of particular poverty groups.

In focusing on these needs, it became clear that measured income and its growth is only a part of basic needs. Adequate nutrition and safe water at hand, continuing employment, secure and adequate livelihoods for the self-employed, more and better schooling for their children, better preventive medical services, adequate shelter, cheap transport and (but not only) a higher *and* growing level of measured income: some or all of these would figure on the list of urgently felt needs of poor people.

In addition to these specific "economic" objectives, there was now a new emphasis on "nonmaterial" needs that cannot be dispensed, but, in addition to being valued in their own right, may be the conditions for meeting "material" needs, like self-determination, self-reliance, political freedom and security, participation in making the decisions that affect workers and citizens, national and cultural identity, and a sense of purpose in life and work. This was accompanied by attempts to evolve human and social indicators of development that would reflect the extent to which some of these needs were met.[20]

3.   A third shift in interest and emphasis was away from the specific economic problems of development and toward the world's common problems and shared constraints: resources and, in particular, energy, the environment and its global pollution, the sea and the sea bed, and world population. The new emphasis was on scarcity and interdependence.

The new emphasis on interdependence was regarded by some as calling for greater solidarity and cooperation ("spaceship earth," "one world"), by others, such as the advocates of *triage* and of the lifeboat philosophy, as calling for partial contracting out of human obligations, and by others again as a shift of attention from positive-sum to zero-sum games. The renewed emphasis after 1972 on scarcities of resources and exhaustion of raw materials extended not only to food, energy and certain metals, but also to some previously free goods, like clean air and clean water, with the resulting concern for environmental protection.

Interdependence does not necessarily point to solidarity; on the contrary, it may give rise to threats, "blackmail," the demand for ransoms, and attempts at isolation. But whatever the response, the fact is that many problems are now global and are shared by all men. Whereas, with the growing interest in different societies in the Sixties, many had argued that there is no single, universal "science" of economics, applicable from China to Peru, and Dudley Seers wrote on "the economics of the special case," the wheel has now turned full circle and we (with Dudley Seers in the lead) now acknowledge that many of the issues that we had considered as belonging to the poor countries are seen to be universal, of concern to the rich, too. Alienation, pollution and crime can spring from underdevelopment as well as from overdevelopment; "intermediate technology" is just as relevant to high-income societies suffering from unemployment in the face of resource limitations, pollution and alienation from work; all states confront the new phenomenon of the transnational corporation; we are all affected by the energy crisis; there are diseases of affluence as well as diseases of poverty; migration of workers and professionals affects rich and poor countries; there is global experimentation with new lifestyles; there is a heritage common to all mankind and the unexploited resources of the sea and the sea bed can be allocated according to worldwide priorities.

4. A fourth and closely related change is that from a tacitly or explicitly assumed international harmony of interests (which was built into the stages-of-growth model) and positive-sum games, to greater emphasis on actual or potential conflict and zero-sum games. There was much talk of cooperation versus confrontation. The new perception was brought out vividly by the actions of the Organization of Petroleum Exporting Countries (OPEC) and by the Intergovernmental Council of Copper Exporting Countries (CIPEC) as well as similar attempts with bauxite, phosphate and iron ore; by attempts or threats of the developing countries to use bargaining power in other fields with refusals to participate in drug control, or the control of nuclear weapons, or patent conventions; by threats of expropriation or tougher terms for transnational companies; and by the support by a few governments of terrorists and hijackers. As the old harmony has benefited the haves, the new confrontation was intended to be used to change the rules of the game in favor of the have-nots.

The fact that economists point to potential joint gains from, say, trade liberalization or commodity price stabilization, and thus to positive-sum games does not, of course, mean that governments perceive such policies as in their national interest. Policies are shaped by pressure groups and lobbies and the ubiquity of protection testifies to the power of these interests. On the other hand, developing countries may on occasion have an interest in show-downs rather than negotiations of common interest. There are political advantages in the publicity of such confrontations. In any case, sovereign political power is in its nature a zero-sum game and the added strength of one country is often perceived ipso facto as a defeat for a rival.

At the same time, negotiations do appeal, if not to common interests, at least to common norms and to acceptable rules. Most nations realize that a world in which each nation and group of allied nations exercises to the full its bargaining power to extract maximum concessions from others is a world in which most nations will be worse off. Bargaining must, therefore, appeal not only to national self-interest but also to widely acceptable principles, rules, and norms on which tacit agreement can either be assumed or assumed to be more readily reached than is possible with selfish demands and threats. If bargaining is seen and conducted in this light, its power to disintegrate the world community is greatly weakened, even if the game is, in economic terms, a zero-sum one. Properly used, bargaining can strengthen world cooperation through joint attempts to evolve a more acceptable set of rules and institutions.

5.   A fifth change was that from treating the Third World as a homogenous group of countries with common interests to the acknowledgement of the wide variety of experiences, interests and stakes in the world order—in spite of the growth of solidarity of the "Group of 77" at United Nations Conference on Trade and Development (UNCTAD) and other international forums. Gaps in income per head opened up more widely within the Third World than between the developed and the developing countries.

The unprecedentedly high average rate of growth of income per head in the developing countries between 1950 and 1975 masked a wide diversity of experience. In Korea, Taiwan, Hong Kong, Singapore, some OPEC countries and the People's Republic of China, income per head rose rapidly and the fruits of this growth were fairly evenly distributed (though the high growth rates for China are crucial and disputed). This group of countries contains about one billion people, or 35 percent of the population of the developing countries.

In a second group of countries, including Pakistan, the Philippines, Thailand, Turkey and many Latin American countries, especially Brazil, containing about 25 percent of the developing world's population, moderate to rapid growth was combined with growing inequality, though it is controversial whether absolute poverty increased.

In a third group of countries, comprising some of the large countries of South Asia (India, Bangladesh) and some of the poorer countries of Africa (incorporating about 40 percent of the developing countries' population) slow growth was probably combined with growing poverty in absolute terms. This group contains some of the largest countries and it remains a disputed issue whether the proportion of absolutely poor increased.

The distribution of the benefits of the commodity boom, especially the oil price rise, and the incidence of the damage done by the world recession were highly uneven and further sharpened differences within the Third World. The hoped-for benefits of the New International Economic Order (NIEO) also are likely to be unequally distributed.

6.   The sixth change in the perception of the development process, closely related to the other five changes, is that from abounding optimism[21] about development prospects and the contribution to them by the rich (through aid, trade and private investment) and by economic analysis, which dominated the Fifties and Sixties, to the deep pessimism of the Seventies. Both optimism and pessimism have their social origins. The optimism of the early decades, as Gunnar Myrdal has pointed out, had its origin not only in the excitement of the discovery of new areas but also in the desire of the governments in the industrial countries to please the new elites in the newly independent countries and to reinforce the view that transfer of capital, skills and technology from rich to poor countries will soon lead to self-sustained growth and thereby get rid of the need for future aid. When faced with the real problems and difficulties of development, which transcended the economic variables—and, at the same time, in their own countries, faced with what has come to be known as "stagflation," together with a host of new problems such as urban ghettoes, student unrest, a growing number of industrial strikes, drug addiction, racial tensions, etc.—the pessimism of the rich countries was a convenient excuse for falling and failing commitments to development cooperation and for contracting out of or for reducing contributions.

As far as economic theory was concerned, neither the Keynesian nor the monetarist approaches had much to offer in analyzing and solving the problems of inflation accompanied by an intractable form of unemployment, the energy crisis, pollution, and the dwindling consensus underlying a social order.

In addition to these six fundamental shifts in perceptions, there have been shifts in fads and fashions. Just as fashion setters emphasize, display and conceal at different times different parts of the female anatomy (though presumably all are there all the time), so economic and social research tends to be preoccupied with different aspects of the variables in the social system, to the neglect of others. Certain subjects or views, at any given time, have "sex appeal." The emphasis on industrial import substitution, followed by recommendations of industrial export promotion and, now, the beginnings of some disenchantment with industrial export-led growth and a new turn to primary export restrictions is one illustration. Another fashion cycle is the switch from investment in physical capital to investment in formal education and a turn to informal education and motivation; from emphasis on output growth to calculations of the social costs and benefits of birth control; also the swings between functional literacy and mass literacy campaigns. Yet another cycle is that between pessimism and euphoria about world food production. The debates on agriculture versus industry,[22] large-scale versus small-scale techniques, formal versus "informal" sector, deteriorating versus improving terms of trade, material versus social objectives, growth versus the environment, etc., have found in turn a clustering of views round alternating sides of the pendulum. The importance and the irrelevance or damage of development aid, as viewed by both donors and recipients, represents yet another swing. One could go on, and to some of these debates I shall return later.

To the extent that these swings of the pendulum are indications of important underlying forces, they clearly raise important questions. But often, they bypass the important issues and, looking back only a few years, or even months, one is astonished at the problems that vexed the profession and by the absence of the discussion of problems that vex us today. With the wisdom of hindsight it is now clear that the really important issues lay elsewhere. It would be nice to be able to predict where the next breakthrough in research is going to be, so that we can prepare ourselves for it. Yet, such a forecast would involve a

logical contradiction. If I, or anyone else, knew where the *next* breakthrough was going to be, we should already have performed it and it
would be the *latest* breakthrough.

Very few indeed would have predicted in 1950 that the preoccupations of the mid-Seventies would be transnational companies, "stagflation," protection of the environment, energy shortages, and the
intractable nature of the development process. One safe prediction is
that few, if any, of the problems that concern us now will stand high
on the agenda in the year 2000.

KEY ISSUES

Another useful way to trace changes in thinking about development
during the last 30 years is to select certain key concepts and examine
how they have provided a focus for development thinking and policy
making. This section reviews some of these key concepts and their
impact on the study of development.

Capital

In the early literature, capital was regarded as the key to development and lack of it as an essential—or the main, or even the only—constraint. Nurkse[23] argued that poor countries were poor because they
were poor. Behind this apparent tautology lies a theory of the vicious
circle of poverty or the low-level equilibrium trap. Poor people can
save only a small proportion of their income, if anything at all. As a
result, there is little capital to invest. This in turn keeps the productivity of workers low and leads to low incomes per head.

This view of capital as the "missing component" fitted well into the
linear stages-of-growth doctrine: "[I] n technical discussions and
writings, in analytical models as well as in policy papers, the relationship between capital formation and economic development is stressed
to the exclusion of all other causal factors and relations."[24]

A powerful influence was Arthur Lewis' model of the dual economy.[25]
A rise in the savings and investment ratio from about five percent to
about fifteen percent and the accumulation of capital, combined with
unlimited amounts of labor drawn from the traditional, subsistence
sector, are the necessary and sufficient conditions of development
according to this model. The model reestablished a classical mechanism

of reinvested profits by capitalists who save, and justified urban industrialization up to the point when the reserve army of labor is exhausted and neoclassical principles come into their own.

The strategic role of capital was questioned both by theory and by statistical findings. Theoretical analysis showed that there is no reason to expect poor people to save a lower proportion of their income than the rich. The relative preference of future consumption over present consumption is not necessarily affected by the current level of income.[26] It was also observed that even quite poor people saved in the form of holding gold and silver ornaments. Furthermore, Abramovitz and Solow[27] showed that capital, as measured, played only a relatively small part in the growth of output and a substantial part must be attributed to the residual or the "Coefficient of Ignorance."[28] A. K. Cairncross and Albert O. Hirschman[29] had questioned early the strategic or autonomous importance of capital, compared with techniques, attitudes, institutions and entrepreneurial motivation. Likewise, T. W. Schultz and others had extended the concept "capital" first to investment in human beings and later to other fields.

At the same time, experience showed that a good deal of productive capital was underutilized, and that capital was not as scarce as the above analysis had led one to expect. Moreover, the capital/output ratio in manufacturing industry turned out to be considerably lower than expected, partly because of the transfer and adaptation of existing, very productive technology from advanced countries, partly because capital-intensive infrastructure with excess capacity already existed in some areas, and where it did not, expenditure on housing and capital-intensive public services was kept low, and partly because countries with uncultivated but fertile land could simply bring more land under cultivation. Rostow had argued that "take-off into self-sustained growth" would require raising the savings ratio from five to ten percent, yet countries with low levels of income succeeded in saving, on average, fifteen percent of their income (though developed countries saved 22 percent).

Not only was capital more plentiful and more productive than anticipated, but foreign aid, a postwar innovation in international relations, was substantial compared with earlier periods and contributed to capital accumulation. On a very crude calculation, using the Harrod-Domar model, the savings and investment ratio of fifteen percent was made up of one percent official aid, two percent private foreign investment, and twelve percent domestic savings. With a capital/output ratio of three, this yielded an annual growth rate of five percent, to which external resources contributed one-fifth. (This contribution was gradually reduced in later years to one-tenth.) Such a model does, of course, assume that capital is the mainspring of economic growth, that foreign contributions are additional to domestic savings and that the capital/output ratio is low and constant. All three assumptions were later questioned.

As both theoretical reasoning and empirical evidence showed that capital does not play the crucial role that had been allotted to it, the debate about "missing components" broadened. The importance of physical capital was downgraded and other missing components were added, such as foreign exchange, entrepreneurship, skills, investment in "human capital," innovation, know-how, technology, institutions, and even birth control.

Entrepreneurship

It was difficult to maintain that entrepreneurship, as such, or the willingness to take risks or the desire to make more money were absent in the underdeveloped countries, for there was considerable evidence to show that plenty of entrepreneurial talent was applied to trade, to small-scale industry and to gambling, and that farmers do respond to price incentives and profit opportunities. It was misdirection and lack of opportunities, rather than absence that seemed to be the trouble. In particular, large-scale manufacturing enterprise was missing. This gap was filled in many countries by state and foreign enterprises. But these presented their own problems. State enterprises were subjected to political pressure to keep prices of their products and services down. Under the guise of rendering a social service, they merely subsidized the private sector, strengthening monopoly power. At the same time, salaries were kept low and retired civil servants or other worthy claimants for patronage were appointed as managers. This did not help efficient management.

Foreign enterprises were more efficient, but the desire to maintain control over indigenous resources and for economic, as well as political, independence of foreign decision makers conflicted with the admission and expansion of foreign firms. In some countries the most enterprising groups were ethnic minorities which attracted the envy and hatred of the indigenous population. The Chinese in Southeast Asia, the Asians in East Africa, the Ibos in Nigeria were maltreated, discriminated against or exiled.

Skills and Education

As attention shifted from physical to human capital,[30] excessively aggregate treatment soon showed up a difficulty. In many countries there were not too few but too many educated. But they either had the wrong kind of education, or the wrong location from the point of view of contributing to development. (England's industrialization took place before the Education Act, when the country had a much smaller proportion of literate people in the labor force than many developing countries today.) The problem in Asia was too many educated unemployed who had received a university education of low quality (though some of them had been educated in developed countries) which had contributed to aspirations that could not be fulfilled. Nor could it be argued that the fault lay with the *content* of education, e.g., too much Sanskrit, law or ancient languages and too little science and technology. India had 40,000 unemployed engineers.

In Africa there was excessive stress on primary education which contributed to a flight from the land to the towns. Skilled manpower was needed in the rural sector, but the aspiration of those who had learned to read and write was to become clerks in the civil service. The difficulty was not to educate more people, but to keep schooling and motivation in step with the changes in the rest of the economy. As in the previously false stress on capital, against the evidence of physical capacity standing idle and underutilized, so the emphasis on formal school education was accompanied by a growing army of unemployed school leavers. There was also too much emphasis on acquired learning, compared with the capacity to inquire and add to knowledge.

Foreign Trade

The early period was steeped in trade pessimism. It was thought that foreign trade had ceased to be an "engine of growth," as protectionist policies in industrial countries and the thrust of science and technology made exporting natural primary products increasingly difficult and unprofitable. In fact, trade grew at quite high rates. Total exports of developing countries in the Sixties grew by seven percent per annum (though those of the developed countries grew by nine percent). The exports of manufactured goods grew even faster. Between 1960 and 1966 they grew at a rate of twelve percent per annum, and between 1966 and 1973 at 25 percent per annum, compared with a rate of growth of seventeen percent per annum for the developed countries. (These rates are in money terms.) Nevertheless, the relative share in world trade of the developing countries fell from thirty percent in 1948 to eighteen percent in 1969. If petroleum exporters are excluded, the share of the developing countries in world exports fell from 24.3 percent in 1950 to 14.7 in 1960 to 11.7 in 1969 and to 9.7 in 1975. This gave rise to complaints. Yet, it is not clear why shares should matter. The criterion should be import requirements rather than shares in world trade which are bound to change with changing incomes and technology.

A good test of "obstacles to development" came in 1973 when the oil-exporting countries enjoyed large increases in financial resources, foreign exchange and government revenue.[31] The constraints that earlier writers on development had seen in the way of the big push advocated by others were suddenly removed, and it became possible to invest à la Nurkse and Rosenstein-Rodan, on a broad front. Mutually supporting investments could be carried out, in principle, so that the demand by industries for one another's products could be generated and supply bottlenecks could be eliminated by complementary investments or imports.

In spite of this great opportunity, development did not occur as swiftly and as harmoniously as the doctrine of the big push would have predicted. New types of imbalances became evident. Administrative, organizational and technological skills and appropriate institutions to direct them to the required areas were lacking, and the surplus oil revenues did little to stimulate or create them swiftly. Finance, foreign exchange and government revenue are not substitutes for all required inputs, and a large advance in foreign exchange spending generates bottlenecks in complementary resources, such as nontradable goods.

More subtly, it was discovered that resources are not just an abstract entity, but it matters how they are generated, earned and used. Oil revenue depends on the actions of governments and is not linked to the responses and motivations of farmers, businessmen, workers or households. And the imbalances that it creates—between tradable and nontradable goods, between high and low incomes, between income generation and its distribution, between present strength and future vulnerability, between finance and administration, between wealth and underdevelopment—present constraints of a different kind from those normally considered by economists.

Even before the opportunity to test the doctrine of the big push presented by the large increase in oil earnings and revenues, attention of development economists had shifted increasingly to variables not previously emphasized by mainstream economists. Among these new concerns were human attitudes, social institutions, power structures, cultural and religious beliefs and the impulses enjoyed or suffered that originated in the advanced countries. The "new" problems on which work was now focused were population growth, unemployment, inequality, and rural underdevelopment.

Population

From the beginning of history until 1850, world population rose slowly to 1,000 million. (It is estimated that at the end of the last Ice Age, about 10,000 B.C., it was less than ten million and in A.D. 250 it was between 200 and 250 million.) By 1960 it had more than trebled to over 3,000 million, and by the year 2000 it will be about 5,000 million. It has been pointed out that the present world population could all find standing room, though somewhat uncomfortably packed, on the 147 square miles of the Isle of Wight. At the present rate of increase of 1.7 percent per year, in 850 years the whole 196,836,000 square miles of the world's land surface would be needed to provide standing room on the same cramped scale for 4×10^{15} people.[32]

The rapid growth of the population could, however, be slowed down, as the situation in some countries showed. Successful programs of limiting population growth were launched in South Korea, Taiwan, Singapore and Hong Kong. The precise relationships between higher income levels, government expenditure on family planning, attitudes to birth control and availability of appropriate techniques are still highly controversial, but there is no doubt that there are statistical correlations between success in other fields (such as income growth, reduced inequality, export performance and, more specifically, women's education, reduced infant mortality and other health measures) and success in bringing down fertility rates.

Nor was it entirely clear or noncontroversial precisely why it was desired to bring down birth rates. Malthusian limitations of food and land played a less important part as it was found that there are large potential reserves of both. Attention shifted to savings and it was argued that a rapidly growing population (or, more correctly, a population growing at an accelerating rate) generates lower savings and, of what savings there are, a higher proportion has to be devoted to welfare rather than productive investment. It was also thought that rapidly growing populations presented more serious employment problems and made policies aimed at reducing inequality more difficult. The most convincing arguments are possibly not to be found in macroeconomics, but in the reduced burden on mothers and the improved quality of family life.

Unemployment

However successful population policy is in reducing population growth, the employment problem remains, because the entrants into the labor force in fourteen years' time have already been born. The sources of the problem were identified as (1) the high rate of growth of the labor force; (2) the inappropriately high wages in the organized, urban sector; (3) the absence of appropriate technologies for low-income countries. To this, some authors added (4) the limitations on international trade of labor-intensive products.

The analysis of unemployment and underemployment was refined as it was found that the standard categories and measurements of unemployment did not apply to the developing countries. Gunnar Myrdal, who found that the obstacles lay as much on the side of supply as on the side of demand (though he also questioned the basis of this distinction), pleaded for the replacement of the misleading concept "employment" by "labor utilization," which draws attention to the multidimensional obstacles to mobilizing labor. Obstacles were to be found in bad health, malnutrition, poor education, caste prejudice, attitudes to women, absence of labor markets, etc., as well as absence of effective demand and machinery.

The social structure within which the Green Revolution occurred, in some areas aggravated the problem of labor utilization by removing small subsistance farmers from their plots.

The ILO missions under the World Employment Programme contributed to a refinement of the concept "unemployment" and to our knowledge. It became clear that unemployment and underemployment were only a small part of the problem. The trouble was not so much absence of work, as unremunerative and unproductive work. Indeed, only those who had some other means of support could afford to be unemployed. In a market economy, the command over food and other necessities of life by the poor depends on the value of the goods and services they produce and sell.

Rural Underdevelopment

Agricultural growth was, until the middle Sixties, the main brake on economic growth. This was partly the result of low growth in agricultural productivity and partly the result of the sheer size of the agricultural sector in low-income countries. Even spectacularly high rates of urban, industrial growth could not absorb the growing numbers in the rural sector because the starting base of the industrial sector was so small. This led to a revision of the early fallacy that industrialization is the remedy for underdevelopment, indeed is almost synonymous with development. So strong was the hold of this myth that Myrdal regarded his view in the Sixties that "the employment effects of industrialization cannot be expected to be large for several decades" as "unorthodox." Eighteen years ago, Folke Dovring had shown that the size of agriculture relative to the rest of the economy imposes a ceiling on the rate at which labor can be absorbed outside agriculture, and he predicted that in most developing countries a continued increase in the size of the agricultural population could be expected for a considerable time.[33]

The majority of the poorest people in the world—the sharecropper, the landowner with a tiny plot, the landless laborer—lived on the land and were bound to continue living there for some time. The Green Revolution, on which the technocratically minded had pinned so much hope, benefited often the large and rich farmers, occasionally at the expense of the small, poor farmers and the landless laborers. In any case, since it is a seed, water, fertilizer revolution, it applies only to the wet tropics where water is available and its supply can be controlled. Seventy-five percent of India and 50 percent of Pakistan are without irrigation. No technology has yet been found that can increase yields in the arid tropics. Such a technology (combined, of course, with the other necessary measures such as land reform, incentives, institutions, information, provision of inputs, access to markets, improvement of health, education and nutrition) would make an important contribution to eradicating poverty in the Third World.

The Distressing Political Record and
Other Neglected Obstacles

Side by side with the new "economic" focus on poverty, underemployment, and inequality went certain political developments. In the international debates on the widening income "gap" between rich and poor countries and in the domestic debates on growing inequality, inequality stood to some extent as a proxy for discontent with political (or tribal or ethnic) results. Systematic denial of dignity or freedom to certain groups reinforced disadvantages of low incomes and denial of access to public services. Both domestically and internationally, the uneven process of development had important, and in some cases disastrous, side effects. The development disasters of the Nigerian civil war and the war of the secession of Bangladesh are extreme instances of the discontent and frustration generated by unequal access to the opportunities offered by development and growing intolerance of this inequality.[34] The same forces encouraged a turn toward greater authoritarianism and military dictatorships.[35] While the aggregate growth record, therefore, has been spectacular and the evidence on distribution ambiguous, the political record has been distressing.

Moreover, there are important areas for analysis which tend to be either neglected ("opportunistic ignorance"), treated in separate compartments as "exogenous" variables, not integrated into development analysis and policy, or dismissed as biased partisan views. Yet, any serious, objective analysis of development ought to incorporate them, because they are closely linked to the development process. Here they can only be enumerated.

1. The unwillingness of governments to grasp firmly the political nettles: land reform; taxation, especially of large landowners; excessive protection; labor mobilization.

2. Linked with the first, nepotism and corruption.

3. Behind these, again, various forms of oligopoly and monopoly power: the power of large landowners; of big industrialists; and of the transnational enterprises.

4. In a different field, but often equally disruptive to development efforts, the power of organized urban labor unions and the obstacles to incomes and employment policy and to a wider spread of employment opportunities, particularly to the rural poor.

5. Restricted access to educational opportunities and the resulting job certification that both reflect and reinforce the unequal structure of power and wealth. Similar restrictions in access to health, housing and other public services.

6. Weak entrepreneurship and defective management and administration of public sector enterprises, of the civil service and of private firms granted protection or other forms of monopoly power.

7. Lack of coordination between central plans and executing min-

istries, central plans and regional, local and project plans, and between the activities of different ministries.

8. The weakness of the structure, areas of competence, recruitment, training and administration of the United Nations specialized agencies charged with development, combined, too often, with a narrowly technocratic approach, encouraged by the historical origin and organization of these agencies and their politically "noncontroversial" approach.

9. There are also the terrible facts of mass slaughter, expulsion of ethnic minorities (often entrepreneurial and therefore hated) and political opponents, imprisonment without trial, torture, and other violations of basic human rights, and the $370 billion spent on armaments, compared with $17 billion on net concessional transfers (in 1975).

This list is not exhaustive but merely illustrative. It is intended to indicate some of the obstacles to human and social development in the full sense and to pinpoint some of the reasons for the disenchantment with what has turned out to be, by narrow economic criteria, unexpectedly and unprecedentedly high growth.

DISCARDED IDEAS

Let us summarize the elements in earlier thinking on development which have largely been discarded.

1. Analysis and policy were originally dominated by the experience of the rapid recovery from the war, supported by Marshall Plan aid, of the industrial countries of Western Europe, by the high postwar reconstruction. The problem of development is, however, fundamentally different from the problem of reconstructing war-damaged advanced economies.

2. Priority was given to industrialization and infrastructure (power and transport) which came to be almost synonymous with development. The savings ratio and the capital/output ratio together were thought to determine the rate of growth of output, which was the main objective of development. It was found, however, that capital accounted for only a relatively small portion of growth, and that growth was not synonymous with development.

3. Central government planning from the top down and the need for a big-push dominated thinking and policy making, and the limita-

tions of administrative capacity, of human and institutional constraints, and the need for participation, decentralization and mobilization of local labor were not recognized.

4. Policies were dominated by the reaction to colonialism. The governments of many newly independent states wanted to do what the colonial powers had neglected to do. This reinforced the desire for planning, for industrialization and for import substitution. It also fed the desire, after the achievement of political independence, for economic self-sufficiency. Latin American countries, which had been independent for a long time, felt that economic independence, which did not follow from political independence, was elusive.

5. Thinking was deeply influenced by foreign trade pessimism, which led to the formulation of two-gap models. Pessimism about export prospects and the terms of trade reinforced policies of import-substituting industrialization, which in turn created strongly entrenched vested urban interests that resisted efforts to liberalize trade.

6. There was a belief that high average growth rates of production will lead to reduced poverty either as a result of trickle-down or of government policies: that the best way to attack poverty was indirectly, by supporting growth, and that the spin-offs would, after a time lag, benefit the poor.

7. The rate of population growth and the problems generated by it were underestimated, and diplomacy ruled out the topic for both bilateral and multilateral development agencies.

8. The goals of development were defined narrowly in terms of GNP and its growth, and other goals such as greater equality, eradication of poverty, meeting basic human needs, conservation of natural resources, abating pollution, and the enhancement of the environment, as well as nonmaterial goals, were neglected or not emphasized sufficiently.

9. The contribution by the developed countries was seen too narrowly in terms of capital aid and technical assistance, instead of as the impact of all policies pursued by the rich countries, whether or not they were pursued with the express purpose of assisting development efforts. These would include science policies, the thrust of research and development expenditure, policies toward transnational companies, migration policy, monetary policy, regional policy, trade and employment policies, agricultural policy, as well as foreign policy and military alliances generally.

10. The Third World was considered, rather monolithically, as an

area with common problems, whereas it became increasingly clear that some of the differences within the group of developing countries were at least as great as those between them and the developed countries.

11.   Development was considered exclusively a problem of underdeveloped countries becoming less so. In contrast, development is now beginning to be viewed as a problem common to the whole world: it gives rise to problems that are shared by the rich and by the poor, with some interests in common, others conflicting.

THE NEW STRATEGY

The new development strategy, which reflects a fair degree of consensus among scholars, may be summarized in the following way:

1.   We must start with meeting the basic needs of the majority of the people who are very poor. The needs are more and better food, safe water at hand, security of livelihood, health, sanitation, education, decent shelter, adequate transport. In addition there are nonmaterial needs like self-confidence, self-reliance, dignity, capacity to make one's own decisions, to participate in the decisions that affect one's life and work, and to develop fully one's talents, all of which interact in a variety of ways with material needs.

2.   Meeting the basic needs of the billion poor people requires changes not only in the income distribution, but also in the structure of production (including distribution and foreign trade). It calls for increases in basic goods bought in the market, as well as in the purchasing power to buy them, and for an expansion in public services. To ensure that these actually reach the poor, restructuring public services will be necessary, as well as greater participation at the local level, better access to these services, and an appropriate delivery system.

3.   Since the majority of the poor live (and will continue to live for some time) by agriculture in the countryside, priority has to be given to growing food for domestic consumption. Agriculture has been the lagging sector; it has been holding up development and its produce has been unevenly spread. Agriculture also forms an important potential mass market for industrial goods.

4.   In order to meet the needs of the rural population, credit, extension services, fertilizer, water, power, and seeds must be made available so that these reach the small farmer. He must also be given security of tenure or secure ownership of his land and a guarantee that

he gains from the improvements that he makes. He needs inputs including information, appropriate institutions and incentives.

5. The small farmer must also be provided with access to markets in market towns and regional cities through feeder roads and marketing facilities.

6. A group of small holdings should be serviced by modern centers of processing, marketing, financial services and extension services, but this must be done in a way which does not call excessively for scarce managerial resources.

7. Efforts should be made to develop efficient labor-intensive technologies or, more accurately, technologies that economize in the use of capital and sophisticated skills and management and are appropriate for the social, cultural and climatic conditions of developing countries. Construction with appropriate building materials also offers opportunities for creating efficient employment.

8. The rural towns should provide middle-level social services, such as health and family clinics, secondary schools and technical colleges.

9. The new structure will reduce the rush to the large cities, economize in the heavy costs of certain services, and will increase the scope for regional and local participation.

10. The whole process should embrace human and social, as well as economic development. More particularly, hundreds of millions of people will not be more productive, for some time to come. They need social help.

All policies, such as price controls, allocation of inputs, financial and fiscal measure, credit control, foreign exchange controls, etc., should be scrutinized with respect to their final impact on the specified goals. Although some increase in inequality may be inevitable in the early stages and tolerable as long as it does not impoverish the poor, those measures whose incidence is to benefit the rich at the expense of the poor should be abandoned or redesigned.

GENERAL CONCLUSIONS

No doubt there were errors, false starts and dead ends in the development story of the last three decades. In accounting for these, there are Keynesians and Marxists. Keynes attributed (at least in a much-quoted passage in the *General Theory*) the errors of "practical men, who believe themselves quite exempt from any intellectual influences" to "some defunct economist." He thought "that the power of vested interests is vastly exaggerated compared with the gradual encroachment of ideas." According to this interpretation it was the mistaken doctrines of Nurkse, Singer and Rosenstein-Rodan that led governments to subsidize industrial capital equipment, support high urban wages, overvalue exchange rates, raise the costs of farm inputs by protecting domestic industry, lower the prices of farm outputs and generally neglect or, worse, exploit, agriculture and the rural poor.

Marxists believe that it is the power of class interests that is reflected in ideas. The above-mentioned doctrines, on this view, are merely an ideological superstructure, reflecting the powerful vested interests of the urban industrialists and their workers.

But there is a third way of looking at the succession of problems and difficulties: there is a Hydra-like aspect to development (and perhaps to all human endeavor). Many of the difficulties encountered in the path of development were neither the result of economic errors, nor attributable to vested interests, but were the offspring of the successful solution of previous problems. Scientific confidence asserts that there is a solution to every problem, but history (and not only the obstructionist official) teaches us that there is a problem to every solution.

The solution of one problem creates a series of new ones. Success in manufacturing industry has brought out the lag in agriculture. The need to expand the production of food for domestic consumption became so acute partly because of the remarkable growth of industrial output. The seed-fertilizer revolution has spawned a collection of new problems about plant diseases, inequality, unemployment and the other so-called second-generation problems. The need for population control arose from the successful attack on mortality through cheap and efficient methods of malaria eradication. Growing unemployment is (partly) the result of high productivity and growth of manufacturing investment. Education raises excessive aspirations and contributes to the movement to the cities and the consequent unemployment of the educated. The success and the attractions of urban development have shown up the need to accelerate rural development, which by the turmoil it creates, may further accelerate the migration to the cities.

The Hirschmanesque generalized doctrine of unbalanced growth cannot, of course, be used to justify and legitimize errors in development thinking and policy. Of these there were plenty. But, on the other hand, not all difficulties are the result of past mistakes, and some are the consequences of the successful solution of preceding problems.

"Hydra" may be the wrong metaphor, for it suggests the hopelessness of all endeavors. "Second-generation" problems, on the other hand, may be too optimistic a term. The question is whether, in spite of the subsequent emergence of new problems, the series converges to, or diverges from, a solution. While some solutions are worse than the problems, others represent progress. It is important to bear in mind that solutions are not readily transferable between places and periods.

Another lesson is what more sophisticated colleagues like to call "the counter-intuitive character of systems analysis." Things are not necessarily true because they are paradoxical, but in development studies, as in other fields, common sense does not always lead to the correct answer. Job creation may cause more, rather than less unemployment. Import restrictions and physical allocations, intended to reduce inequalities, may strengthen monopoly power. A strategy that sacrifices economic growth of consumption in order to create more jobs may require *faster*, not slower, growth. Policies designed to help the poor may benefit the middle and upper classes, and so on. As these illustrations show, the implications of this view can be profoundly conservative or startlingly revolutionary. In a given power structure, attempts at piecemeal reform *may* be self-cancelling and the system will tend to reestablish the initial wealth and power distribution. Only a deep, structural change *may* enable reform to take root.

On the other hand, piecemeal reform *may* trigger pressures that lead to further reforms, whereas revolutionary change, as the many revolutions that failed show, may fail to achieve its objective.

A third lesson is that in many areas only a concerted, properly phased attack on several fronts yields the desired result and the application of some measures without certain others may make things worse. "Correct" prices in a society with a fairly equal distribution of assets and available appropriate technologies may raise efficiency and reduce inequality, but to use "correct" prices in a society with very unequal ownership of assets will only change the manifestation of inequality.

Not only are there Myrdalian cumulative processes, but the processes require packages; the causation is cumulative and joint. The appropriate metaphor is the jigsaw puzzle, the fitting together of different parts, not the toothpaste or the sausage machine which respond to pressures with homogenous outputs. To do something in a certain sequence, together with other things, brings success; to do it in isolation may be worse than doing nothing. A program of education without employ-

ment opportunities will only accelerate the brain drain. What is needed
is a range of interrelated, properly phased, measures. There are no simple remedies. The solution of underdevelopment is not to be found in
making the soil more—and women less—fertile in a combination of
fertilizer and pill (the technocratic solution); nor, for that matter, by
staging a revolution (the revolutionary solution), or implementing a
radical land reform (the radical solution), nor by "getting prices right"
(the economist's solution), though each, in conjunction with the others,
may have something to contribute to a total solution.

A fourth lesson is that few problems are narrowly economic ones.
The difficulties often lie with human attitudes, social institutions and
political power structures, more than, or as well as, with scarcities of
productive inputs and their correct allocation. Scarce inputs—capital
and skills—will probably also be needed to attack social and political
obstacles, but the link between resources and outcomes is a tenuous
one: there are no fixed capital coefficients between resources spent
and an effective land reform, or between money and a successful birth
control campaign.

Finally, the response of the rich countries to the challenge of development is not to be found in development aid alone, whether it consists of capital or brains, even if it were two percent instead of one-third
percent of GNP, or in freer access to the markets of the rich countries.
It is the *total* relationship, the impact of *all policies* of the rich countries, that is relevant, and that has to be our concern if we are serious
about international cooperation.

Chapter 2

THE ORIGINALITY OF THE COPY: THE ECONOMIC COMMISSION FOR LATIN AMERICA AND THE IDEA OF DEVELOPMENT[1]

Fernando Henrique Cardoso

Among the critics of culture in Latin America an intermittent, but not uninteresting, debate is going on about the effects of dependency on the production of ideas. Some specialists in the theory of Brazilian literature[2] have been attempting to show how the *same* idea, once transferred from the centers of the international production of culture to periphery nations, becomes something else. Perhaps the classical example of this—as pointed out by another researcher in the history of ideas, Professor João Cruz Costa—is the transference of Auguste Comte's positivism to Latin America.[3]

In this chapter we are going to discuss just the opposite in the history of Latin American ideas, for we are going to discuss ideas in their rightful place. I will trace the origins and history of one major body of Latin American ideas on development since the early 1950s. As such, this chapter is a literal companion piece to Professor Streeten's survey (Chapter 1)—which focuses heavily on economic thought produced in the *developed* nations. The alternative material presented in the present chapter is noteworthy because at least some important ideas about economic development did originate in Latin America. I should at once point out that I shall also take care to show that even the most original Latin American thinking on economic development has its roots outside the continent. I shall not, however, take ideas on development as mere "reflections" of the blazing sun of western thought. What is new in ideas is often the "rewarming," provided that a little seasoning is added to the water which is used for this purpose, in order to prevent the old ideas from being burned to a frazzle in the process. It is in this sense that I shall be concerned with the "originality of the copy." I will return to this theme in the conclusion, when considering how we should interpret the importance of indigenous Latin American thinking on development.

IDEAS ON ECLA DEVELOPMENT

During the 1950s the United Nation's Economic Commission for Latin America (ECLA) acquired a registered trademark in Latin American economic thought as a channel for the diffusion of a set of theses concerning development—its causes, its conditions, and the obstacles to it.

What were the key ideas concerning development put forward by ECLA, and why did they prove to be so controversial?

The main ECLA text on the relations between center and periphery, and therefore on development and underdevelopment, is the *Economic Study of Latin America* written in 1949 and published by the United Nations in 1951. It has exactly the same theoretical foundation regarding Latin American development as an article published in 1950 by Dr. Raul Prebisch—undoubtedly ECLA's predominant economist during that period.[4] In these texts, forming the basis of what came to be known as the Prebisch-ECLA doctrine, there are two or three ideas that were fundamental and innovative.[5]

In *opposition* to orthodox liberal ideas such as the fundamental premise of market theory concerning the comparative advantages of the international division of labor, Prebisch argued that the economic relations between center and periphery nations tend to reproduce the conditions of underdevelopment and increase the gap between developed and underdeveloped countries. The invisible arm of the market does not appear, according to Prebisch, in the role of fairy godmother. On the contrary, instead of correcting inequalities, it aggravates them.

Why is this so? Because the countries of the center appropriate the majority of the fruits of technological progress. How? Starting from evidence presented in United Nation documents that showed a trend of deterioration in the terms of trade between primary and manufactured goods, Prebisch reviewed the factors which cause this situation.[6] They include:

1.   The rate of productivity growth in manufacturing production was higher than in the production of agricultural goods.
2.   The rise in productivity should be transmitted to the prices of manufactured products, via the lower value incorporated in each unit produced.
3.   In the industrialized countries there is, however, trade union pressure to maintain wage levels, and industrial production is organized so that oligopolies can defend their profit rates. Thus, prices do not fall in proportion to the rise in productivity.

In other words, what Prebisch calls the agents of production—workers and employers—of the industrialized countries manage, thanks to their *political and organizational* strength, to block the functioning of the market and produce a specific effect on international trades. That effect is the constant deterioration of the terms of trade, preventing the international diffusion of technological progress. This explains why the prices of primary products tend to *fall* as a proportion of the prices of manufactured products.

The above synthesis shows that Prebisch started from a basic classical assumption.   The latter forecast a relative fall in international prices compared with primary commodities.[7] If such a relative fall occurred, it could be expected to result in a trend toward international equalization of resource prices (given that the commodity-producing countries have a lower income).

The ECLA position is clear that the consequences of falling prices of primary products in conditions of abundant labor will be growth that is lower than that of the developed countries. This tendency gives rise to a *lower* capacity for accumulation on the periphery since, for Prebisch, savings are primarily dependent on growth in productivity.

If there is a questionable element in the ECLA reasoning, it is perhaps the failure to explain in more detail the mechanisms of exploitation of the periphery by the center. It cannot be said, however, that ECLA neglected the fundamental role of accumulation in market economies. Nor was there any lack of references to the specific social and historical circumstances in capitalist countries which underlay accumulation. Greater capacity of trade unions to fight for their own class interests and the political and organizational strength of the big capitalist firms to resist the fall in the profit rate constituted obstacles, according to ECLA, to the automatic transference of the gains from rising productivity. The latter transference was taken for granted in the classical theory of international trade.

CRITIQUES OF THE ECLA THEORIES

ECLA's theses on international trade and development were not accepted without opposition—far from it. The more orthodox economists (both liberals and Marxists) were always critical (from opposite points of view) of what came to be known as the "ECLA theories." For zealous defenders of the idea that the "logic of the market" is the best mechanism to propel *true* development, ECLA always represented the Trojan horse of leftism. Behind its recommendations concerning the necessity for state intervention to correct distortions, the defense of protectionist policies, and the insistence on the structural nature of inflation in Latin America, orthodox liberals always saw the risk of bureaucratic socialism.

Later on, no less zealously, the theoreticians of the ultra-Left "unmasked" the class character of ECLA's formulations, alleging that they did not expose the mechanisms of social and economic exploitation that maintain the working-class subordinated to the bourgeoisie and the latter subordinated to the imperialist centers. To understand more clearly the controversial nature of ECLA's "doctrine" and the criticisms to which it was subjected, we must examine the reactions from distinct schools of economic thought.

The "Orthodox" Line

It was not long before ECLA's formulations were rebutted by the representatives of orthodoxy. Professor Gottfried Haberler, of Harvard, peremptorily denied that economists possessed "any kind of law that permits them to predict price tendencies in favor of or against producers of raw materials."[8] He accepted the existence of short-term variations which disfavored underdeveloped countries, since during phases of world economic depression the relative prices of primary products tended to worsen, but he denied the possibility of inferring a constant trend toward decline. Haberler believed that the extent of the deterioration of the terms of trade of primary exporting countries had been exaggerated. He advised underdeveloped countries to live with their adversity and take comfort in the hope that the rich countries also are subject to hard times.

Notwithstanding the bias of Haberler's conclusions, he does put forward one pertinent argument, if in mistaken terms, when he touches on a controversial point of the ECLA theory: the inevitability of the gap between center and periphery. Indeed, Haberler argues that a worsening in one country's terms of trade on the international market within a given period does not signify that this country by the end of such a period will have suffered damage to its economic welfare.[9] In other words there may be an unequal distribution of gains in favor of the center via foreign trade. *At the same time*, as a result of rises in productivity, there may in theory be economic growth and even an improvement in the standard of living in the periphery. Thus, the gap between developed and developing countries may increase and standards of living in the latter could at the time be rising.

Haberler also tried to attack the idea that the transference of the benefits from technological progress is blocked by defense of wage and profit levels in the industrialized countries. He argued that competition between capitalists and the breaking of Britain's monopoly of technological progress invalidated ECLA's position. According to him, the producers of raw materials are perfectly capable of looking after themselves; the ones who suffer are the fixed-income groups in the developed countries!

In spite of their conservative bias and their misleading interpretation of Prebisch's views, Haberler's arguments also indicate an important lacuna in the early work of ECLA: the lack of a more explicit analysis of the role and nature of economic cycles, and the distinction between such cycles and tendencies towards constant deterioration. Later on, in the works of ECLA's followers, the effects of recessions were taken as expressions of irreversible tendencies. This conception led to the illusion of continuous and growing deterioration, not only in the relation between developed and underdeveloped countries, but in the very situation of underdevelopment itself.[10]

In his advocacy of *economic policy*, Prebisch vigorously defended the creation of conditions to reduce the gap between center and periphery. The theoretical argument, however, left room for ambiguous interpretations, and these were in fact the basis of Haberler's critique. Other economists did the same as Haberler: they took a step backwards in the debate. Among them, the most conspicuous was Professor Jacob Viner.[11] To repeat Viner's words:

"All that I find in Prebisch's studies and in the other literature along similar lines emanating from the United Nations and elsewhere is the dogmatic identification of agriculture with poverty, and the explanation of agricultural poverty by inherent natural historical laws, by virtue of which agricultural products tend to exchange on ever-deteriorating terms for manufactures, technological progress tends to confine its blessings to manufacturing industries, and agricultural populations do not get the benefit of technological progress in manufactures even as purchasers, because the prices of manufactured products do not fall with the decline in their real costs." And, he adds, "This is no more nor less than mistaking a simple conjecture for non-existent tendential laws."[12]

Having seen no more in Prebisch's argument, Viner went on to "demonstrate" that the real problem was not *agriculture* as such, or *industrialization* as such, but "poverty and backwardness." How in a nontautological way, could poverty and backwardness be presented as a cause of themselves? Nevertheless, he was wrong in his representation of Prebisch's argument. The latter was founded on the differential rates of *productivity* increases (or of development of the productive forces) in developed and underdeveloped countries. The example of agriculture was introduced to underline the fact that in Latin America, in general, productivity was low in agriculture compared with that of the urban industrial sector, and that *therefore* there was greater poverty in the countryside. Furthermore, Prebisch has always maintained that increasing productivity in agriculture is a good way of increasing living standards.

The "Heterodox" Liberal Line

It is worth remembering that the economic formulations prevalent at the time (leaving aside Marxist analysis) focused on the formation of capital to break the inexorable circle of underdevelopment. Capital formation was seen as depending on two mechanisms: foreign investment and exports to generate "surplus." Concerning exports and imports, it was emphasized that even without industrialization the periphery could benefit from the center's progress, because there were equalizing mechanisms in the international trading system. As to foreign investment, even the most orthodox advocates of its advantages recognized that it tended to be concentrated in the colonial-exporting sectors and that the limited internal market was an obstacle to the attraction of industrial investments to underdeveloped countries. Thus, the prevailing development theories were either based on the advantages of international trade or, in one way or another, ended up accepting the vicious circle of poverty as a fundamental limiting element in peripheral economies.

The most prestigious critical formulation on underdevelopment from liberal quarters in the early Fifties was produced by Gunnar Myrdal. With the critical eye which he had developed in his masterly work on the American Negro, Myrdal had incorporated a "structural" perspective into his work. His analyses became more and more politically dense, as evidenced in *The Political Element in the Development of Economic Theory*.[13] But when he worked out his hypothesis on "circular causation with cumulative effects"—which gave more sophisticated theoretical grounds and added critical elements from political theory to the old idea of the vicious circle of poverty—Myrdal was emphasizing obstacles rather than possibilities of development.[14]

In the Latin American debate—which bore on a more urbanized region which was also more of an appendix to capitalist development in the center—the major academic argument was related to the circularity of poverty due to the restriction of the markets. The weight of extra-economic factors was less visible and had less impact on economic theory.

Ragnar Nurkse, in lectures he gave in Rio de Janeiro in 1951, stated the issue clearly: the limited size of the internal market would be the greatest obstacle to development.[15] How were Latin American nations to break this barrier?

Nurkse's answer is also clear. In situations marked by the vicious circle of poverty, only a rise in productivity really generates an expansion of the market. (Monetary inflows produce nothing more than inflation, and exports in themselves do not resolve, and may even reproduce, the vicious circle.) However, an isolated rise in productivity is not enough. Only a chain reaction produced by a "wave of capital investment in various industries" can break the circle. Schumpeter's theory of the innovating entrepreneur and the successive waves of business action would give sociological and economic support to the theory of the initial thrust.

In this way, there arose an elegant formulation of the so-called "theory of balanced growth," based on an amplification of the size of the market and increased stimuli to investments in industry in general.[16]

The discussion—the development of which cannot be followed in this short chapter—of what was meant by "size of the market" in relation to the size of the population and geographical space, was an intense one in the early Fifties. Not all economists from the developed countries agreed with Nurkse. Although, as we shall see below, he put more emphasis on the need for foreign capital than internal saving to increase productivity per capita and break the iron circle of backwardness, he arrived at a formulation which favored industrialization through the theory of "balanced development."

Albert O. Hirschman, for example, proposed in 1954 a different strategy of development. Instead of taking the "balanced growth" view with its obvious concern for capital, Hirschman pointed out that *imbalances* sometimes promote corrective reactions. He suggested that a chain of technological requirements could induce new investments. So it is important to take into consideration backward and forward linkages derived from investments.

Hirschman was more a critical supporter of ECLA's claims in favor of industrialization than an opponent. He showed that internal creativity in the process of capital accumulation is more important for development than the continuous lament about capital scarcity. Writing in the late Fifties, Hirschman was a pioneer among non-Latin American economists in advocating planning and public intervention in the economy. Some of his explanations, with respect to inflation and the balance of payments problems, are close to ECLA's structuralist views, although they have been proposed independently.

Both Nurkse and Hirschman began, then, to concentrate their interest less on the "automatic" effects of the theory of comparative advantages than on the real problems of development: how to accumulate or make better use of the surplus in order—through industrialization—to break with backwardness and underdevelopment.

The Marxists

It was on the basis of Lenin's second version of the effects of imperialism that Marxist economists contemporary with ECLA's early formulations made their proposals. Dobb used the classical Marxist approach: capital expansion will occur on the periphery because the rise in the organic composition of capital in the industrialized countries accelerates the fall of the profit rate. Thus, the colonial countries, where there is cheap and abundant labor and a lower organic composition of capital, should attract foreign investors.[17]

Paul Baran, on the other hand, sees the narrow limits of the market as an obstacle to development: "The shortage of investable funds and the lack of investment opportunities represent two aspects of the same problem. A great number of investment projects, unprofitable under prevailing conditions, could be most promising in a general environment of economic expansion."[18] Consequently, Baran becomes an "industrialist" and argues for increasing productivity and industrialization in order to develop agriculture. He accepts protection policies and tax reforms, but subordinates their importance to that of the prevailing power structures. Without radically modifying the latter, any reform program is an illusion:

"For backward countries to enter the road of economic growth and social progress, the political framework of their existence has to be drastically revamped. The alliance between feudal landlords, industrial royalties, and the capitalist middle classes has to be broken."[19]

In a book published in 1957, Baran reformulated his point of view. He upheld his critical analysis of political conditions detrimental to development, but refuted Nurkse and Hans Singer, replacing the idea of the absence of capital funds (narrow limits of the market) with that of inadequate use of the "economic surplus" in underdeveloped countries. He also argued that deterioration of the terms of trade is not of general importance, given that this does not affect all underdeveloped countries in the same way and that many of them have little need of exchange controls.[20]

Introducing the idea of "economic surplus," Baran shows that it is often used irrationally in Third World countries—as in the luxury goods consumption of the wealthy classes. A proper application of this surplus, he argued, would solve the alleged shortage of capital. Furthermore, foreign investments do not resolve, but rather aggravate, distortions in the use of the surplus according to this view.

Thus, while the classical Marxist view diverges from ECLA's analysis because it did not see the scarcity of capital as a problem, the more political tradition based on Lenin, and accepted by Baran, perceived that there was a problem in the market and in the dynamic insufficiency of capital funds. In contrast with Prebisch, Baran did not believe that reforms, increased productivity, and foreign capital could drastically alter the prevailing conditions of underdevelopment. Only a socialist revolution could liberate the productive forces and permit the elevation of the masses' standard of living, through a more rational use of the available surplus.

ECLA'S IDEAS IN PRACTICE

It is interesting to note that Prebisch and ECLA's policy of increased productivity per capita and capital accumulation (in order to raise the standard of living of the mass of the population) was highly criticized by both Left and Right. The Left criticized it because there was no explication of the mechanisms by which the two goals—capital accumulation and improvement of popular living standards—would be made compatible. The Right criticized this policy because it did not see in the Latin American Manifesto (as the 1949 document was called by Hirschman) any more than an accusation of the rich countries.

Nevertheless, Prebisch was explicit. He showed that:

1. International trade should give active aid to Latin American growth.
2. Increased productivity was indispensable.
3. Without accumulation there would be no development.
4. This process should not be realized through a compression in popular consumption, which was already very low.

ECLA's Development Policies

When it began to advocate specific policies, ECLA's proposals were even more exposed to criticism than they had been during the theoretical debate.[21] This was largely because ECLA's policies emphasized the problems of structural imbalance between center and periphery. Those economists who were concerned about the short term and the monetary aspects of development saw in such proposals the risk of anticapitalist rhetoric.

In terms of basic objectives and of the economic policy instruments to reach them, ECLA's position varied little during the Fifties. Those objectives were:

1. industrialization and "healthy" protectionism;
2. adequate foreign currency allocation policy;
3. programming of import substitution; and
4. a desire to avoid cutting wages in the process of industrialization and to avoid a reduction in the masses' capacity to consume.

Obviously, these were important issues. Until the end of the Fifties ECLA was discreet in advocating socially and politically thorny measures, such as agrarian reform and policies to achieve social equality. Even so, the idea of exchange controls and/or programming investments seemed to conservative eyes to be wholly heretical.

Aside from declarations about the standard of living of the masses, the emphasis of ECLA's policies was laid on the need for "programmed" industrialization, with the necessary exchange control mechanisms. The implementation of these policies, however, presupposed moving the centers of decision to the periphery nations and strengthening the decision-making and regulating capacity of the state. So it is not difficult to understand the reason for the liberal-conservative reaction to ECLA.

In this respect, it is curious to note that there was a certain coincidence on the purely ideological level between some of ECLA's positions and the solutions proposed by Marxists, insofar as the latter also criticized the "feudal-imperialist" alliance. The two used distinct languages and based their explanations on distinct premises, but both located the principal enemy *overseas*. Both also agreed that without an internal effort to remove "obstacles to development" embodied in the traditional sectors there would be no improvement in the standard of living of the masses. These coincidences were what made ECLA's thinking "pink."

Prebisch and ECLA, as well as the representatives of its thinking in various countries—the most brilliant example was that of Furtado at the head of Brazil's Superintendence of Development for the North-East (SUDENE)—stood their ground as to the need for industrialization and programming. And they kept to their objective of raising the welfare of the masses.[22] However, they did not draw up specific policies for this purpose. Nor is it right to say, on the other hand, that they defended protectionism to excess. Prebisch always defended the need for a certain amount of competition. His distrust of Soviet-style state control led him to question whether the undeniable economic achievements of the Soviet Union—which amazed him—were not due more to the opening of the educational system and the mobility of

Soviet society than to excessive centralization.[23]

Later, around the end of the decade, ECLA insisted on the importance of economic integration between countries to assist industrialization and economic programming. It began to propose and implement the formation of Latin American "common markets": Latin American Free Trade Association (LAFTA) and the Central American Common Market. It is easy to see behind these efforts ECLA's concern for the narrow limits of the market—the search for the desired scale for investments—and the political notion that it was perhaps easier to offer resistance to the interests of the center through the formation of "blocs."

In the early ECLA documents technological dependency was taken for granted as a characteristic of underdevelopment. Nevertheless, there is considerable indecision in later ECLA thinking on development policy in relation to foreign capital, and the explanation of the nature of the proposed accumulation.

In Prebisch's 1949 article, the following idea of how to accumulate is put forward:

> In order to form the necessary capital for industrialization and for technological progress in agriculture, it would not seem indispensable to compress the consumption of the masses which is in general already too low. In addition to present savings, foreign investments, *if well employed* [my emphasis], could contribute to an immediate rise in productivity per man. Once a certain initial improvement had been achieved in this way, an important part of production could be channelled off for the formation of capital, thus avoiding premature consumption.[24]

Prebisch's realism led him to be cautious about the contribution of foreign capital. In the early formulations of his doctrine, it appears as a temporary resource necessary to increase the internal formation of capital to raise productivity. The state is the primary agent of acceleration in this process, but since there are distortions in the process (due to inflation, high propensity to consume, and so on), it will be necessary to resort to foreign capital.

In 1952 Prebisch pointed out a positive tendency not taken up for discussion again until the Sixties: that there was an emerging new market for commodities produced by foreign investments and that this market was *internal*.[25] He was critical, however, of foreign capital for failing to accelerate this process. In this sense he singles out the role of foreign capital in transferring technology.

"There is a need to stimulate these investments, not only for the capital, but also for the technological aid they bring with them and for the spreading of know-how which is so essential for these countries."[26]

In other words, the theory did not make quite explicit what was meant by the internal division of labor which could facilitate accumulation. It did remain faithful, on the other hand, to the imperative need for increased productivity and endeavored to avoid cutting the real wages of the mass of workers. Hence, the way out of the circle would be:

1. control and reallocation of the resources obtained by exports;

2. diversion of resources from consumer goods to the capital goods sector; and

3. additional, but important, recourse to foreign capital to accelerate both the formation of capital and technological progress.

The goals later sought by Prebisch (which do not come within the objectives of this chapter) were fully in line with this vision: multilateral treaties on international trade to defend the prices of primary goods, for example, the United Nation's Conference on Trade and Development (UNCTAD) and proposals to increase "foreign aid" and make it multilateral. These proposals would obtain the minimum of extra capital and technology to guarantee the great leap forward in terms of industrialization and development.

Adaptations of ECLA's Thinking to Emerging Situations

The preceding pages give a general summary of ECLA's thinking during its heyday.[27] When they are put alongside the prevailing ideas of their time, the originality of ECLA's proposals become clear, as well as their sources and limitations. Undoubtedly, however, the theoretical arguments and the solutions put forward, although I have not analyzed the latter in detail, show a certain capacity to renovate themes and solutions as a function of a given historical situation. In this sense, it does not seem exaggerated to say that there is such a thing as Latin American economic thought. It would be ingenuous to believe that this thought was not nourished by the classical models and their continuation. But this theoretical inheritance was "rewarmed" and made more malleable and more capable of explaining the new situations that were emerging.

From around the mid-Fifties onward, there was change in the rhythm and form of the international movement of capital and in the very organization of international capitalist firms. These transformations altered the relations between center and periphery. I shall not even attempt to make a synthesis of this process here. It is sufficient to point out that the activity of what have come to be known as multinational companies has considerably increased. More than this, these companies—a handful of former trusts transformed into conglomerates which diversify their investments on a world scale, along with new organizations of the same brand which have arisen—began to intensify *industrial investments on the periphery.*

Thus, after the Second World War, the Marxist theorists' "optimism" as to the effects of the expansion of capital on the industrialization of the periphery *seemed* to be justified. If until the mid-Fifties the struggle to industrialize the periphery was *at the same time* an anti-imperialist struggle, because the trusts invested little in the periphery's secondary sector, from this time on industrialization became one of the *goals* of foreign capital in some countries of the periphery.[28] The relations between public policy, state enterprise and foreign capital became more and more complex after this development.

Nevertheless, it took some time for this process to be well recognized in Latin America. North American policy, especially during Kennedy's time and that of the Alliance for Progress, had accepted part of the original critique in ECLA analyses, but had *changed their emphasis.* The discussions on the "internal obstacles" to development, both social and political ones, were brought to the fore, and the United States government explicitly patronized more active forms of international cooperation through the Inter-American Development Bank. As a consequence, the bank began to finance health projects, agrarian reforms, roads, and similar projects.

In a sense, ECLA was overwhelmed by this policy. The OAS meeting at Punta del Este in 1961 represents the most splendid moment of North American sociopolitical reformist zeal in its encounter with ECLA's critique. Previously dangerous themes, such as agrarian and tax reform and planning, became legitimate. But the basic structural questions were momentarily forgotten: the terms of trade, the disparity in technological progress and the level of real wages in center and periphery. So much so, that it seems justifiable to say that ECLA's thinking in this period entered a phase of relative decline. The consistency and simplicity of the heyday was succeeded by a period of growing prolixity and theoretical imprecision in ECLA's production.

At the same time that relations between center and periphery were changing, Latin American economists saw in some local economies "tendencies to structural stagnation"—mistaking the recession cycle which began in the early Sixties for a law implying the difficulty, if not impossibility, of development on the periphery.

At the beginning of the Sixties, statistics showed that the per capita dollar value of exports was *diminishing*, that there had been an accentuation in the deterioration of the terms of trade, and that agricultural exports had diminished. These problems arose because international demand in this sector was declining in the rich countries (Engel's Law) without any decline in the industrial import requirements of the periphery. Undoubtedly these were real phenomena. Linking them all together, however, led to interpretations which asserted the absence of any real capitalist dynamic and the difficulty of obtaining *real* effects of development.

At this time, it became popular to make a distinction (basically a moral one) between "growth" and "development." The latter process would only occur if there were a better distribution of income and of property, which would permit a more complete development of mankind. This, of course, was never the version officially endorsed by ECLA, but it was commonly adopted by Latin American critical thought. The fragility of such a formulation consists in its mistaking the socialist critique of capitalism for the inviability of capitalism. In practice, the multinationals at the same time had launched the energetic process of capitalist accumulation on the periphery, by means of forms of exploitation which contained all the ingredients criticized above.

Pessimism was, then, the keynote of the works written in this period. In the decade 1965-75, however, not only was world trade extremely dynamic, but in a few years the terms of trade became *favorable* to agricultural and mineral products.

Thus, history had prepared a trap for the pessimists. This occurred as a result of confusing reformist ideals—which gradually became more explicit in ECLA documents—and the specific analysis of capitalist development. The latter's incompatibility with the desired reforms motivated feelings of frustration. Yet the national product of industrialized countries did not stop growing, and technological progress was consolidated, despite the "distortions."

ONCE AGAIN INNOVATING IDEAS?

The "Perverse" Style of Development

The theoretical crisis undergone by the ECLA position and its failure to understand the transformations which were occurring in the world economy were not, however, entirely negative. It was in this period, too, that a new critical reevaluation of the social critique argument about "styles" of development was formulated. The most creative contribution to this critique was that of Aníbal Pinto,[29] who emphasized the internal inequality of the distribution of the advantages obtained from increased productivity.

Pinto argued that there is a "malignant style" of development, in the expression of Ignacy Sachs, which does not presuppose, on the national level, the trickle-down caused by investments and economic growth. The style of development in Latin America is "concentrative and exclusive." This point of view, empirically recognized and proclaimed previously by sociologists and critical economists, produced innumerable studies and discussions, emphasizing the inability of the prevailing type of industrial development to absorb labor and, hence, its consequences for the concentration of income.

In its 1968 report, ECLA took note of this discussion and summed up current interpretations. Pedro Vuskovic[30] adhered to Aníbal Pinto's critical theoretical line, adding to it somewhat catastrophic connotations concerning the employment capacity generated by this style of development and concerning the investment capacity of Latin American economies.

This is not the place to make a detailed review of the developments in ECLA thinking since the formulation of this concept of "perverse development."[31] It is important, however, to stress that the diagnosis was brilliant in comparison with the earlier revisionist thinking and out-of-place pessimism at the beginning of the Sixties. The work of Aníbal Pinto and Pedro Vuskovic, quoted above, indicates the direction which Latin American economic thought was to take from that time on.

Structural Dependency

Around the mid-Sixties, outside and inside ECLA, another more sociological and political line of interpretation began. Even though it was not incorporated at once into the "House" line of thinking, it was to appear later on in texts by Vuskovic, Furtado, Sunkel, and others. This line became known as "dependency theory."[32]

There were several versions of the same theme. As I have pointed out elsewhere,[33] the early versions written in ECLA itself between 1965 and 1966 tried to take up again the question of why some of the presumed consequences of industrialization on the periphery were not being produced. In their answer they emphasized several explanatory factors.

The first one is the fact that foreign investment was applied to the production of durable consumer goods, with the result that the accumulation cycle has to be completed on a world scale, since to keep the pace of economic growth implies an expansion of the importation of capital goods. More specifically, this process means that the peripheral economies were industrializing, but the capital goods sector continued to function only in the center nations. Thus, the dynamism derived from investments in the internal market spread *to the center nations*. There is no obvious reason why this should correspond to a rigid obstacle that will never be overcome. But up to now the crucial technological advances and financial support to assure them have been achieved only by already industrialized economies.

The implication of this situation is that central and peripheral economies are "interdependent," but with a specific assymmetry which may induce deterioration in the terms of trade if, in the industrial sectors, there are real differences in wages and productivity between center and periphery.

This was not the only version of "dependency." There were others, just as or more stagnationist and catastrophist as some of the ECLA hypotheses criticized before. There were even some interpretations elaborated more in terms of "national dependency" and the difficulties with "foreign dependency" than in terms of "structural dependency" as I have summarized above.[34]

For better or for worse, though, these studies attempted to elaborate some of the elements already contained in ECLA's explanations and to make explicit both the role of foreign capital and that of the class basis of capitalist development.

CONCLUSIONS

The comparison between ECLA's analyses of international trade and development, and the conceptions which prevailed in the academic world of the time (the Fifties) shows that there was something original in ECLA's formulations. Later critiques recognized how advanced these formulations were in relation to neoclassical and marginalist theories but tried, nevertheless, to play down the novelty of Latin American thought and show that its theoretical formulations fell short of what

Marx had said a century before. The argument may be correct insofar as the theory of accumulation is concerned, but it lacks historical perspective when it refers to the problems created by the industrialization of the periphery and the fetters imposed on the latter by the prevailing theory of international trade. While ECLA's formulations have obvious roots in classical economic thought and in Marxism, they are permeated by Keynesian language. This ambiguity makes it difficult to identify the theoretical framework in which the analysis is inserted.

On the other hand, the originality of ECLA's thinking did not consist merely of its emphasizing the tendency for international trade to reproduce the inequality between nations, nor in its explaining this process by the existence of differential wage rates and distinct degrees of technological progress in the center and the periphery. This in itself constitutes a more comprehensive analytical perspective than that implicit in the alternative interpretations which prevailed at the time. But the originality of ECLA also resides in its efforts to transform this interpretation into a complete set of policies to promote industrialization. In this sense, ECLA's thinking generated *ideologies* and motivated action by providing an opening for political practice. For this very reason, it became easier to see the weaknesses of an analysis which pointed to the causes of inequality, but restricted its critique to the threshold of the subject without revealing the class content of the economic exploitation of the periphery by the center.[35]

On the strictly theoretical level, the originality of ECLA's version of development theory remained more implicit than explicit. In the same decade as that in which it was formulated, other economists were working on related theoretical critiques of neoclassical economic positions. In 1960 Piero Sraffa, for example, in *Production of Commodities by Means of Commodities*, illustrated how some problems related to value theory and relative prices—problems which were implicit in ECLA's analysis—could be dealt with in a rigorous manner by making a thorough critique of marginalist theories. Instead of pursuing such theoretical matters in detail, ECLA economists restricted themselves to practical problems.

In ECLA's analyses there is a coexistence without integration of classical, Marxist, Keynesian, neoclassical and properly marginalist explanations of the mechanisms of market prices and of economic growth. The scant attention paid to consistent economic theory— explicable as a consequence of the historical and institutional contest— made it difficult for the international academic world to recognize the originality of ECLA's version of underdevelopment and international inequality. It is time to recognize that, even without theoretically explicating its discoveries, the ECLA school made sound critiques of the neoclassical theory of international trade. Reformulating those critiques should be a tempting task for economists who want to use old models to say original things.

The restatement of ideas in new contexts, far from being a merely repetitive process, implies enrichment. If there is a world for which the simile of perpetual motion is useless, it is that of thought: the trajectory of the "same" idea in another historical and cultural universe makes it into something else. In this sense ECLA's formulations constitute a good example of originality: they offered new themes in the search for ways to confront the problems which arose in economic practice. Furthermore, although they were based on analytical instruments originated in other contexts, ECLA's methods and views elaborate the latter to explain a situation of inequality in international trade and to justify policies which promoted the industrialization of the periphery. If more was not done, it was—as I have stressed—because ECLA's critical radicalism was hemmed in by its political-institutional position. After all, it is an intergovernmental organ. It also lacked the intellectual élan to present its themes in the perspective of an economic theory of the accumulation process. Even within the narrow political-institutional limits of ECLA, it would seem possible to have made more progress with more rigorous critiques of the vulgar academic theories which predominated in those days—as they do today.

To say, however, that a perspective for intellectual analysis could have gone further does not deny the advances it has made. On the contrary, I believe that it is a characteristic of good theory to make the reader's mouth water. Only dogmatists are intent on closing the circle of knowledge and only they produce systems which create the illusion of the old sphinx who said, "Decipher me, or I shall devour thee." Creativity in science is measured by how much greed a theory awakens in its followers to supersede it and, in so doing, to say: Without this shortcut, I would not have been able to open up this possibility of seeing further ahead. ECLA produced ideas which, at that moment, aided the understanding of some of the central problems of capitalist accumulation on the periphery and some of the obstacles which stand in its way. There is no reason, then, to write epitaphs for ECLA's ideas. They have changed and, in the usual way of all seminal ideas, they have molted. Yet, they have remained very much alive, often in other institutions or in other colors, while at the same time they have left their sloughed-off parts by the wayside, as normally occurs with all scientific interpretations.

Part II
Debating Development

Chapter 3

THE CURRENT DEVELOPMENT DEBATE[1]

Bagicha S. Minhas

From the predominant attitude of "more of the same but at an accelerated pace," which prevailed from the mid-1950s to the publication of the Pearson Commission Report[2] in 1969, to the advocacy of "another development" in the 1975 Dag Hammarskjold Foundation Report,[3] the nature of perception in the West of the Third World development problem would seem to have undergone a major change. In order to understand the genesis of this change in perception, a number of questions need to be answered: What are the main elements of this new perception? How is it different from what has gone on before? To what extent are these differences grounded in the changed social and economic circumstances of the Western countries in the late 1960s and early 1970s? To what extent are the new perceptions in the West a product of reaction to changes in indigenous thinking on development in the Third World itself? Or, is the new perception still another attempt to establish in the ideological battleground of the Third World a mirror image of the "good society" of the West? This paper is addressed to some of these questions but not necessarily in the order in which they have been listed here.

BIG PUSH FOR MORE OF THE SAME

A typical expression of the understanding, ideological interests and attitude of the West toward the development of poor countries in the 1950s and 1960s can be found in a study[4] from the Center for International Studies, Massachusetts Institute of Technology. *The Emerging Nations* was authored by ten[5] distinguished intellectuals, most of whom wielded considerable influence in the academic world as well as the American Administration. A documented statement of the position of these authors is given in Appendix A. A stylized summary of their views may be rendered in the following manner:

1. The problems of achieving sustained economic growth in the underdeveloped countries at mid-twentieth century are similar to those that the developed countries faced in the past.

2. Once growth has been built in as a regular and inherent feature of the underdeveloped economies, and has been continuing for some time, these nations will start to look (except for some differences in descriptive detail) like the developed countries of the West.[6]

3. In three critical aspects of population pressure, technology and politics, the current environment is unlike that in which the industrialized Western countries entered the stage of rapid growth. These differences underscore the importance of outside help and the need for a "big push." The United States and the rest of the free world can afford to provide this help.

4. The United States and the rest of the free world should be concerned to see that their influence "is exerted to help these societies move in directions compatible both with their long-run interests and with our own."

5. The overall political objective of the free world in the development of the Third World was described "as an effort to maximize the attractiveness and feasibility of the third choice: to help make the evolution to modernization successful enough so that major groups will not struggle either to repress change entirely or to promote it by ruthless and extremist measures."

It is this perception of the Third World economic and political development problems as a mirror image (of course, blurred here and there by distance in time) of the West which provided the basic ideology for the formulation of aid and other policies in the United States and many of her partners in the cold war.

The Commission on International Development (Pearson Commission) submitted their report to the president of the World Bank in September, 1969. The perception of Third World development embodied in this report was a close replica of the thesis advanced by the authors of *The Emerging Nations* eight years earlier. "The widening gap between the developed and the developing countries" was seen as "a central issue of our times" by the Commission and they observed that "the attempt to do something about this gap was based on the assumption that economic underdevelopment would yield to a determined national effort to change it, with external help from those whose economic strength made this possible." The Pearson Commission further observed that "the experience which we have gained in the last two decades bears out the premise—and the promise—of the effort that has been made. Economic growth in many of the developing countries has proceeded at faster rates than the industrialized countries ever enjoyed at a similar stage in their own history."[7]

Although, in the eyes of the Pearson Commission, the old model of industrialization and modernization, buttressed with foreign aid, stood vindicated in the new experiences of the poor countries in the 1950s and 1960s, they were concerned about fast developing aid-weariness and flagging of international support. The most important question which the Commission raised for themselves and tried to answer was "whether the rich and developed nations will continue their efforts to assist the developing countries or whether they will allow the structure built up for development cooperation to deteriorate and fall apart."[8] The signs were not propitious. The volume of official aid had been stagnant and had not "kept pace with the growth of national product in the wealthy nations." The "commitments by the United States, which had been much the largest provider of aid funds"[9] were declining.

It was against this background of the understanding of the process of development in the Third World and the trend of aid from the rich countries that the Pearson Commission outlined their strategy for international development and cooperation. A number of valuable recommendations were made concerning a framework for free and equitable international trade, promotion of private foreign investment, effective aid administration, redirection of technical assistance, revitalization of aid to education and research, population control and the strengthening of the multilateral aid system. However, the commission's main points relevant to the theme of this paper can be summarized as follows:

Many of the underdeveloped countries should be able to raise the annual rate of growth of their national product to at least six percent.

If they give adequate attention to export promotion, they should achieve self-reliance in the balance of payments sense before the end of the century. There is need for external resources of the order of magnitude of one percent of GNP of the wealthier countries. The official assistance, which was 0.38 percent of donor GNP in 1968, should be raised to 0.70 percent by 1975.[10] Although the motives and purposes of aid policies in the past have been many and varied, a primary objective of aid in the future should be the promotion of economic development. Increases in development aid should be linked to the economic objectives and development performance of the aid-receivers and the monitoring and assessment of performance is best done in a multilateral context in which donors and aid-receivers jointly review the past and plan for the future.

The Pearson Commission's perception of Third World development was clearly an affirmation of the earlier views, which I characterized as "more of the same but at an accelerated pace." The commission, of course, tried to convince the West that, in the ideological battleground of the Third World, their aid objectives should be reoriented and more closely focused on the economic objectives and the development performance of the aid-receivers.

RICH WORLD ISOLATIONISM

While the Pearson Commission was underscoring the need for higher levels of international aid to raise the rates of growth in the Third World, a strong sentiment to look inward was beginning to emerge in a number of rich countries in the West. This sentiment was the strongest in the United States but by no means unique to that country. Its emergence was a reaction to the politics of the cold war, the war in Vietnam, domestic problems of environmental pollution, the degradation of central cities and the existence of social injustice and inequality at home. In Europe, the development of the European Economic Community (EEC) and, more generally, the rapid expansion of trade among the developed countries was also a factor.

The emergence of this isolationist sentiment has been subjected to scholarly debate. A lucid account, which also tries to relate it to the problems of Third World development, is available in W. W. Rostow's *Politics and the Stages of Growth*:

> Thus, the year 1968 saw in America each of the abiding elements of politics enflamed and in mutual conflict: a debate on security

policy and security outlays, focused around Vietnam, but implicit with a general isolationist sentiment; a debate on a tax increase which could only be obtained from the Congress by constraints on welfare outlays. . . ; a debate on the appropriate constitutional balance between justice and order, with respect to race and the cities.[11]

Rostow argued that American society was "entering the complex transition from high mass-consumption to the search for quality—in a world in unresolved transition from Cold War to the chaos or order that lies beyond—there emerged voices demanding urgently, at once: a domestic life of quality and justice; a wider range of freedoms for the individual; and world peace."[12] He went on to observe:

As in the United States, a radical youth exists in other advanced nations, which tends to believe that the Cold War is outmoded and a bore. . . . Even before the bulk of the citizens of their societies have come fully to share in high mass-consumption, they are drawn to revolt against its values.[13]

Rostow expressed his concern for Third World development in this environment of the politics of the search for quality in the West in the following words:

If we turn inward and grow lax in the laborious struggle to move from Cold War to stable world order, if we fail to reach out in brotherhood to those coming up behind us, notably those who have not yet completed successfully the take-off, if we fail to respect the vulnerability of this precious global community, with its national components at very different stages of growth and aspiration, living in the shadow of nuclear weapons—then, surely, we face evils greater even than those generated during high mass-consumption, pressing hard upon us now during the early phase of the search for quality.[14]

Whatever the *source* of rich world isolationism, the most important observations for this chapter concern its likely *effect* on Third World development. Both *The Emerging Nations* and Pearson Commission perspectives view developed world assistance as a critical element in any strategy of development. A continuation or hardening of this isolationist posture (manifest in the greater use of import quotas as well as restrictions on aid budgets) would seem, therefore, to impose a significant constraint upon both the choice of any nation's development strategy, and, as I shall point out in more detail below, the likelihood of success of *any* chosen strategy.

SOME INDIGENOUS THIRD WORLD
PERCEPTIONS AND THEIR IMPACT

While the strongly inward-oriented domestic pressures in the Western world came to restrict the availability of aid needed for a big push to raise the overall growth of GNP in many countries of the Third World after the mid-1960s, serious questions also began to be raised about the viability of the proposition that improved living standards for all and higher levels of employment would automatically result from un-differentiated growth. These questions were first raised in some Third World countries, which by the early 1960s, had had a decade or more of experience with planned development.

An early and important example of this view was presented in the 1962 paper[15] of the Perspective Planning Division (PPD) of the Indian Planning Commission, done in collaboration with the planning unit of the Indian Statistical Institute (ISI). This paper drew pointed atten-tion to the problem of absolute poverty and quantified its magnitude on the basis of a minimum normative level of private per capita con-sumption. It also worked out the composition and profile of output and investment for a fifteen-year period (1961-1976) which would be consistent with pulling up all but the last two deciles of the population above the poverty line. The problems of the lowest two deciles—only loosely integrated with the growing sectors of the economy and living in remote hill and tribal areas and certain sections of rural society—were to be tackled with a different range of policies outside the purview of the basic model presented in the paper. This paper had a poor recep-tion from academic economists[16] and it was not until many years later that the government of India moved in the direction of the lead indi-cated in this seminal document.

The political consensus, which the Indian National Congress Party maintained for a long time, was shattered in 1967. During the next few years, the poor in India emerged as the darling of all political parties. These political developments, the phenomenon of abject poverty and the relevant strategies of national development became the subject of intense study and debate[17] in India. The Indian National Congress (which went through a split in 1969 and ruled as a minority government in Parliament while many Indian States had already been under non-Congress governments since the 1967 general elections) regained its hold on Parliament with a two-thirds majority in the March 1971 elections on the basis of a manifesto whose centerpiece was the elimination of abject poverty. Election manifestos of all other parties, both on the Left and the Right, gave prominence to the problems of the poor. This political consensus, although largely populist, on the problem of poverty was further strengthened in the elections to the State Assemblies in 1972.[18] In May 1972, the top political leadership of India in the National Development Council accepted a document[19] of the Planning Commission outlining a strategy of self-reliant and participative development for the removal of absolute poverty through the provision of better employment opportunities, particularly in agriculture; special programs for specific poverty groups; and a program of basic minimum needs in the field of primary education, health, nutrition and family planning, clean drinking water, sanitation and slum improvement, house sites for the landless, rural roads and electrification. This strategy was further elaborated in other documents of the Indian Planning Commission in 1973.[20] Unfortunately, the final document of the Fifth Five Year Plan, which appeared two and a half years too late in September 1976 under the emergency regime, is almost silent on removal of poverty and the basic minimum needs strategy.

A number of interesting changes also occurred in the perception of development in some African countries in the 1960s. The Arusha Declaration of February 1967, for instance, marked a significant watershed in the development strategy of Tanzania. The old model of urban-based industrial development, aided by foreign finance and technical know-how, was criticized in the declaration in the following terms:

> The mistake we are making is to think that development begins with industries. It is a mistake because we do not have the means to establish many modern industries in our country. We do not have either the necessary finances or the technical know-how. . . .
> It is stupid to rely on money as the major instrument of development when we know only too well that our country is poor. It is equally stupid, indeed, it is even more stupid, for us to imagine that we shall rid ourselves of our poverty through foreign financial assistance. . . .

After the Arusha Declaration, particularly since 1971, Tanzania has been trying to chart and execute a new strategy of development with stress on self-reliance through improvement of her human and land resources. The main thrust in agriculture and rural development has been the establishment of Ujamaa villages, where the main principles of organization are cooperation, participatory democracy and communal ownership of land. A number of imaginative programs relating to educational reform, health care, sanitation and drinking water have been the other features of the new strategy. While materials suitable to assess the performance of Tanzania under the new strategy are not generally available, such an assessment is not necessary for this chapter. Our purpose here has been to give a significant African example of the changing perception of thinking about the content and meaning of development in the Third World.

From its overwhelming emphasis on import-substituting industrialization in the 1950s and early 1960s, Latin American thought on development during the last ten years has been undergoing substantial change.[21] A number of scholars in Latin America have pushed ahead on the thesis of transnationalization and dependent development. Arguments have also been advanced to delink the "periphery" nations from the "center" nations and to organize Third World nations to achieve collective self-reliance. The inability of the prevailing style of Latin American development (characterized as "concentrative and exclusive") to absorb labor and to produce an effective trickle-down has been adequately recognized. Questions relating to marginalization, poverty, income distribution, emphasis on reducing dependence, and the establishment of a "new society" are now an important part of the development debate in Latin America.

The serious questioning of the meaning of undifferentiated growth in the underdeveloped countries (as a reduced mirror image of the developed countries) has not remained confined to the Third World. The relevance of the trickle-down from undifferentiated growth was also seriously challenged around the turn of this decade by some Western scholars.[22] The work of the Pilot Missions under the International Labor Organization (ILO) World Employment Program in Colombia (1970), Ceylon (1971), and Kenya (1972) helped to show how the problems of employment, poverty and inequality are varied and require very different priorities in development—different from those suggested by perceptions which are obsessively concerned with GNP growth alone.

Lately, the march of events seems to have induced some Western development theorists to rethink their values concerning development in the Third World. Witness the following statement from Professor Hirschman:

A drastic transvaluation of values is in process in the study of economic and political development. It has been forced upon us by a series of disasters that have occurred in countries in which development seemed to be vigorously underway. The civil war in Nigeria and the bloody falling apart of Pakistan are only the most spectacular instances of such "development disasters." ... As a result, one reads with increasing frequency pronouncements about the bankruptcy of the "old" development economics, with its accent on growth rates, industrialization, and international assistance, and about the need for a wholly new doctrine that would emphasize income distribution, employment, and self-reliance.[23]

A significant change occurred, then, between 1970 and 1974. The international financial institutions have also revised their diagnoses and perceptions of the development process. Professor Chenery, in his introduction to a joint study[24] of the World Bank's Development Research Center and the Institute of Development Studies at the University of Sussex, made the following observations in 1974:

It is now clear that more than a decade of rapid growth in under-developed countries has been of little or no benefit to perhaps a third of their population. . . . Paradoxically, while growth policies have succeeded beyond the expectations of the first development decade, the very idea of aggregate growth as a social objective has increasingly been called into question.[25]

He went on further to observe that "our diagnosis of the causes and dimensions of poverty calls into serious question the accepted approaches to policy-making" and

leads us to propose a fundamental redirection of development strategy. Before this can be undertaken, the general diagnosis must first be refined to fit the conditions of each country. This requires a specific analysis of the characteristics of the principal poverty groups, which vary greatly between rural and urban areas and according to their response to different policies. . . . While the tools for analyzing the sectors that employ most of the poor—small-scale agriculture and the urban "informal sector"—are primitive, the available studies suggest that there is considerable scope for expanding the productive use of resources in these activities. . . . Our rural strategy, therefore, focuses on increasing the productivity of the small farmer and the self-employed through better access to land, water, credit and markets, and other facilities. The urban poor require a more diversified strategy. . . . However, even with optimal policies, the modern sector cannot provide employment for the bulk of the rapidly growing urban labor force. A second range of policies designed to reach the self-employed and to make small producers more efficient is therefore necessary.[26]

THE NEW INTERNATIONAL CHORUS: BASIC NEEDS

The withdrawal symptoms, which Rostow attributed to the politics of the search for quality in the rich countries in the 1960s, were further accentuated in the 1970s. The international environment was complicated by the chaos in the international monetary system. Reconciliation of high rates of growth with price stability and accepted levels of unemployment became difficult. The state of confusion was further compounded by the energy and food crises of 1973 and 1974. This was not the environment for increasing international assistance for the development of the poor countries. Instead serious theses on *triage* and the analogy of the lifeboat became fashionable.[27] The development of detente, attempts at rapprochement between the United States and China and the defeat in Vietnam further diminished the attractiveness of the Third World as an ideological battleground. The old model of global development, with its national components at very different stages of growth to be helped along with a big push to successively higher stages through large injections of foreign resources, has few adherents left.

New global manifestos have begun to appear. The Dag Hammarskjold Foundation version (1975) advocates "another development."[28] The main issue for "another development" is introduced in these terms:

In a world whose gross product trebled over the last twenty-five or thirty years, whereas population increased by barely two-thirds, resources are available to satisfy basic needs without transgressing the "outer limits." The question is primarily one of distributing them more equitably.[29]

This issue is not new. But it is now considered urgent to turn toward another development—another development, which should be (a) geared to the satisfaction of needs (such as food, shelter, drinking water, sanitation, health and education), beginning with the eradication of poverty, (b) endogenous and self-reliant, that is, relying on the strength of societies which undertake it, and (c) in harmony with the environment. Although different countries would need to vary their path toward "another development," yet, "However diverse the paths, a common orientation is needed."

This is the basic content of "another development" for all societies. As for the Third World, two parallel strategies are recommended. "One is the reallocation of resources to meet basic needs, to reduce inequality internally and dependence externally and to increase the scope and depth of participation in decision making. The other is raising the level of productive forces in accordance with the objectives of another development."[30] It is further argued that since "the international market mechanism is in fact a power play scenario," the Third World countries should participate in the international system only on a selective basis and work toward Third World collective self-reliance.

The report of the Director-General of the International Labor Office to the Tripartite World Conference on Employment, Income Distribution and Social Progress and the International Division of Labor, held in the summer of 1976, also recommended the adoption of new approaches to development:

> The approach which is now proposed to this conference is that development planning should include, as an explicit goal, the satisfaction of an absolute level of basic needs.[31]

Basic needs include two elements:

> First, they include certain minimum requirements of a family for private consumption: adequate food, shelter and clothing are obviously included, as would be certain household equipment and furniture. Second, they include essential services provided by and for the community at large, such as safe drinking water, sanitation, public transport, and health and educational facilities.[32]

This basic needs approach has been recommended by the ILO for each of its member countries. It is hoped by the ILO that the employment policy would be so directed and supplemented by other policies (sug-

gestions for developing European socialist and industrialized market-
economy countries are contained in the report) as to achieve adequate
levels of consumption of certain goods and services by the year 2000.

SELF-RELIANCE AND COLLECTIVE
SELF-RELIANCE

In view of the declining commitments and willingness of the rich
countries to give aid, some of the self-reliance talk in the Third World
would appear in the nature of an effort to make a virtue out of necessity. However, it is not for negative reasons alone that the concept of
self-reliance has achieved prominence in the current development
debate. In this interdependent world, self-reliance does not mean
autarky. Although freer international trade may produce more efficient
allocation of world resources, it is no longer possible to say these days
that free trade is "good" for all. The distribution of gains from international trade is not independent of the power play scenario aspects of
the international market mechanism. All one may be able to assert is
that some trade is always better than no trade. The notion of collective
self-reliance among Third World countries is one manifestation of the
qualifying "some" in "some trade is better than no trade."

Self-reliance also does not mean total rejection of foreign aid in
development. Looked at in a positive way, self-reliance means the
choice of a strategy of development which is relevant to the initial
conditions of a particular country and can be executed (with or without foreign aid) without risking undue vulnerability in its strategic,
long-run interests.[33] Having chosen the relevant strategy of development, the amount of external resources that any country may be able
to attract is a function of (a) its desire to attract these resources, (b)
its finesse in diplomacy, and (c) the state of the international political
environment. What the policy makers of a country need to do is to
clarify the terms and conditions on which they will accept aid and not
overdraw the virtues of self-reliance in personal behavior into national
policy. Economic and political implications of alternative paths to self-
reliance must, of course, be analyzed and studied. A smaller amount of
aid by itself does not necessarily reduce the impact of uncertainties
arising in the foreign sector. A better approach to self-reliant development would be to indulge in contingency planning assuming different

levels of aid and keep plans and policies ready to deal with different contingent situations. There is no special merit in a development strategy which is aimed at reducing aid requirements if larger aid were available on terms and conditions acceptable to the developing country.

In view of the abject poverty in many Third World countries, self-reliance at levels which sacrifice growth, other things being equal, will cause more problems than it can tackle. The crucial problem of choice is in the selection of a relevant and self-confident strategy of development. Once this choice is made a poor country should try to augment domestic savings with as much external resources as it can usefully absorb on terms and conditions consistent with its economic and political objectives. It should, nevertheless, be quite clear that even if the overall objective of development strategy in the Third World were the removal of abject poverty, the patterns of self-reliant development would have to be different in different countries. A self-reliant pattern of development in India would differ from its content in Singapore. Similarly, Tanzania and Nepal would see self-reliance in different perspectives.

It was noted in passing that the idea of *collective* self-reliance among Third World countries is a reflection of the power politics aspects of the international market mechanism. This notion has been discussed in the international political arena for some time, but it is yet amorphous and conceptually opaque. An in-depth discussion of this concept would seem to be outside the scope of this chapter. I shall, nevertheless, note a few points which might help in understanding some practical aspects of the relationship of collective self-reliance to various political and economic linkages among nations.

In this unequal world of ours, where the flow of goods, people, and technical know-how is terribly restricted by all kinds of barriers, the economic advantages of trade, monetary and technical cooperation among groups of countries are well known. Conditions under which such cooperation may succeed are outlined in a fairly well-developed body of literature on the theory of customs unions, free trade areas, clearing and payments unions, pooled reserves, commodity associations, etc. Some practical experience with these tools of mutual cooperation among countries in some areas of the world is also available. However, by far the largest payoff from this body of economic knowledge will remain unrealized unless some viable principles of limited political federation among sovereign nations are researched and elaborated. Thus, significant political constraints probably exist which, if not resolved, would limit the chances for success of Third World collective self-reliance initiatives. Our understanding of these constraints is also not sufficiently sophisticated to indicate the most viable solutions to eliminate them.

In an attempt to puzzle out the meaning of collective self-reliance, it may also be instructive to inquire why, after nearly a quarter-century of effort to attain self-reliance, the poor nations of the Third World today are no less dependent on the rich. This dependence is not confined to developmental assistance alone. It is even more pervasive in the field of machines and technology. The Third World's incapacity to turn to other developing countries among themselves for machines and technology is *not* to be explained solely by the phenomenon of source-tying of aid. Some of the Third World countries today are using free foreign exchange to import capital goods and new technology. The tendency among them, however, is to hire the services of prestigious consulting firms at fantastic costs or to buy machines and machine tools made by well-known companies of the rich countries at relatively higher prices. One of India's public-sector concerns which manufactures quality machine tools has, for instance, already learned that it is easier to sell those in rich countries such as the United States than in Africa and Asia. The engineers in the United States and other developed countries are able to assess independently the quality of the sophisticated products of the Third World. The firms in Africa and many parts of Asia lack the necessary expertise to do so. The cause of collective self-reliance can be pushed forward by pinpointing areas of technology and products where assistance from other Third World countries could be of benefit to its members: there is an urgent need to develop a vehicle for the collection, evaluation, and dissemination of relevant information.

Cooperation among the poor countries can lead to faster growth of trade and exports, as well, The faster growth of export revenues will certainly be desirable. Nevertheless, it is useful to make a distinction between the growth of exports when it furnishes an opportunity for technological liberation and economic independence as against the compulsion to export more in order to pay for the imports of sophisticated armaments and the latest machines for imitative industrialization. The more they use exports to fulfill the former goal, the sooner the Third World countries will achieve self-reliance. Unfortunately, the experience of the past 30 years as well as the current trends point to the opposite direction. Most of the world's fighting since the end of the Second World War has been waged in the developing countries, and these countries have been spending significant proportions of their export earnings in buying armaments from the rich countries. By winding down their mutual hostilities through collective efforts and by cutting down their imports of arms from the rich, the poor countries could pave the way toward collective self-reliance in development. The gains from a few short steps in this direction should ensure far more success with the objective of collective self-reliance than many novel schemes of trade cooperation among the Third World countries that we might be able to suggest.

Examples of wasteful uses of export proceeds to import sophisticated technology and machines for imitative industrialization and modernization are legion. The poor countries must decide if, for instance, it is necessary for their people to consume mechanically baked bread, to wear factory-made shoes, to build houses of machine-made bricks, and to travel even short distances in cars and tube railway rather than on bicycles and scooters. The desire for mechanized brick kilns, automated bakeries, shoe factories with little use of labor, a car industry in each developing country, buildings and cities built in a style which *may* have use for mechanically made bricks or urban transport systems terribly wasteful of energy is a consequence of the elitist and imitative orientation to industrialization and modernization.

One can give many more examples of the uses of export proceeds which have drawn poor nations more and more into the technological bondage of the rich rather than to self-reliance. However, it is unnecessary to do so. The straightforward moral to be drawn is a simple one. In order to achieve self-reliance, collectively or individually, the poor nations need to think again, and think hard, about their social values and lifestyles. Unless the poor countries are able to get rid of the elitist and imitative thrust of their strategies of development and modernization, the growth of exports as such would not assure self-reliant development.

SOCIOLOGY OF KNOWLEDGE OF DEVELOPMENT STRATEGIES: SUMMARY CONCLUSIONS

The overall political objective of the West in the development of the Third World, particularly until the mid-1960s, was to maximize the attractiveness of the so-called third choice—to help the poor countries to grow fast enough so that change is neither "suppressed" nor permitted to be promoted "by ruthless and extremist measures." The promotion of this process of growth and modernization in an "orderly" fashion, with financial, military and technical assistance, was seen as a necessary effort to win sympathy and to align the new independent countries on the side of the ideological and cold war interests of the rich world. The "big push for more of the same" attitude of the West found a ready coincidence and willingness on the part of the elitist regimes in the Third World to adopt imitative, urban-based strategies of industrialization and modernization. These concentrative patterns of development did not produce the expected trickle-down. Nor did these patterns turn out to be self-generative and less dependent. In the mid-1960s, when the need for outside assistance to Third World growth was most acute, the cold war interests of the rich world began to shift. A strong isolationist sentiment started to emerge and the wherewithal for a big push to Third World growth began to evaporate. Among other things, an important reaction to these changes was the emergence of a renewed search for alternative perceptions and strategies of development in the poor countries. The new emphasis on self-reliance is a part of this perspective.

In the early phases of the postcolonial era, when political consensus on domestic questions of economic and social policy could emerge as a by-product of the rhetoric of national consolidation or anticolonialism, the elitist regimes in the Third World did not find it difficult to bypass the interests of their poor. This rhetoric has, more or less, lost its appeal now. The majority among the populations of the Third World are poor. The bulk of them are absolutely poor and destitute. Although the poor do not have strong political organizations of their own, nevertheless, the elitist regimes, as long as they find it necessary to face their electorates to seek their mandate to rule, cannot ignore the poor who are in the majority. An almost populist, competitively radical style of politics should be the order of the day as long as some form of popular, representative structure of government is maintained. The Third World governments' concern with the poor and the eradication of absolute poverty as an objective of development would, therefore, seem to be in the nature of a sociopolitical compulsion. Recent changes in indigenous development thought (bearing on questions of mass poverty) in many Third World countries are a reflection of these sociopolitical compulsions.

Although the new mood of self-reliance in the poor countries has not yet been translated into concrete patterns of self-reliant development, the willingness of the rich countries to give aid has declined much further. Unlike the 1950s and 1960s, aid for a big push is no longer the central concern of the development lobbies in the rich world. These lobbies would seem to have found, instead, a more virtuous source of excitement: they are busy developing suitable designs for the penny-packets and the systems for their delivery to the poor of the Third World. The rich world's *new* concern for the poor has also begun to be reflected in the policy statements of some Western governments. Sweden and Holland were the first to shift the emphasis in their aid policies to the problems of the poor. The British government, in October 1975, published a White Paper entitled, "The Changing Emphasis in British Aid Policies: More Help for the Poorest." The policy laid down in this White Paper places emphasis on aid to the poorest countries, the poorest groups within these countries, and especially rural development. There is also some evidence (in 1976) that the United States Agency for International Development is stressing the need to shift the direction of their aid policy more toward the poor, particularly the rural poor.

Because of the lack of effective political instruments at their command, the poorest of the poor countries have not yet begun to reap, in any significant measure, the benefits from the antipoverty strategies of their governments. Although the recent shift in emphasis toward the problems of the poor in the aid policies of some Western governments and international financial institutions may be considered a welcome development, these donors do not yet seem to have had sufficient time to identify the poorest groups within the poorest countries, or to refine their general diagnoses of the causes and dimensions of poverty to fit the particular conditions of different aid-receiving countries. In their meticulous concern for the vast multitudes of the poor, the aid-giving agencies seem to be becoming oblivious of any virtue in the resource fungibility argument. In spite of sharp cuts in the overseas aid budgets they are finding it difficult even to disburse the amounts actually provided for international assistance! Sufficient intellectual effort has not yet been put in to digest the full implications of the eradication of abject poverty as the dominant objective of development policy. One cannot find many examples of countries where the interrelationships and trade-offs between the objective of poverty eradication and other objectives such as growth and self-reliance have been worked out in relevant detail. However, in their unbounded enthusiasm, a significant section of the developmentalist lobby have started to advocate in high gear a universal doctrine of basic needs as the cornerstone of an antipoverty, worldwide development strategy.

The love and enthusiasm of international agencies and their well-endowed bureaucracies for universal, worldwide strategies is not difficult to understand. This enables them to operate, dispense advice and distribute funds among their member nations with an easy and seemingly impartial conscience. They have learned to make their task still easier by commissioning roving bands of international experts to do thematic and repetitive research for them on lucrative terms. The results of this activity often get reported in well-advertised and trend-setting conferences organized by these agencies. The new international chorus of basic needs for all is the newest joint product of the activities of the international agencies and their hired consultants.

Is it possible that the problem of basic minimal needs in the Third World is also being seen as a mirror image of the solutions evolved in the West? One hopes not. Undoubtedly some advanced welfare states have gone a long way in providing the basic needs of their populations in the fields of job security, educational opportunities, medical care, housing, etc. The concept of the welfare state, as it has evolved in the West, has consisted primarily of an effort to redistribute in an environment of plenty in order to reduce inequality, whereas the problem of eradication of abject poverty in the Third World is *not* primarily a matter of redistribution. There is no plenty from which to start. The main problem is one of focusing efforts on the absolutely poor to increase their productivity and therewith their levels of living. The provision of minimal basic needs of social consumption through collective means is better seen as a useful supplement and incentive to the poorest to increase their efforts to help themselves to grow.

While "to each according to his or her need" as a right rather than as charity may not be far off in some rich welfare states, one is not sure if they are succeeding in getting "from each according to his or her ability." It is not uncommon these days to hear of the British (who ruled the world not too long ago) being referred to in almost the same way as the Westerners used to talk about "those lazy Orientals." Of course, these days even the lazy Orientals have to be non-Chinese!

The Mainland Chinese, in an environment of poverty, are said to have pushed far ahead on the provision of basic needs as an integral part of their development strategy. However, revolutionary China has a significantly different concept of basic freedoms. Her structure of sanctions and incentives to get work out of people does not run against the kind of difficulties which the welfare states and the mixed economies of the Third World often experience. The moot question is therefore: What concept of basic freedoms is consistent with a generalized doctrine of basic needs for all societies? The advocates of the universality of the "basic needs first" approach must ponder this question.

ABSOLUTE POVERTY, DEVELOPMENT STRATEGY AND POLITICS

In view of the initial conditions that prevail in most of the Third World countries, basic needs cannot be the central concept around which poverty-focused development strategies can be organized. The focal point for strategic thinking about development issues would have to be the improvement of the capacities of the poorest groups to earn and attain socially acceptable, minimum levels of living through the expansion of employment opportunities. The earning capacities of producers with poor resource bases will have to be augmented through measures such as land reform and other programs of resource transfers. These measures for improving the incomes of the poor will have to be supplemented through the provision of collective means which assure the poor over a period of time certain minimum standards of social consumption and investment (the basic needs) in the form of health care, sanitation, drinking water, shelter, education, etc.

While these essential services should figure in any reasonable concept of a minimum standard of living, even with expanded employment opportunities, the poor will not be able, with their level of earnings, to buy them. The collective provision of these basic needs can go a long way in the establishment of conditions which help the poor to increase their ability to help themselves and grow. However, the size of the bundle of basic needs envisaged to be delivered during a period of time will have to be worked out in the light of a number of factors—the organizational capacity of a country, the availability of material resources and the extent of mass participation in the construction, operation and maintenance of these facilities are some of the important factors. A bundle of basic needs that appears feasible on these considerations can then be fed into the overall development program as a prior, hence inviolable, constraint. This is one helpful way in which some practical planners have looked upon the basic needs problem: not as the centerpiece but as an important aspect of the poverty-focused development strategy.

Quite aside from the obvious point that food is the most basic need, the renewed emphasis on rural development and agriculture in the current development debate derives from the fact that accrual of income from agriculture is fairly widespread and so is participation. Generally over two-thirds of the populations of the poor countries work in rural areas and produce 40 to 50 percent of the national product. The bulk of the poor live in the rural areas and are only loosely integrated with the nonagricultural sectors of the economy. The major thrust of the poverty eradication strategy, and of the specific programs for particular poverty groups, will have to be in the rural areas. The detailed content of rural development in different countries, however, would have to be different. One can talk about ideal types: e.g., the Chinese experience in rural development has been very much praised in the last few years. Nevertheless, the initial conditions, social and political, of different countries would largely determine the choice of models of rural development.

The most important point that deserves to be understood in connection with the eradication of absolute poverty as a goal of development in the Third World is the fact that for the elitist regimes this goal is a fairly radical one. The emerging political consensus for the execution of development policy in favor of the poor will last as long as the ruling apparatus feels compelled to go back to the people for their mandate to rule, or feels otherwise threatened by the poor. Furthermore, this goal does not seem to undermine the advent of revolution as and when the true radical is able to bring it about. He will have a better and more politically conscious ally in the poor when they are less destitute. However, the situation would also seem not entirely free from the risk of slipping into elitist dictatorships. Much would depend on how populism is politically managed. The commitment needs to be translated not only into changed flows of resources, but primarily into a reorganized structure of the responsible agencies of the government, proper means for horizontal and vertical coordination, and effective instruments for the participation of the potential beneficiaries in the planning and implementation of the efforts on their behalf. This is not something aid providers can do or instigate: the political considerations are too critical for them to be associated with the preparation of this groundwork. However, for strengthening the resolve of the Third World in favor of policies to remove absolute poverty, both increasing levels of material assistance and the adoption of enlightened policies on commodities, quota restrictions and migration by the rich countries could make a crucial difference. In formulating their aid and military policies, the rich countries must nevertheless understand the substantial lack of predictability in the political dynamics of Third World regimes. Will they learn not to interfere with the Third World in order to mold it in their image? This would undoubtedly be a hard discipline for the rich countries to practice. But it is equally idealistic to expect the rich countries to help the poor of the other lands on purely humanitarian grounds.

APPENDIX A

Extracts from Max F. Millikan and Donald L. N. Blackmer, eds., *The Emerging Nations: Their Growth and United States Policy* (London: Asia Publishing House, 1961):

We can start by underlining the essential economic difference between the developed and the underdeveloped countries. The most significant difference is not to be found in the commonly cited difference in levels of per capita income, or in degrees of industrialization and urbanization, or in the relative state of technology in the two kinds of countries. Although these are all present and important, the essential difference is that in the developed societies continuing growth of output is a regular and normal feature of the economy, whereas the national per capita product of traditional societies fluctuate erratically around a static norm. Once growth has been built in as a regular and inherent feature of an economy, and has been continuing for some time, all the other economically descriptive differences between developed and underdeveloped countries follow as a logical consequence. If an annual increase averaging two or three percent per capita can be regularly counted upon in a developing country, it does not take many decades to separate by very wide margins levels of living there from those in the underdeveloped countries. [p. 45]

Many of the problems of achieving take-off in the mid-twentieth century are similar to those that countries faced in the past. The early economic tasks still center around social overhead capital and around technological change in agriculture and in the export industries. The necessary social and psychological transformations, too, are in many ways similar to those of the past. But in three critical respects—population pressure, technology, and politics—the current environment is quite unlike that in which the industrialized Western countries entered the stage of rapid growth. In fact, the importance of outside help and the need for a "big push" rather than gradual and piecemeal change are in part consequences of the differences. [p. 60]

The most vital interests of the United States will be affected in critical ways by the manner in which the transition to modern life occurs throughout the world. Our political influence, our military position, our economic health, the entire quality of life in our society will depend in some measure on how the evolution of the traditional societies proceeds. In consequence, therefore, we should be concerned to see that the influence of the United States is exerted to help these societies move in directions compatible both with their long-run interests and with our own. [p. ix-x]

Our concern with world-wide economic, social, and political change is not, however, America's concern alone. It is the concern of every modern society in the free world, for these other nations must also reconcile their international policies with the rising tide of change in the underdeveloped countries. [p. x]

This summary review of the major alternatives perceived by men in transitional societies can be related to the interests of the United States and the rest of the free world in the evolution of the under-developed nations. From this perspective, our overall objective can be described as an effort to maximize the attractiveness and feasibility of the third choice: to help make the evolution to modernization successful enough that major groups will not struggle either to repress change entirely or to promote it by ruthless and extremist measures. [p. 98]

Chapter 4

URBAN BIAS, RURAL BIAS, AND
THE REGIONAL DIMENSION:
TO THE HOUSE OF TWEEDLEDEE[1]

Harold Brookfield

This chapter differs in some ways from others in this collection in that it concerns itself overwhelmingly with internal issues of development within countries, rather than with issues that arise at the whole-nation scale or between countries. Discussion of within-country issues is not new, but it is nonetheless a departure to rank them among the *major* issues of the development debate. The last few years, however, have seen not only a revitalization of the old argument between urban-industrial and rural priority in development—an argument that to many seemed long-since settled in favor of the former, but also a new surge into consciousness of the regional issue. As Lasuen remarked in 1974, "suddenly in the decade of the seventies without any transition... the urban-regional theme in almost all countries has moved up the scale of national aspirations from the base to the top."[2] This is true in developed as well as developing countries, as witness the new concern for the European periphery, but it is in the developing countries that social concern

97

with rural and peripheral poverty, economic concern over the growing problems of the crowded national centers, and sometimes chauvinist concern to ensure more effective occupation of the whole of national space, have come together most dramatically in this decade.

In his chapter, B. S. Minhas stresses the current emphasis on "basic needs" and the belated realization that national development cannot arise where "rural development" is neglected. Throughout this book, indeed, the persistence of poverty despite the rapid economic growth of the last quarter-century has been a major theme. More than any other single fact of the world developmental situation in the 1970s it is the failure of growth to eliminate poverty that is responsible for the major rethinking of developmental goals and strategies that is now in progress across the world. There is a new insistence, most clearly expressed by Lipton, on the conflict between rural and urban interests, for it is "the rural sector [that] contains most of the poverty, and most of the low-cost sources of potential advance [while] the urban sector contains most of the articulateness, organization and power."[3] Though the reality of a rural contradiction would be disputed by Marxist theoreticians such as Castells,[4] who sees an identity of interest between peasant workers and urban proletariat in a whole economy increasingly dominated by monopoly capital, Lipton's argument against what he calls the "urban bias" in development theory and practice is strongly persuasive. It challenges one of the most fundamental development dogmas of the whole period since World War II, that of the prior place of industrial growth, and the desirability of shifting people out of agriculture into the "modern sector" as the principal path to progress.

Minhas outlines the growing disenchantment with macroeconomic models based on growth, and the rise of new policy considerations at the international level. In this chapter a different approach is adopted. Because the theoretical background of regional development is not widely familiar, even among many development specialists, a brief preliminary discussion is necessary, in which the interrelation of existing regional theory with "urban bias" is first traced out, then questioned. The alternative case for "rural bias" in development is then presented, and it is shown that while this, too, has obvious regional dimensions—especially since the largest part of almost every country is rural—there is no theory of "rural regional development" on which to draw. In an attempt to fill this gap, the actual development problems relating to these issues are traced out for two contrasted countries, and the difficulties in the way of reaching an adequate regional development policy are then faced in the conclusion.

THE STATE OF REGIONAL DEVELOPMENT THEORY: THE CASE FOR URBAN BIAS

Notwithstanding antecedents going back even into the nineteenth century, the theory of regional development may properly be said to have begun with the near-simultaneous appearance of books by Myrdal[5] and Hirschman.[6] Though the analysis of the latter is the more rigorous, the impact of the former has been greater, perhaps because he wrote for the nonspecialist. Essentially, the argument is that development begins and takes root only at certain places; this sets up a cumulative set of processes under which entrepreneurs concentrate at the growing points, savings from the whole national space are invested at these points, and labor is drawn thither. Since the manufactures produced at the "growth points" have higher income elasticity of demand (are demanded in greater quantity relative to other goods as incomes rise) the rest of the country suffers by paying progressively more for the goods imported from the growth centers than they receive for their own exports to these centers (i.e., the terms of trade are set against the periphery). These backwash effects, therefore, impoverish the periphery, and in time (so it was argued) the increasing cost of factors of production (land, capital and labor) at the center will cause entrepreneurs to look more closely at opportunities in the periphery, so that "spread" effects will ultimately overcome the backwash and lead to a more uniform pattern of growth. Hirschman thought this would occur of necessity; Myrdal that it would require the intervention of governments.

In the emphasis implicitly placed on industry and towns in this formulation, these ideas meshed with the "growth-pole" theory of Perroux,[7] so that it swiftly became established that the proper method of obtaining a "spread" of development was through reconstruction of the national urban system.[8] This doctrine, which underwent its most important step forward with the publication of John Friedmann's[9] design for the regional development of Venezuela has perhaps received its most elegant formulation in the hands of Hermansen[10] who sought to link the dynamic theory of growth poles and the static-equilibrium theory of central place patterns. Underlying this entire approach is the notion that a fully structured urban system embracing the full range from metropolitan cities to closely spaced rural service centers will "provide the requisite incentives for increased application of labor, capital and human skills" throughout national space, and so spread the effects of development uniformly.[11] The great city is the focus of all development impulses, which are diffused outward through the hierarchy. The rapid growth of town-creating activities—industry and commerce—and their distribution through national space thus leads most readily to the spread of development.

This conception of regional development, with its heavy urban bias, has continued to be argued in a massive literature going well forward into the 1970s. It rests firmly on the notion that polarized development is an initial stage and that true "development" will be achieved through the spread of the "modern" or urbanized system. Geographers and others have sought indicators of the spread of urbanism to trace the progress of the trickle-down effects that are supposed to follow. An extensive literature in this field has been reviewed critically by Brookfield,[12] Porter and de Souza,[13] and several others. Tests have been few, but one, by Gilbert,[14] has concluded that there is little evidence of widespread benefit from "growth center" development. Indeed, Gilbert's data suggest that the effective "benefit" is limited to a radius of only some 50 kilometers from the large and spontaneous growth center of Medellin, Colombia.

The point to be emphasized here is that the urban-biased theory of regional development has evolved within a growth-biased theory of development as a whole. Therefore, indicators of economic growth are also indicators of development, and the most important single piece of "validation" had been Williamson's[15] examination of spatial inequality in regional income data, using cross-section data of variable quality for 24 countries in the 1950s and time-series data for a smaller number of countries (mostly highly developed ones, including only Brazil as a true representative of the developing countries). Williamson's hypothesis is that spatial inequality in income levels is low at an initial stage of development, increases rapidly during the "take-off" period, and subsequently diminishes again as countries achieve maturity. As elaborated by Gilbert and Goodman,[16] who used data from additional developing countries, this breaks down into two hypotheses: first, that spatial inequality is initially low but increases rapidly as the gross national product (GNP) increases; second, that beyond the middle levels of the GNP ladder there is convergence in the regional income indicators. Williamson's initial analysis seemed to support the second hypothesis, though with the rider that the convergence of regional incomes is slow and halting even in the most advanced countries. A Canadian study, however, employing a wider range of data[17] flatly contradicts his conclusion that regional income levels are tending to converge in that country, even in the same year as Williamson's paper.

Subsequently, the mounting body of evidence on varying regional income levels within the European Economic Community (EEC) can scarcely be interpreted as a tendency toward convergence in this the oldest of the world's "developed" regions. The first hypothesis, on the other hand, had little empirical validation in Williamson's paper for sheer want of data. Gilbert and Goodman's[18] subsequent analysis finds little evidence with which to support it; variance is as great in countries of very low per capita GNP as in "middle rung" countries with ten times their income per head.

Moreover, there are other objections to Williamson's much quoted survey. There is no reason at all to suppose that regional gross domestic product (GDP) is a better indicator of welfare levels than is national GDP or GNP. In the study cited above, Gilbert and Goodman argue forcibly that improvement in other regional development indicators does not necessarily correspond with improvement in the distribution of incomes within regions. Indeed, in the specific case of the Brazilian northeast where there has been economic growth as part of the "Brazilian miracle"—albeit at a lower rate than in the nation as a whole—they demonstrate quite conclusively that income distribution has simultaneously become more concentrated, so that the poor are worse off than they were. Almost everywhere in the Third World, studies of income distribution with or without a regional breakdown have established that whatever trends toward regional convergence there may be, the poor remain poor, disproportionately located in rural areas, and in agriculture.[19] An Organization of American States (OAS) survey of employment growth[20] comes to a parallel conclusion and favors a regional development policy based on growth poles. However, Ahluwalia's policy conclusion is fast becoming the new conventional wisdom: ". . . given the scale of the problem, and the limited capacity of other sectors to expand productive employment, it follows that a viable strategy for raising income of the lowest 40 percent of the population must necessarily focus on the agricultural sector."[21] Therefore, they must also focus on agricultural regions, or on areas of national periphery in urban-centered national systems.

What, then, does this do to the whole painfully evolved urban-industrial model of regional development? The basic assumptions of the whole theoretical system have been brought into question even as it was at last becoming soundly established.[22] Some of its principal theorists, outstandingly Friedmann himself, certainly survive, but in strong opposition to a whole set of new approaches.

This confrontation has been long in emerging. Now that it has emerged it promises to be very fruitful in terms of the generation of new approaches to the practical problems of Third World development. Efforts are being made to evolve regional development strategies of a very different kind. Any such strategy, and any new theoretical system on which new strategies might be based, needs to be grounded in empirical reality. Part of this chapter is, therefore, devoted to empiricism, but it will first be useful to review briefly the history of another argument—that for rural bias in development; this is fundamental to what follows.

THE CASE FOR A RURAL BIAS

The Cambridge conferences on development in the 1960s discussed issues such as priority for agriculture or for industry, and the question of appropriate technology, in a manner that remains illuminating today.[23] The consensus was in favor of industrialization, but in a mixed strategy in which agricultural exports would bear the load of earning foreign exchange for industrialization. The argument was for greater emphasis on industrialization "to redress the balance and achieve a better rate of expansion." Concerning location, it was argued that a single large industrial center may find it cheaper to import food rather than buy from remote agriculturalists within the same country. The balance of opinion was, therefore, in favor of a small number of large industrial centers, enjoying economies of scale, the better to "increase the impact of industrialization on the rest of the economy." The "agriculture-first" argument was also advanced by those who felt that increase of per capita food production and disposable income is the surest way of producing a large and ever-increasing demand for manufactures. The consensus, however, was that agriculture is never likely to be able to supply the main drive for industry, and that industrialization is the only hope of releasing agriculture from the stranglehold of population pressure.

There was a major dissenting voice, that of E. F. Schumacher.[24] Schumacher argued strongly against massive urbanization and the use of high-cost technology in industry. In making a case for "intermediate technology" in industry he was also arguing for a dispersal of industry into the countryside, so that "workplaces have to be created in the areas where the people are living now, and not primarily in the metropolitan areas into which they tend to emigrate."[25] This, he maintained, required a regional approach to development, based on the employment of a suitable technology. Schumacher did not convince the conference, but as Robinson remarked, he "emerged as the agricultural developer par excellence. We had all complained about the painfully slow progress in agriculture and hoped that industry would stimulate quicker results. Dr. Schumacher's enthusiasm for dispersed manufacturing, using intermediate technology to revitalize agrarian economies, suggested how this might be done."[26]

The Rise of Dissent

Schumacher's arguments of the late 1960s find many echoes in the present day. Several reasons may be identified. First, is the evident failure of "growth" to lead into comprehensive national "development," and the failure of industrialization strategies in a number of countries, outstandingly India as described by Minhas (Chapter 3) elsewhere in this volume. Second, is the realization that the rapid urbanization of most Third World countries greatly exceeds the rate of industrial growth, creating an urban situation without historical precedent. The Economic Commission for Latin America (ECLA)[27] survey of Latin America in 1970 examined the growing divergence between the structure of production and that of employment; it suggests that the problem of employment comes before that of income distribution, because "part of the labor force of the countries of the region is either unemployed or engaged in what are to all intents and purposes marginal activities."[28] Castells[29] has argued that the real cause of "over-urbanization" lies not in the growth of urban activities themselves but rather in the "smashing up" of rural society under the impact of monopoly capitalism.

Also important is growing acceptance of the view first solidly advanced by Galbraith[30] that theory based on the individual firm freely competing in a self-equilibrating market bears no relation to modern reality. In most developing countries it never did, as Puthucheary[31] has amply demonstrated in the case of Malaysia. What we have instead is a limited number of firms which make the market rather than respond to it, and whose operations can, in the view of some,[32] lead to cumulative imbalance between countries and between regions within countries. In these circumstances the "center-periphery" model needs to be rewritten in very different terms.

More positively, the experience of China, and to a lesser extent other countries such as North Vietnam[33] which have adopted strategies of rural priority, have come to be better known. While recent studies such as that of Mesa-Lago and Hernandes have cast some doubt on the success of socialist policies in Cuba in equalizing income between occupations—and, hence, between regions—there seems to be general agreement that the Chinese have at least achieved the goal of rural full employment via Schumacher's strategy of creating workplaces in the areas where people are living. Perhaps, the principal value of the Chinese experience for development thinking as a whole is that it has demonstrated a viable alternative to an urban-industrial strategy in which the only role for the rural periphery is to supply cash crops to boost export earnings, while exporting its own poor to fill the cities.

ADDITIONAL INFLUENCES ON REGIONAL DEVELOPMENT POLICY

The theoretical system reviewed up to this point is based primarily on economic arguments. An important omission in such theory is the lack of concern for noneconomic issues which impinge upon the choice of development strategy. There are two such sets of considerations that should be introduced. One has found little place so far in the argument that we are examining; the other has been offered, by an economist, as an all-embracing "general theory" to explain the growth of regional, or urban/rural, inequalities and their persistence. Both need to be examined before we go further.

The Environmental Dimension

During the late 1960s a powerful force of world opinion emerged, one that should have allied itself to the new thinking about regional development and the rural/urban argument, yet has somehow failed to do so. This force was the rising concern for natural ecology and for the stock of future resources of the sort for economic growth that had characterized the preceding 20 years. Schumacher's case, cited above,[34] formed part of it, and was carried further in his last major works into alliance with such thinkers as Ivan Illich. An essentially idealistic case for life and economy organized around self-sufficient small communities acquired a wholly new dimension when it was also espoused by the distinguished signatories of the *Blueprint for Survival*.[35] The case now rested not only on greater human well-being, but on reversal of tendencies which many saw as destructive of the conditions of human life itself.[36]

The new issues relate first to the massive pollution generated by urban-industrial society, especially in its great cities, and secondly and perhaps more importantly the enormous energy and resource consumption required to fuel growth and support bigness. In the developed countries, not only industry but also agriculture is a massive consumer of energy. In 1910 the United States food supply system still produced and delivered about as much energy as it used in farm inputs, food processing, transportation and preparation. Yet, by 1970 there was an average of about ten joules input per joule's worth of food put on the table.[37] The larger part of this input was required between farm gate and consumer. On the farm alone the level of inputs was still below the output in energy terms for arable production, though far above the output for livestock. The specialization of food production between regions—under which foodstuffs are transported long distances, and are processed and frequently also packaged before marketing—is thus the principal source of energy loss in the food system. Since a high proportion of the energy required is derived from formerly cheap oil, much of which is imported, the situation has acquired a wholly new dimension since 1973.

At the time of the Stockholm Conference on the Human Environment in 1972, the developing countries as a whole were reluctant to share the developed countries' concern with either pollution or resource scarcity. The former nations were fearful that a large measure of this concern represented a wish by interests in the already industrialized countries to pull up the ladder behind themselves, and so preserve their own affluence at the cost of keeping the rest of the world in poverty. Such a "lifeboat philosophy" on the part of many environmentalists in the developed countries is a reality, albeit often an unconscious one, as O'Riordan[38] demonstrates brilliantly from an analysis of the positions of the several different classes of environmentalists. It is widely held that since there is simply not enough to go around, it is "unrealistic" of the Third World to aim at the consumption standards of the West, and there is satisfaction that few Third World countries have yet evolved the energy-intensive urban-industrial systems which constitute such an energy sink in the developed countries.

Such thinking, however, ignores two important trends in the contemporary Third World. First is the massive urbanization described previously. Somewhere during the 1970s there has occurred or will occur an important event, perhaps a watershed point in the history of the world. Before the decade is out the Third World share of the whole world population living in cities larger than one million will have exceeded the share in the developed countries. By the end of the century it is likely, based on current trends, that some three-quarters of the world's large-city dwellers will be residents of countries now classed as "developing." While the structure and economy of these new great cities differs sharply from those of the older great cities of the West, and their consumption of energy per capita is far lower, no one familiar with such cities as Manila, Mexico City, Bangkok or Calcutta can doubt that the effects of such hyper-urbanization on world energy and resource demands will be of a massive order.

The second trend is embodied in the Green Revolution. There are many who believe that the solution to the food problem posed by population growth and hyper-urbanization in the Third World will be provided by means of continuation of this process of agricultural transformation. The success of the new varieties—first of wheat developed in Mexico, then of rice developed in the Philippines—is proven, but at the cost of heavy consumption of water, fertilizer, pesticides, herbicides, insecticides, and fungicides. The energy input required is derived primarily from oil, requiring an application to the Third World of some of the technology which has already formed the basis of the "second agricultural revolution" in the West. While the Green Revolution continues to be heralded as a success, and by some as merely the beginning of an enormous expansion in the world food output, there are others[39] who regard it as no more than a breathing space. Moreover, not only the food-production system itself, but also the transportation and distribution system allied to it in the support of large-city growth, will enormously increase the energy consumption of developing countries. Between 1950 and 1965, energy consumption in underdeveloped countries grew at an annual rate of 7.7 percent compared with 3.9 percent in the developed countries.[40] All indications are that the differential has since increased further.

The spatial aspects of these processes of rapid urbanization and agricultural revolution in the Third World seem not to have been subjected to any close examination; indeed, the issue has scarcely been raised. However, on prima facie grounds it would seem to follow that the greater is the level of urbanization, the larger will be the area from which food is drawn, requiring greater use of energy in transportation and distribution on top of the input required to increase production. In view of the rising cost of energy, and the prospect that real shortages of oil will arise somewhere between 1980 and 1995, it would seem highly desirable to contemplate energy-saving strategies of development as a matter of urgency. A regional policy based on self-reliance, and on the creation of workplaces where people now live rather than in the large cities patently fits this requirement.

The Political Dimension

Any major shift away from urban-industrial strategies of economic growth and polarization requires, however, political somersaults of a major order. Governments and their advisers may declare an intention to make such major changes, but actually to undertake them is another matter, requiring action that will inevitably hurt the most vocal and influential power groups. The fate of Allende must be in the minds of all leaders of developing countries who contemplate strategies that will hurt the urban middle classes and the large corporations.

One of the leading theoreticians of regional development, John Friedmann, has offered a schema of the evolution of a center-periphery situation which incorporates political considerations. This chapter, several times modified, represents something of a midpoint in Friedmann's progress from neoclassical economics to Maoism.[41] In it he proposes what is termed a "general theory of polarized development" which relies basically on a model of political conflict between center and periphery. Following Schumpeter, the argument is that development arises through a concentrated flow of innovative forces, localized at a place that becomes the center. Successful innovation increases the potential power of the innovators, and when this power is exercised it becomes socially legitimized as authority. The remainder of the national spatial system thus falls into a relation of dependency on the core. Dominance of the core over the periphery then becomes entrenched through transfer of resources from periphery to center, the creation at the center of an attractive reward structure for innovation, and the corresponding transformation of social values and behavior which extends the dominance of the center from the economic into the social and cultural spheres. Conflict then arises as attempts are made within the periphery to gain access to the benefits of innovation. These attempts include demands for peripheral autonomy. Such demands may encourage the core elites to adopt decentralization measures or may lead to armed uprisings. Friedmann concludes, rejecting his own earlier models, by stating that:

> In the context of the General Theory, contemporary regional growth theory may, therefore, be treated as a special case, applicable only to situations where the dualism of core and periphery is of relatively little consequence, such as the reasonably advanced and integrated spatial systems of the United States, West Germany or Sweden. It is applicable neither to the industrializing countries nor to multi-national regions where core-periphery dependency relations are still predominant influences.[42]

Friedmann's "general theory" has value in relegating economic forces to a role which, while initially crucial, ultimately becomes subordinate. But it fails to give proper significance to the manner in which a rural oligarchy can control both center and periphery in alliance with a national bourgeoisie. Furtado[43] has demonstrated the latter situation to be the case in Brazil, where wealth generated in the center can be used to maintain extreme inequality in the periphery. It is of only secondary importance whether this be interpreted as the "center buying off the rural elites and bourgeoisie"[44] or as the rural oligarchy extending their power base to the center, as has been argued in the case of Peru. The net effect is much the same in that there is, in fact, an integrated power system over the whole of national space, sustaining inequality in both center and periphery. Friedmann's search for a way out through spatial conflict, like Lipton's "class" conflict between city and countryside, is negated by such a system. The reality of the political dimension is more subtle, then, than these polarizing models would suggest.

There are countries in which regional political forces are important in the way described by Friedmann; most of them, however, are developed countries where resurgent regional movements have become of major importance in recent years. Canada, Great Britain, Yugoslavia, Spain and even France are striking examples. Even in "homogenous" Australia the divergence between Queensland and Western Australian politics and those of the core region of the nation has sharpened in recent years. In developing countries regional movements are often complicated by foreign intervention, as in Zaire, Nigeria, Ethiopia, and Indonesia. There are developing countries with spontaneous regionalism at the political level, and we shall examine one of them below, but they are rare. For the most part the all-important political element in regionalism, and hence also in the rural/urban contradiction, is played out among opposing forces each of which has a power base shared between center and periphery. The sharp dichotomy is easier to identify in the abstract than in the real world.

THE ISSUES IN CONTRASTED SITUATIONS

Theory From the Ground Up

The deductive theory of regional development fails because it takes account of too limited a range of variables. In these circumstances, it is best to begin from the bottom up and see what can be done by generation of "grounded theory" from the examination of particular cases. This approach has the advantage that it is able to take account of a wider range of evidence within the confines of a particular instance, but the disadvantage that it can support truly general propositions only by rigorous use of comparative method over a large number of cases. However, the examination of only one or two particular instances can yield insights, especially when the selection of material is contrasted with available theory. In what follows the evidence from two countries is looked at in this way; these are not simply "case studies," but form the basis for the general propositions offered in the conclusion.

The two countries selected are sharply contrasted. Mexico is a large country, has undergone strikingly rapid economic growth since 1950, experienced the first "modern" political revolution in the developing countries during the years 1910-17, was the place of origin of the Green Revolution in food production and has a center-periphery dichotomy that has evolved through time but has retained some constant elements for almost a thousand years. Papua New Guinea, by contrast, is a creation of colonialism; its small population is divided into groups speaking several hundred distinct languages, with no history of political fusion. Its modern economic growth is virtually the creation of external aid and enterprise. It is still without an integrated system of overland communications and its urban/rural dichotomy has truly emerged only in the present decade. There is still no national core region or single center-periphery system. Within the range of situations found in the developing countries, these two are close to the two ends of a spectrum that excludes only those small and poor countries, most of them island groups or landlocked states, that are wholly within the periphery of some more powerful neighbor.

Background of the Mexican Case

The history of Mexico has an enormous literature, most of it concerned with the 1910-17 revolution and its aftermath, but including
also a great number of titles on colonial history, the conquest, and the
pre-Columbian period. There is no need to review this literature here.[45]
However, certain elements are of major importance from the present
point of view. First is the persistence of the central plateau as national
heartland through all changes from pre-Aztec times to the present day;
half the population lives there and half of this in turn now lives in and
around the capital. Cities were the core of pre-Columbian civilization
as well as of the present. Except for modern developments in the north
and on the two coasts, a rural/urban dichotomy has persisted in very
much the same spatial distribution throughout Mexico's history. This
is a European or Middle-Eastern situation, and is in sharp contrast with
the rest of Latin America, Africa and most of Asia. In spite of this
continuity, however, it is only since the revolution that control of the
economy and society has fallen into the hands of the bourgeoisie.
The Spanish Empire created two main foci of power: the landed
aristocracy[46] and the Roman Catholic Church. The power of the
latter was eliminated during the nineteenth century; the revolution
undid the great landholders, but in stages extending from 1910 to 1950
so that the rural revolution was always partial. Foreign control of the
"modern sector," almost total in 1910, was progressively eliminated
during the first 40 years of the revolutionary period, but then partly
re-established in the period of rapid industrialization after 1950.

Not conflict, but compromise and "flexibility" have been the keys
to understanding both the development history of Mexico and the contemporary state of crisis. From the overthrow of Emperor Maximilian
in 1867 until the revolution, the national leaders played class and regional interests, foreign and national interests, and competing foreign
interests themselves against one another. The revolution was brought
about by a shifting alliance of forces in which the strongest elements
were the "liberal" bourgeoisie, the peasantry of the sugar districts south
of Mexico City, the cattle barons and small businessmen of the arid
north, and the small urban working class. The new constitution of 1917
was also a compromise. Thus, while the army continued to provide
the presidents for more than 20 years thereafter, the political direction
ranged from an inactive conservatism under which landed interests
regained some strength, to a pragmatic neo-Marxism under which

peasants and urban workers made gains and foreign interests were nationalized. Throughout, however, it was the new national bourgeoisie that scored the most consistent benefits.

Later, in the boom of the 1950s and 1960s, we find a number of writers, including Higgins,[47] placing the credit for success in achieving rapid growth on an alliance between national financial institutions and foreign capital. The assumption of a greater economic role by government accompanied first the national acquisition of foreign interests in the railways and oil, and later partnership with a second wave of foreign capital in the establishment of secondary industry, export agriculture, and large-scale tourism. At the same time a strongly nationalist ideology has been constantly maintained. A rural ideology originating in the land-reform aspirations of the peasant revolutionaries and some intellectuals[48] has been expressed in the halting progress of the land distribution program, but the real benefits of government activity have generally been felt elsewhere.

Many foreign observers have praised this skillful balancing of social needs and the demands of progress. In 1970, Barkin and King, for example, remarked that:

> . . . by placing great stress on this effort to carry out the goals of the Revolution by redistributing land, the government has convinced the peasants of the intention to improve rural incomes. This official concern and interest in the problems of the peasant is constantly stressed in the face of accumulating evidence that the relative standard of living of this group is deteriorating. The substitution of ideology for economic achievements thus permitted the government to divert fewer resources to programs of social welfare than might otherwise have been necessary. Moreover, Mexico has been successful in devising a policy toward foreign investment that enables it both to satisfy strong nationalist feelings and to exploit the benefits that foreign investment can bring.[49]

Already in 1968, however, the Mexican "consensus" had come to an abrupt end. A series of peasant, worker and student troubles broke out in different parts of the country and in Mexico City itself. Behind this mass disorder lay grave problems. These were apparent at the national level in an increasingly unequal distribution of income which affected principally the share of the lowest 30 percent of earners.[50] The "modern sector," despite its large growth, has expanded only to occupy some 15 percent of the labor force. Despite the high rate of urbanization, and the emigration of several million Mexicans to the United States, the agricultural population continued to increase at about two percent per annum. In the early 1970s it was estimated that some 60 percent of the agricultural work force was either without land or was on holdings too small to offer more than a subsistence income with present technology. And although most of the poor were in the countryside, inequality of incomes was greater in the towns. From the mid-1960s onward, the growth of food production ceased to keep pace with population growth so that a rising share had to be imported. Consumer prices of foodstuffs increased sharply though the farmers received little more, so that hardship was spread among urban and rural poor alike. The policy of compromise and consensus, of concentrating investment in the areas of highest return while relying mainly on land reform to appease peasant discontent and low prices to relieve urban poverty, had at last failed to deliver the goods.

Urban Bias or Rural Bias?

Heavy emphasis on industry in the allocation of investment and inducements to invest have given Mexico a dualistic industrial structure. Over 80 percent of factories have fewer than five employees, while a small sector using imported high technology dominates the field. Industry as a whole is, however, highly concentrated. About half the wages paid, production and value-added are accounted for by industry in the capital city and its region alone. This region, together with the states of Jalisco (Guadalajara) and Nuevo Leon (Monterrey), have half the industrial plants, 65 percent of employment, and approximately three-quarters of the wages and salaries, gross production and value-added.[51] Efforts to obtain greater "dispersal" have for the most part led only to some spread around the existing centers.

The dominance of the capital city is overwhelming, even though more rapid growth rates are recorded in the towns along the United States border where major efforts have been made to create employment, in the new resorts on the Pacific coast and the oilfield towns of the Gulf Coast. Mexico City and its immediate region has almost half the urban population of the country, and in a highly centralized political system virtually all real decision making is concentrated there. It is significant that approximately half the newspaper circulation in the country is in the capital alone.

These facts certainly provide strong indication of urban-industrial bias. The integration of the nation's economy achieved by public invest-ment has been paralleled by political integration which has reduced the power of the army and has virtually eliminated the regional *caudillos* and *caciques*, who were still a dominant force as late as the 1930s, from any effective participation in national politics.[52] Power has in-stead gravitated into the hands of the organized business sector and the leaders of the public corporations—virtually all located in Mexico City. The growth of industry, the cities and the national communications network had absorbed the major portion of social infrastructure in-vestment as well as productive investment.[53] Mexico has also achieved an agricultural revolution, and has done this at remarkably small cost. The fact of rather limited resource allocation to agriculture has, however, meant that this revolution has been highly concentrated geographically in areas offering the most favorable capital/output ratios.

Many Mexican writers, and foreigners who write about Mexico, virtually ignore this achievement and concentrate their attention on urban-industrial growth on the one hand, and on rural deprivation on the other. Stavenhagen[54] finds it necessary to insist that there has, in fact, been substantial progress in the agricultural sector. The first and major drive has been in irrigation, especially in the arid north, and since the 1940s this has been coupled with the breeding and introduction of new strains (first of wheat, then of corn), of new crops (particularly sorghum), and major increase in cotton production—all aided by a heavy application of fertilizers to increase yields and eliminate fallow. Nitrogenous fertilizers, which are the most important, are produced by the national petrochemical industry. Wheat yields quadrupled between 1950 and 1970 but after 1965 the rate of expansion began to level off. One problem seems to lie in the close link between Mexico's Green Revolution and irrigation. Irrigated cropland generates more than half the commercial output of Mexico's farms, but it comprises less than a third of the total area. In addition, the research effort declined in the 1960s while official "guaranteed prices" were kept low in the interest of providing cheap food for the urban population. Since 1972 these "guaranteed prices" have at last been allowed to rise sharply, forcing up the real but lower prices received by most farmers, and there has been a renewed surge in the growth rate of fertilizer use. At the same time, the administration of land reform was changed to break up the "new *latifundia*" that were coming into being especially in the irrigated areas.[55] These measures have had some effect, but the marginal returns are now much less than in the early days in the 1950s. Wellhausen is probably correct when he asks rhetorically: "Could it be that under present circumstances the rate of growth in the production of food crops has diminished because the rural sector is running out of clients who can make use of the technological package in the form in which it is now being offered?"[56]

Mexico has developed a dualistic agriculture, in which a minority of "efficient" farmers is distinguished from the mass of small-holders mainly working unirrigated land. Whereas 75 percent of the total area affected by the land reform has gone to the communal *ejidos*, only 47 percent of the irrigated land was held by these small-holders in 1973. This latter share had 273,000 owners against 115,000 who held the remaining 53 percent. Twenty-five percent of the irrigated area was held by only 9,200 individuals.[57]

There is widespread agreement that wholly new initiatives are demanded, involving a major increase in the proportion of national expenditure devoted to agriculture, and with emphasis especially on improving the productivity of dry-land small farmers in the marginal-to-adequate rainfall areas of the central plateau and the south, where the bulk of Mexico's rural population resides. Greater reliance on energy imports to the farm seems inescapable given the needs of the situation, but Mexico is at least fortunate in that 30 years of modest production following nationalization of the oil companies in 1938 has left the country with resources in the ground amply sufficient through at least the 1980s. However, these resources are limited; present development is increasingly for export especially to the ever-hungry American oil-and-gas market to which even the new fields in Chiapas in the far south may soon be linked by gas pipeline. Given the continued rapid population growth, at or above 3.5 percent per annum, it would seem important that long-term food needs be placed ahead of short-term gain, and that the growth of urban-industrial energy consumption also be restrained. Present indications are that the application of new technology in the rain-fed areas could triple Mexican food production, but this will not be achieved without a new sort of national planning, involving a genuine rural bias in place of the tokenism of the past.

Mexican regional development policies have hitherto been of rather limited scope, concerned with the development of irrigation, the generation of power and the dispersal of industry, and mainly organized through "river basin projects."[58] They now need to embrace much more general rural development, both agricultural and industrial; new forms of encouragement to the rural and small-town entrepreneur; an active family planning policy; and also the decentralization of decision making. The latter is politically risky, but the nettle has been grasped elsewhere, even in one of the world's most newly independent countries to which we now turn.

The Genesis of Regionalism in Papua New Guinea

As its name implies, Papua New Guinea is an amalgam of two colonial territories, separately administered until World War II. Prewar foci of development around Rabaul, Lae, Madang and Port Moresby were augmented by the opening up of the central highlands along the axis of the new highway constructed during the 1950s and 1960s, and after 1969 also by the major copper mining enterprise in Bougainville, which after it came into full production in 1972 transformed the balance-of-payments situation. Nonetheless, both economic and special development continued through independence in 1975 to depend heavily on Australian aid, enterprise and technical support. Some private and public elements in Australia continued until the end to treat Papua New Guinea as though it were a peripheral part of Australian economic space. A significant part of the history of the country in the period 1950-75 could be written around such a theme of *internal* colonialism. Government itself, especially under the direction of a forceful minister long in office,[59] took a major role in creating national institutions and in securing a more even spread of social services and infrastructure. The "uniform development" policy was essentially a gradualist policy. When the prospect of political independence began to emerge after 1960, such equity-based policies had increasingly to give way to a drive for economic growth. This is turn led to a new reaction, so that when local politicians began to assume power in the early 1970s, the old "uniform development" aims were again written into the plans.[60] The brief statement of aims, the so-called "eight-point plan," therefore, included the following:

1. More equal distribution of economic benefits, including movement toward equalization in incomes among people and toward equalization of services among different areas of the country (point 2).
2. Decentralization of economic activity, planning and government spending with emphasis on agricultural development, village industry, better internal trade, and more spending channeled to local and area bodies (point 3).

3. A more self-reliant economy, less dependent for its needs on imported goods and services, and better able to meet the needs of its people through local production (point 5).

In practice, this is to say that Papua New Guinea attained independence with the economic-planning ideas of the 1970s, and with no deep commitment to an earlier set of notions needing first to be overcome. There were also other reasons for the determination with which ideas of equalization and decentralization were espoused. Even though there was no history of exploitation of one region by another, there was considerable hostility toward migrant workers from other parts of the country in the less developed areas. The central highlanders as a whole had long been reluctant to accept independence under conditions which would lead to control of government by coastal people; a strong separatist movement in Bougainville in the 1970s was only "defused" after large concessions had been made. Active separatist movements have also flourished in New Britain and in central Papua itself, around the capital. Government became a coalition of regions rather than of parties, even though broadly "radical" and "conservative" groups could be discerned. The 1977 election appeared at first to be a clear win for the Prime Minister's party and its supporters. Even so, the following weeks were marked by shifting coalitions for and against the government, and resolution was achieved only shortly before the opening of Parliament, by means of the surprising decision of the Bougainville separatists and the New Britain autonomists to support the government.

The regional issue is inherent in the political geography of the country and its colonial history, but it is increasingly complicated by a fast-growing urban/rural dichotomy that has come to prominence only in the 1970s. In 1966 the urban population was only 128,000, six percent of the whole. Among these were only 104,000 Papua New Guineans. Since then the growth rate has been very rapid, though it is open to dispute and current estimates vary between five and 12 percent per annum. While there has been some slackening in the rate of growth in the mid-1970s due to a diminution of employment opportunities, projections indicate that by the mid to late 1980s the urban population of the country will reach one million, comprising some 30 percent of the whole population. The capital, Port Moresby, which had a population of only 40,000 in 1966, now has at least 120,000 inhabitants. It follows that most townspeople are immigrants. Political control, however, is retained largely by the local people in each case—a situation that is inevitably productive of conflict. The rapid growth of towns has placed a heavy burden on government for the provision of infra-structure and services, and one official study has suggested that 56 percent of all public spending in 1974-75 went to thirteen towns which had only 9.3 percent of the population.[61]

Rural Development and the Provincial Policy

The relatively more developed geographic areas have a higher de-mand for services and their leaders are able to express this more effec-tively than are those who need everything and do not know what to seek first. The ten-year-old Rural Improvement Program has been greatly expanded by the Papua New Guinea government; its purpose is to fund self-help projects arising in the rural areas, and allocation has been increasingly decentralized to the provincial level. The principle is excellent, but as Colebatch[62] points out, the effect of this effort at decentralization in a highly centralized administration may simply be to put more money into the hands of the political forces dominant at provincial levels. Since these latter forces are drawn mainly from the more central and wealthier areas of each province, the results of the program may actually be a new form of centralization.

At the same time, much greater legislative power is also to be given to the province, in the aftermath of the 1977 election and the political compromises on which the new national government rests. The question of provincial autonomy has been a major issue in Papua New Guinea since well before independence.[63] It is now being resolved in favor of a devolution of power which, it is hoped, will permit the unified country with its national institutions to survive. Tensions between these institutions, such as between the police and the army against the govern-ment, have already arisen—both at the level of regional politics and of the independent decision-making power of the army. The provincial policy may or may not succeed at the political level. It is certain, how-ever, that it will create serious problems in the management and control of governmental structures in a country where administrative and other skills remain in very short supply.

In Mexico, the creation of a modern nation demanded that the sectional power of both regional leaders and the army be curtailed; the result was highly successful in national terms, but has permitted great inequalities to survive and has led to neglect of possibilities for rural development in large and populous regions of the country. Papua New Guinea is forced by political realities to proceed directly to provincial devolution without yet having consolidated a power structure at the center, or even created a national "center." Provincial, or regional, devolution is fraught with serious political risks and undoubtedly creates opportunity for the local concentration of wealth and power in a few hands. Nonetheless, the situation in both these countries seems to demand such devolution at the present time. The new development ideas of the later 1970s reinforce the local conditions which make devolution necessary, but no sure way forward is to be seen. Federal solutions are not necessarily helpful, since—like Friedmann's[64] "national urban system"—they may merely transfer polarization down to a more local level. The question, therefore, remains: Is it possible to derive some general principles from this discussion of the realities of regional development problems in two particular nations?

CONCLUSION

Different elements of the regional development theory which we outlined in the first section of this chapter crop up at various points in the empirical analysis, but often in the wrong place and out of context. Mexico has created a nationally integrated spatial system, has developed resources in its frontier regions, and has even taken steps to create a development "corridor" along the Veracruz-Mexico City-Guadalajara line; yet none of this has eliminated rural poverty even from the central plateau. As Gilbert[65] found in Colombia, the spatial trickle-down effect of growth centers seems to be very limited in Mexico; it is still more limited in Papua New Guinea, even in the immediate hinterland of the capital. One aspect of the problem was, perhaps, identified in a study carried out by the writer in Malaysia.[66] While new developments certainly create regional demand and have multiplier effects, the backwash linkages tend to run to the national or—in the Papua New Guinea case—external metropolitan centers. Forward and even final-demand linkages[67] may also "jump space" so that the ends of a distribution and collection system are all that develop around the "motive industry" at the new "growth center." As Myrdal[68] suggested at the very beginning of the regional development argument, "trickle-down" is something that happens only if governments intervene to make it happen. Often the effect of government intervention has been in the opposite direction, controlling the prices of rural goods in order to keep exports competitive and subsidize the living costs of the urban population.

Nor is Friedmann's "general theory of polarized development" of much use in analyzing the actual course of events in these countries. In Papua New Guinea, the demands for peripheral autonomy have arisen before a center has been properly created. By contrast no strong centers of peripheral opposition to the center have emerged in post-revolutionary Mexico, and most of the idealists and pragmatists who now call for a "new deal" for the periphery live in Mexico City itself. Even the physical conflicts of 1968, which brought the consensus era to an end, took place mainly in the capital. Perhaps Friedmann was wrong in the way that Marx was wrong: the conflicts between exploiter and exploited, which he saw as the end point of capitalist evolution, in fact take place in their sharpest form at intermediate stages in the process.

There is a parallel weakness in Lipton's[69] view of the conflict between the rural and the urban classes. This argument neglects the deep inter-penetration of people and mutual support between city and country that studies of the informal sector[70] have demonstrated, and which certainly characterizes Mexico. Even in Papua New Guinea the new towns are still controlled mainly by the old "local" people, and the political bargaining is between regional interest groups, wherever their members are now located. The Papuan independence movement is strongest in and around Port Moresby, but does not represent the migrant majority of the city's population; rather, it gains strength from fear that this majority will in time dominate the regional political process.

Likewise, the interests of the rural poor and urban poor may be opposed in some areas, but are interdependent in others. Enclave industries and interest groups tied to foreign patrons may be found in both city and countryside. Simple dichotomies of rural versus urban interests obscure these interdependencies, and in constructing a new approach they must be cast aside.

Rural and regional problems are, therefore, national problems. The first step should be to examine in what ways the rural areas and the whole national periphery can best contribute to national needs, defined as the greater welfare of all the people, with minimal dislocation. Import substitution, not only at the national level but also at the regional, regains an important place in this context. Supply of the national market and the elimination of unnecessary interregional exchange are both potential goals of regional development policy.

Of additional importance for understanding the realities of regional development problems would be a change in the way the problems are traditionally conceptualized. The linkage of regional with urban development is outmoded; it needs to be augmented, at least in regard to the developing countries, with a new linkage between rural and regional development. The base of regional planning needs to be the land itself, its resources, and their proper utilization in relation to properly assessed national and regional needs. Urban planning should grow out of this base, and not be imposed on it as though in a vacuum.

There are also political corollaries. The Papua New Guinea experiment certainly has its risks, but it points a way that should also be explored by others. It is easy to recognize weaknesses, as it has always been with new experiments made in that country. The writer has, in the past, doubted and even opposed developments there which he now regards as successful. The problem is to create a coalition between center and periphery, so that the center can collaborate with the periphery and integrate disparate ambitions into national goals. Coalition politics are less easy than central direction, but the problems of peripheral dependence and "internal colonialism" will not be solved without them. Consultation with the rural people by the planners, as is advocated by many writers,[71] by itself is not enough.

Redistribution at a national scale, reversal of urban bias, and the proper development of the rural sector and of areas of national periphery, therefore, all require an overturn of many of the basic assumptions of three decades of development theory and practice. To the several objective functions of "development" another must be added: to make the best use of natural and human resources where they are to be found. Rural development and regional development thus become two faces of the same coin; redistribution with growth and the problem of finding a development strategy that is economical in its use of energy may also be served in the same way.

It would now be foolish to make light of such a task, but given that there is now very general realization of the need for intervention to obtain redistribution, spread development, and put a far greater proportion of national effort into the rural sector, it may be helpful to reduce the scale of the problem by demonstrating the close interrelations of these several needs. The urban problem and the rural problem, the ills of crowded centers and impoverished peripheries the intractability of persistent poverty in village and urban slum alike— all are amenable to attack through a strategy which begins with a proper understanding of the regional dimension and its dominantly rural component. The largest obstacle is the political decision to share power between center and periphery and to allow the marginalized to find a voice along with groups that are already powerful. This problem too can perhaps best be handled pragmatically, by taking one decision at a time. Lewis Carroll mapped out the path more than a century ago and also its goal:

> "However, I know my name now," she said: "that's some comfort. Alice—Alice—I won't forget it again. And now, which of these finger posts ought I to follow, I wonder?"
>
> It was not a difficult question to answer, as there was only one road, and the finger posts both pointed along it. "I'll settle it," Alice said to herself, "when the road divides and they point different ways."
>
> But this did not seem likely to happen. She went on and on, a long way, but wherever the road divided there were sure to be two finger posts pointing the same way, one marked "TO TWEEDLEDUM'S HOUSE," and the other "TO THE HOUSE OF TWEEDLEDEE."
>
> "I do believe," said Alice at last, "that they live in the same house! I wonder I never thought of that before—but I can't stay there long. I'll just call and say 'how d'yer do?' and ask them the way out of the wood."

Part III
The "Facts" of Development

Chapter 5

DEVELOPMENT IN RETROSPECT

Goran Ohlin

THE AGE OF DEVELOPMENT

It is thought of some semantic interest that the countries now referred to as "developed" never thought of themselves as developing.
If there were other ways of describing what happened to them, why do
we now talk so much about "development," what do we actually mean
by it, and how might we possibly assess it?

A reasonable suggestion might be that "development" is a shorthand
term to describe something not previously recognized, such as an all-
embracing social change for the better, not confined to mere growth of
production but encompassing every kind of social improvement. But
there were words in the past to serve that purpose, such as "progress"
and "reform." Does "development" really involve anything different?

Probably not. The real reason why "development" and its derivatives gained acceptance as a basic notion for our time seems rather to
be that it suited a number of political purposes in the age of decolonization. It had antecedents in the form of "colonial development,"

and yet it had a ring of novelty and challenge and was ambiguously transitive and intransitive. Civil servants and secretariats of international organizations who in the 1950s were faced with a momentous change of the world's political map needed a new terminology. The nations emerging from colonial status were at first described as underdeveloped, and their common denominator was that of requiring development assistance. Semantic diplomacy then turned them into "developing countries," and development became the art and science of engineering social progress in poor countries.

One unanticipated consequence of the new terminology was that the countries which were lumped together as "undeveloped" or "developing" emerged as an international block in which extreme disparities of cultural, social, and political characteristics were subordinated to a common denominator of essentially economic content. Another consequence was that the terminology that was suited to purposes of international diplomacy made it more difficult to think clearly about the underlying problems. Political language is designed to conceal and mitigate conflict, not to lay bare the essential elements of policy problems.

Extensive concern with the problems of "development" on the part of international agencies and academicians drawn into the study of the subject led to two additional unfortunate results. One was a belief that when there is a word for something, it must exist. Given this belief, it becomes sensible to ask what development really is and how it is best pursued. This is but one example of how secretariats of international organizations are under constant pressure to provide answers to questions that, perhaps, should not have been put.

The second result of this extensive concern came with the discovery that the idea of development was, in fact, quite complex and subject to great disagreement as to its meaning. This discovery led to interminable wrangles about the intellectual neocolonialism of imposing foreign ideas of social growth on new nations.

If one wants to let common sense be one's guide, he might recall Robert Heilbroner's suggestive description of development as the history of the future. The record of development is, then, no more and no less than the history of Africa, Asia, and Latin America in recent decades. Accepting this view of "development" should help one resist the value-laden and assumption-ridden perspectives which have dominated most prior discussions of the topic. In this same spirit, the intention of this essay is to survey some of the more notable aspects of this historical record. This exercise should highlight both the salient features of the recent past and the implications of these same phenomena for the immediate future.

It is too early, of course, to say with certainty what have been the most crucial features of this historical period, but it seems probable that the emphasis will not fall on the common record of the so-called developing countries. Rather, the contrasts and disparities that mark them in so many respects will probably be seen as more important. Futhermore, it is probable that the political transformation of the Third World, rather than its economic one, will ultimately be seen as the principal occurrence of this era. This change has set the stage for whatever other alterations in the life of these nations have occurred. Thus, it is to a consideration of the political record that we initially turn.

AN AGE OF POLITICAL AGONY

It is no exaggeration to say that the international concern with development largely originated in apprehensions about the anarchy which might be expected from the sudden transition to political independence of whole continents. How one should now appraise the record of political development also depends on what might reasonably have been expected. Latin American history has demonstrated the likelihood of considerable political instability in countries with extensive poverty and a dualistic social structure with profound inequality, but it also showed great national diversity. In the new African and Asian countries, ethnic and cultural conflicts were contained at first by alien rule and then by the elation over political independence. It would have been naive, however, to expect continued stability.

When the experience of the Third World is couched only in terms of economic development, the result is to obscure the political problems or to suggest that the latter constitute only minor complications. Yet, the opposite is closer to the truth. The political process has absorbed much of the energy of national leadership, just as military expenditure has absorbed much of the available resources. Not surprisingly, democratic forms of government have generally not evolved. Civilian authority has frequently yielded to military control or rests on strong police powers. Freedom of expression is the exception rather than the rule, and the opposite holds for the detention or even extermination of political opponents. Conflicts and rivalries among and within new nations have erupted into bloody conflicts.

To be sure, there are exceptions and nuances to add to this picture, but by and large the crystallization of viable political structures in the poor continents is turning out to be at least as painful as it was in Western experience, perhaps even more so, as modern technology has contributed more efficient means of oppression. This is not the place to draw up a balance sheet of the political evolution of the Third World. But its pervasive instability and the precariousness of its political institutions are highly pertinent to the record of economic and social change. Although lessons of history can only be read with difficulty, it is obvious that the slow secular growth of the West was one in which the political and economic dimensions were closely intertwined. A climate of order and stability was especially indispensable in the mobilization of individual initiative, innovation, and investment.

AN AGE OF MILITARY RULE

The prominence of the military in the developing countries deserves more than passing attention, not only because it is important for its own sake but also for what it reveals about the fundamental constraints within which the political process operates in the Third World.

At the time of the emancipation of the colonies in Asia and Africa in the 1950s and 1960s it was not widely anticipated that most of them would in a few years be ruled by military oligarchies or dictators. The struggle for independence had mostly been a political, not a military one, and in some countries there was no native officer corps whatever. Moreover, the prevailing frameworks of social thought, whether Marxist or other, did not see armies and their officers as autonomous classes or political forces.

If Latin American experience had been taken more seriously, the drift toward military rule would have come as less of a surprise.[1] In most of Latin America, the military have played a dominant political role ever since the wars of independence in the early nineteenth century. The social changes accompanying urbanization and industrialization have, of course, affected the military and their aspirations, but their role as wielders and arbiters of power has remained decisive except in a very few countries—Costa Rica, Venezuela, and Mexico. Permanent military or pseudo-military rule may, judging by this evidence, be a very probable outcome in modernizing countries.

Reasons for the emergence of military government in new nations are not hard to find. The weaknesses of the polity are evident. The economic dualism, the ethnic conflicts, the erosion of traditional authority, and the lack of institutions that would make ambitious modern constitutions viable create a power vacuum into which the armed forces are drawn. They have the guns, they alone incarnate national unity, and they make liberal use of its symbols.[2] The corruption and inefficiency of civilian power-brokers may rouse the impatience of military leaders, but if the political process stalls by itself officers may also find that any remaining effective power is in their hands by default.

In a longer historical perspective it is not unusual that military leaders exercise political power—it was the essential characteristic of European feudalism—and the tangled relations between military, religious, and other sources of authority is what much of history is all about. The fateful role of the army in the decline of the Roman Empire also comes easily to mind, and army rule in some African countries has been described as a praetorian system.[3]

Military government in the Third World today is variously regarded as an abomination, a regrettable but hopefully temporary lapse from grace, or as a guarantor of order and efficiency. But military regimes are as dissimilar as civilian ones, and their variety also reflects important aspects of the societies in which they function.

In Latin America, military politics has a tradition going back to the personal rule of the nineteenth-century *caudillos*. Gradually, a symbiosis with the civilian oligarchies usually evolved. The military sometimes seized power at the request of civilian governments unable to stem a drift toward anarchy, and they sometimes intervened from the conviction that their interpretation of the national interest was of greater legitimacy than that conferred on civilian authorities by ephemeral constitutions.

In the latter part of the nineteenth century, the professionalization of military officers was promoted by scientific and technical training in military schools, by the influence of European instructors and by Comtean positivism, with its stress on order and progress.[4] Naval officers continued to be recruited among the upper classes, but the armies were more sensitive to social change and increasingly drew their officers from the new middle classes.

Rebellious younger officers began to question the traditional institutions with which their superiors had identified, as in the case of the Brazilian *tenentes* in the 1920s, and eventually reformist military regimes came to alternate with conservative ones. Personal rule was replaced by institutionalized *juntas* incorporating representatives of various armed forces and sometimes civilians, as well. But generally a "strong man" would assume increasingly dictatorial power—until he was ousted, not seldom by the same, now disaffected officer brethren who once helped him into office.

International influences were important. In the 1930s, Nazi and Fascist impulses spread in Latin America with the exchange of military missions and overseas training of young officers. In the navies, links with the United States were stronger. In the period after World War II, radical militarist ideology all over the world has in part been a response to the new forms of guerilla warfare.

The objectives of military regimes at the present time range from traditional caretaker tasks of restoring or preserving internal order until civilian rule can be resumed, to clearly antidemocratic and national-socialist schemes for social reform, and to more revolutionary ambitions to promote social justice on behalf of the masses.

It is natural to ask whether military rule has contributed to the economic development of Latin America or set it back. An adequate answer would require a difficult exercise in conjectural history for it is hard to know what the alternatives would have been. Taken by itself, the record of the vast range of military rulers in Latin America is obviously mixed. The *transformadores* of earlier times often used the armies, as they are still being used, in the construction of roads and bridges, the development of telecommunications, and internal colonization. The educational functions of the military have extended down into the ranks. And in many countries the military have served an antidespotic function which may have been essential to the orderly evolution of economic institutions.

But the predatory side is also starkly in evidence. Even civilian governments have had little or no influence over military expenditures which have been called a "parasitic appropriation of the surplus produced by the economically productive civilian sectors."[5] Exiled military dictators are alleged to have absconded with spectacular fortunes, such as $700 million in the case of Perón, but one hesitates to assume that such abuse has been the prerogative only of the military.

The financial policies of military rulers in Latin America have often been disastrous but the same thing goes for many civilian ones, and for that matter the distinction between the two kinds of government is not always very clear. One view is that by and large military governments tend to do no better and no worse than civilian ones in the same circumstances. Corruption is particularly interesting because new military regimes almost invariably, and in many cases probably quite sincerely, invoke the corruption of their predecessors as one of the compelling reasons for intervening. Yet, with rare exceptions, the need to consolidate political support results in the deflection of public funds for such purposes. Only rigorous systems of accountability, auditing, and checks and balances in the field of political power are likely to stem such practices in countries which are involved in the creation of new wealth.

The two fundamental features of military rule in Latin America seem to have been the weakness of alternative power structures and the transformation, in time, of the army into one of the instruments of change and modernization. Those features are also common elsewhere, although the historical circumstances vary. Parts of the Middle East have been ruled by soldiers for a thousand years, and in the last phase of the Ottoman Empire the Sultan's invitation of European instructors to officer training schools started the transformation of the military "from praetorian guard to advance guard."[6] Kemal Atatürk of Turkey was a product of such training and was, in his day, the very model of a modern nation builder. He is exceptional, however, in leaving behind a tradition of civilian rule in Turkey which has only briefly been broken by military caretakers who have seen their task as watching over this legacy.

Elsewhere in the Middle East, the recent international tensions making for a colossal expansion of the armed forces have created large classes of officers drawn from the rural sector, animated by a distrust of civilian politicians and sometimes reinforced by religious fanaticism. In the domestic instability of what used to be called the Fertile Crescent, the discontent and frustration of the military makes it a potent force which is strengthened by the perpetual state of emergency. In the new states born after World War II in Asia and Africa, charismatic civilian leaders associated with the struggle for independence have gradually been replaced with military men.

In South Asia, India is the great exception, perhaps because officers there have not been as dominant in the modern intelligentsia as in most of the other countries, because the Congress party managed for long to preserve the momentum of the struggle for independence, and because there was no disintegration into anarchy. In Pakistan, on the other hand, the army assumed control at an early time, making it clear that civilian government was at the sufferance of the military. In East Asia,

with the possible exception of Sri Lanka, officers have similarly formed
a dominant part of the elite and set the style of politics even when
authority has been restored to civilian politicians.

The African situation is the most alarming one. In most of the
former colonies south of the Sahara, the armed forces had no native
officers at the time of independence—in some cases not even non-
commissioned officers. The hasty training and promotion of officers
did not instill professionalism and discipline. Military aid extended to
the young nations by the United Kingdom, France, the United States,
the Soviet Union, China, and Cuba put powerful arms in the hands of
young men suddenly promoted to high rank and also subjected the
officer corps to a bewildering variety of ideological impulses, making
for even greater internal friction than tribal and ethnic conflict tended
to create in the first place.

In such circumstances, most African military takeovers have borne
little resemblance to those of Atatürk or other military reformers.
Many contemporary African armies can be described as coteries of
armed gangs with unstable allegiances to officers of different ranks who
are themselves divided by tribal and personal rivalries.[7] When they
take power, their first measures are usually to raise army and police
salaries and to slash development expenditure. In these "praetorian
systems" the jockeying for power within the junta and the effort to
stay in power tend to lead to governmental paralysis in the socioeconomic field.

The repression of opposition, real or imagined, has usually been
brutal. Idi Amin's regime in Uganda has been so eccentric and extreme
as to reach international attention, but it is not unique in its cruelty.
Bloody expurgation of opponents is not, however, the monopoly of
military regimes. The distinction between police and military is fuzzy
and the complicity of the military in massive repression is usually
indispensable. In the unstructured and feverish climate of many young
African countries violence and anarchy is also engendered by attempts
at mobilizing the population in youth organizations and militias. In
the French Congo, officers of the regular army were eventually pushed
to step in to check a populist take-over of the entire military machinery.

Military governments are sometimes not very different from their
civilian predecessors or successors, especially when the officers who
take over the key posts in government and administration have much
the same social background as those civilians they replace. They might
bring to the task a fresh combination of technocratic dedication and

inexperience, but they will make their peace with the civil service and the elite and a return to civilian rule is not excluded.

But this is not true of military governments in states where both political and military systems are rudimentary—such as in most of Black Africa. A military take-over may in such circumstances put power in the hands of a soldiery with no experience of government. If the army has been deliberately recruited in the hinterland, tribal animosities against the urbanized populations may be so strong and the previous elite so thin that the latter is annihilated in repressive actions. In such circumstances, military rule may thwart prospects of development for the foreseeable future. Social discontent may cause rumblings in the barracks and internal coups, but it will not alter the situation significantly.

Even in the best of circumstances military rule is a flawed political system. It holds no room for constitutional opposition and tends to make no provision for succession. By stifling public opinion it throttles the development of a civilian tradition of government and becomes self-perpetuating. Social conflicts may indeed be reflected in the struggle inside the military complex, and there may be important and lasting socioeconomic development, but a measure of instability is bound to persist where the coup d'état is the only way to change government.

Whether on balance military rules have made a positive contribution to development or served to retard it is a question that probably does not allow of a simple answer.[8] Emile Benoit has found a positive correlation between military spending and the rate of growth of civilian incomes in developing countries.[9] This in itself is proof of nothing—military expenditure does not, for instance, create oil wells—but Benoit argues that many of the resources devoted to military users would not otherwise have gone into investment, that idle capacity has been put to use and aggregate demand stimulated, that attitudes have been modernized and nation-building assisted.

Others have disputed the alleged efficiency and stability of military as compared to civilian government, or argued in various case studies that military governments have indeed attained more rapid industrial growth, but only at the expense of the poor or with the help of massive foreign aid.[10]

But "the military" is a deceptive term. Although the armed forces of the Third World share several similarities, there is also a variety of political orientations among them similar to that among civilian regimes. Sweeping generalizations are not appropriate.

Merely to condemn or regret a phenomenon which is nearly universal in the Third World can serve no good purpose. But the training of the officers in the Third World, their competence, and their attitudes toward social and economic development are obviously matters of great consequence.

AN AGE OF WEAPONRY

The enormous expenditure on armaments in the Third World is another feature of the development record which causes both bewilderment and criticism. How can countries which are desperately poor give priorities to arms and spend more for military purposes than for education and health?

The situation is actually quite complex—the military build-up is highly concentrated in the Middle East; on the other hand, in the Latin American countries with long traditions of military rule but fairly high incomes, military spending is fairly low.

Average military spending in the Third World has grown at about ten percent a year in the last 20 years (1957-1976); that in the rest of the world by some three to four percent. So the Third World share in world military expenditure has about doubled. In 1976 it was about fourteen percent.[11]

Per capita, developing countries spend very little on arms compared to industrialized countries—probably less than one-tenth. As a proportion of gross domestic product (GDP), their average military spendings in the 1970s has been about four percent which is also a good deal lower than the six percent of the rest of the world. But armaments in the Middle East were spectacular even before the rise in oil revenues which led to a new escalation of rearmament, and not only among the oil-rich.

Most of the arms in the Third World are supplied by imports. In fact, the overwhelming part of the world's arms trade consists of shipments to the Third World. "Major weapons" probably account for about half, and practically all of these come from the United States, the Soviet Union, the United Kingdom, and France.[12] The growth of such sales has been explosive in the 1970s. Orders for American arms from non-OPEC developing countries increased from $240 million in 1972 to $2.3 billion in 1976 which, even if prices doubled, is a remarkable increase.[13]

But several developing countries—Argentina, Brazil, India, Egypt,

Taiwan, and others—already have industries producing sophisticated weapons, and many others are building them. Small arms and trainer aircraft are produced in a great number of countries; missiles and combat planes by a few. Nuclear technology is rapidly spreading beyond those countries—Argentina, India, and Pakistan—which already operate reactors and produce plutonium.

The political tensions in the Third World are not caused by armaments. Nonetheless, the major powers' readiness to supply the most modern equipment to countries in the most unstable regions of the world is in part responsible for the colossal economic drain this arms race has turned into and for making armed conflicts in the Third World bloodier and more destructive.

AN AGE OF ECONOMIC GROWTH

Even with all the above borne in mind, it must be said that the economic record has been surprisingly good when viewed in the aggregate. Although it is commonly asserted that development is not a matter of economic growth alone, it seems that per capita income sums up surprisingly well much of what is associated with the idea of development. When countries are ranked on social indicators such as life expectancy at birth, literacy, or social amenities, the result is not very different from the ranking by per capita product.[14]

Contrary to dire prophecies and well-intentioned suggestions that the situation is going from bad to worse, the overall economic growth of the developing countries was impressive in the 1960s and has accelerated in the 1970s. Table 5.1 indicates the recent growth record for regional groupings of developing nations.

TABLE 5.1.   GROWTH OF GROSS DOMESTIC PRODUCT (GDP) AT CONSTANT PRICES

	1961-65	1966-71	1972	1973	1974	1975
All developing countries	5.9	6.1	6.5	7.5	6.4	2.6
Africa (south of Sahara)	4.0	5.5	4.5	4.8	5.2	2.9
East Asia	5.3	7.2	6.3	10.9	5.1	4.0
Latin America	5.3	5.8	6.8	7.1	6.4	2.7
Middle East	6.6	7.9	12.4	10.9	14.0	-0.2
South Asia	3.8	4.2	-1.6	4.6	1.5	4.4

Source: World Bank, *Annual Report* (1976).

TABLE 5.2. THE DISTRIBUTION OF DEVELOPING COUNTRIES
BY RATES OF GROWTH IN GROSS DOMESTIC PRODUCT (GDP),
1960-1973

	0-2%	2-4%	4-6%	6-8%	8-10%	above 10%
Africa	4	12	12	6	2	-
Middle East	-	-	7	1	-	5
South Asia	-	5	2	1	-	-
East Asia	1	1	4	2	2	3
Latin America	1	2	13	5	-	-

Source: World Bank, *World Tables* (1976).

But behind the averages in Table 5.1 there is actually a stupendous diversity. Table 5.2 indicates the distribution of nations in each region by their average growth rate in the period 1960-1973. Arranged in this order, African countries are spread out fairly evenly from total stagnation to an average rate of growth close to ten percent. The slow growth of most of the countries in South Asia stands out, as does the rapid growth of the oil countries and of the East Asian export economies. Most developing countries are in the range between four and six percent, ahead of population growth by one to two percent, while about one-third of them grow faster than that.

The diversity of experience appears even more striking when one examines the distribution of nations by per capita growth in Table 5.3. About two-fifths of the developing countries showed per capita growth rates of three to five percent or higher. They did as well as or better

TABLE 5.3. DISTRIBUTION OF RATES OF GROWTH OF GDP
PER CAPITA IN NINETY-NINE DEVELOPING COUNTRIES, 1960-1973.

	below -3%	-3 to -2%	-1 to 1%	1 to 3%	3 to 5%	5 to 7%	7 to 9%	above 9%
Ninety-nine developing countries	3	4	17	36	20	10	4	5
Middle East	1	1		2	1	1	1	2
Africa	1	2	11	14	11	3	1	2
South Asia		1	2	4				
East Asia	1		1	2	3	3	2	1
Western hemisphere			3	14	5	3		

Source: World Bank, *World Tables* (1976).

than industrialized countries (which had an average of 3.6 percent), or the socialist bloc (which had an average of 3.2 percent over the same period). But close to two-fifths of the developing countries showed per capita growth closer to two percent, and more than one-fifth showed stagnation or declining per capita growth.

Unless countries which initially were the poorest registered the fastest growth, which we know not to have been the case, these disparities in growth rates must have led to growing inequality among countries (leaving apart the question of inequalities within them). This is borne out by studies of changing per capita product levels in the period 1958-1968 which showed a marked increase in inequality among 78 developing countries at the same time as there was growing equality among the developed ones.[15]

Table 5.4 suggests that the richest countries have been the fastest growers—which is, of course, in part why they are richer. If the past record is any guide to the future, these figures suggest that there are a number of countries in the middle and upper ranges of the developing world which have shown great capacity for growth—so great that in another decade they may well overtake some of the old industrialized countries. At the other extreme, among the poorest countries, some of which are among the most populous, growth and development have not taken root, and they are emerging as the hard-core problems. One must thus prepare for the graduation of some developing countries while recognizing that the problem of world poverty will be with us for a long time.

Growth has not only been unevenly distributed among countries, but also within countries and among individuals. This has attracted

TABLE 5.4. AVERAGE GROWTH RATES OF
GROSS DOMESTIC PRODUCT (GDP) PER CAPITA
FOR DEVELOPING COUNTRIES IN DIFFERENT
INCOME GROUPS[a]

GNP/capita 1973	Growth Rate of GNP/capita, 1965-1973
Over $800	5.5%
$400-$800	3.0
$200-$400	2.7
$100-$200	1.2
Below $100	0.3

[a] Unweighted averages of the growth rates given in World Bank, *World Tables* (1976).

much attention in recent years, and the World Bank's major report on the matter opens with the bold claim that growth since 1960 has been of little or no benefit to perhaps one-third of the population in developing countries.[16] No general statement seems possible about whether inequality within countries has increased or decreased, and it cannot be claimed with certainty that the poorest groups have generally suffered from rapid growth in their countries. Although it has been claimed that large numbers of people have been impoverished rather than helped, the evidence is contradictory.[17] In India, for example, Ahluwalia finds the proportion living below a poverty line to have fluctuated between 40 and nearly 60 percent between 1956-57 and 1973-74, without any trend.[18] But then India was not a country of vigorous growth. In Brazil, sustained growth seems to have produced a greater inequality but it is not clear whether absolute incomes of the poor have been reduced. On the other hand, in Korea and Taiwan, which have both been growing rapidly, benefits have been remarkably equitably distributed.

The share of income accruing to the lowest 40 percent seems to be higher in countries with very low incomes than in the middle range, and then higher again in the high-income-level nations. But the deviations are too large and numerous to permit the conclusion that this is a law of development.

The record simply does not confirm any grand hypothesis about equity and growth. Growth does not necessarily produce more inequality or impoverishment of the poor; nor is equity a prerequisite of growth or even of growth that benefits the poor. The issue is, as might be expected, more complex.

It remains true that growth has made no dent on poverty in India, Pakistan, and Bangladesh, where the absolute poverty of the world is largely concentrated. The same is probably true in parts of Africa and Latin America where little is known.

The concern with basic needs of the rural and urban poor that has emerged in recent years does not necessarily conflict with the growth objective. Growth should make redistribution easier, and the record shows that the two goals can be reconciled.

The reasons why some countries have succeeded better than others are varied. In some cases, a favorable resource base and operations by transnational companies have been enough to confer substantial incomes on countries without any significant domestic development. But of greater importance for particular countries has been successful implementation of policies for agricultural and industrial growth, or of import substitution and export promotion.

Great strides have also been made in the technical and administrative capacity to manage economies. International efforts to help countries strengthen their machinery for economic planning and administration have helped to transform the situation in this respect. But here, too, improvement has been uneven. Ideological and theoretical disputes about priorities, about the place of the private sector, and about the wisdom and feasibility of export-oriented strategies have been intense. It is not difficult for foreign observers to list weaknesses and mistakes that continue to mar economic policies in many developing countries, but often these are primarily due to the rigidities of the internal political situation.

It would be dangerously wrong to dismiss the political problem as a mere obstacle to the implementation of the policies which technocrats and economic experts find advisable. Yet it often is just that, as the result of a pervasive tension between power and development. Governments with a precarious political base are naturally wedded to the status quo and are not given to visions of development and social change with vast and unpredictable consequences. Without political stability and efficiency, economic planning will not matter much, no matter how brilliant. Political crisis accounts for several of the extreme cases of stagnation.

As a result, developing countries offer a spectrum from success to failure with regard to economic and social development. No verdict suits them all, least of all one based on statistical averages. Their common label is losing plausibility, and one must distinguish between regions and even individual countries.

What has been demonstrated is that countries can, from the most varied base of departure, be mobilized into growth rates of six to ten percent when they are not torn by political dissent, ridden with corrupt and inefficient administration, or paralyzed in such matters as taxation, exchange rate policy, land reform and education.

AN AGE OF EXPANDING POPULATION

There is little doubt that one of the obstacles to achieving more rapid improvements of economic and social conditions in developing countries has been the inexorable growth of population and that, in a historical perspective, this will stand out as one of the most dramatic aspects of the first decades of independence of Africa and Asia.

But even rapid population growth is not necessarily incompatible with economic progress, as is sometimes naively asserted. It is enough to recall that at the beginning of this century the rate of natural increase of the United States was about the same as that of India today, or 2.5 percent, and that a century earlier it was well over three percent. And today, the fastest-growing economies of the Third World are not distinguished by slower population growth than more stagnant economies.

Nor should it be overlooked that the declining mortality which is the dominant feature of the present phase of the demographic transition in the Third World is itself the result of incontrovertible social progress.

Hypotheses about the retarding effects of population growth usually rest on the assumption that with large families and high dependency ratios, resources will be used for child rearing which would otherwise be saved and invested, but there is really no evidence of such a link.

It is often suggested that developing countries have directed inadequate attention to the population problem, and that energetic policies to check population growth should be part of their strategy. Such policies are certainly advisable, if only because access to family planning is an important social service in its own right. But it should also be realized that even an all-out effort to check fertility by coercive methods is not likely to bring down birth rates very fast or very much. Few developing countries have the social discipline of China, and in most of them even extensive population programs will only marginally affect the situation.

Fortunately, birth rates seem destined to decline on their own eventually. They are already doing so in 78 of 89 countries for which data are available, and the decline is gathering strength. It is probable, then, that population growth may be the principal determinant of whether the development gap between rich and poor countries will continue to widen.

AN AGE OF TRANSITION

So far, accelerated economic growth in most developing countries has been accompanied by a growth in the labor force which has been difficult to absorb, and by political instability and widespread inequality. Many have already drawn the conclusion that the patterns of growth and the general strategies by which it has been pursued must inevitably fail to meet the high expectations that are placed on development. The growth model of the industrialized countries is derided and said to be infeasible. In its place, some suggest the need for a "bicycle economy" with appropriate technology and low resource needs. It is true that indiscriminate transfer of modern industrial technology can easily absorb the savings of a poor country without creating much employment and without making a dent in the social and economic framework. But this was never the "growth model" of the countries already industrialized. There may be numerous other objections—moral, ideological, or aesthetic—to the notion that the road to development should be basically similar today, but it would be wrong to argue that the road is not passable.

Political leaders have good reason to underline the uniqueness of each country's particular situation. They are correct, of course, as social and political issues are bound to be of infinite variety. Yet social scientists cannot fail to be impressed with the strong patterns evident in the growth of consumption and production all over the world.

Kuznets, Chenery and others have pointed out that structures of industrialized countries are now quite similar, although they started their industrialization at different times and have shown great differences in their rates of growth. The same similarity by and large holds for thoroughly underdeveloped countries. But the developing countries today find themselves in a situation where taking advantage of technological opportunities and the international division of labor involves major change in the structure of demand and production.[19] To some, this need for momentous structural transformation is the distinctive difference between development and mere growth.

Some countries are well launched on this transition. Large parts of Latin America now have more in common with southern Europe than with Africa or Asia. Along with some of the smaller countries in East Asia they have shown that it is possible to break into world markets by combining modern technology and low labor costs into a formidable comparative advantage. Of the nonfuel exports from developing countries no less than 40 percent now consist of manufactures, which is twice the portion of ten years ago.

To be sure, the "outward-looking" development strategies which have so far been the most successful are not unproblematic. Their export orientation makes them vulnerable to the instability of world demand and the precariousness of access to other markets. In the old industrialized countries, the capacity for rapid contraction of key industries is limited by social and political constraints, and other developing countries wish to reserve home markets for their own infant industries.

There is thus a real risk that the world trade in manufactures will be overloaded by the very success of developing-country export capacity. A sharp rise of trade barriers would be a serious blow to countries where the growth momentum stems from exports, and it would discourage others from following their example. The future of development performance is thus closely linked to the prospects for world trade.

CONCLUSION

The experience to date of the developing nations has not been entirely what was hoped for by many of the leaders of these nations or by officers of international organizations of the early 1950s. Perhaps, the most striking events have been in the political sphere. The military has come to hold power or to influence civilian politics significantly in a very large number of these nations. Furthermore, the general problems of political instability—both at the mass and the elite level—have plagued an even larger number of countries. As a consequence of these political difficulties, civilian governmental institutions remain poorly developed or legitimized in many developing nations. Likewise, western conceptions of individual political liberties are rarely entertained in the Third World.

In terms of strictly economic changes, the record has been rather uneven. Some nations have moved forward dramatically. Some have made real but limited progress—often held back as much by rapid population growth as by the difficulty of choosing the optimal development strategy. Yet, another set of nations remains today much as they were when independence was achieved.

Unfortunately, many of those nations which have experienced accelerated economic growth have found it to be accompanied by some unanticipated and severe secondary consequences. Certain segments of the labor force have grown dramatically and have been difficult to absorb into the economy. Inequality within the nation has frequently been increased rather than diminished in the early stages of growth. Finally, the already tenuous political balance has been rocked by the social and economic transformations attendant to rapid development.

There is little point in referring to the developing countries as a group. They are quite diverse in terms of past economic performance, social structure, economic infrastructure, natural resource endowments, and consequently prospects for future progress. This diversity of character means also that Third World nations have a diversity of interest. It means, as well, that no single set of economic policies is adequate to the development needs of all these nations.

The political unity and solidarity demonstrated by developing countries in their demands for a new economic world order may or may not survive the growing divergence and the conflicts of interest *within* the Third World. To students of the developing world it should, in any case, be clear that some of them are about to "graduate," if they have not already done so. This is, in itself, a demonstration that development is possible.

Attention, then, must focus on the genuinely poor countries. With an arbitrary dividing line of some $200 annual income per capita, they have about two-thirds of the population of the Third World. There has been a tendency for the poor countries to grow more slowly than the rich ones. But there are also examples of small, poor countries which have been able to grow quite rapidly, achieving growth rates around ten percent per year. When, where, and whether the poorest countries will repeat such performances are questions which cannot be answered on the basis of their experience so far. To break the vicious circle of poverty by outside assistance from international organizations or bilateral aid agencies will certainly prove impossible where the growth of a viable political and social community is thwarted by endemic instability and the stranglehold of praetorian despots.

Chapter 6

THE POSTWAR ECONOMIC EXPERIENCE OF
THE THIRD WORLD[1]

Bill Warren

A widespread view prevails that the postwar record of economic development in the Third World has been one of failure, of failure moreover developing inexorably toward catastrophe in some versions. The major components of this view can be summarized straightforwardly.

1. In terms of material advance, as measured by the (formerly) standard indicator of gross national product (GNP) per capita, the record for the developing countries has been disappointingly poor, in some cases negative, resulting in, among other things, a growing absolute and relative gap between developed and underdeveloped countries.

2. More importantly, the absolute rise in GNP per capita of the developing countries has not been reflected in rising absolute standards of welfare for the mass of the populations of the developing countries as a result of a range of causes, among the most important of which have been increasingly regressive income distribution and patterns of output irrelevant to basic social needs, as well as types of economic development tending towards an increasing marginalization of growing sections of the population. On the contrary, Third World postwar

economic development has been characterized by negligible improvement or even increasing material misery for the majority, with only a small minority benefiting from development.

3. Even where (or if) material standards have improved, the result is "growth without development," i.e., a process whereby average purchasing power over goods and services increases but without an improvement, with perhaps a decline, in the quality of life for the majority. Thus, growth without development entails unjust income distribution, the shattering of traditional values and communities without any worthwhile alternatives, growing crime rates, the loss of human dignity resulting from growing unemployment and underemployment, and in general, the imposition of unsuitable Western modern capitalist industrial culture, including consumption patterns, on Third World societies.

4. In any case such material progress as has been achieved, disappointingly small as it may be, is likely to be ephemeral, threatened as it is by the specters of starvation, ever-growing mass unemployment and dwindling resources.[2]

5. Starvation threatens as a result of rapidly accelerating population growth, the pattern of international trade which favors cash crop production by the developing countries and the dominance in the political system of privileged elites whose interests and consumption patterns are not directed toward the development of domestic food production. The reality of this threat is evidenced by the failure of Third World agriculture in the postwar period to date.

6. Mass unemployment, including large-scale urban and rural underemployment, is already characteristic of Third World countries on a scale never before witnessed since the localized experience of the advanced capitalist countries in the 1930s. Currently accelerating rates of population growth and the capital-intensive character of modern industry (together with a host of other factors, not least of which has been uneven income distribution) make it a near certainty that by 1990 Third World overall unemployment rates will total anywhere between 50 and 73 percent.[3]

Insofar as it can be distinguished from this populist-liberal view, the specifically "Marxist" or neo-Marxist version of this outlook emphasizes that the alleged failure of postwar Third World development is evidence of the socially retrogressive character of capitalist development to accomplish imperialism and the consequent inability of such development to accomplish even the material success which early, non-imperialist capitalism in the West accomplished. One conceptualization of this neo-Marxist approach is Gundar Frank's "development of under-development," which postulates that underdevelopment is not simply a failure to develop as compared with the economically more advanced continents of Europe, North America, Australasia and Japan, but is a state *sui generis* of distorted development caused by Western imperialism. A corollary of the neo-Marxist view is that capitalism in Third World countries, being an externally introduced (and generally forcibly imposed) system, has no healthy internal roots or vigorous autonomous dynamic of its own.

In what follows we shall argue that the empirical data belie this picture and that in the Third World the postwar period has witnessed substantial, accelerating and historically unprecedented improvements in the growth of productive capacity and of the material welfare of the mass of the population. The developing capitalist societies of Asia, Africa and Latin America have, moreover, proved themselves increasingly capable of generating powerful internal sources of economic expansion and of achieving an increasingly independent status in the world, economically and politically.[4] This progress has, however, been extremely uneven as between states, classes, regions and ethnic groups and has been accompanied by new and varied tensions, individually and within and between societies and social groups. This latter point touches on a range of phenomena both favorable and detrimental to human progress and is beyond the scope of this chapter. The fact of markedly uneven development, however, together with the immense heterogeneity of the societies of the Third World (a heterogeneity far greater than that of the advanced capitalist countries taken as a group) poses the question of the appositeness of treating these societies in aggregate, and of the related conceptual division of the world into developed and underdeveloped countries. So rapid and fundamental has been postwar international economic change that the core of truth in the division of the world into developed and underdeveloped is rapidly crumbling as the situation gives way to one which could more appropriately be conceptualized as a spectrum in which the location of individual countries is constantly shifting. Nevertheless, the core of truth yet remains substantial[5] and justifies an aggregative treatment, provided the elements of change qualifying such a treatment are duly taken into account.[6]

MATERIAL PROGRESS—GNP PER CAPITA

Cross-national comparisons of the poor countries with the rich in terms of GNP per capita, infant mortality, access to running water, or calorie intake per capita, etc., are only too frequently used to argue or suggest poor performance or failure of Third World development efforts. Yet such comparisons throw no light on the performance of the poor countries in attempting to change this condition, since it takes no account of the state of affairs before the effort to improve began, nor of the time span which has since elapsed. Indeed such cross-country comparisons, presented as evidence of the failure of Third World development, are all the more absurd in view of the comparatively cheerful picture painted by the relevant data relating to progress over time.

In terms of the standard measure of economic progress, GNP per capita,[7] it must be stated unequivocally that the record of the Third World postwar has been reasonably, and perhaps outstandingly, successful as compared *either* with their pre-Second World War twentieth-century record *or* with whatever past period one cares to take as relevant for comparison in the now developed market economies (DMEs). *Any argument that the postwar economic growth of the developing countries has been a relative or absolute failure must rest on other grounds.*[8]

Comparison of postwar Third World economic growth with prewar (twentieth-century) growth is necessarily based on scanty evidence but is fairly conclusive: postwar economic growth in terms of gross domestic product (GDP) per capita has in general been faster than prewar economic growth for the developing countries. Kuznets[9] summarizes the evidence for seven underdeveloped countries for which long-term records are available. Of the four (or perhaps five) countries for which the data permit pre- and postwar comparisons (Jamaica, Philippines, United Arab Republic, India and perhaps Ghana), all show markedly accelerated growth rates of real product per capita postwar as compared with prewar, with the possible exception of Ghana, where there was probably very little change on average. Aggregate data for Latin America for a more limited period show the same postwar acceleration. According to the Economic Commission for Latin America (ECLA), GNP per capita increased at two percent per annum from 1935-53, while in the period 1945-55, GNP per head increased by 1.4 percent.[10] Bairoch's estimates for all noncommunist developing countries taken as a whole shows the same prewar to postwar contrast, with per capita GNP increasing at a rate of 1.3 percent per annum, 1900-13; 0.9 percent per annum, 1913-19; 2.2 percent per annum, 1929-52/4; 4.8 percent per annum 1960-70.[11] These results are all the more impressive in that the pre- and post-Second World War comparisons show an acceleration as compared to a period (*circa* 1900-1945) which itself witnessed, as far as the scattered evidence goes, unprecendented growth rates as compared with any earlier period in the history of the developing countries.[12]

Comparison of the recent developmental experience of the Third World with that of the now developed capitalist economies at an earlier stage of the latter's economic growth, generally the period of their industrialization, is not a comparison of like with like since the industrialization of the now developed countries was the culmination of a process of modern socioeconomic change stretching over several centuries. Since most of the developing countries start or have started the development process from a position far more primitive than the developed capitalist countries, then *if other things were equal* (see below) the comparison would be bound to minimize such achievements as the developing countries could demonstrate. Despite this, the developing countries come out of such a comparison rather well. Their postwar growth rates of product per head have in general been higher than those of the industrializing capitalist countries of the eighteenth and nineteenth centuries. Summarizing the evidence for all the noncommunist developed countries for which there are long-term records, and excluding very small countries with a population of less that two million, Kuznets notes that the rate of growth of per capita product for the long period covering the modern economic growth of the 14 countries concerned ranges from 1.0 to 1.2 percent per annum[13] for Australia, the Netherlands and Great Britain-United Kingdom, to 2.9 to 3.2 percent for Sweden and Japan, with the rates for the remaining nine countries[14] clustering between 1.4 and 2.3 percent per annum.[15] This compares with average postwar per capita growth rates in the Third World ranging from 2.4 percent per annum in the 1950s to 2.6 percent per annum in the 1960s and 3.8 percent per annum in the early 1970s,[16] averaging 2.8 percent per annum in the years 1963 to 1973.[17] Limited indeed as is the value of these comparisons, they serve to suggest *the extent to which in fact other things were not equal* (see above) as regards the capacity for material advance and, in particular, the extent to which new elements have improved the prospects of material advance at a faster rate and generally from a considerably less appropriate base than was the case with the countries of Western Europe, North America, Australasia and Japan in the eighteenth and nineteenth centuries. In a broad perspective "the advantages of backwardness" thesis appears to have much more relevance to current Third World economic growth than has often been supposed—both as regards technology and the increased opportunities and stimuli provided by the expansion of the world market.[18]

Bearing in mind, still, the much more inappropriate technological, economic, institutional and cultural base for modern economic development from which today's developing countries started, the comparison of their current growth rates of per capita product with those of the developed world clearly has limited value as a measure of economic achievement or performance. Quite a substantial divergence in favor of the latter countries would not by itself suggest a poor performance of the former, particularly in view of the differences in population growth rates. Nevertheless, such an alleged divergence has been taken to be a reasonable criterion of performance, and quite specific economic and political conclusions have been drawn from it.[19] Without in any way subscribing to this approach, we may nevertheless note that in the 1970s "depolarization" occurred, with per capita growth rates of developing countries rising faster than those in developed market economies (DMEs), a development which started in the late 1960s.[20]

More fundamentally, however, the notion of a "growing gap," or rich world-poor world polarization, implies both a marked discontinuity in the total range of growth rates and the grouping of all or most of the countries commonly classed as less developed at the lower end of the range, with most of the developed market economies bracketed at the upper end of the range. If this is not the case, and particularly if the second condition is not fulfilled, then the thesis of growing polarization must be discarded. There is in fact a continuous spectrum of growth rates with no marked discontinuities.[21] Further, although the greater proportion of the developing countries are bunched in the lower ranges of the growth spectrum for the period 1960-1973, between one-quarter and one-third are to be found in the upper and middle ranges.[22] Only about a quarter of the developed market countries are to be found in the higher growth rate ranges, the vast majority of them being in the middle range with a few in the lower ranges. While all this indicates uneven development and continuing polarization, at least up to the late 1960s, it certainly does not indicate either economic stagnation or *growing* polarization.

MATERIAL PROGRESS—GROWING INEQUALITY

Has this rapid expansion of output been nullified in terms of material welfare by growing inequality and marginalization, so that the mass of the population—or the lowest 20 percent[23]—is worse off than before? Is it the case that the "type of growth" so far pursued in most developing countries has itself been a cause of growing domestic inequality?

The widespread belief that the rapid Third World economic progress of the postwar period has been generally associated with growing aggregate inequality is not borne out by either the (extremely scanty and unreliable) time-series data or by the more plentiful cross-section data. Summarizing time-series data for 18 countries on a graph relating the annual growth rate of income of the lowest 40 percent against the rate of growth of GNP, Ahluwalia notes that "the scatter suggests considerable diversity of country experience in terms of relative equality. Several countries show a deterioration in relative equality but there are others showing improvement."[24]

Ahluwalia's cross-section evidence covering 66 countries is used to examine the statistical relationship between distribution and per capita income and between distribution and growth of GNP at given levels of per capita income, the former being taken as an indicator of the short-term impact of economic growth on income distribution. Concerning the *secular* relationship of economic growth to inequality, Ahluwalia finds that "there is some confirmation that income inequality first increases and then decreases with development."[25] Further, "there is no strong pattern relating changes in the distribution of income to the rate of growth of GNP. In both high-growth and low-growth countries there are some which have experienced improvements and others that have experienced deteriorations in relative equality. The absence of any marked relationship between income growth and changes in income shares is important for policy purposes. It suggests that there is little firm empirical basis for the view that higher rates of growth inevitably generate greater inequality."[26]

Ahluwalia's findings thus buttress earlier studies[27] to the effect that the earlier stages of growth are likely to be characterized by increasing inequality with the trend being reversed as higher levels of development are reached. The turning point toward the emergence of substantial middle-income groups and the stabilization and improvement of the lower quartiles appears to occur at about the $500 per capita income level.[28] It is of interest that well over one-quarter of the 80-odd developing countries listed in the *World Bank Atlas* had already passed that level by 1973.[29]

Furthermore, concerning the short-term impact of growth on redistribution, "the cross-section evidence does not support the view that a high rate of economic growth has an adverse effect upon relative equality. Quite the contrary; the rate of growth of GDP in our sample was positively related to the share of the lowest 40 percent, suggesting that the objectives of growth and equity may not be in conflict."[30]

The secular scenario of initially growing inequality followed by declining inequality as growth proceeds is not only hopeful in itself, but, when allied with the postwar tendency for growth to accelerate in Third World countries, implies that the turning point to stable and eventually improved distribution is likely to take place relatively sooner for such countries than it did in the historical past of the now developed nations. In other words, the sequential development of initially rising and subsequently falling income concentration is likely to become compressed so that the initial period of rising inequality will become foreshortened. In some cases, e.g., perhaps postwar Taiwan, it may well be that the equalizing aspects of modern development are strong enough almost from the start to outweigh the initial concentration aspects so that the sequential *aggregate* development of income redistribution does not take place and there is no initial concentration of overall distribution.[31] We must repeat, however, that there is no implication here of general, widespread, early and even "improvements" in distribution as economic growth proceeds. On the contrary, it is extremely likely that there will be traumatic disruptions in previously accepted relative incomes within and between sectors (whether these previous relativities were "good" or "bad") and particularly marked development of social differentiation in agriculture as commercialization penetrates it further, although in some cases, of course, this will not lead to increased concentration but to the replacement of one type of social differentiation by another.

Nevertheless, the rejection of a Panglossian approach should not blur the logical implications of the empirical data discussed above. And these are that, far from curtailing growth to improve income distribution (the "basic needs" approach), growth ought to be speeded up to bring more rapidly into play the economic and institutional[32] forces which tend to ensure that the more economically advanced societies are also the more economically egalitarian, and the more egalitarian at higher absolute standards of living.[33]

It has been argued or implied that since the evidence does not show rapid growth to be incompatible with more equal income distribution, this justifies extensive egalitarian policy measures.[34] But this ignores the fact that the move toward more equal income distribution is in the general case the by-product of high levels of economic achievement and of measures to promote economic growth per se rather than the reverse, especially the extensive development of relevant education.[35]

Changing and probably increasing income differences are, in fact, likely to contribute to economic growth in the following ways: by promoting the necessary diversification of skills and occupations; by mobilizing latent energies previously relatively dormant in non- or only partly commercialized sectors of the economy where previously custom and habit had prevailed; by mobilizing for economic activity scarce or underutilized entrepreneurial talents; and by promoting rapid changes in resource allocation at minimum cost (as compared with bureaucratic methods). These unequalizing aspects of economic growth are likely to be strongest in the earliest stages of growth as the expansion of the nascent, high-productivity modern sector creates sectoral inequalities; while commercialization of agriculture and the development of the urban informal sector produce increasing inequality as social differentiation proceeds and as entrepreneurs emerge. Within the modern sector, too, there may be increasing initial differentiation as new skills and industries develop, while trade unions have not yet developed sufficiently to counteract this trend. Such processes, while increasing income inequality, are likely to expand material welfare for the majority,[36] eventually, or perhaps immediately, creating conditions for raising the standards of those who have failed to acquire new skills, or failed to respond to new opportunities or have not initially had new opportunities to respond to.[37] These unequalizing forces will tend to decline as the proportion of the labor force in the modern sector rises, as productivity levels in the agricultural and urban informal sectors rise in relative terms, as educational and training opportunities expand, as trade unions become stronger, and as barriers to resource mobility become weaker. This highly stylized picture is lent support not only by the cross-sectional evidence but by the evidence relating to causes of income differences which show such differences to be highly correlated particularly with geographical location, sectoral location and education.

None of these points depends on the thesis that the wealthy save a higher proportion of their income than other groups—on which the evidence is not clear and which, even if it were, would still leave the direction of causation an open question. Where savings and investment decisions are highly interdependent then the presence of actual savings signified by high incomes will be far less important to the growth of output than the inducement both to save and invest encouraged by new opportunities which mobilize *latent* savings.[38]

It is certainly true that not all income differences or growing income differences serve to promote economic growth. Even in the case of self-made men, their offspring will inherit advantages not necessarily related to their own ability to contribute comparably to the exchange economy. But the business and professional classes necessary for noncommunist economic development will also hand down from generation to generation experience, traditions, and cultural traits appropriate to their calling and socioeconomic locations in competitive societies which, especially in the case of businessmen, demand that they keep advancing as a necessary condition of at least maintaining their position. In the longer term, the stabilization of a substantial capitalist class promotes the institutionalization of economic innovation and accumulation on a continuous and cumulative basis.[39] Thus, it does not strengthen the equation of growing inequality with declining welfare to narrow down the relevant concept of inequality to that arising from ownership structures or structures of political authority (classes and elites), since the development of ownership and power structures in a capitalist society is inseparable from the acquisition of new skills and behavioral traits adapted to the economic requirements of this type of society. Even where economic inequalities arise from morally unjust and/or economically irrelevant factors, the attempt to discriminate closely between such inequalities and those arising from economically functional income differences may be very difficult in practice, in some respects impossible, and even where possible, is likely to mean an immense strain on weak administrative apparatuses and an enormous cost in terms of alternative uses of such administrative apparatuses and especially of wastefully used skilled manpower. In general, this consumption-oriented egalitarian approach ignores the economic costs of egalitarian policies,[40] both direct and indirect. These costs are likely to be very high if some of the policies now being advocated are attempted.[41]

Moreover, the pursuit of income equality per se is both unjust and undemocratic. It is unjust in the sense that it would tend to reward equally in material terms different groups and individuals with different value judgments about consumption, leisure, intensity of work, acquisition of new skills and of the desirability of changing long-held customs and beliefs. The separation of reward from individual effort in societies characterized by extreme poverty would unjustly prevent the individual from fulfilling his social and personal obligations (e.g., toward his family). It is undemocratic in the sense that it is exceed-

ingly unlikely that the current preoccupation of development economists with equality reflects the value judgments of the majority of the
Third World currently emerging into or adapting to the exchange
economy. An aspiration to keep up with the Joneses or even to prevent
oneself from starving neither logically implies a desire for an egalitarian
economic policy, nor particularly the desire for equality for those
worse off than oneself.[42] Yet increased "participation" by the population at large in government is illogically assumed to be consistent with
egalitarian policies.

In sum, such increasing income inequalities as have been developing
in the Third World postwar—and the evidence does not support the
view that they dominate over trends towards greater equality—cannot
be assumed to be generally detrimental to the poorest sections of the
community, except in an arithmetical sense (i.e., the top five percent
have gained "at the expense of" the bottom 40 percent). There are
strong grounds for arguing that, analogously to the historically unprecedented economic achievement of the Western world in the eighteenth and nineteenth centuries, these inequalities are as much a cause
as a consequence of economic growth and therefore of an absolute
improvement in the living standards of those relatively worse off.

MATERIAL PROGRESS—MARGINALIZATION

"Marginalization" implies that an increasing proportion of the labor
force is becoming unemployed or underemployed, either in the sense
of working short hours (or a small number of working days in the year)
or in the sense of being engaged in comparatively unproductive or low-
paying occupations. This latter conception of underemployment is
often inaccurately confused with a situation in which an increasing
proportion of the labor force is regarded as being engaged in activities
such as crime or beggary which effectively amount to obtaining a share
of the productively earned income obtained by the rest of the labor
force. In a descriptive sense an increasing proportion of the total
potential work force is becoming marginal to the national economy and
thus decreasingly able to share meaningfully in its material or cultural
progress (if any).

Concerning open unemployment proper, a misleading impression
has been given of extremely high and currently rising rates, especially

for urban areas, often based on the use of employment exchange statistics. For the great majority of developing countries the only worthwhile evidence actually shows that open unemployment in urban areas is considerably less than has generally been supposed, often comparable to rates in DMEs.

The latest International Labor Office (ILO) estimate of aggregate Third World open unemployment (based on such "hard" data) at 1976 puts the figure as low as five percent,[43] a figure consistent with a number of studies which have revealed unexpectedly low rates in individual countries.[44] The relative scarcity of hard data of this type means that trends over time for the poor countries as a whole are difficult to establish, but the limited evidence available lends no support to the view that unemployment rates have been rising and instead rather suggests the contrary.[45] The United Nations Food and Agricultural Organization (FAO) *Report on the State of Food and Agriculture, 1973* noted that of the thirteen developing countries which carried out regular labor force sample surveys in the 1960s, five showed a downward trend of the rate of open unemployment, one an upward trend, and the trend for the remainder was unclear.[46] It does not seem likely that this can be principally explained by changing participation rates (as the potential job-seekers withdrew from or failed to enter the labor market) [47] since the decline in crude participation rates which actually occurred in developing markets economies in the 1960s was mainly due to a reduction in the proportion of the population of working age, together with a widespread tendency toward decreasing activity rates for males in the youngest and oldest brackets. There was little variation in activity rates of men in the central age groups who provide most of the labor supply in most countries.[48]

The case for such remarkable prophecies as those of Singer cited earlier (unemployment rates of up to 50 percent by 1980) must rest then upon underemployment within urban and/or rural areas. If we examine the short-hours definition of underemployment, a survey of the available evidence shows that average hours worked by the total urban labor force tend to be high, that those wishing to work longer hours are frequently already doing so, that there is no particular relationship between time worked and extra time wanted, that estimates of the extra work demanded tend to be rather small proportions of full-time employment equivalents, and that those working short hours tend to be concentrated at the extremes of the age range of the labor force. Moreover, average hours worked are high despite genuine short-time working and despite the fact that some groups such as teachers have short working hours by agreement.[49] Turnham advances the important suggestion that since the gap between "hours worked" and "hours available for work" does not appear to be particularly wide, especially among those working few hours, then the application of conventional unemployment methodology (as in the developed economies) may be quite appropriate to the developing countries.[50] This, of course, would enhance the significance of the comparatively low and probably declining unemployment rates we have earlier seen to prevail.

It is also now clear from recent research[51] that it cannot simply be assumed that urban informal sector activities are predominantly of a time-filling, redistributive (e.g., beggars and thieves)[52] or duplicatory (e.g., hawkers) character.[53] The relative importance of such parasitic activities is unknown, but at the least it can be said that in most of the large cities of the Third World a wide variety of essential goods and services are provided economically to a substantial proportion of the population by the informal sector.[54] There is disagreement as to whether the informal sector is basically of a residual and stagnant character or whether it incorporates significant elements of internal dynamism in terms of innovation, accumulation and the upward expansion of the more successful operators.[55] A strong case can be made out for the latter view,[56] which implies the existence and expansion of a wage labor force in the informal sector[57] and suggests that the formal-informal sector dichotomy may be excessively rigid. A wide range of service activities, which are often taken as prima facie evidence of underemployment, appear to be functional to the general growth of the urban economy, many of them directly linked to the needs and growth of the secondary sector.[58] The multiplication of trades of various types has been convincingly argued to be an economically efficient adaptation to the structure of the economy.[59] Modern, as well as traditional, occupations are undertaken involving the use of modern technologies, from photography and cab-driving to small-scale engineering,[60] and profit maximization is found even among the self-employed traders and craftsmen.[61] Thriving indigenous "informal" apprenticeship systems testify indirectly to the nonephemeral, productive and expansive character of some important informal sector activities.[62] Scattered but increasing evidence of a spectrum of earnings, numbers employed and productivity are suggestive of dynamic processes leading to the emergence and growth of the more efficient entrepreneurs.[63] It thus remains to be established that those working in the informal sector are marginal except in the tautological sense that underemployment is defined as relatively low levels of productivity or income. The view that the existence of the informal sector reflects widespread underemployment appears, in the present state of knowledge, to be a distorted reflection of the fact that the range of productivity and earnings levels within and between occupations and industries is much greater in developing countries than in developed market economies—itself a result of dynamic process at work rather than of processes of "developing underdevelopment."

It is widely held that underemployment in the Third World is growing as the urban work forces expand faster than formal sector employment, and that this implies a secular trend toward declining average levels of productivity and remuneration. But it is not clear either that the informal sector labor force is increasing proportionately to the urban labor force over time or that productivity in the informal sector is declining over time. The United Kingdom *1974 Report on the World Social Situation* points out, for example, for Latin America (citing occupational data for the 1900s for Brazil, Chile, Venezuela, Cost Rica, Ecuador, and Uruguay), the birthplace of "marginalization," that "the available occupational statistics do not indicate a disproportionate relative increase in those forms of self-employment and tertiary-sector labor which are most likely to contain disguised unemployment and poverty...."[64] Little or nothing is known about productivity and real earnings *trends* in the urban informal sector but it has been rather generally found that per capita remuneration there is higher than that for the openings available in the rural sector,[65] so that the possibility of obtaining a formal sector job is not the only economic rationale for rural-urban migration. However, this leaves open the possibility of declining average informal urban sector earnings over time if average earnings are declining in the rural sector. As to the trend of real earnings in agriculture, as well as other rural activities, very little is known. There is a slight presumption that average real earnings in agriculture will have tended to rise somewhat throughout the Third World postwar in view of the fact that both overall agricultural output per head of the population and food output per head of the population have risen slightly, while the proportion of the total labor force in agriculture has substantially declined from 73.3 percent in 1950 to 60 percent in 1970.[66] Moreover, discussing the employment situation in agriculture, Turnham, surveying the evidence, remarks on the lack of empirical basis for the widely held opinions about the prevalence of unemployment and underemployment in agriculture, particularly the view that labor has little to do for four to six months of the year in the rural areas.[67] But changing terms of trade between manufactures and agricultural products, changing income distribution in the countryside, government fiscal policies, etc. will all have affected the situation, as well as the fact that in particular cases there will be no alternative openings in agriculture, i.e., there will be open unemployment. A pertinent point here, however, is that the spectrum of earnings within the informal sector and the overlap between formal and informal sector earnings,[68] together with the fact that the length of residence tends to be positively correlated with the urban immigrants' average earnings,[69] imply an upward mobility which would ensure that the informal sector average earnings would not be rigidly tied to rural income level trends.

To interpret growing urban underemployment over time as a shift from previous more highly productive and remunerative occupations to less remunerative, less productive occupations is consistent with the concept of "disguised unemployment" from which the underemployment approach originated.[70] In the original conception this move from higher to lower productivity occupations was due to a decline in effective demand. It is more likely that what is called underemployment in the Third World, at least in the urban areas, is the result of a process of moving from less to more remunerative occupations, at least for the bulk of rural-urban immigrants. The principal basis for characterizing such people as "underemployed" is that they fall below some arbitrary dividing line which separates them from the rest of the urban labor force with higher average earnings or productivity, even if their remuneration has actually improved over time.

The concept of marginalization implies the effective disruption of the linkages of a significant and growing number of the (generally urban) population with the central activities of the economy. As is common in development economics, a term which has started life with a valid descriptive function (describing shantytowns on the outskirts of Third World cities), has acquired an immense, sophisticated, conceptual superstructure erected on its shaky base.[71] In fact, so-called "marginalization" is a way of referring to the anarchic, chaotic, unplanned and sometimes brutal but nevertheless vigorous fashion in which urbanization expands the market, stimulates commercialization of the whole of society and thereby increases the division of labor and thus the *integration* of society, as Adam Smith long ago noted. The process is exactly the opposite of what is implied by the word. It is a process of increasing *integration*. The shantytowns are not, like slums, the result of deterioration. They are improvements as compared with rural conditions[72] and many are themselves improved over time.[73] Rural-urban migration, together with the return flows to the villages, is a progressive force in breaking up subsistence activities, institutions, and attitudes which held up material progress so that rural life generally and agricultural practice in particular are transformed. In place of relatively self-sufficient communities, the growth of towns leads to specialization and reintegration of separate economic activities with the breaking down of the economic isolation characteristic of precapitalist societies.[74]

MATERIAL PROGRESS—
"BASIC NEEDS" AND WELFARE

Related to the marginalization approach, another major source of some development economists' dissatisfaction with the first development decade has been the feeling that the increasing volume of goods and services made available by Third World postwar economic development has not in general been oriented toward the "basic needs" of the majority of the population (i.e., food, health care, housing and education). This argument is closely related to the point that GNP per capita is an inadequate proxy for "welfare" or "development," if those concepts are regarded as referring in some sense to the needs of the great majority of the population rather than the privileged few. Uneven distribution alone ensures that GNP per capita is a value-loaded proxy, insofar as the market valuations are inherently biased to give greater weighting to consumption by the rich. Moreover, the very incomplete development of the market in developing countries and the high degree of market imperfections there weaken the value of GNP calculations even on their own terms, quite apart from important defects in market valuation common to all market economies. Finally, of course, the statistical base of such calculations in many, perhaps most, developing countries is so weak as to render measures of levels of GNP per capita liable to errors of several hundred percent.

These points are all valid, but they leave open the problem of the *extent* to which GNP per capita figures give a misleading impression as to the level and pace of development and welfare over time and as between countries.

As regards the large element of statistical error, however, this point is far less serious for rates of change than for absolute levels of GNP per capita, so that relative progress over time by this measure is liable to be much more adequately assessed than cross-national differences at a point in time. More fundamentally, however, composite measures of development or welfare based on physical indicators show a high degree of association between per capita GNP and the level of living index or the development index. A 1966 study by the United Nations Research Institute for Social Development (UNRISD)[75] covering 20 countries about 1960, demonstrated very high intercorrelations between per capita GNP and a "level of living" index covering nutrition, education, housing, leisure, and health as well as a distributional component. This correlation must imply that, insofar as the level of living index provides a trustworthy indication of welfare, then so also does GNP per capita on average.

Subsequently, UNRISD has produced a more ambitious development index.[76] This index related to 1959-61 and covered 58 countries, 29 of them underdeveloped. It differs from the 1966 level of living index in that the former was basically a normative index, whereas the latter specifically eschews any attempt to measure the level of culture, civilization, human welfare, happiness or the "better life." It is essentially a measure of those characteristics that distinguish more developed from less developed countries. It is based on 18 core physical indicators of both levels of living and structural features associated with development.[77] No distributive component is explicitly incorporated, but a number of the indicators, e.g., percentage of children in school, literacy rate, percentage of dwellings with electricity and life expectancy rates, reflect the spread or distribution of socially favorable conditions in society in a rough way.

The overall correlation between this development index and GNP per capita is 0.86, with a lower (although still respectable) correlation of 0.67 for the developing countries taken alone. Differences between the development index and per capita GNP for some individual countries do appear to be sufficient, together with judgment based on other criteria, to justify use of the former instead of the latter as a measure of development as defined. Furthermore, as the original authors emphasize, these development and level-of-living indexes must be regarded as extremely tentative because of both conceptual problems and data availability limitations. Nonetheless, the correlation results suggest that GNP per capita, although liable to produce wild results for some individual countries, may not be so bad a guide in assessing the pace of development for the developing countries in general as has been widely supposed. It is noteworthy that the range (between the upper and lower values) of both the level of living index and the development index is very much narrower than that of per capita GNP, which is consistent with the recent ILO reestimates of the per capita GNP gap between DME and developing countries, the effect of which is to reduce estimated average income differences from about 13:1 to about 4:1. Furthermore, while the development index may not be a strictly normative one, insofar as it does reflect progress of the developing countries toward the characteristics of the already developed countries, it necessarily incorporates progress toward the removal of poverty, unemployment and inequality, the basic normative elements of development as defined, e.g., by Dudley Seers,[78] values which are widely accepted by development economists. The onus lies with the critics to show that advances in monetary per capita GNP do not have at least a rough and ready positive correlation with welfare and development.[79]

Changes in various individual fundamental indicators of welfare in recent years are also consistent with the view that there has been considerable progress in material welfare for the population as a whole and not just a privileged few. Thus, kilocalories intake as a percentage of requirements in *developing* market economies taken as a whole increased from 93 percent in 1961 to 97 percent in 1969-1971,[80] following a much steeper improvement in the previous period, 1948-1952 to 1957-1958.[81]

The United Kingdom *Report on the World Social Situation* for 1963 and for 1974 indicates truly remarkable advances in education (with increasing proportions of the appropriate age groups enrolled), in health where the data show marked improvements in the highly significant indicators of infant mortality and life expectancy at birth, and to a lesser extent in housing where the available data are much less complete.[82]

The preceding findings are further supported by an ILO study of the proportions of developing nation populations classed as "poor," "seriously poor," and "destitute." For the period 1963-1972 there were decreases in the percentages of the population accounted for by all these categories, for all *developing* market economies in the aggregate, and for Asia, Africa, and Latin America separately—the only exception being for the percentage of the population classified as "poor" in Asia.

The rise in *absolute* numbers below the highest poverty line in Asia (estimated at 208 million) in any case is itself a product of past general welfare improvements insofar as the increasing numbers are associated with increasing expectation of life at birth which in turn is the best single indicator of health available. Since health is affected by such factors as literacy, housing, food consumption, water supply, and personal income as much or more than direct health services and also in turn affects all these variables, there is a high correlation between both expectation of life at birth and the infant mortality rate and 41 other selected development indicators.[83] This indicates a strong causal link from rising general welfare to rapid population growth, the latter implying the former, and the relevant indicators relatively free of distributional bias. Thus, so far from basic needs being neglected, the accelerating population growth which is regarded by many as the fundamental cause or sign of underdevelopment arises solely from increasingly effective attention to basic needs in the most "basic" sense.

On the other hand, the relative neglect of agriculture and indeed the promotion of policies the effect of which has been to mitigate against a growth of agricultural output adequate to the needs of the expanding Third World economies has caused relative food prices to rise in recent years and has left significant proportions of the Third World population at risk of starvation should there be a conjuncture of unfavorable circumstances. The improvements in calorie consumption intake per capita which took place in the 1950s and 1960s were in part dependent on increasing gross food imports which grew at a rate of 3.5 percent per annum for the developing countries as a whole from 1961-1963 to 1972. On the other hand, this represents a slackening over the period 1955-1966 when such imports almost doubled; and indeed between 1966 and 1969-1971 the number of food surplus countries in the developing world rose from 20 to 38 while the number of food deficit countries fell from 72 to 55.[84]

Another argument supporting the view of declining welfare in developing nations arises from certain criticisms of manufacturing development in such nations. As is well known, the growth of the manufacturing sector has been very vigorous and increasingly diversified, extending to a wide range of intermediate and producer goods and creating substantial capital goods industries in some developing countries. It is, however, argued that much, if not most, of this industrial growth is oriented toward providing for the consumption needs of wealthy elites. Such individuals are seen as having a political-economic stranglehold over the nation, ensuring the continuation of this pattern of growth which leads to greater capital intensity, in turn, raising unemployment and keeping wages depressed.[85] The argument is plainly incorrect for the Third World countries which account for the vast majority of the population in Africa and Asia, where the market for "luxury goods"[86] is too small to sustain profitable production and where the manufacturing sector has been built up on the basis of a mass market catering to lower- and middle-income consumers.

In some developing countries with relatively high per capita income levels and a substantial degree of industrialization, production of durable consumer goods has been growing rather rapidly. A very important and detailed study[87] of consumption patterns in one such country (Brazil) shows that for a wide range of durable consumer goods, the diffusion of a modern style of consumption is not confined to a small minority—the market extends to include at least 60 percent of all Brazilian households. Although there is a fairly marked discontinuity in the profile of demand, such as to exclude households in the rural sector and the poorer regions, there is no such discontinuity for *urban* households even in the poorer northeastern cities. We should note, further, that Brazil is now predominantly an urbanized country as are, to an even greater extent, all the other major countries of Latin America. A very wide market diffusion of durable consumer goods[88] was found, reaching well down to the lower-income urban groups. In the late Sixties the household goods and appliances sector grew rapidly despite the redistribution which occurred in favor of the rich, owing to the large average size of the Brazilian household, to the relatively limited proportion of consumption devoted to public consumption and to the ability of the financial system to ensure that the savings of the rich help finance the purchases of the poor. Wells concludes:

> Provided the process of urbanization continues there appear to be few limits to the process of market deepening. The data reviewed are not consistent with the pessimistic views of writers, such as Furtado, concerning the possibility of generalizing this pattern of consumption.[89]

If this kind of demand profile for durable consumer goods is characteristic of other developing countries as their industrial sector grows (and there have been too few studies to permit any judgment on the matter), then we must consider the growth of the durable consumer goods industry as likely to benefit substantially increasing sections of the lower-income groups and not merely a small elite plus limited sections of the middle-income groups.[90]

The fact that purchase of consumer durables by low-income households is, to some extent, at the expense of public and perhaps other forms of consumption may be regarded as a distortion of resource allocation due to Western influence. But it cannot be denied that most durable consumer goods such as bicycles, sewing machines, motorbikes, radios, even television and refrigerators, etc., add immensely to the quality of life of the poor households. It is only those who have such goods in abundance who feel it appropriate to suggest that it is not desirable for others to have them, i.e., the well-off middle classes of Europe and America.[91]

CONCLUDING REMARKS— THE SPREAD OF CAPITALISM

Of necessity, the preceding survey could not but be impressionistic. But it seems justifiable to draw the following conclusions:

In conventional terms, economic progress, as measured by GNP per capita, was rather fast and fairly generalized throughout the Third World in the postwar period (although very uneven as between countries)—as compared with the prewar period for the same group of countries, as compared with the now fully industrialized countries during their period of industrialization in the eighteenth and nineteenth centuries and, even to a lesser extent, as compared with the DMEs today.

There are at least prima facie grounds for believing that GNP per capita, although a highly imperfect measure of progress toward greater all-round material welfare for the majority of the population or for development as conceived in terms of movement toward the present dominant characteristics of the now developed countries, is nevertheless a closer rough and ready approximation than has been widely considered. Moreover, movement toward the present main characteristics of present economically advanced countries does imply a measure of progress toward such widely accepted normative aims as greater equality, reduction of poverty and of unemployment.

This last point, together with scattered and patchy evidence of physical indicators of fulfillment of the basic needs of the Third World population relating to health, education, nutrition and housing, and with fairly definite aggregate evidence of substantial declines in the proportions of those falling below various poverty lines, leads to a strong presumption that there have been major postwar advances in the material welfare of the majority of the population of the Third World, advances which have been uneven in their incidence as between economic groups but which have nevertheless reached deep down to the lower-income groups. Moreover, there is some evidence that the rapid growth in some countries, especially of Latin America, of the production of durable consumer goods by no means simply benefits the wealthy or the middle classes but again penetrates downwards to the market formed by the lower-income groups in the urban areas (which includes the majority of the population of Latin America, for example).

The widespread belief that economic progress in terms of improvement in the average availability of goods and services per capita has been in large part nullified for the poor majority of the Third World by an increasingly uneven income distribution is not borne out by the admittedly scanty time-series or cross-section data. Tendencies toward more even income distribution, as far as the evidence goes, have been at least as important, certainly more important in the long run, and just possibly becoming slightly more important in the short run, as growth in GNP per capita accelerates. The increase in income inequality which frequently characterizes the earliest stages of growth, moreover, cannot be regarded automatically as a negative occurrence, since there are strong, though not as yet conclusive reasons, for considering that such growing inequality is as much a cause as a consequence of growth and thereby benefits absolutely, if not relatively, the poorest sections of the population.

An important dimension of the view that per capita income growth has not contributed substantially to general welfare is encapsulated in the concept of "marginalization." However, the relevant measurable indicators show very little evidence of marginalization, practically none in the case of short hours, with possibly declining unemployment rates for the majority of countries, although the evidence here is slender. Nor is there definite evidence that the size of the informal sector is increasing significantly as a proportion of the urban population. Further, the informal or unenumerated sector, which is generally taken to include the bulk of the underemployed, is now considered by some scholars to provide a wide range of necessary goods and services for a substantial section of the urban population. The same scholars argue that the informal sector has within it significant dynamic features resulting in the advance of accumulation, innovation, productivity, earnings, and entrepreneurship.

More generally, it can be argued that the apparent "marginalization" in urban areas is in reality a progressive phenomenon representing the fuller *integration* of the population into the market economy as the market widens and economic activities become more interdependent through increasing specialization.

Thus, contrary to widespread liberal populist opinion, stagnation, relative or absolute, has not been characteristic of the postwar Third World. On the contrary, significant progress in material welfare and the development of the productive forces has taken place, representing an acceleration of prewar trends. This also runs against the grain of current neo-Marxist outlooks which have stressed the impossibility of vigorous national development for the Third World within a capitalist framework or, alternatively, have argued that the development of capitalism in the Third World is itself impossible except as a distorted and feeble caricature of Western capitalism, without any indigenous roots or significant internal dynamic.

The period we have been discussing has witnessed titanic strides forward in the establishment, consolidation and growth of capitalism in the Third World, with corresponding advances in material welfare and the development of the productive forces. The development has been highly uneven, as is entirely characteristic of capitalism, and perhaps every type of human development, and many countries at the beginning of our period were still predominantly subsistence, while others, such as Argentina and Uruguay, were already largely capitalist. Although the capitalist system was initially largely externally introduced, and often by force, its underlying superior dynamic, as compared with precapitalist societies, is even more marked now than it was for Europe and Japan when capitalism there succeeded feudalism. The result is that what is initially an external force quickly develops deep internal roots and a continuing and deepening internal momentum. The reality of this picture of a vigorous, irreversible, "grass-roots" development of capitalism is supported by the abundant evidence of rapidly growing commercialization and resulting social differentiation (especially in the rural areas of Asia and Africa), coupled with the relative expansion of the wage labor force at the expense of family or self-employment.[92]

The attention now, correctly, being focused on agriculture's relatively poor performance should not distract attention from the profound underlying changes in agrarian social structure gradually gathering momentum. These changes will sooner or later result in major advances as agrarian capitalism becomes sufficiently developed to utilize more productive methods and inputs.

In retrospect, the enormous wastes of postwar economic development and the many major policy blunders have signally failed to halt the gathering momentum of capitalist advance and associated material progress. Many of these blunders are now widely recognized by all schools of thought (including those ideological trends in development economics which promoted them in the first place)—blunders such as the neglect of agriculture in favor of industrialization and the pessimistic bias against development of an exporting manufacturing sector and the over-valuation of exchange rates. The character of these errors (and their origin) suggests the nature of the underlying problem. Development economics in the Fifties and Sixties had within it conflicting schools of thought. That school favoring rapid industrialization primarily for the home market as a first priority (Prebisch and Mahalanobit) became extremely influential. This approach was strongly influenced by the Soviet example of development by rapid industrialization, by Western liberal-egalitarian ideals, and by an anti-imperialist approach related to both Leninism and liberalism which tended to regard underdevelopment as in large part caused by the character of international economic relations between wealthy capitalist countries and the countries of Latin America, Asia and Africa. For obvious reasons this liberal-populist trend in development economics met with considerable response from governments of underdeveloped states.

But the main problem with the liberal-populist approach, which its proponents did not always squarely face, was that the economies they were concerned with were developing in a *capitalist* direction. An explicit recognition of this fact would have permitted the promotion of a more efficient and more humane capitalist development, as distinct from the inappropriate imposition of a welfare approach plus the Soviet model on countries which have neither the advanced economic basis required for the one nor the communist leadership required for the other.

Failure to recognize the above situation has caused neglect of the elementary requirements of promoting capitalist development, especially the expansion of commercialization in agriculture (so crucial to the spread of growth-conducive attitudes and habits) and to the expansion of the agricultural surplus, itself essential for successful industrial-

ization. The continued relative slowness of economic advance in South
Asia testifies to the failure of the liberal-populist school of development economics[93] which has undoubtedly had serious adverse effects
on potential welfare. Indeed, development virtually throughout the
Third World has been held below its potential by the failure to promote
adequately rural commercialization and the consequent enlargement of
the agricultural surplus. Nor is this all. The garbled liberal-populist
outlook is still dominant in development economics and it is clear that
a new set of blunders is rapidly becoming or has already become,
part of development orthodoxy: an excessive and impractical emphasis
on equal income distribution, the retardation of economic growth
for employment reasons and counter-productive proposals for debt
cancellation or default. Whatever is to be the new world being created
in Latin America, Asia, and Africa, nothing is to be gained from a refusal
to recognize the existence of the developing capitalisms already there.

Part IV
The Revolt of the Periphery

Chapter 7

REVOLT OF THE PERIPHERY

Nurul Islam

INEQUITIES OF THE EXISTING INTERNATIONAL ECONOMIC ORDER

The Third World is in a state of ferment; it demands change in the existing international economic order. It seeks to do so through either unilateral action or by a process of negotiation with the Developed World. The Third World considers the prevailing rules and practices governing the working of the international economy to be inequitable and discriminatory in a cumulative way in favor of the rich nations which have a greater command over resources and technology. Moreover, the disparity in income and wealth between the rich and poor nations instead of narrowing, as a result of the working of the international economic system, continues to be large and widening.

Exports of the Third World, both agricultural and manufactures, face barriers to entry in the markets of the developed countries; manufactured exports face trade restrictions which escalate or are "cascaded" according to the degree of processing. In the export markets for many

primary products, the Third World is confronted often with oligopsoni-
cally organized purchasers such as the giant international trading companies. Frequently the multinational corporations vertically integrate
all operations from the stages of production of raw materials in the
Third World to that of their fabrication into finished manufactured
goods, often located in the developed countries.[1] Furthermore, the
developing countries are faced with highly unstable markets for their
primary exports, which introduce uncertainties and destabilize the
planning of production and investment in raw materials.[2] Low income
and price elasticity of demand for primary exports, combined with the
growth of synthetic substitutes, have contributed to slow growth or
relative stagnation in the earnings from raw material exports. The terms
of trade of the primary exports of many developing countries in relation to their manufactured imports from the developed countries have
shown a downward trend, especially since the mid-Fifties until the
commodity boom in the early 1970s. To a large extent this is due to
imperfections in the markets of manufactured goods as well as in the
factor markets of the developed countries, which prevent the trans-
mission of the gains in productivity or the benefits of technological
progress to the Third World. Furthermore, the lack of diversification
as well as the limited substitution possibilities in the developing economies severely inhibit their ability to respond to changes in demand and
supply conditions in world markets or to take advantage of the expanding but changing world market conditions.

The developed nations put restrictions—discriminatory restrictions—
on the flow of unskilled labor from developing countries whereas they
facilitate or encourage the flow of professionally skilled and technically
trained personnel from the poor countries. At the same time, they
encourage the flow of corporate investment by multinational corporations in the Third World whereas no such encouragement or incentives
are provided for enlarging the access of the latter to developed-world
private capital markets. The multinational corporations play a critical
role in the unequal distribution of gains from trade and investment
flows between the Third World and the Developed World. They not
only determine the magnitude, the pattern and costs of the international transfer of capital and technology but also affect the pattern
and terms of trade. They introduce significant monopolistic and oligopolistic elements into international trade due to their size, economies
of scale, vertical and horizontal integration, and their control over
technology, marketing and sales outlets. They also control access to
intermediate inputs and, therefore, the location of economic activities

based upon such inputs. The intercompany or interfirm trade which bypasses the market transactions in international trade ranges anywhere between one-third to one-half of world trade in manufactures.[3]

It is in respect of technology and its transfer cost that the Third World finds itself at the greatest disadvantage. The cost of transfer of technology is high; moreover, the imported technology and the products associated with it are not always appropriate in view of income levels and factor endowments of the Third World.[4] The multinationals do not make the maximum use of indigenous resources or raw materials nor are they oriented toward meeting the basic needs of the masses in the Third World. As the purveyors of the sophisticated products of the advanced countries, they prefer to manipulate the tastes and preferences of the affluent minority by "demonstration effect" and advertising rather than innovating products and processes which are suitable for the Third World.

Under the prevailing international monetary regime, not only do the developing countries have a small absolute share in global liquidity in relation to their needs, but also the available liquidity is highly unequally distributed.[5] The International Monetary Fund (IMF) has a system of quotas highly weighted in favor of the rich countries, which determine not only their voting power but also their access to liquidity as well. Moreover, the "reserve currency" countries in the Developed World enjoy the privilege of creating liquidity for themselves by the mere act of running deficits in their balance of payments.

GENESIS OF REVOLT AND THE NEW INTERNATIONAL ECONOMIC ORDER

Apart from the growing dissatisfaction with the existing economic order, there are a number of factors which have shaped the attitudes of the Third World toward the developed countries. The countries of the Third World share common experiences and aspirations in their relationships with the Developed World.[6] These have contributed to the sense of cohesion and the growth of united efforts on the part of the Third World in their struggle for the new international economic order (NIEO). Firstly, the vast majority of them share in common a history of colonial domination by the developed European countries with its attendant humiliation, indignity and inequalities. The majority of them gained independence only in the period following the Second World War (70 countries gained independence in this period).[7] Secondly, irrespective of the levels of income and endowment of natural resources they are technologically inferior to the Developed World in terms of command over and access to science and technology in the widest sense of the term. Military and technological capability are interrelated and the prestige of a nation state in international affairs is closely related with both. Thirdly, Third World nations lack participation in the decision-making processes of the affairs of the world; and they are at the receiving end of all the major decisions in world affairs. For example, the General Agreement on Tariffs and Trade (GATT) as a forum for negotiations on trade and tariffs is very largely, if not exclusively, controlled by rich nations. Again, in the Security Council of the United Nations or in the international financial institutions, like the International Bank for Reconstruction and Development (IBRD), underdeveloped nations play a very minor or insignificant role in the decision-making process.

Apart from common experiences mentioned above, the Third World also shares common aspirations as well as frustrations. Political independence has not been associated with rapid economic advancement or eradication of poverty and unemployment in many of the developing countries. Even in countries which have achieved moderate rates of development, there is a heightened awareness of relative deprivation and an expectation for further improvement. Secondly, political independence has not brought economic independence. The Third World needs and depends heavily upon the capital, technology and resources of the Developed World. It requires from the Developed World imports of critical materials and equipment for its development and imports of foodgrains for its survival. Great expectations were raised in the 1950s and 1960s following the example of the Marshall Plan in Europe, that the developed countries would provide substantial and sustained assistance to the poor countries for raising their living standards. The much-heralded partnership in development never materialized; witness, for example, the disappointing performance in meeting the aid targets proposed by the United Nations International Development Strategy (IDS) in 1970.

The shared aspirations and experiences of the Third World in their relationship with the Developed World have been strengthened by increasing perception of how the developed countries make conscious efforts at coordination and cooperation among themselves on major economic and political issues confronting them. This is evidenced in the activity of the Organization for Economic Cooperation and Development (OECD), the European Economic Community (EEC), the Group of 10 and periodic summit meetings amongst the most important developed countries. There is a much closer economic interdependence, as evidenced by the volume of trade and capital movements, amongst the developed countries than between them, on the one hand, and the developing countries, on the other.[8]

The beginnings of cooperative action amongst the developing countries was the nonaligned conference, with its founding meeting in Bandung in 1955. It started with an overwhelmingly political motiviation: the primary, initial objective was to form a neutral block independent of the big-power rivalry between the Soviet Union and the United States. It excluded a number of developing countries which had political and military alliances with one of the two big powers. Over the years the nonaligned conference added economic issues to its agenda.[9] It was, in fact, at the meeting of the nonaligned heads of state in Algeria in 1973 that the major issues relating to trade in raw materials and development of the Third World were formulated as a prelude to the United Nations debate on the NIEO in 1973.

The role of the United Nations system, including its various specialized agencies and regional commissions, in promoting frequent contacts, interchange of views, and common approach amongst the developing countries to the obstacles and problems they face in the international economy, can hardly be overemphasized. Amongst the regional commissions, the Economic Commission for Latin America (ECLA) and its dynamic executive secretary, Dr. Raul Prebisch, played a unique role in the 1950s in analyzing and articulating the external constraints on the development of the Third World. The most prominent amongst the institutions which provided fora for a coordination of Third World strategies for bargaining with the developed countries were the United Nations Conference on Trade and Development (UNCTAD) and the Group of 77 (now expanded to more than 112 members), the latter constituted at the time of the first UNCTAD Conference in 1964.[10]

The systematic articulation of the demand for a change in the prevailing international economic system had its origins in the first UNCTAD in 1964. It was, however, the Sixth and Seventh Special Sessions of the United Nations General Assembly in 1974 which marked the high point in the struggle of the Third World for securing greater equity in the international economic system. These sessions provided an opportunity for the consolidation, in a comprehensive framework, of all the demands relating to different aspects of the international economic system. Unlike the various specialized international agencies dealing with specific aspects of the international economic system, the United Nations General Assembly has as members all the countries of the world. International economic issues never before occupied the center of the stage in the United Nations General Assembly—which has been traditionally concerned with political and security issues. Obviously, by bringing the discussion of international economic issues to the General Assembly, the developing countries attempted to place economic issues in the overall framework of the totality of relations, political, strategic and economic, of the Third World with the developed countries.[11]

Recent developments in the world economy have contributed to a consciousness of strength on the part of the Third World. The most important amongst them is the phenomenon of rising prices of raw materials and minerals during 1971-73, accompanying the gloomy forecasts by the various studies of the Club of Rome about the future scarcity of raw materials.[12] The Developed World consumes a disproportionately large share of the world's scarce natural resources, especially nonrenewable resources; its imports from the Third World for meeting the requirements of scarce natural resources are expected to increase over time. The continuation of the present trends in growth of income and consumption in the Developed World, combined with the impact of increasing population in the Third World, is likely to accentuate the future scarcity of natural resources.[13]

It was in a general climate of concern about the scarcity of resources and its adverse impact on economic growth in the Developed World that OPEC quadrupled the price of oil in 1973; a few producers imposed embargos on exports of oil as well. OPEC demonstrated the possibility of transfer of resources from the Developed World by collective action. Also, no less significant was their ability to renegotiate with the multinational oil companies the terms of contract for the exploitation of oil resources, including increased participation by the oil-producing countries in the ownership and management of oil production.

Increased confidence on the part of the Third World is partly due to their perception that the developed countries, either singly or together, are unlikely to use military force either to gain economic advantages or deter attempts to inflict economic damage on them, through disruptions of supply or raising prices. OPEC could succeed with the most drastic cartel-type action without any military intervention by the developed countries, even though it involved a commodity of vital importance to their economies.[14] The decline in the threat of the use of force is partly explainable by the increased ability and willingness on the part of the Third World to resist force as well as to bear the economic costs of resistance.

SPECIFIC NIEO PROPOSALS

The proposals for the new international economic order (NIEO) have ranged over a wide area: increased earnings from the exports of raw materials and manufactured goods, acceleration in agricultural development and food production in the developing countries, rapid industrialization, improved terms for the transfer of technology, regulation of multinationals, increased transfer of resources to the developing countries including the rescheduling of debt and reform of the international monetary system, etc.[15] The proposed measures in the field of trade in raw materials and manufactures have been on the agenda of UNCTAD since its beginning. These include the stabilization and expansion of the export earnings of the developing countries through international commodity agreements, buffer stocks and common financing arrangements (Common Fund being the most important integrating mechanism for individual commodity agreements), the progressive elimination of trade barriers against agricultural exports, increased processing of raw materials in the Third World and a greater share in the marketing and distribution of primary exports.

There are, however, a number of new elements in NIEO proposals as well as different emphasis on a few old ideas. For example, there is a great concern in the proposals for the NIEO about scarcity of resources, about food shortage, increasing world population, energy, and environmental pollution in a way which was absent in earlier United Nations or UNCTAD discussions. A significant new element in this context is the suggestion for indexing the prices of primary exports to the prices of manufactured imports. Similarly, a much greater emphasis than in the past is placed on the role of producers' associations for increasing the real earnings from primary exports. These producers' associations are to include a wide variety of cooperative activities, including collective bargaining with developed countries as well as cartel-type action, wherever possible or feasible.

In the field of trade in manufactures, the old proposal for a reduction of the trade barriers in a preferential manner is combined with a new proposal for increasing the share of the Third World in the world's manufactured output from about eight percent in the 1970s to 15 percent by the end of the century. The emphasis on science and technology, i.e., not only on transfer of technology from the advanced countries but also the growth of scientific and technological capability in the Third World, is new compared to earlier discussions on the subject, especially the need for technological self-reliance in the Third World.

In the field of monetary reform and development assistance, earlier proposals are reemphasized. These include fulfillment of the aid target (set at 0.7 percent of the GNP of the developed countries), linking of development assistance to the provision of additional liquidity by the IMF through the creation of Special Drawing Rights (SDRs), and the liberalization of the IMF scheme for compensating for shortfalls in exchange earnings. The emphasis in this area is to make the flow of resources more automatic, assured, stable, and less discretionary, and, therefore, less dependent on the fluctuating political will of the developed countries. Faced with greatly worsened balance of payments deficits, the Third World has added to its accumulated debt burden by extensive recourse to short-term borrowing since 1973. Therefore, the need for large-scale debt relief is high on the agenda of the NIEO.

With respect to multinational corporations, the developed countries are called upon to promote foreign investment, "in accordance with the needs and requirements in sectors of their [Third World] economies as determined by the recipient countries," as well as "to encourage investors to finance industrial production projects, particularly export-oriented production, in developing countries in agreement with the latter and within the context of their laws and regulations." The major emphasis is on the formulation of an international code of conduct in order to regulate restrictive business practices, to facilitate the transfer of technology, and to regulate the transfer of profits. The developed countries are called upon to facilitate, if necessary, the revision and review of previously concluded agreements with the multinationals. The NIEO asserts the right of the Third World to nationalize foreign direct investment without any external intervention or without any threat of external political or economic sanction by the developed countries. Any dispute between the host country and foreign investors is to be settled according to the domestic laws of the host country, without any external interference.

The promotion of intra-Third World economic cooperation (which has been on the agenda of the UNCTAD for many years) is placed in the context of a new concept of collective self-reliance implying reduced dependence on the developed countries for imports of commodities, capital, and technology. The Developed World is urged to promote economic cooperation amongst the Third World countries by means of financial and technical assistance.

The NIEO is concerned not only with obtaining a greater share of the world's resources for the developing countries, but also for a greater role in the decision-making processes in the international institutions which set the rules of international economic relations. For example, it is suggested that in such financial institutions as the IMF and the IBRD voting rights should be divorced from strict adherence to capital participation in the capital resources of these organizations. In other words, there is a demand not only for a greater share of economic resources but also for greater status and power in the international sphere—a demand for equality. There is a new emphasis on two elements of international economic relations. One is the right of every country to adopt the economic and social systems it deems to be most appropriate for its own development and not to be subjected to discrimination of any kind as a result. The other is the right of full sovereignty of every state over its natural resources and all economic activities, including the right of nationalization of foreign-owned assets without being subject to any kind of external coercion.

In general, the Third World wants to bring the rules and practices governing the international flow of commodities, labor, capital, and technology under broad international control and away from unilateral determination by the developed countries as has been the case hitherto. At the same time, they want to democratize the decision-making process in international institutions so that the developing countries have a much larger share in the decision-making process. The most recent example of the assertion of their right to participate in the international decision-making process has been in the field of negotiations for international monetary reform. The Group of 10 deliberating on international monetary reform, consisted mainly of the rich, industrialized countries. It was expanded to the Group of 20, to include the developing countries, while at the same time the developing countries constituted their own Group of 24 to coordinate their approach on the issues of monetary reform and to put pressure on the Group of 20. Participation by the Third World in decisions on international monetary reforms relating to the role of gold, SDRs, and exchange rate flexibility required the revision of the original articles of agreement of the IMF. While the day-to-day decisions by the IMF were governed by weighted voting (weighted in favor of the rich countries), the revision of the articles of agreement required unweighted, majority rule voting.

IS THERE A NEW IDEOLOGY AND A NEW CLASS STRUCTURE?

The confrontation between the Developed World and the Third World on the question of international economic equity and allocation of resources does not reflect a uniform new ideology sweeping through the entire Third World; nor does it indicate the rise of a new class structure. There is wide diversity among the countries of the Third World, both in terms of ideologies and class structure including the composition of the dominant class or the ruling elite. The wide spectrum of ideologies within the Third World ranges from communist countries to predominantly private-enterprise countries run by an alliance of the big landed interests and industrialists, with a major role played by the multinationals. A large number of Third World countries belong to an intermediate category which is characterized by large public ownership, especially in the industrial sector, and by the absence of large landed interests. These nations operate a wide variety of controls on economic activities.[16] Such regimes are often dominated by an alliance between medium-sized, surplus farmers and medium-scale industrialists, supported by the mercantile and trading classes as well as middle-income professionals. The multinationals do not play an important role in these countries; they are often hedged with restrictions.

The dominant groups in all the non-communist states, including the intermediate types of countries discussed above, are under varying degrees of pressure for improvements in the conditions of living of the masses. The strength of this pressure varies widely amongst these countries, depending upon the degree of education, political consciousness, and organization amongst the masses. Moreover, the intensity with which the ruling elite feels and responds to this pressure varies from country to country. There are countries where the elite feels itself securely entrenched and, therefore, is indifferent to such pressure. In many other nations, they feel insecure and make sporadic responses to the demands of the poor. Again, some governing classes are more farsighted than others. However, in all the Third World states, irrespective of class structures and ideologies, there is a consensus behind the demand for restructuring of the international economic order which would augment the resources available at the disposal of these nation states. Whether the additional resources and opportunities secured through a change in the international economic system would in fact be used for the alleviation of poverty in the Third World cannot be guaranteed. It is a reasonable presumption that the Third World governments or their ruling elites are, on the whole, interested in promoting economic growth. This is not to suggest that they are disinterested in status, equality, and political power in the international arena. They are interested in all of these as well as in wealth and economic growth. Moreover, economic growth by itself enhances their economic strength, status, and political influence in the international arena. However, search for status through economic growth may not be accompanied by greater equity in the domestic economy. Additional resources at the disposal of Third World governments may generate a pattern of growth which further accentuates inequalities. This may strengthen both the economic position and political power of the dominant groups with a resultant increase in tensions and conflicts.

The fact that there are inequities in the international economic system is not entirely irrelevant to the political economy of growth in the Third World. The elite can utilize the phenomenon of international inequities as a rationale for the problems of underdevelopment and poverty in their own nations. Thus, it can attempt to divert the attention of the masses away from the inequities and failures of the internal socioeconomic system. As international inequities and discrimination diminish, it would become increasingly difficult for the elite in the Third World to point toward them as causes of domestic poverty and inequity. More and more they would have to turn to internal policy measures in order to respond to domestic pressures for greater equalities of opportunity.

When discussing class relationships, it is important to observe that the relationship of the Third World with the Developed World has characteristics closely analogous to that of trade unions toward the property-owning classes or employers. The comparison is with the situation of trade unionism in the early days of capitalism in the eighteenth and nineteenth centuries—during the period of Industrial Revolution in Britain. Today's counterpart of the capitalist of industrial Britain is the group of industrial advanced states; the developed states typify the role of the employers or owners of capital and power. Of course, it is the elites in the industrial states, those who control the levers of power and decision-making authority, who represent the advanced states in the international political and economic arena. This way of looking at the relationship between the two sets of countries ignores the role of classes other than the elite groups in the advanced countries. The demands of the Third World for a greater share of world income and output, greater equality of opportunities in expanding volume of world trade and investment, and for higher and more stable earnings from primary exports bear resemblance to the demands of the trade unions for higher wages, security of employment, unemployment insurance benefits as well as a greater share of free social services. As the trade unions increased their demands beyond higher and stable wages and security of employment to participation in the decision-making process of the management and ownership of the industrial enterprises, the Third World likewise increasingly demands its greater participation in the decision-making process in the international economic system.

As in the trade union movement, so also in the Third World, there are differences of view regarding the future pattern of international economy and society. There are those who believe that the future world order should be one of socialism spreading throughout the rich and poor countries of the world. There are those who believe that irrespective of whether different countries have the same sociopolitical system or not, there must be a fundamental redistribution of world wealth and income. Again, there are those who do not emphasize so much inequalities amongst nations as the satisfaction of basic human needs in the poor countries and an improvement in their absolute standards of living. The latter group puts special emphasis on internal reforms and policy measures, on the one hand, and on the elimination of inequalities and discrimination in the international economic system, on the other. That is, they tend to deemphasize financial assistance or aid. Again, there are others who believe that the development of the poor countries requires that they break out of the international economy. Participation in the international economy, which is and would continue to be dominated in the foreseeable future by the developed countries, would accentuate the dependence of the Third World and prevent the growth of indigenous technology or of production and consumption based upon domestic resources and value systems. Such critics advocate a reduction, if not a total elimination of links with the Developed World.

At this moment in time, however, the great majority of the Third World is interested in maximizing the gains from their participation in the international economic system and the minimization of the negative effects. They recognize that there are differences amongst them in terms of their ability to take advantage of more favorable development in the international economic system. As evidenced in the past history of internal struggle for redistribution of income within the advanced societies, the initial benefits accrued predominantly to the elites. Similarly, in the international sphere, the initial gains from changes in the international economic system would accrue more to the middle-income than to the poorest countries.

In the early stages of trade unionism, there were differences of interest or lack of complete harmony amongst the different skills and occupational groups in their relationship with the employers. In the same way, there are developing countries today which have special relationships and preferential economic arrangements with groups of developed countries, as evidenced by the special relationships of France and Great Britain with a few of their ex-colonies or of the relationship of the EEC with the African, Caribbean, and Pacific countries or of the United States with the Latin American countries.[17]

POWER OF THE PERIPHERY: ECONOMIC AND NONECONOMIC FACTORS

Among the sources of power residing in the Third World for bringing about a change in world economic order is the power of rational argument and appeal to the morality issue. The counterpart of this power in the Third World is the concern in the Developed World with the question of international equity on moral grounds.[18] The hard core of this moral argument is that there is an ethical responsibility of the rich to help the poor. There is an even more fundamental sense in which equity in the international distribution of income is a moral issue. The prevailing distribution of income and wealth is arbitrarily determined by the division of the world into states. Those nations which are lucky enough to be endowed with abundant physical resources relative to population pursue policies with respect to movement of labor, capital, and technology which prevent others from sharing in their wealth and opportunities. Initial natural advantages, including natural resources in the broadest sense of the term, produce cumulatively beneficent effects. They, in turn, generate resources for capital accumulation and for the acquisition of skill and technology.[19]

A part of the indirect leverage which the Third World enjoys in relation to the Developed World relates to the threat or fear that poverty causes political instability and violence and that such violence is not necessarily confined to the borders of the individual Third World states. A particular state or its ruling elite, confronted with poverty-generated domestic pressures, might undertake adventurism abroad, especially in neighboring states, in order to diffuse domestic threats. Most of the "mini-wars" in the post-Second World War era have been fought between states in the Third World. They frequently threaten to be internationalized, involving the developed countries. The threat or occurrence of violence and sociopolitical instability in the developing world may jeopardize the material interests of the rich countries by creating uncertainty in or actually disrupting the flow of trade and investments.

It is in the context of the importance of the Third World in the economic field, however, that the major source of its bargaining strength has been sought. The Third World is important to the Developed World as a source of raw materials, as a market for exports, and as an outlet for investment resources, especially private investment through the multinational corporations. Total imports from the Third World were 31 percent of the aggregate imports of the Developed World in 1974, having increased from 26 percent in 1961. The proportion of manufactured imports obtained from the Third World was much less (ten percent in 1974) than that for primary products (54 percent in 1974). The United States and Japan depended on the Third World for slightly less that two-thirds of their aggregate imports of primary commodities; the dependence of the EEC is less since only about 45 percent of the primary imports of the EEC came from the Third World.[20]

A different indicator of dependence of the Developed World is the proportion of total domestic consumption which is accounted for by imports from the Third World. Imports from the Third World constituted 20 percent of the total domestic consumption of primary products in the Developed World in 1974. The percentage was much less, i.e., only two percent, for manufactured products. In terms of specific products, however, the dependence was greater, the percentage being 51 percent in the case of fuels and 25 percent for other minerals. Moreover, Japan and the EEC were considerably more dependent than the United States in the case of fuels (with imports constituting 77 percent of consumption for Japan and 70 percent for EEC as against

10 percent for the United States). In the case of other minerals taken together, the percentage varied between 39 and 27 percent for the former and 14 percent for the latter. For five minerals (copper, tin, manganese, chromium, cobalt) Japan and the EEC depended on imports from the Third World to an extent varying between 65 percent and 90 percent of their total consumption.[21]

Several factors are relevant in evaluating the dependence of the Developed World on the Third World. Firstly, the commodities may be crucial for the working of the modern industrial economy and for the maintenance of the standards of living in the developed countries. Secondly, while some imports may be a small percentage of total consumption in the Developed World, those who consume or use them may be powerful interest groups; the governments of the developed countries need to respond to their pressures. Thirdly, there is the question whether the magnitude of dependence, while small at present, may increase over time in the future. Fourthly, even though the average dependence of the Developed World as a whole is low, the fact that one or two developed countries depend substantially on the Third World has implications for the entire Developed World, because of the close interdependence between the developed countries themselves.

The minerals discussed above are considered critical for the industrial, developed economies, as evidenced from the fact that in most of these commodities, the richest amongst the developed countries, the United States, holds large strategic stockpiles to guard against the disruption of supplies from abroad. Moreover, in the case of a few raw materials and minerals, even if the dependence of the Developed World as a whole on the Third World is not very large, the dependence of a few multinational corporations is substantial. Likewise, certain important industries in the developed countries depend heavily on imported materials from the Third World. About 70 percent of the total resource use, direct and indirect, in eight specific industries is accounted for by zinc; about 65 percent in ten industries is accounted for by copper; and aluminum accounts for 72 percent of the total resource use in ten industries.[22]

Though in the case of many agricultural products the same degree of essentiality may not apply, attempts to promote synthetic substitutes in their place involve risks of pollution and environmental degradation. Looking to the future, it appears that if present trading patterns continue, and if growth rates in the Developed World follow past trends, dependence on the developing countries for materials and minerals will increase.[23]

The future magnitude and pattern of dependence of the Developed World on imports from the Third World partly rests on the policies pursued by developed and developing countries. These policies, in turn, depend upon how they perceive their mutual interrelationship in the various economic, political and strategic areas. At the same time, the availability and costs of alternative sources of supply, including synthetic substitutes, compared with the prices of imports from the Third World is an important determinant. In many cases technological innovations are necessary, requiring large research and development expenditure. Imponderables in these matters are many. How long would it take to develop new technologies? What would be the adverse side effects, if any, of new technology? How would the social consequences of new technology be accomodated? How would it be shared among the individual developed countries?

With the dependence of the Developed World on imports from the Third World probably increasing in the future, there is a real risk of an interruption of supplies of such imports and consequent dislocations in domestic economies. In the colonial periods most of the countries producing raw materials were the colonies of the rich, industrialized nations. In the subsequent period of decolonization, it was the multinationals located in the Developed World which owned and controlled to a very large extent the production, marketing and distribution of many of the raw materials and primary products. In the post-Second World War period and especially in the 1970s, the Third World has increasingly asserted the right of national sovereignty over natural resources located in their territories. Associated with this claim has been increasing participation by the host countries in the management and ownership of multinationals. Therefore, over the years, the degree of direct control by the Developed World over the ownership and use of natural resources located in the Third World has diminished.

The most important conditions necessary for the Third World to be able to interrupt supplies or to regulate exports with a view to raising prices is their ability to join together and maintain cohesion. The standard conditions for the exercise of monopoly or cartel power in international trade are well known: essentialness of products, inelasticity of demand, inelasticity of supplies from alternative sources or from synthetic substitutes, and a limited number of suppliers controlling a large proportion of world trade. Analysis of supply and demand characteristics in the long or medium run suggests that only a few primary commodities are eligible for cartel-type action. For example, iron ore, copper, tin, bauxite, manganese, phosphate, timber, bananas, pepper, tea, coffee, and cocoa are likely candidates.[24]

However, in many cases even though the long-term demand and supply elasticities may be high, the Third World may nevertheless combine to regulate supply and price in the short run. The time horizon of most of these nations, in desperate need of resources, is very short run. They have a strong incentive for maximizing short run revenues or profits, especially in the case of export products which face either stagnation or an absolute decline in demand in the future. Short-term gains in financial resources could then be used for diversifying the domestic economy. In any case there is considerable uncertainty and lack of firm information about price elasticities of demand and supply or about future changes in demand and supply conditions, including changes in technology.

Projections of shortages in the near future owing to a fall in the rate of investment in raw materials and minerals, combined with a forecast of increases in future demand, provide opportunity as well as incentive for restrictive action. This is especially so in view of a gestation lag in the production of substitutes or in securing an increased output from alternative sources of supply.[25]

The fact remains that the Third World could undertake, in the short run, actions which would disrupt the flow of trade; they could inhibit the planning of production and investment by creating a sense of uncertainty in the minds of investors. The risks of failure of cartel-type action owing to miscalculations regarding supply and demand are easier borne if the developing countries concerned are able to sustain losses without serious domestic strain or distress. The countries which have natural resources in short supply and in great demand in the developed countries are also mostly middle-income countries.[26] The Third World could take concerted action to discourage the emergence of synthetic substitutes or increased production from alternative sources of supply by the threat of dumping in the future. The fear that a cartel could reduce prices in the future to inflict losses on the potential competitors could deter them from undertaking long-term investments to increase output and supply. It is the possibility of such a threat that has led to the demand for a floor price for petroleum on the part of the new high-cost producers of petroleum in North America and Western Europe.

The Third World is less important to the developed countries as a market for exports than as a source of imports. The percentage of the developed countries' total exports absorbed by the Third World was about 20 percent in 1974; the percentages for the United States, the EEC, and Japan were respectively 26 percent, 15 percent, and 39 percent. While the proportion of imports obtained from the Third World increased between 1963 and 1974, the proportion of exports going to them stagnated or slightly declined. Exports of the Developed World consisted overwhelmingly of manufactured goods.

The Third World is important to the developed countries not only as a market for their exports but also as an outlet for savings and investment and for the sale of technology. Twenty percent or more of the total foreign direct investment of the major industrialized countries was located in the Third World in 1970. About 29 percent of the total foreign investment of the Western European countries was located in the Third World; the percentages for the United States and Japan were respectively 25 percent and 20 percent. By the end of 1970 their direct investment in the Third World was worth about $39 billion, out of a total of $153 billion in aggregate total foreign investment. As an outlet for savings the importance of the Third World is different for the different economic sectors in the developed economies. Petroleum, mining, and manufacturing activities have a greater stake in investment in the Third World than other economic sectors.

It is not only the search for markets and materials which encouraged investment in the Third World. Increasing militancy among trade unions in the advanced countries, accompanied by higher wages, has prompted the multinationals to move into the Third World, especially to those countries in the Third World which have a disciplined labor force and are able to maintain low wages. The question whether, in the absence of investment opportunities for the multinational corporations in the Third World, the growth prospects of the Developed World would be adversely affected cannot be answered easily. One can, however, hypothesize that for individual multinational corporations the investment and market opportunities provided by the Third World are often crucial. They provide the opportunities for growth and market expansion to oligopolistic firms as well as access to and control over the sources of supply of raw materials.[27] In this respect there is scope for bargaining between multinationals and the Third World. The Third World has leverage over the multinationals operating in their territories; they could impose fiscal burdens on them or impose restrictions of various kinds on their operations, including participation by the nationals of the host country in the management of multinationals and, in the extreme case, the Third World countries could expropriate the foreign enterprises located in their territories. The bargaining power of the Third World is increased whenever there is competition between individual multinational corporations; the multinationals from the United States, EEC, and Japan sometimes compete with each other in the Third World. On the other hand, competition among Third World countries for encouraging investments by the multinationals weakens their bargaining power. Therefore, a coordinated policy on their part in relation to the multinationals would add to their bargaining strength. Also, the bargaining power of the Third World vis-à-vis the multinationals is strengthened if they have well-developed domestic enterprises and technological capability of their own. Obviously, their bargaining power in getting a large share of returns on past investments already made in their territories is greater than in the case of prospective investments which are under negotiation.

The large and growing debt burden of the Third World ironically increases the dependence of the Developed World on the financial and economic stability of the Third World. The Third World's public and publicly guaranteed debt burden amounted to about $150 billion in 1975. In addition, there is a large amount of private debt, and either willful default or unintentional default would disrupt the financial markets of the developed countries. Losses and bankruptcies might result from defaults on debt due to supplier credits granted by non-banking and industrial enterprises as well as from default on debts due to banks. Moreover, bank failures owing to default by Third World countries could spread, through speculative repercussions, to the whole economic system.

AREAS OF COMMON CONCERN AND BARGAINING POWER OF THIRD WORLD

The Third World can also exercise bargaining power by united action on issues of common concern to both the developed and developing countries. The most important among such issues are the control of environmental pollution and the exploitation of resources of the sea. Environmental pollution has no national frontiers.[28] Air and ocean space carry the effects of pollution far and wide. Those who possess more also stand to lose more from the disturbance of the ecological balance and from increasing hazards to health and life. The poor countries can, therefore, bargain for advantageous deals with the rich countries while participating in international measures for the control of pollution. In the case of negotiations on the Law of the Sea, experience to date has demonstrated various aspects of the bargaining process. Even though the developed countries have a major share of the continental shelf and economic zones around the world, their interests extend far beyond the ocean space in areas adjoining their territories. The developed countries have far-flung security and commercial interests and want rights of passage or navigation around the world for both military and civilian purposes. With exclusive control over their territorial waters, those Third World countries which control straits might impede the free passage of ships or hamper the navigational facilities needed by the Developed World. The developed countries want both opportunities for scientific research in the sea waters of the developing countries and access to natural resources and minerals lying under the seabed in the extraterritorial zones. Admittedly, the Third World lacks the capital and technology to exploit fully the resources in the seabed. Therefore, as a part of their agreement to the international regime for oceans, they need to bargain for access to the capital and technology as well as for their participation in the decision-making process.

Nuclear proliferation is also a subject of common concern to the world as a whole. The cooperation and participation of the Third World is urgently needed in view of the loss of monopoly over nuclear weapons on the part of the few selected developed countries.[29] It is suspected that the Third World countries are likely to be more adventurous than the Developed World in the use of nuclear weapons, especially in the cases where extreme poverty leads to desperation. Desperation might lead to local wars. Furthermore, there could be non-state use of nuclear weapons by terrorist groups.[30] The use of nuclear weapons could cause a great deal of harm to the world economy and environment. The developed countries which consume the largest share of the world's resources and make the greatest demand on the world's economy and ecology would be the greatest sufferers. Furthermore, the possession of nuclear weapons or nuclear capability increases the importance of the Third World in the arena of international power politics, which affects, in turn, their role in international economic relations.

THIRD WORLD BARGAINING POWER AND
DIFFERENCES AMONG DEVELOPED COUNTRIES

The Third World could also attempt to exploit possible differences among the developed countries in order to improve its bargaining power. With the termination of the cold war, there has been an increasing competition between the three big economic powers, namely, the United States, the EEC, and Japan, in the field of international trade and investment. There is a possibility that the EEC and Japan, being more dependent on the Third World, would be more amenable than the United States to making concessions to Third World demands. Again, some members of the Developed World such as the United States and West Germany are more ideologically committed to free market forces than others. Because of their superior economic power and efficiency they gain more from free markets than France or other European countries. France has always believed in the "organization of markets." Japan has traditionally been accustomed to long-term sales and purchase contracts for materials and minerals tied to her manufactured exports and financed by long-term credits.[31]

There are limits, however, to the extent to which the Third World can exploit the differences among the developed countries. There is a close economic interdependence between developed nations. Moreover, there is a sense of solidarity as well as political and ideological identity of interests which is further strengthened by common security interests vis-à-vis the Soviet Union and China.[32]

It is the Scandinavian countries which have shown greater responsiveness to the demands of the Third World than any of the major developed countries, partly on the basis of moral convictions regarding equity in international economic relations. For example, the Netherlands and the Scandinavian countries have been active in softening the hardliners like West Germany, the United States, the United Kingdom, and Japan in their negotiations on the UNCTAD's integrated commodity program.

With the decline of cold war rivalry and the emergence of detente the opportunities to take advantage of the differences between the socialist and capitalist countries have diminished but have not disappeared. During the 1950s and 1960s, rivalry and competition between the big powers, especially the United States and the Soviet Union, resulted in a great deal of attention being paid to the Third World. The superpowers competed in order to win friends and allies in the Third World and carve out spheres of influence including preferential or closer economic relationships. The latter in some cases were expected to provide in turn access to raw materials which might have contributed to the respective military might of the big powers. In the course of competing for influence, the major powers provided both aid and commercial concessions to Third World countries. Military alliances built up with groups of Third World countries by the superpowers were accompanied by substantial economic advantages in terms of aid flows and trade concessions. The intense rivalry between the superpowers has declined but the struggle for influence continues, albeit on a reduced scale, especially in the Middle East, in the Indian Ocean, and in the continent of Africa. Moreover, the rise of China as a big power partly offsets the impact of detente in reducing the interest of the Developed World in the Third World. New tensions and rivalry have been created between China and the Soviet Union and should, hopefully, increase the scope for maneuver on the part of the Third World. Competition between China and the United States in Asia might increase in the future. Furthermore, China consistently supports the demands of the Third World in international fora as against the active opposition of the United States and the lukewarm or indifferent attitude of the Soviet Union. It is true, of course, that in terms of economic benefits, through either trade or aid, China at the present time could contribute little to augment the resources of the Third World countries in their relationship with the advanced, capitalistic countries.

The reactions of the socialist countries to the various proposals in the NIEO are ambivalent. They object to being treated on a par with the capitalist countries with respect to Third World demands. Since, according to them, the present plight of the Third World is largely, if not wholly, due to past colonial exploitation, and since the socialist countries were not colonial powers, they should not be called upon to compensate for past injustices. Secondly, any transfer of resources from highly egalitarian socialist countries cannot be equated with an equivalent transfer from the capitalist societies, in which the rich and affluent groups can make concessions without much hardship. Increasing integration of the socialist countries in the international economy has contradictory effects insofar as the Third World's bargaining strength is concerned. While they provide alternative sources of capital and technology to the Third World, in competition with the developed countries, at the same time they compete with the Third World as sources of scarce materials or natural resources to trade with the capitalist powers.[33] Socialist nations borrow in the Euro-currency market and increasingly enter into licensing and contractual agreements with the multinationals. Therefore, they provide alternative outlets or markets in competition with the Third World for the capital and technology of the developed, capitalist countries.

While the Third World can strive to benefit from whatever divergence of interests exists between the groups of developed countries, it can also try to build up alliances with the various interest groups in the Developed World. Producers of capital goods in the developed countries have an interest in the expansion of their sales: hence, they should be in favor of aid to the Third World, since it is spent on the import of capital goods. This is of special importance at times of recession, unemployment, and excess capacity in the manufacturing sector in the Developed World. Similarly, the producers and exporters of food grains in the rich countries should have an interest in aid which would stimulate their export of food grains. Moreover, consumers in the Developed World have an interest in cheap imports and, therefore, may be sympathetic with the Third World's expanded exports of light consumer's goods. Wholesalers and retailers in the Developed World could also be their allies in this respect.

THE FUTURE OF THIRD WORLD REVOLT

The foregoing pages analyze the factors contributing to building up a united front among Third World countries in their relationship with the Developed World. The future of Third World unity and its success in effecting structural changes in the international economic system would also depend upon the extent to which divisive forces in the Third World can be contained.[34] There are several divisive factors at work in the Third World. There is a widening of the economic gap among the developing countries; in addition, there is an increasing differentiation in terms of political ideologies and military strength. On the one hand, there has been an increase in the number of Third World governments which have adopted a pronounced radical-leftist ideology. On the other hand, in a large number of Third World countries liberal-democratic governments have been replaced by authoritarian regimes run by an alliance between the military and the bureaucracy. In the area of military strength, there are a very few with nuclear capacity and a few others with considerable conventional military power compared with the remainder of Third World countries. These developments have already raised fears among the weaker members of the Third World about the more powerful among them attempting to secure a position of dominance or hegemony. This situation is prone to create tensions and strains in the Third World so that the countries which feel insecure would try to build special alliances with the developed countries. Thus, the cohesion and the solidarity of the Third World is likely to be undermined.

The most important differentiation underway in the Third World is, however, in the economic field. This is due to the growing disparity between the middle-income and poorer members of the Third World. Between 1965 and 1975, average per capita incomes in the poorer countries (with per capita income below $200) increased at an annual rate of only 1.51 percent ($2 per year). The non-oil, middle-income developing countries (with per capita income above $200) achieved a per capita growth rate of 4 percent per year. The world economic crisis since 1972 has widened the divergence between these two groups of countries. The poorer countries have been faced not only with a deterioration in the terms of trade but also with a slow growth of exports; this has led to severe balance of payments deficits, falling import capacity, and consequently an adverse turn in future growth prospects. The middle-income countries have done better in dealing with the effects of worldwide recession and inflation because they have had access to private capital markets (in view of their greater credit worthiness) and resorted to extensive borrowing. In some cases, they have enjoyed increased prices of a few of their exports, which partially offset the rising prices of imports. The more industrialized amongst the middle-income countries have been able to take advantage of the expanding OPEC markets. The prospects for the future indicate divergencies in the prospective growth rates and economic performance of these two groups of countries.[35]

At the apex of the middle-income developing countries stands the Organization of Petroleum Exporting Countries (OPEC). However, the growing investment of the OPEC surplus in the financial markets of the developed countries strengthens its ties with, and gives it a long-run interest in, the economic viability and growth of the Developed World. OPEC dependence on technology and on imports from the developed countries is also on the increase as these developing nations attempt to diversify and develop their economies. No less important is their dependence on the imports of military hardware from the Developed World. However, too close an integration with the developed countries carries a risk for OPEC to the extent that it reduces its maneuverability and flexibility. The more its future economic prospects are tied to the developed countries, the less effective becomes the weapon of the oil cartel. This situation increases the risk involved in a possible retaliatory action on the part of the developed countries. Viewed in this light, OPEC has an incentive to diversify its investments toward the Third World and thereby to reduce its risks, both political and economic.

The ability of OPEC to diversify the sources of their investments in the Third World has been partly inhibited by the latter's under-development. The opportunities for short-term and highly profitable investments are not abundant in the Third World. OPEC would need to take a much longer-term view of the security and profitability of their investments if they were to successfully diversify their invest-ments in the Third World. It will be in the middle-income developing countries that OPEC is likely to find investment opportunities which would be directly productive and would repay within a relatively short period. Similarly, the latter nations would also be able to meet the requirements of OPEC for technology as well as for trained manpower so that their current heavy dependence for skill and management on the developed countries can be reduced. On the other hand, the poorer developing countries would be in a better position to meet the growing requirements of unskilled labor in the OPEC countries. Already migrant workers constitute more than one-third of the labor force in the majority of the Arab OPEC countries; in a few OPEC coun-tries such as Kuwait the majority of the labor force are foreigners.[36]

Politically the OPEC countries are pulled in two opposite directions. On the one hand, it is unwise for them to be too close to the developed countries in a period when the rest of the Third World is engaged in a struggle to gain concessions from and to drive advantageous bargains with the developed countries. Moreover, support of the Third World helped the success of the oil cartel in its confrontation with the Devel-oped World. At the same time, a close relationship with the rest of the Arab World is politically important for internal stability in the OPEC countries and for regional peace. Moreover, there is an active movement for the integration, both political and economic, of the Arab countries. The confrontation of the Arab members of OPEC with Israel puts them in a special relationship with the rest of the Third World. Faced with strong material and diplomatic support of Israel on the part of the Developed World, they need the diplomatic support of the Third World in their efforts to ensure an advantageous bargain with Israel. They have used the oil weapon to put pressure on the western world, especially the United States, to help negotiate with Israel. On the other hand, they have used the leverage of financial assistance to the Third World, especially the African countires, in winning their political support against Israel. Yet, most of the OPEC countries have relatively conservative regimes and are politically adverse to the growth of radicalism in the Third World. They would prefer to be politically close to the western capitalist countries.

Faced with these opposing pulls, OPEC is most likely to follow a middle course: Continuing to support Third World solidarity and expand the scope and range of economic cooperation with it, while at the same time avoiding a break with the Developed World. The Developed World on its part is likely increasingly to attempt to provide a greater—a marginally greater—role in the decision-making process on international issues to OPEC and the middle-income countries.[37]

Recent developments in the international economic scene mark only the first step in the structural changes desired by the Third World in the international economic system. It will take years before the end of the road is reached and the exact time span is difficult to predict. The solidarity among the Third World countries in international fora with respect to the broad range of global issues must continue. Limited concessions will probably be obtained by the Third World in the field of trade as well as of transfer of capital and technology.[38] At the same time, groups of countries in the Third World should be able to strike limited and more specific bargains with groups of developed countries. Such "deals" or bargains may be more advantageous than the global bargains reached for the entire Third World. The "Lome Convention," incorporating trade and financial agreements between the EEC and the associated territories in the Caribbean, Pacific, and Africa, is a case in point. The greater the degree of cohesion, the greater is the likelihood that the specific, limited bargains or agreements between groups of countries in the developed and developing world would be supplementary to and not substitute for the global bargain. The full realization of the potential for an increased inter-Third World cooperation will take time.

It is most likely that concession in the first round of international negotiations would benefit the middle-income countries more than the poorer developing countries. The greater the success of domestic efforts of the Third World in mobilizing resources and in accelerating the development process on the basis of self-help, the greater will be the possibility of turning the external economic forces to advantage. The greater the equity in the internal socioeconomic system, the greater will be the degree of cohesion and solidarity within an individual Third World country. National solidarity and self-reliance is a prelude to collective solidarity and self-reliance among the Third World countries. For the poorer developing countries, the future is more uncertain. The possibility of violent internal changes which involve departures from liberal democratic practices toward authoritarianism are likely. In these countries, the elite is likely to be more insecure and will have smaller resources to diffuse tensions and pressures for redistribution. Hence, an insecure elite with insufficient resources might resort to an authoritarian and inegalitarian political and economic system. In a few cases the existing structure may break down; the elite may be overthrown, resulting in chaos or the emergence of leadership from the masses. There will be individual cases where violent internal change may cause links with the external world to be disrupted, probably temporarily, either in the wake of or as a prelude to radical internal structural transformation. There is likely to be an alternation of contact with and isolation from the Developed World, arising from changes in the economic and political structure. A wholesale delinking of the entire Third World from the international economy, even temporarily, is, however, extremely unlikely.

Chapter 8

THIRD WORLD REVOLT AND SELF-RELIANT
AUTO-CENTERED STRATEGY OF DEVELOPMENT[1]

Fawzy Mansour

The main concern of this chapter is to fit together an adequate
conceptual framework for understanding the Third World revolt. I
propose that in order to understand the motivations for this revolt or
its prospects for success, one must appreciate the history of socioeconomic change in the Third World. The most important historical
forces have been economic and political relationships with the now
developed industrial nations. Both the historical and continuing linkages of the developed to the underdeveloped world determine what
strategies will and will not bring about desired economic changes in the
less-advanced regions. This chapter initially will describe the nature of
these linkages and their past and continuing effects on the Third World,
and then, will examine several broad proposals for Third World development and their individual prospects for success. This examination
will point out how continuing ties to the advanced nations limit the
feasibility of some popular proposals for change, many of which have

arisen in the Third World itself. I argue that the only strategy which can ultimately be successful in providing for the material needs of the people of the Third World is one joining domestic control of the means of production by the producing classes, national self-reliance, and certain kinds of active cooperation among Third World nations. Some initial steps requisite to following such a strategy are outlined at the end of this chapter.

THE CONCEPTUAL FRAMEWORK: THE THIRD WORLD REVOLT AS A REACTION TO THE WORLD CAPITALIST SYSTEM

Understanding the Third World revolt requires a proper grasp of the world economic system of which the Third World is an integral part, and to which, by that revolt, it is reacting.

The world capitalist system is the economic system to which the Third World is reacting. It is a complex economic system, and an old one, dating back to the sixteenth century and, in contrast to all previous economic systems, was *born* a complex, not a simple, one. A *simple* economic system is a system of social division of labor, held together by the way an economic surplus is regularly generated, circulated, and disposed of. It constitutes the economic base of a particular social formation, or class configuration, having its own specific pattern of political power, individual culture and ideology. A *complex* economic system is, likewise, a system of social division of labor, held together by a regular unidirectional flow of surplus—not between different social classes but between distinct, usually differently organized, social formations. Since, however, surpluses are produced by classes and are disposed of by classes, tracing the flow of surplus from one simple economic system to another within a complex economic system necessarily involves the scrutiny of class relationships within each simple economic system and across their respective borders.

The very emergence of the capitalist system in the West was inextricably linked with an unprecedented flow of surplus from other, differently organized societies in other parts of the world. Its development continued to be sustained by the inflow, on an ever-widening scale, of surplus. The forms surplus assumed, the channels through which it was transmitted and the means guaranteeing its extraction and flow, and with them the class configurations in the giving societies and even the class relationships within the receiving countries themselves, differed from one stage to another.

The Recapitulation Hypothesis

As the capitalist system developed from one stage to another, it tended to recapitulate on a world scale, and in the course of a few centuries, the three main modes of surplus extraction which succeeded one another on a smaller scale, in as many millenia of human history; they are: the use of arbitrary violence, as in slavery; the use of organized, institutionalized violence, as in tributary systems; and the use of economic constraints, the specific mode of capitalist surplus extraction.

The essence of slavery is the denial of any rights to slaves, the arbitrary appropriation of their labor by the slave holders, and the continued necessity for violence, or the threat of it, to coerce the slaves into performing the day-to-day productive activities which they neither will, nor do benefit from. To that mode of surplus extraction corresponds the first stage of the development of the world capitalist system: that of primitive accumulation. Direct plunder, the imposition of tributes and fines, the use of slave labor in plantations and mines, the eviction from their lands of native populations in the Old as well as the New World—these as well as other forms of the use of arbitrary violence for surplus extraction belong to that period.

To the tributary modes of surplus extraction (feudalism, the oriental modes of production, etc.) corresponds the intermediate or colonial stage in the development of the world capitalist system. In feudalism, the serf has to work a certain number of days on the lord's fields, grind his grains at the lord's mill, present him with gifts at festive occasions, and so on. Likewise, the colony has to produce cotton for the colonial power, buy its textiles, deposit gold with its central bank, and so on. In both cases, violence is institutionalized into political power, and political power is the means which ensures the regular flow of surplus.

The third—and contemporary—stage reproduces on a world scale a development which corresponds to the victory of the capitalist mode of production on the national level in Western countries. Within the national capitalist economies, economic constraints replaced political constraints as the guarantor and regulator of surplus flow between classes. In the same manner colonialism (that is, direct political rule) gives way to formal political independence, and economic constraints replace political constraints as the guarantor and regulator of surplus flow from the periphery of the world capitalist system, now become the Third World, to its center, the advanced capitalist countries. Violence, of course, still looms in the background, ready for use whenever and wherever the existence of the system is seriously threatened.

As in all attempts at periodization, no hard and fast line between these three stages in the development of the world capitalist system can be drawn nor, when looked at from the perspective of this or that Third World country or region, is a necessary order of succession implied. Present Third World countries were drawn into the world capitalist system at different points of time to fulfill different functions.

By the nineteenth century, most Latin American countries had reached the third stage, that of political independence coupled with economic subordination, while parts of Africa—north and south, east as well as west—were having their first taste of the arbitrary violence stage. At present, though most of the Third World has been more or less ushered into the third stage, the three modes of encroachment still coexist side by side with and reinforce each other in certain areas, e.g., southern Africa.

The first stage of this process, that of arbitrary violence, need not detain us here. The third stage, the replacement of political constraints by economic constraints within the world capitalist system, will be examined in the following section. Attention now will be turned to the intermediate stage or mode of encroachment. It was during that stage that the two parts of the world capitalist system, the developed center and the underdeveloped periphery, really began to be organically linked to each other, and yet to part ways, and that the foundations for the present stage were solidly laid.

The Impact of Colonialism on Capitalist Development in the Colonies

Contrary to widely held views, both on the Left and on the Right, in this century as well as the last, the main impact of integration into the world capitalist system of the various regions, countries, and societies which now constitute the Third World was not to introduce capitalist development, much less to accelerate it "through the export of capital," but to block the way. As the example of Japan shows, the very fact of the appearance of capitalism in one region, with its inner achievements and outer menace, would have made it spread as a form of socioeconomic organization in most other regions had central capitalism not battled with all its might against this spreading.

The blockage of capitalist development in Third World countries during the intermediate stage of encroachment had two effects: the prevention of the process of reorganization of the social division of labor (called accumulation) from taking place on any considerable scale, and the introduction of a pattern of trade in which man's labor in the advanced capitalist economies was increasingly exchanged for more and more of the labor of the Third World. The facts that trade—both ways—between the advanced capitalist countries and their dependencies was controlled by the former countries, and that these advanced countries usually exported manufactures which were subject to various degrees of monopoly, whereas the exports of the dependent countries were produced under conditions approximating perfect competition, are often invoked to explain this secular trend, and they do indeed partially explain it. The main reason, however, lies in the nature of the encounter between two modes of production, the precapitalist and the capitalist. Whereas any accumulation that took place within the former mode of production was immediately translated into lower prices, the surplus—the increased productivity—resulting from accumulation within the capitalist mode of production was appropriated in the form of profits and interest, and lately, with the increasing power of organized labor in the capitalist centers, also in the form of higher wages. This analysis, of course, does not apply to those sectors in the dependent countries which were organized on a capitalist basis; but then, it is characteristic that those sectors were organized and retained by foreign capital, which appropriated to itself the major gains in productivity resulting from accumulation. The whole mechanism of colonial exploitation saw to it that capitalist development remained restricted to narrow, isolated sectors serving the metropolitan economy, strictly owned and/or controlled by foreign capital.

The Political Basis for Colonial Exploitation

The mechanism of colonial exploitation was essentially political, based on the direct use of institutionalized violence rather than economic constraints. The design of tariff systems in the periphery, the granting of concessions and awarding of contracts, the patterns of public expenditure, public investment and taxation, the linking of currencies, the monetary and credit policies, all of these and others were *political* acts tailored to serve one economic aim: facilitating the generation and flow of various kinds of surpluses from the periphery to the center. Foreign business, in its turn, returned the compliment: in its choice and location of investments, its recruitment and employment policies, its allocation of credit facilities, etc. Short-run and even long-run profit considerations were usually subordinated to the overall strategies designed for each dependent country or region by the foreign chancelleries which held sway over them. Here the role the colonial state played in directly shaping economic development—or under-development—in the colonies or semicolonies stands in clear contrast to the relatively restrained role it played on its own metropolitan territory, and justifies the expression "colonial social formation."

The Colonial Social Formation

A colonial social formation is one in which the various sectors of the economy (agriculture, industry, trade, finance, etc.) as well as the various instances of social life (productive techniques, relations of production, class stratification, power distribution, culture and ideo-logy, etc.) are not allowed to develop freely and interact in accordance with their own inner logic. Instead, they are consciously controlled or fashioned by outside forces in the interest of creating and maintaining the maximum surplus flow to the dominant capitalist center nations.

A colonial social formation, in contrast to a developed capitalist one, contains a number of potentially antagonistic modes of production—communal, involving elements of slavery, feudal and semifeudal, "colonial," small-commodity, capitalist—which persist side by side. Their main relationships (when they are not closed upon themselves, as in the subsistence communal mode of production) are oriented toward the outside world and not toward each other. Hence, the extraordinary coexistence—otherwise difficult to explain—of extremely varied levels of productive techniques.

There is a consumption-goods sector producing essentially subsis-tence goods and marked by a great simplification of function, even compared with precolonial times, as a result of the progressive dis-appearance in the face of foreign competition of traditional crafts and industries. There is also an export sector, producing one, two, or three raw materials and quite divorced from the rest of the economy.

A multitude of classes and social forces exists, corresponding to the multiplicity of modes of production. In densely populated countries, where private ownership of land has long prevailed or has been introduced by colonial rule, a feudal or semifeudal class of landlords dominates and exploits a large mass of poor or middle-income peasants. An intermediate rich peasant class may or may not exist. Where land is abundant and special agricultural products are needed for the world market, either the colonial administration or colonial trading companies indirectly organize production on the basis of peasant farming and trade monopoly, thus creating what came to be known as "colonial trade" (*l'économie de traite*). Wherever capitalist farming proper appears— using wage labor, sometimes forced labor, modern techniques and business accounting methods—it is the preserve of either colonial settlers or foreign enterprises exploiting large estates or plantations. Outside of agriculture, capitalist industry (that is, mining, simple raw-material transformation processes, public utilities and transport) is likewise in the hands of foreign capital.

Thus, where conditions allow it, a working class appears long before its own national bourgeoisie. When foreign trade is not completely in the hands of foreign capital, a *compradore* class appears whose function it is to mediate between foreign capital and the national economy. This class is often made up of national minorities, transplanted or encouraged to migrate from other equally colonized regions, such as the Chinese in some parts of Southeast Asia, the Levantines in Egypt, the Arabs and Indians in East Africa, and the Syrians and Lebanese in West Africa.

A petty bourgeois class also exists, made up of petty traders, the remnants of the ancient *artisanat*, professional people, employees of the colonial or semicolonial administration, etc. The size, composition and weight of this class varies considerably from one colonial social formation to another.

Except where there was direct colonial rule, often resting on a broad base of colonial settlers, foreign capitalist domination always managed to forge an alliance with certain dominant classes, originally found and strengthened, or especially created, within the colonial social formation: feudal and semifeudal landlords and *compradore* traders.

The Development, Differentiation and Equivocal Role of the Local Bourgeoisie

Since the bourgeoisie is the class destined to bring about capitalist transformation, one of the main results of colonial rule was to liquidate the national bourgeoisie in the colonies and semicolonies where it had begun to make its appearance, and to prevent its emergence where it did not exist. However, within the world capitalist system various contradictions were at work which brought to an end the ability of the center to extract the surplus from the dominated territories with the direct exercise of institutionalized violence and in the process gave the national bourgeoisie in certain parts of the non-Third World the chance to make a reentrance or a first appearance.

The First World War caused a certain degree of dislocation of normal lines of supply. Manufacturing activities began to spring up in various peripheral regions of the world to meet civilian needs—hitherto fed by metropolitan centers—as well as to supply armies fighting or being formed and trained on their territories. Construction relating to the war effort—building military roads, railways, ports, barracks, warehouses, etc.—and involving the use of considerable amounts of local labor and material, had to be delegated to local entrepreneurs. Funds began to accumulate in their hands, which were fed from another source: the rise in food and certain raw material prices, exclusively benefiting landlords, traders and businessmen. The same trend continued during the postwar construction years. Where these developments were particularly marked, e.g., in Egypt, India, and certain parts of China, a national bourgeoisie arose or was reinforced which led other classes such as the peasants, the workers and the petty bourgeoisie, in the struggle for national liberation. These latter classes were not acquiescent to foreign domination, but they could not, as yet, provide the necessary leadership. They were the classes which bore—as far as the dependent territories' share was concerned—the main burden of the war effort, in the form of shortages of necessities, higher prices, requisitions, forced or directed labor, etc. Thus, an active anti-imperialist alliance was formed between those who benefited most and those who suffered most from war and postwar conditions, each for his own reasons. In the course of that struggle, concessions were extracted from colonial powers which gave the national bourgeoisie greater scope for self-development and for the development of the national economy. The possibilities for growth and development open to the newly emergent bourgeoisie proved, however, to be more and more limited. The main levers of the economy—the monetary and financial system, much of the foreign trade, mining industries and the like—were still in the hands of foreign capital, draining away much of the available surplus. A great deal of what was left of that surplus was wasted on imported luxury goods by feudal and semifeudal classes (which, supported as they were by colonial rule, could not be dislodged from their position of internal political and economic eminence), thus limiting still more both the availability of surplus for investment and the market for goods produced by the emerging local industries.

This complex situation led to a marked differentiation within the peripheral nations' bourgeoisie. Part of this bourgeoisie, those who had the means, the know-how, the suitable line of business, sought protection and strength in some form or other of local monopolistic organization. This was usually a conglomeration of enterprises grouped around a financial institution, a "banque d'affaires." That, naturally, was the part which drew the most hostile reaction from foreign capital and which succumbed, within a decade or two, both to its threats and enticements. Alongside the feudal, semifeudal and *compradore* classes, with which on the personal level it became increasingly interchangeable, it ended by becoming another local ally of foreign domination.

The position of the middle section of the bourgeoisie was much more complex. They were subjected to the various forms of pressure and encirclement exercised by foreign capital, yet denied the possibility of a workable compromise; for they were not compact enough to fit into the role of agents, collaborators, and junior partners of foreign capital, which fell to local monopolies. Hence, they had to fight for the possibility of their further growth, even for their very existence. They could not, however, lead a consistent, consequential and thoroughgoing fight against foreign domination, for another danger now appeared on their left flank. A fight to the finish could only be won if the popular masses—the peasants, the workers, the petty bourgeoisie—were drawn into it. That meant their progressive radicalization, and the appearance of another model of development arising from the example of the Russian revolution: a type of development, and of revolution, quite different from that on which the national bourgeoisie was ready to stake its own fortunes.

The Appearance of a New, Socialist Model of Development

The Russian revolution, besides constituting a break with the world capitalist system, presented to peripheral countries an alternative model of development which seemed peculiarly suited to their conditions and requirements. By dispossessing the propertied classes, who gathered in their hands all the surplus that was spared by the foreign connection, it could channel that surplus toward development purposes: no part of it need be wasted on unnecessary consumption, whether taking the form of imported luxury goods or of unproductive local menial services. The surplus—always directed toward accumulation—could be increased significantly, inasmuch as a different management of the economy can mobilize into productive activities the various forms of unemployment: disguised, seasonal, and outright chronic unemployment so characteristic of peripheral economies. It could be used in a much more efficient way, since the uncertainties, lack of information, lack of coordination and short-time horizons (which lead to duplicated, misplaced or unbalanced investment patterns in an atomized market economy) would be replaced in a planned economy by coordination between projects, sectors, magnitudes and flows.

The Appearance of Socialism in Developing Rather Than Developed Countries

That the first socialist revolution took place in a relatively backward country and, in the face of various potent forms of outside hostile reaction, shortly transformed it to a modern industrialized economy, revealed the true nature of the basic contradiction governing the contemporary world. It was not, as previously thought, the contradiction between *developed* forces of production and relations of production no longer capable of matching them. It was the contradiction between *underdeveloped forces of production*, potentially capable of enormous development, and the complex network of relations of production—combining *both* external and internal elements with foreign-dominated underpinnings—which held them in check. That contradiction was localized in the underdeveloped part of the world capitalist system, not in its developed part. It is there that it called for radical change of relations of production, those characteristic of the colonial social formation. Rather than rectifying, so to speak, its initial mistake, and moving to the West as it was expected to do, the socialist revolution moved more and more eastward and southward *where the tensions between the actual and the potential were greatest.*

The Situation on the Eve of the Second World War

Were we to terminate our discussion in the midst of the colonial stage of development, several conclusions would be warranted. First, it should be clear that colonialism *and* its local allies were the main obstacle to development in the dominated countries. Second, since the

colonial powers were not willing voluntarily to give up their domination, armed struggle for liberation appeared necessary to achieve that
end. Third, such a struggle would also pit some indigenous classes in
dominated countries against one another—the local allies of imperialism
(feudal classes, *compradores,* and local monopoly capitalists) siding
with the colonial powers.

The indigenous bourgeoisie was not in a position to lead the struggle
for liberation to the finish. The only classes which could present a
viable alternative with the potential of bringing it about were the
working class—to the extent it existed at all—and the peasants. These
groups are crucial because the only satisfactory domestic alternative to
colonial rule is one in which the actual producing classes assume control
over all aspects of the economic process and decide how its fruits—
especially any surplus—should be used.

All colonial, semicolonial and dependent countries are potentially
ripe for following this revolutionary path, irrespective of the level of
development of their productive forces, or of the relative weight of
their working class. Whether a revolution will take place or not depends
on the existence of a revolutionary organization capable of perceiving
the proper strategy for each revolutionary phase, of serving it with the
proper tactics, of transmitting this knowledge to the potentially revolutionary forces within society in terms which can be understood by
them and which correspond with their preoccupations and aspirations,
and of gaining their trust and being able to work with and mobilize them.

Although external conditions are an important factor in determining
the path and outcome of a revolutionary struggle, during the colonial
era the main role had to be that of national liberation movements, each
doing battle on its own ground, in relative isolation from the others.
The Third World had not yet made its appearance as an organized group.
There were various colonies, semicolonies and dependencies, each tied
to the center or to the particular part of the center which dominated it,
but with no horizontal connections among them. Since none of them,
by definition, was master of its own house, a unified or synchronized
economic struggle was not within reach.

The Post-World War II Transformation
of the World Capitalist System

Within the last two or three decades, however, the world capitalist
system has undergone a considerable transformation, both at the center

and in the periphery. That transformation calls for a corresponding modification of the above-cited premises, especially as they affect the Third World revolt. *The key to that transformation is what we have have termed the shift from a colonial mode of surplus transfer to the capitalist mode, which has its roots in economic constraints.*

No doubt the major factor which brought about this transformation was the manifest determination of the dominated peoples to bring colonial rule to an end, and the support national liberation movements were getting from socialist countries. It must, however, also be recognized that the United States, in particular, hastened the end of colonial rule in its traditional form and, in doing that, gave that transformation in many countries the twist it has taken: away from socialist transformation and toward a greater integration at the lower end of the scale—in a full-fledged world capitalist system. In this, the United States was sometimes unwittingly helped by the underestimation of some socialist countries of the revolutionary potential of the periphery.

The United States was mainly motivated by two considerations. First, a growing realization that a protracted armed struggle for national liberation is likely to lead to the radicalization of the masses. The second consideration is the disparity in the development of forces of production between the center and the periphery, and the form that development has taken in the former, especially in the United States itself, as compared, for example, with old colonial countries. Given a favorable class alignment within peripheral countries, the spontaneous tendencies within the world capitalist system in its new form would lead to a greater flow of surplus to the center without the provocative, potentially dangerous, and costly trappings which went with the colonial form. This new aspect will be considered in the following section.

The analogy between the latest stage of the development of the world capitalist system and the development of capitalism on a micro (that is, national) level, however, goes beyond the replacement of one mode of surplus flow by another. In the same way as it happened at the micro level, political power at the world level became at once more centralized and eventually more democratic. Global institutions begin to appear which, alongside various forms of common economic action, can be used by the periphery for gaining a better position within the system, in the same way as they are used by the working classes in micro-capitalist systems. This aspect, which we call global social democracy, will be examined in a third section, in order to see both its potentialities and limitations.

That analogy, however, should not be pushed to extremes. A world economic system, by definition, is much more complex than a simple one, and its transformations can be much more varied. Two possibilities remain open to peripheral social formations which are closed to the working classes within a micro-social formation. One of them is to opt out altogether from the system, or at least to keep at a distance from it, in what has come to be called auto-centered, self-reliant development. The other is to devise common lines of independent action: the equivalent, not of trade unionism, but of tried and mostly failed nineteenth-century producers' cooperatives, self-help schemes, etc., in what has come to be called collective self-reliance. The needs, potentialities, and limitations of these aspects of the Third World revolt will be examined in the fourth and fifth sections.

THE BASIC TENDENCIES OF THE CONTEMPORARY WORLD CAPITALIST ECONOMIC SYSTEM

The Effects of the Contemporary Technical-Scientific Revolution on Center-Periphery Relationships

The enormous leap in productive forces during the last two or three decades, unparalleled in its impact on human affairs except perhaps by the early development of agriculture, need not be dwelt upon here. Certain features, however, need to be underlined, since they explain the increasing imbalance of power and disparity in income between the central and peripheral parts of the world economic system, as well as the new pattern of international division of labor which is gradually replacing the old one, with its new peripheral class structures and class alliances. These features, constituting together what has aptly been termed the technical-scientific revolution, can be listed as follows:

a) the enormous quantitative growth of scientific knowledge;

b) the qualitatively new spheres to which scientific knowledge has been extending;

c) the equally rapid advance in technology and the equally broad front on which this advance is taking place; and

d) most important of all, the increasingly close connection between science and technology as manifested in the unprecedented speed with which scientific discoveries are translated into technical innovations and the interdependence between scientific advance and technical advance.

The implications of this technical-scientific revolution for the under-developed part of the world capitalist system have been—and are still—enormous. Leaving aside the socialist countries, the technological base sufficient to carry the weight of modern scientific research exists only in the developed part of that system. The oft-noted brain drain from the periphery to the center certainly supports this pattern. As a result, the capitalist centers now have a new monopoly position vis-à-vis the periphery which is more dangerous, concentrated and intractable than the old monopoly of manufacturing, heavy industry, and capital goods. The new monopoly exists in such fields as electronics, automation, cybernetics and synthetics, and still more important, in general scientific advance and technological innovation. Because that monopoly is so great, self-protecting and self-perpetuating, it is a de facto monopoly, economic rather than legal, which need not rely on force though both force and law may play their part. It calls forth a new pattern of division of labor between the scientific research and industrial technology centers and the periphery which imports their achievements. The old international division of labor—except in the case of strategic raw materials or specific agricultural products for which no economic substitute is readily available—becomes neither necessary nor, in some cases, desirable.

The pattern of unequal exchange characterizing the colonialist mode can be maintained even when the two kinds of goods exchanged between the center and the periphery are produced under capitalist (cost-accounting) conditions, so long as the goods exported by the center to the periphery embody a higher "capital-cost" element (as is the case with capital goods, usually the product of heavy industry, and of certain luxury goods, embodying, as well, up-to-date technical innovations). In fact, to understand the nature of this type of unequal exchange, it must be recognized that "knowledge" enters with an ever-increasing weight as an element of cost, with as little justification as far as society is concerned (though not for the purposes of resource allocation) as capital itself, both being merely the expression of a certain pattern of social division of labor—hence, of class stratification—within the advanced society. No permanent cost is incurred in the case of knowledge beyond the differential remunerations which might be necessary to secure and maintain the required training and application. Technological knowledge is now being marketed to peripheral countries as a separate commodity, with a price of its own. Whether it is sold as an element in the cost of other commodities or as a separate commodity, the price at which it is being sold goes far beyond its cost to the society producing it and is becoming an increasingly important element in the increasing differentiation between the center and the periphery.

In the same context, organizational knowledge is no less important than technical knowledge, especially of how the various parts of a branch or sector or aspect of the world economy function and fit together. The latter type of knowledge is most effective in securing surplus in three fields: world commerce; world finance, traditionally the almost exclusive preserve of the advanced center; and multinational business, where technical, organizational, and economic knowledge, research and development, and, of course, power of decision are concentrated in the center and used to its advantage.

Under these conditions, then, the old type of international division is no longer necessary for securing a flow of surplus from the periphery to the center. It is also no longer desirable as an exclusive form, for the great expansion of heavy, capital-goods industries in the center creates a marketing problem similar to that created by the growth of manufacturing industry in a previous age.

The Spontaneous Reproduction of Underdevelopment Gradually Replaces Its Production. The Appearance of the Peripheral Social Formation

Two other major developments were instrumental in bringing about this new pattern of international division of labor. One was the shift in power within the center itself, and the other, not unrelated to it, was the pattern of industrialization chosen by the peripheral countries themselves, or rather by the new classes which rose to power in them in the wake of the victory of the national liberation movements.

Long before the middle of the century, the United States had emerged as the most powerful economy within the center; World War II merely gave it the political predominance which corresponds to that position. It had its own enormous sources of raw materials, its highly developed agriculture and its extensive internal market; hence, it was less dependent on a monopoly position in foreign trade. Its scientific-technical base was so far advanced, even in comparison with other central capitalist countries, that it could well afford to relinquish a monopoly position in the traditional industrial consumption goods. What it needed most was an outlet for its capital-goods industries, preferably going hand in hand with an outlet for investment. This ideal combination would be achieved through the activities of multinational firms, establishing and controlling manufacturing industries abroad (beside, of course, the other traditional extractive activities) and supplying them with the necessary capital goods and know-how. But capital goods could be equally supplied to peripheral countries even where the multinationals could not secure partial or complete control, whenever it was a good or a necessary risk to allow dependent local capitalism to develop. Because of these reasons, the United States sometimes looked with favor at the disintegration of the old colonial system and the feudal and semifeudal classes and modes or production associated with it— provided, of course, that the alternative was a congenial one: *a peripheral, not an independent socioeconomic formation.*

Three new varieties of peripheral socioeconomic formations emerged (which, while still moving within the orbit of the world capitalist system, succeeded the old colonial social formation): neocolonial, liberal-capitalist, and bureaucratic-capitalist. They all have this in common: they are drawn, wittingly or unwittingly, toward a closer and closer integration into the world capitalist system; they are, to a greater or lesser degree, becoming part of the new pattern of international division of labor; they foster a certain degree of dependent capitalist development; and they are the vehicle at differing levels for the *spontaneous reproduction of underdevelopment.*

The Neocolonial Variety

A neocolonial system is one in which foreign capital, especially in the form of multinational firms, dominates the economy of the country. It differs from the old colonial system in that foreign political domination is neither directly nor totally exercised; hence, a certain degree of freedom to maneuver between capital belonging to various central countries is open to local interests. Nationalization of foreign companies, even on an extensive scale, is not incompatible with such a system.

In the neocolonial social formation, industry, aside from traditional extractive and primary processing destined for export, is usually limited to simple manufacturing processes serving the local market or, at most, neighboring markets: food, beverages, textiles, footwear, soap and other consumer goods. Intermediate goods such as cement, fertilizers and chemical products are sometimes ventured upon, but durable consumer goods are very underdeveloped—that is why, in the first place, an old colonial system is replaced by a neocolonial one instead of by either of the two other alternatives considered below. Apparent power is held by a local *state* bureaucracy which replaces the old colonial administration. It is mostly drawn from the petty bourgeoisie, which also spreads out into the professions, from which it was previously barred or crowded out, and is sometimes called upon to perform ceremonial or public relations functions on the boards of foreign firms or in their administration. It provides a national facade for the neocolonial system. This facade was often precision-engineered by the old colonial power, which carefully groomed the future "national" leaders, sometimes going to the extent of thoughtfully equipping them with the mandatory prison terms or banishments. The "fruits of independence," consisting mainly of various kinds of occupational privileges, fall essentially into the hands of this petty bourgeoisie, including part of the intelligentisia. By satisfying the economic ambitions of these groups, their revolutionary potential was removed, a critically important development.

The neocolonial situation is more likely to arise where neither a national bourgeoisie, nor a significant working class was allowed to develop and where independence was readily granted or easily won. The political form it assumes can be either semiliberal or, more often, authoritarian, in which military coups based on personal intrigue and ambition succeed one another, but in both cases there is ruthless suppression of the Left. A working class develops only to the extent that foreign capital finds it advantageous to develop industry. The main source of surplus, besides extracting and simple manufacturing industries wherever they exist, is still the countryside which is called upon to increase its exports to the world market in order to provide the expanding local bureaucracy with the foreign currency needed to finance its imported luxury goods. The overall result is the increasing poverty of the peasantry and nomads; their increased exposure—since extensive agriculture, deforestation, and soil erosion on a large scale accompany these developments—to climatic risks such as drought which the traditional balanced way of cultivation and the habit of household or communal stockkeeping used to alleviate; their reluctance to pursue agricultural activity or to put much effort into it, since its pattern is not their traditional one but a pattern imposed on them; increased migration to the towns where they become marginalized and drawn into unproductive employment; and, most important of all, the failure of food production to keep up with the increase in population or for food production actually to decrease, thus creating a new kind of dependency: dependency on food imports.

The Liberal-Capitalist Variety

A liberal-capitalist system is one in which the main modern means of production are privately owned and power is in the hands of the local bourgeoisie. Liberalism here refers to the way the economy is run, but not to the way the political system functions: political liberalism is such a rare and vanishing species in Third World countries. This is not because Third World people are "not ripe for democracy" or that authoritarianism is traditional there. It is because, in view of the basic contradiction which can only be solved by a thoroughgoing socialist system, political liberalism is certain to lead to a rapid growth of mass movements which eventually bring about socialism. The economy in a liberal-capitalist system is run according to the well-known principles of free enterprise. They do not exclude various forms of state intervention, the existence of a public sector, or even the exercise of some sort of planning—all of which are used in the long-term interests of capital. The latter include creating certain conditions favorable to growth, undertaking certain economic activities which would be unprofitable for private capital, gaining a more powerful position vis-à-vis foreign capital, favoring one sector of the bourgeoisie (the one that is more directly associated with power) against the others, and conceding certain advantages to the masses or sections thereof whenever that would be a more suitable and practical way of meeting an otherwise acute class conflict.

The relationship of a liberal-capitalist system with foreign capital is a complex love-hate relationship. It is the new pattern of international division of labor, it must be remembered, which, by allowing industrialization of a certain kind to take place, is giving the bourgeoisie in Third World countries a new lease on life. That type of industrialization, at the same time, accords well with the basic tendencies and mechanisms of liberal capitalism (as well as those, as we shall see, of bureaucratic capitalism); hence, a common ground with foreign capital is established. But it is the ground for a game in which the stakes are the degree of direct involvement of foreign capital in running the economy, and the terms upon which loans, capital goods, technology and expertise are obtained from it. It is a game in which foreign capital is the ultimate winner—on all fronts. Since, by its very class nature, the local bourgeoisie is unwilling to quit the game, it seeks a modification of its rules in association with like-minded and similarly positioned Third World countries, though some of them may have different internal social structures. Hence, its enthusiastic support for the call for a new international economic order (NIEO).

The reasons for complaint against the old order, and the areas for modification, are manifold: deteriorating terms of trade, aggravated by the export of inflation from the center; the harsh terms of foreign loans; the increasing burden of foreign debt; the exorbitant price and selective nature of technological transfer; the control by the capitalist center of world finance, commerce and transport; the barriers raised against Third World exports; etc. The grievances against the rules of the game are real enough, but their roots must be located, not only in the nature of the world economic system, but also in the policies pursued by the ruling classes in Third World countries. These policies are symbolized though not exhaustively described by the strategy of industrialization through import substitution.

Industrialization through import substitution is the normal choice of the liberal bourgeoisie in an underdeveloped country. Since its activities are guided by market demand, it naturally opts for those industries which produce goods for which a market already exists. All it needs is to protect this market from foreign competition. In the interwar period, wherever the local bourgeoisie managed to embark on an industrialization course, the industries chosen were those producing goods for popular consumption: textiles, footwear, food processing, beverages, etc. These usually used local raw material, their capital requirements were relatively modest, their technology was relatively simple; hence, they created a certain amount of industrial employment and had a beneficial effect on the balance of payments. After the Second World War, a new mode of consumption, originating in the highly developed capitalist countries and symbolized by the motorcar and by durable household goods, had begun to filter down and spread wherever a local bourgeoisie was growing. Industrialization through import substitution was centered around industries producing these goods: an industrialization determined by an imported pattern of consumption and an unequal pattern of income distribution. The new industries, in contrast to the old ones, were characterized by large capital requirements; by reliance on imported raw materials, intermediate goods and capital-intensive, relatively advanced technology; and by their large energy requirements, whether at the stage of production or at the stage of consumption. Thus, it was mostly through importation from developed countries, and that in the field of luxury consumption goods, and not through a self-generating process, that the technical achievements of these countries became available to developing countries. The imported techniques are those which were developed in response to conditions prevailing in the center, and are inappropriate—especially because of their reliance on nonlocal materials and their feeble employment-generating power—for the countries to which they are transplanted. Since their main linkages are elsewhere, in the developed centers, their spread is limited to the sector in which they are directly applied and cannot exert a positive effect on the transformation of economic structures as a whole. In addition to the immediate burden on the balance of payments, they further contribute to the deterioration of the terms of trade. *This, then, is the way the new pattern of international division of labor manifests itself: a division of labor between centers of industrial technology and scientific research, and a periphery which imports, at an ever-increasing cost, their achievements.*

The main burden of such a policy falls, not on the limited number of workers who find employment in these industries, and who manage to secure for themselves a relatively privileged position, but on the peasantry, who are called upon to pay the main cost of this distorted pattern of accumulation. They become the subject, not only of the traditional exploitation by world capitalism, but also, and increasingly so, of the local bourgeoisie. Where modern technology is also introduced in the countryside, then, as a student of the Green Revolution observed:

technology, public power and market power combine to ensure that it is the landowner who benefits from agricultural innovation. The changes which are at present occurring tend to increase the relative inequality of large sectors of the rural population and even reduce absolutely the standard of living of large sectors of the rural population . . . commercialization will tend to concentrate the function of entrepreneurship into a few hands. In the process, the peasantry will be destroyed. . . . Already there are reports from Ceylon, India, Pakistan and the Philippines of landowners evicting tenants and taking over the land themselves. Sometimes the tenants are paid a small sum of money in compensation for being evicted, and sometimes they are not. But in either case, a tenant entrepreneur is converted into a member of the proletariat, an absentee *rentier* becomes a capitalist farmer.[2]

The Bureaucratic-Capitalist Variety

A planned economy, presumably, can introduce a different pattern of industrialization. Supply can create its own demand in the sense that capital-goods industries and consumption-goods industries can be planned together as one set and synchronized in such a way that the products of the one can be used by the other. Hence, a capital-goods industry can be created which not only makes for a rapid growth of the economy, but lessens its dependency. It is on this ground, as well as on other well-known grounds, such as doing away with the wasteful consumption of the feudalists and the capitalists and increasing the surplus available for investment, that the state has been presenting itself more frequently in newly independent countries as the alternative to capitalism in running the economy. This is the *bureaucratic-capitalist* variety of the peripheral social formation. The results under this formation serve to illustrate the unfailing fact that whenever the state falls into hands other than those of the direct producers (that is, the peasants and the workers, and the intelligentsia who, not just by words and declared ideology, but by their mode of life, completely identify with them) results which are very much similar to those of liberal capitalism are obtained: the development of dependent capitalism and greater integration into the world capitalist system. This is because the alternative to the power of the direct producers, when it is not that of the traditional bourgeoisie, is that of a new class which uses its hold on the state to obtain surplus for its own purposes. That is, it feeds a pattern of consumption aped from advanced capitalist countries and pushes investment in directions which serve this pattern of consumption.

This bureaucratic bourgeoisie is different from the administrative bureaucracy which presides over a neocolonial system in that: (a) it usually gains power in the wake of a protracted national liberation struggle in which it takes a leading part; (b) it shows marked anti-imperialist tendencies which often manifest themselves in the nationalization of foreign assets; and (c) it adopts an ideology of economic growth, which it tries to foster first by using the usual methods of state intervention, then by establishing an ever-growing public sector, and, finally, by adopting some sort of planning. These policies are used, not only for their hoped-for economic results but also because they give the regime a populist, or "socialist" complexion. The public sector is first erected on the basis of nationalized foreign assets. Then it is extended to certain key branches or key activities held by the local bourgeoisie, thus bringing this ruling bureaucracy into sharp conflict with that bourgeoisie or with those sections directly affected by the nationalizations.

Planning, when it is not a mere collection of investment projects, is an imposition from above, bureaucratically conceived and bureaucratically implemented and often sabotaged by the very people entrusted with it. It essentially reflects the interests and limitations of the ruling bureaucracy. If the country is very poor, it is limited to certain investment projects in which foreign capital is induced to take interest, like tourism and extractive industries. If the country has a certain amount of economic resources, a pattern of industrialization through import substitution similar to that of the liberal system is embarked upon, leading to the same results. If, for one reason or another, such as the existence of natural resources much demanded by the world market, the country is so rich that it can afford to start both capital goods and consumption goods industries, dependency and greater integration into the world capital market would nevertheless be the ultimate result. This result occurs because that path requires heavy doses of foreign management contracts, foreign expertise, and (since the consumption industries are not directed to the basic needs of the people, and the capital goods industries are on too big a scale for their products to be absorbed by the home market) reliance on foreign markets, usually through the good offices of the foreign capital which discreetly guides this process of industrialization. In spite of their rich natural resources, countries of this third type, like the first two types, end by experiencing balance-of-payment difficulties and assuming a heavy foreign-debt burden. Tanzania under Nyerere, Egypt under Nasser, present-day Algeria and Iraq, are examples of the three types, in spite of the national sentiment and "socialistic" tendencies of their leaders.

The policy toward the peasants requires some comment. Land reform, wherever a feudal or semifeudal class exists, is introduced by such regimes, usually by stages. At the first stage its main purpose (or result) is to break the political power of the feudal and semifeudal classes and, deliberately or not, promote liberal capitalism in the countryside. At a later stage, the need to draw agricultural surplus increases, the export of modern-type durable goods proves to be illusory, and resort is made again to traditional agricultural exports or to new ones (e.g., fruit or rice instead of cotton) so as to carry the heavy burden imposed on the balance of payments by the policy of import substitution and the necessity to feed the growing cities. To get hold of that surplus, various forms of "socialization" are introduced (marketing cooperatives, production cooperatives, etc.) side by side with such devices as obligatory deliveries, fixed low prices for agricultural products, higher prices for agricultural inputs and consumption goods consumed by the peasantry. Cooperatives are in the hands of the rural bureaucracy who work in close alliance with the rich peasants. The results, as far as the poor and middle-income peasants are concerned, are similar to those obtaining under liberal capitalism, only more so, since the bureaucracy holds all the cards in its hands.

Power in a bureaucratic-capitalist system is in the hands of a certain elite, which uses state power, first to secure a privileged position for itself, based on patterns of consumption borrowed from the West. Secondly, this elite uses state power to obtain, by various unofficial ways, access to primitive accumulation. Outlets are found through the class alliance which such regimes usually maintain to invest the accumulation. These alliances are with the *kulaks* in the countryside and with certain industrial, commerical or "entrepreneurial" sectors which are protected from nationalization—under various high-sounding pretexts—in town. It is characteristic of such regimes that certain sections of the private sectors are preserved simply to siphon off surpluses collected by the public sector. Often two branches of the public sector, rather than dealing directly with each other, require the mediation of a private sector, with *personal* benefit to all concerned.

A bureaucratic-capitalist regime necessarily goes hand in hand with political authoritarianism. Political power is firmly held in the hands of the ruling bureaucracy and its class allies. Unique parties "representing all the people" are the rule. Producers' participation in management of cooperatives or enterprises may be formally introduced. "Peasants" or "workers" may even be required to form the majority of their boards. It is no accident, however, that wherever such participation exists, a class struggle is waged around the definition of a peasant or a worker. The ruling bureaucracy usually denies the very existence of classes, or in accordance with the ethic of "African socialism" or "Arab socialism," etc., insists that anyone who is engaged in agriculture is a peasant, and anyone who receives a salary or wages "from the president to the street-sweeper" is a worker. The practical result is that these boards are kept firmly in the hands of the bureaucracy and its class allies. This can be explained by the fact that the bureaucracy, not directly connected with the process of production, tenaciously keeps state power in its hands, since this is its only source of privileges and of "primitive accumulation."

This, however, is only the immediate explanation. The ultimate one must be sought in the relation of this bureaucracy with the outer world, in its internal class alliances, and more specifically, in the role it plays in relation to the internal class struggle at various junctures. This interpretation is corroborated by the ease with which—despite much thunder and lightning—one kind of capitalism transforms itself into the other: e.g., Egypt moving from bureaucratic capitalism to liberal capitalism while India was moving under Indira Gandhi in the opposite direction. *The two systems may be different in form and class structure; they are similar in basic tendencies.* What initially directs one country toward one form or the other, and what afterward makes for a change of form, is very much relevant to this chapter. It cannot at present receive the attention it deserves.

The Bureaucratic-Capitalist, Not Noncapitalist, Road of Development

One of the reasons for the existence or the maintenance—while it lasted—of the bureaucratic-capitalist form in so many developing countries is the support given to it by socialist countries. Such support arose because of certain habitual patterns of thought: (1) the belief that the main content of the contemporary epoch is the transformation to socialism; and (2) an underestimation of the revolutionary potential of peripheral countries resulting from the old belief that only a developed working class can lead a socialist revolution. Hence, there was a tendency to look favorably on any system which started a vigorous policy of industrialization and a belief that closer relations with socialist countries can somehow bring about some form of socialistic transformation. By supporting such regimes, the socialist countries gave them a certain degree of independence vis-à-vis the capitalist center and, more importantly, also vis-à-vis their own masses.

In the long run, the outcome of such regimes is capitalist, not noncapitalist, development. Capitalist development is proceeding both on the national level, and on the level of the world economic system. One of the manifestations of this double phenomenon is the equally double phenomenon of increasing inequality inside the developing countries *and* between these countries and the developed centers. The original capitalist countries themselves started with a similarly increasing inequality, which tended to decrease at a later stage due to the operation of social democracy within their borders. Whether the worldwide increasing inequality can also be modified by some form of global social democracy will be examined in the following section.

GLOBAL SOCIAL DEMOCRACY

Social Democracy at the National Level

In contrast to feudal society, power in a *national* capitalist system becomes concentrated, and so do certain economic functions, such as the creation of money and control of credit. Though economic constraints govern the relations between bourgeoisie and the working class, these relations operate within a certain legal framework which defines the nature of the system. A central state apparatus appears, which works in the main to maintain the power and further the interests of the bourgeoisie, the dominant class in a capitalist system. In a modern advanced capitalist system, a system of representative democracy gradually develops. The working class makes use of this representative democracy, as well as the other forms of direct *economic* action, such as strikes, to improve its position within that system, *but not to change its nature.* Social democracy becomes a system of *class alliance* between the bourgeoisie and the more privileged sections of the working class. Because of the enormous profits it draws from the periphery, the bourgeoisie can afford to make important concessions to privileged sections of its own working class, although, of course, it is not above using the periphery (e.g., importing labor, exporting certain manufacturing industries to the periphery where labor is cheaper and more docile) when that class becomes uppish and demanding. The fact that the working class at the center also derives certain direct advantages from the center-periphery relationship, such as cheap energy and foodstuffs, also cements that class alliance.

Similar Tendencies at the Level of the World Capitalist System

With the transformation of the *world* capitalist system, especially since the Second World War, from a system based on institutionalized force to one based on economic constraints, similar tendencies are at present manifesting themselves at the global level. Instead of "multiple centers" characterizing the classical period of colonialism, each with its own jealously guarded preserve of a periphery, a more or less unified center has emerged of which the embodiment is the rise to hegemonical power of the United States. No doubt, contradictions do still exist between the advanced capitalist countries (especially between the much more advanced United States and the rest of the center). The intracenter secondary contradictions within the modern world capitalist system are overshadowed, first by the contradictions with the emerging socialist system, but, much more importantly, with the periphery of that capitalist system. Concerted, centralized action with correspondingly centralized institutions is resorted to by the now largely unified center at the military level, at the political level, and on the economic level. The centralized, or at least concerted, action at the economic level has a double function: one is to combat the latent tendencies of the system toward periodic crises and depressions and long-term stagnation; the other is to increase the flow of surplus from the periphery to the center. Nowhere is the centralized economic power and action of the center—vis-à-vis the periphery—more exercised and felt than in such "international" institutions as the International Monetary Fund (IMF) and the World Bank. The activities of these international institutions reinforce the present system of international division of labor, *both* in its old form and in its new form, whichever is the more appropriate for the developed center in the given conditions of the concerned developing country.

Along with this process of centralization of certain strategic economic functions within the world capitalist system, an embryonic world state apparatus and an embryonic political representation system are beginning to make their appearance, characteristically enough, as part of the post-World War II arrangements sponsored chiefly by the United States—with the "tyranny of the majority" and "irresponsible block voting" having taken an unexpected and disconcerting turn during the last few years. With the single exception of UNCTAD—where Third World countries managed to establish for themselves both a forum where their grievances are aired and a technical secretariat where their problems are given special attention—the United Nations Secretariat and its specialized agencies are essentially dominated by the metropolitan center. The executive branch of this embryonic world government is headed by the Security Council, where the superpowers, through the power of veto, have the final say.

It is a different story within the United Nations General Assembly, the political representation branch of the emerging system. There the Third World countries are in the majority and are using this majority to present such declarations as their conception of a new international economic order. The content and impact of the declarations and resolutions emanating from the General Assembly deserve close analysis. For the moment, it is sufficient to remark that little in the way of practical, immediately applicable results has been achieved.

Although—objectively and in the last analysis—the movement for the NIEO forms part of the Third World revolution, it is also part of the process of the transformation of the world capitalist system from the phase of institutionalized violence to the phase of economic constraints. That process is leading, among other things, to: (1) a certain kind of capitalist development *within* the peripheral countries themselves—a dependent, if rapid, capitalist development accompanied by a greater development of productive forces, a greater differentiation between the rich and the poor and a greater marginalization of the masses, etc.; (2) a greater—not lesser—integration of the peripheral countries into the world capitalist system; and (3) a certain mobility within the world capitalist system allowing certain developing countries to occupy intermediate positions, sometimes termed subimperialism.

Nothing illustrates the equivocal nature of the call for a NIEO as well as the current attempts at enacting internationally binding legal rules on such matters as the nationalization of foreign assets, TNC's activities, patent rights, technological transfers, the use of seabeds, etc. The attempts represent both a movement toward a global legal framework for the present phase of the world capitalist system, corresponding to the legal framework of national capitalist systems, and a struggle by Third World countries to secure for themselves through legislative action "a fair deal" within that system.

Among the leaders of the call for a NIEO are often those who, within their own countries, are preserving or introducing neocolonial, traditional-capitalist or bureaucratic-capitalist systems. Though it is the masses in all Third World countries who pay the penalty for the existing IEO, and who would benefit most from a really new international economic order, they are seldom allowed to take an active part in the struggle. Getting them involved, that is, educating them as to the nature of the system, would necessarily also call into question the *internal economic order*. At best, they are kept in the state of enthusiastic spectators of a drama in which they play no part, of repeaters of slogans of which the import and direct connection with their day-to-day lives are not explained: The enthusiasm of some leaders for a NIEO may be partially motivated by the desire to remedy the consequences of policies of their own which they were unable or unwilling to foresee, and by the equally futile desire to replace the old international division of labor by a new one which is basically similar in long-run results. For example, some wish to replace an industrialization based on import substitution by an industrialization based on export promotion, instead of an industrialization intended to meet the basic needs of their own people and to provide the necessary industrial means for transforming agriculture—as well as such other aims as to create productive employment for the increasing population. There can be many new international economic orders. The version that some leaders are really clamoring for is not *essentially* different from the present one, since it is based on the greater integration—though on more favorable terms—into the world capitalist system.

The latest version of the NIEO, now more appropriately called reformed international economic order (RIEO), is not *essentially* opposed by the center, or at least by the more forward-looking sections of it. The various forms of confrontation and dilatory obstructions are in some cases manifestations of short-sighted or sectoral opposition within the center to the RIEO. But in other cases these are negotiating strategems used to obtain overall better terms for the center; to effect a gradual, orderly transformation; or to ensure that the "right" kind of Third World countries, or of Third World political regimes, are the ones to which the RIEO is (selectively) applied. It is on the basis of this RIEO that a new class alliance is emerging at the level of the world capitalist system between the center of that system and the bourgeoisie of Third World countries. This class alliance is the manifestation, on the political level, of global social democracy.

Global Social Democracy and Third World Trade Unionism

The essence of global social democracy, it has been maintained so far, is the preservation of the basic principles of the present world capitalist system while improving the position of Third World countries within that system. One of these is on the political front—the formation of blocks and alliances and the use of various international organizations and instances. The other is on the economic front— various forms of collective Third World economic action which correspond, on the national level, to trade unionism. That latter aspect of the Third World revolt is best exemplified by Organization of Petroleum Exporting Countries (OPEC) action, so far the most spectacular and successful example of Third World trade unionism, and one hailed as the first decision affecting the world economy taken in the last five centuries outside the Western metropolitan center. A lengthy defense of OPEC and OPEC-type action need not be undertaken here. In all respects OPEC action is justifiable and effective. It also is beneficial, not only to the oil-exporting countries themselves, but to the Third World at large. But this is so only at a certain level of analysis. At another level, the overall impact of OPEC action on Third World long-run prospects may acquire a different complexion. A considerable part of the enormous surpluses at the disposal of certain oil-exporting countries is being used to reinforce the domination of the center over the periphery, to influence directly the internal social structures and regimes of at least some Third World countries and, more generally, to further the greater integration of the Third World—hence, the continuation of dependent development—into the world capitalist system. No doubt the latter results are due to the concentration of enormous surpluses in the hands of those few who preside over archaic social structures and regimes, kept in existence by the strategy of the center itself. The formation of other Third World producers' associations dealing with less-strategic and quantitatively less-important export raw materials would not necessarily lead to similar developments. Nevertheless, the OPEC action, with its contradictory aspects, singularly symbolizes the extremely complex nature of the Third World revolt.

Can Global Social Democracy Raise the Standard of Living of Third World Masses?

The main content of the demands for a NIEO, then, is the metamorphosis of the world capitalist system into its third stage of reliance on economic constraints mitigated by some form of global social democracy. An important question, however, needs to be answered. Granted that global social democracy does not aim at a radical transformation of the world capitalist system, can it nevertheless raise the standard of living of the great masses of people living in the Third World? After all, this is what internal social democracy achieved on a national scale in the advanced capitalist center; so why should it not succeed in the same way on a global level?

An affirmative answer to that question requires that two conditions be satisfied. First, Third World countries must be in a position vis-à-vis the world capitalist center as strong as that of the trade unions inside the advanced capitalist center itself. Second, the governments of the former countries must be willing (or forced) to pass on the gains so obtained from a modified (but not radically transformed) IEO to the majority of their own populations.

A number of factors seem to battle against the realization of the first condition. Neither in the short nor in the long run can the bourgeoisie in the advanced capitalist centers do without their own working class. Once the workers get organized (and failing a transfer of power to themselves), the two parties have to negotiate some sort of social contract. Not so in the case of the center and periphery of the world capitalist system, at least when long-run prospects are considered. In the short run, it is true, the center may be dependent on Third World countries for essential supplies of raw materials and energy and certain kinds of foodstuffs. If these countries act in unison, they can modify the terms of trade, and obtain other concessions. In the long run, however, the center seems to be much less vulnerable. It has, can maintain, and can reinforce the monopoly of technical progress—that is, so long as the periphery continues to develop in a dependent manner. It can use its technical superiority for the development of alternative techniques or sources of supply, such as through the exploitation of the oceans. The center has less incentive to meet the demands of the periphery halfway than the central bourgeoisie had when dealing with its own working class, since at the basis of the latter compromise was the establishment of the internal social-democratic class alliance, *essentially financed from the surplus drawn from the periphery*. A similar alliance on a world scale—that is, between the center and the whole, not just sections, of the periphery of the world capitalist system—is almost a contradiction in terms, since there is no other planet from which to draw the enormous surpluses necessary to finance it. No doubt, a "positive-sum game" can be conceived, permitting the formation of a real global "alliance for progress," but for this game to be played, a totally different type of socioeconomic organization would be required, *both* in the center and in the periphery, entailing a totally different type of world economic system.

Even if the Third World builds up a sufficiently stable and strong position to persuade the advanced center to accept a compromise, it is far from certain that the modified international economic order (better terms of trade, alleviation of the debt burden, access of Third World manufacture to advanced markets, etc.) will bring about a long-term improvement in the living conditions of the masses, parallel to that experienced by the national working classes in advanced capitalist countries. It would certainly improve the position of the Third World bourgeoisie and other privileged classes. It may allow these classes to develop the national economy of Third World countries. *But development is not synonymous with raising the standard of living of the masses.* That depends on what type of development the national economy is experiencing. Because of favorable historical conditions, capitalist development in the center was able, through the social-democratic alliance, to raise the standard of living of the majority of the population. Capitalist development in the periphery does not enjoy the same advantages—hence, cannot offer the same compromise. On the contrary: it is capitalist development within capitalist development, burdening the masses of its population with the double weight of the world capitalist system at large and that of itself.

The Struggle for a NIEO

Current efforts to change the present IEO should be encouraged and strengthened. They have three important potential benefits:

1. By drawing attention to the nature and shortcomings of the present IEO they provide a healthy climate of international public opinion which allows important internal transformations to take place in those Third World countries where objective and subjective conditions are ripe for them, without brutal interference from outside forces.

2. Whether by their successes or by their failures, these efforts perform an important educative function, inasmuch as they give all peoples a peculiarly clear insight as to the fundamental causes of underdevelopment, the nature of the forces associated with it or working to combat it, and the proper means to combat it.

3. Not least of all, such efforts to change the present IEO can secure to Third World countries real economic benefits which—marginal as these benefits are bound to remain, considering the present balance of forces and pending the successive internal transformations which will be referred to below—these countries can ill afford to ignore.

But having said this, the essential fact must be faced that the present struggle for a NIEO will not lead to a qualitative transformation of that

order. This is because, now and for the foreseeable future, the nation
(and not the world at large) will remain the basic unit for consequential
revolutionary action. Though underdevelopment, as we have seen,
emerged essentially under the influence of external factors, overcoming
it can take place only as a result of such revolutionary action operating
at the national level, complemented by concerted action directed toward
economic cooperation between Third World countries themselves. This
is the long-term main import of what before we called the basic contradiction operating within Third World countries between their potential
productive forces and their present relations of production. These two
aspects of the Third World revolt, relating to necessary internal transformations and to intra-Third World cooperation, will be considered in
the following two sections.

THE STRATEGY OF AUTO-CENTERED, SELF-RELIANT DEVELOPMENT

A Coherent Whole, Not a Collection of Arbitrary Measures

It will have become apparent from previous discussion that the
strategy of auto-centered, self-reliant development is not a collection
of arbitrary, isolated measures, each to be taken or left at will. It forms
a coherent whole, the main elements of which can only be touched
upon here. The cornerstone of this strategy is that economic activity
should be geared to the satisfaction of the basic needs of the masses—
both material and moral. From this basic premise follows a whole set
of propositions.

We must first recognize that the masses themselves are the best
arbiters of their own basic needs and the order of priority in which
these needs should be satisfied. Not only this, but that for the masses
to have and exercise that right of decision in itself satisfies a basic moral
precept: the freedom of choice. Needed moral rights, however, extend
far beyond that of choosing among various patterns of consumption.
Much more importantly, they cover such things as the right to work,
that is, in the present context, the right to feel that one is a needed
productive member of the community, and the right to have a say as to
what pattern of production should be socially promoted. That latter
right means, for example, the producer's right to decide whether he
prefers a society where he must spend all his work life tending a machine

in an uncongenial environment under the watchful eyes of an overseer, or whether he prefers a different pattern of work, of cooperation and of social division of labor which would develop all his potentialities and make him feel whole and human. Recognition of that elementary right, not only to the privileged minority but to the majority of the population is impossible in capitalist ideology because that recognition undermines the very basis of capitalist society: its class division and the complete subjection of the process of social division of labor to the blind forces of the market. It would mean the replacement of that society by another type where all men are *equally* free to reflect, deliberate and decide on what type of society they want to build. It means, in other words, crossing the line between man's submission to alien and alienating forces and the conscious use of these forces to foster man's—*all men's*—freely chosen ends. It should be clear, then, that if these basic needs or basic rights are to be satisfied, all men must have equal rights over the productive resources of society.

It has been pointed out that accumulation, the most important source of increased productivity, is essentially a process of reorganization of the social division of labor. Labor is the most abundant "factor" in many Third World countries, especially the "overpopulated" ones. But even in Third World countries where labor is not so abundant, relative to other resources, it is to a considerable extent unemployed, under-employed, or employed in socially unproductive activities. Contemporary experience shows that in both types of Third World countries (here again with the exception of sparsely populated oil-rich countries) capitalist development is congenitally incapable of mobilizing all that "surplus" labor available to society, let alone canalizing it in the right direction—that of satisfying the basic needs of the population. On the contrary, it is inextricably linked with mounting labor surpluses in the countryside, mass migration to towns, and the swelling army of the unemployed in both.

There is still another important dimension to the question of mobilization of productive resources resulting from effective social control over the means of production. What is really involved here is much more than simply finding a slot for everybody in the productive apparatus of the community. It is, in addition, the mobilization both of the freely given, consciously developed enthusiasm and the creative abilities of the productive masses. Neither enthusiasm nor creative abilities are, of course, lacking in capitalist societies. They do exist, sometimes in ample measure (though not always of the desirable type), but only at the level of entrepreneurs and perhaps also at the higher level of management. They do not exist to any considerable extent, beyond the narrow confines of wage-rate incentives, at the level of the great majority of producers, where fear of dismissal or of sanctions is the dominant incentive to "stick it out."

In a different type of socioeconomic organization, though direct personal-gain incentives would not be dismissed offhand, other types of social incentives play an increasingly important role. To begin with there is the consciousness of producers that they are not toiling to amass private fortunes for the bosses, but for themselves, in the larger sense of the word. Then there is the fact that the organization of work as well as its aims, is not imposed from above but is the result of multiple processes of democratic deliberation. Third, there is the continuous urge and opportunity to find new ways, more efficient and at the same time more congenial, of doing the same thing, since there is no separation between conception and execution: the same people fulfill both functions either concurrently or on an interchangeable basis. Thus, the man who tends the machine would know from firsthand experience where it can be improved, and the man who conceives the improvement knows in the same way how it feels to work it. And even if the new methods lead to a lessening of tempo or a more relaxed atmosphere of work, this is not necessarily a social loss, given a sane calculation of what constitutes benefits and what constitutes cost.

Effective social control over means of production is a necessary precondition for the full liberation of the enthusiasm and creative abilities of the masses of producers for still another reason: it is impossible to give free play to these forces without a corresponding national organization of existing production units, particularly in agriculture—a task in its turn impossible to achieve within the existing pattern of property relationships in most Third World countries. Ingenuous or naive experiments with auto-centered, self-reliant development schemes show that all attempts at engaging the peasants' enthusiasm, organizational ability, work capacity and creativeness for communal productive endeavors on a purely local or partial basis which do not take into account the all-persuasive surrounding socioeconomic conditions are doomed to failure or frustration. This is true, however high they may raise the banner of voluntary, popular-based, grass-roots socialism. To cite a few examples: schemes undertaken by the Arab Socialist Union in its heyday around the middle of the Sixties in the villages of lower and upper Egypt; by European idealists in the Waneng Hill village of Botswana; or by Chinese-sponsored or World Bank-sponsored rural development projects in middle Casamance, Senegal.

The most important reason, however, why effective social control over the means of production is a precondition for a strategy of auto-centered, self-reliant development is that pursuing such a strategy, given the initial situation prevailing in Third World countries, requires major structural changes in the economy and in society—an impossible feat to achieve without that control. It is well known, for example, that many Third World countries are becoming more and more food deficient, relying on the highly industrialized countries for meeting their food requirements—in spite of the fact that a high percentage of their productive population is engaged in agriculture and that accessible arable lands may exist in abundance. Rectifying this situation may require the breaking up of big estates and the regrouping of inefficient small-holdings in peasants' cooperatives. The results would be to re-orient agriculture from producing raw materials for the world market to the production of foodstuffs and needed local industrial inputs on the one hand, and to raise productive efficiency on the other hand. Industry in its turn would be required to produce basic consumption goods, in particular those needed by the rural population, as well as the inputs needed to raise agricultural efficiency. Certain proportions and balance have to be maintained between the respective rates of growth of industry and agriculture and of the capital-goods and consumption-goods sectors. In highly developed capitalist countries, the market mechanism can be relied upon to introduce such marginal structural changes as are called for, though of course not without its particular type of crisis and penalties. In Third World countries, where fundamental structural changes are indispensable, no such role can be expected from the market mechanism. Central planning is required, not only to initiate and carry out these changes in a balanced way, but to initiate and carry them out at all. Central planning which aims at introducing major structural changes geared to the satisfaction of the needs of the masses cannot be exercised without effective social control over the means of production, that is, control by those producing masses themselves. This, however, is an extremely important and complex subject which cannot be fully explored here.

Auto-Centered, Self-Reliant Development
Does Not Mean Autarky

Control is all the more necessary if a Third World country is to achieve, maintain, and consolidate its economic independence vis-a-vis the outside world. There is no doubt that a strategy of auto-centered, self-reliant development does imply a definite degree of keeping one's distance from the world economy; of "delinking" from it, even, if necessary (that is, if forced to do so), of opting out of it. But it does not mean autarky; nor does it mean ignorance of, or ignoring, the advantages of the international division of labor. It simply is a recognition of the facts that, under present conditions, the IEO is such that it works mainly to the advantage of highly developed metropolitan countries and to the detriment of underdeveloped peripheral countries. The oft-proclaimed and real advantages of the international division of labor cannot be shared by all countries unless that order is fundamentally changed. Furthermore, fundamental changes in that order are not likely to be forthcoming in the near future either as a result of the concerted action of Third World countries, or as a result of negotiated agreements between Third World and advanced metropolitan countries.

Accordingly, rather than just lament the present IEO, the best that each developing country can do for itself is to set its own house in order. Not only will this reordering create the internal conditions most conducive to meaningful development, it will also allow the given developing country to make use of the opportunities presented by the world economy, such as they are, for the purposes of its own development rather than for the greater enrichment of rich metropolitan countries. The aim must be for each developing country to make the world economy marginal to the national economy instead of—as at present—being marginal to it. For that end, control by each society over its own means of production, and over the uses to which they are put, is imperative. More specifically:

1.   It permits the adoption of a sane pattern of consumption rather than allowing cosmopolitan patterns to infiltrate to national consciousness and usage. This entails no less of consumers' surplus, nor is it a plea for isolation from the fruits of human progress. It simply allows a measure of protection against gadgetry. Someone who has never seen a gadget will never miss it; and in most cases it is doubtful, once the novelty wears out, that life has become richer or more meaningful as a result of its acquisition.

2.   National control over the means of production is also necessary if an appropriate technology is to be evolved. This should be one appropriate both to national factor endowments and to the mode of life

sovereignly chosen by the people, not one imposed by outside market forces.

3. National control over the means of production is a preliminary step toward stopping the outward drain of surpluses. This point needs no further elaboration here.

Contemporary history offers living proof both of the potency of the contradiction between potential productive forces and actual relations of production in Third World countries, and of the feasibility of its solution along the lines of auto-centered, self-reliant strategy. The experiments which are taking place on an unprecedented scale, in the face of enormous odds imposed from outside, in many parts of the underdeveloped world—in China, Southeast Asia, Cuba, and (in a more embryonic form and with less success) in certain parts of Africa—would not have been dreamed of even by the most scientifically minded students of social development three-quarters of a century ago. There is no guarantee of their final success: an experiment might collapse here and there or it might change its course, producing a new type of class stratification. But there is little doubt that both the problem and its specific solution are firmly poised as the top priority in present history's agenda. The *objective* conditions are there, at least for a number of countries. Success, initial and consolidated, requires the fulfillment of a stringent set of *subjective* conditions, most notably the development of political consciousness and scientific habits of thought and organizational ability among the masses. But these are not difficult to develop, given the emergence, from among the masses themselves and *always relating to them,* of a dedicated and selfless leadership.

The Barrier of Small Size

Not all Third World countries, as presently constituted, are suitably equipped for a strategy of auto-centered self-reliance. An important objective limiting factor is size. A viable minimum of natural resources, land area and population size is required if this strategy is to result in rising standards of living. A country which attempts to make the world economy marginal to the national economy without possessing the material means needed to build up a diversified economy, eventually capable at reasonable cost of applying modern technology and satisfying a broad variety of legitimate needs, risks living on inflated slogans and deflated expectations. The healthy *cordon sanitaire,* necessary during a prolonged transitional period to isolate and keep away disrupting influences coming from abroad, can solidify into a prison wall shutting out hope and progress.

Unfortunately, many Third World countries are too small in size to support an introverted self-reliant strategy. This is especially true in Africa, where too many "national" frontiers are the accidental results of ancient colonial rivalries or of the legacies of deliberate disruptive colonial designs. One way out of the difficulty is for small countries to seek in economic cooperation with "like-minded" countries adopting the same strategy, a compensation for their own smallness. Failing, however, equality in size, resources and level of socioeconomic development, and indeed failing complete political integration on the basis of absolute equality, such attempts at creating a new, socialist system of international division of labor are bound to raise a number of complicated problems which are far from having received a satisfactory solution, either in theory or in practice.

COLLECTIVE SELF-RELIANCE

To stress the primary importance of internal transformation in each given country does not mean ignoring the effects of external conditions. A reciprocal relation certainly exists between the two, and all efforts toward improving the present IEO should be encouraged. The point so far stressed in this chapter is simply that internal conditions are the decisive factor both for determining the course development takes in each developing country and, eventually, for bringing about the radical transformation of the IEO itself. It is in this context that economic cooperation between Third World countries can now be considered.

Increasing Diversity Among Third World Countries

The most important reason for the currently meager level of active economic cooperation among Third World countries is the great diversity which prevails among them. It is true that some highly developed capitalist countries tend to play up this diversity, classifying the Third World developing countries, for example, into "more developed," "less developed," "resource-rich," "resource-poor," "land-locked" and "island" countries. The aim of such rhetoric is to implement the avowed policy of breaking up the so-called solid block of Third World

countries. Consciousness of this aim, however, should not induce Third
World countries to ignore the real, and even great, diversity of conditions that exist among themselves. *On the contrary, this diversity should
be brought out into the open, objectively analyzed, and practical
measures of active cooperation evolved and implemented which take
full account of it.*

The major forces working for differentiation among Third World
countries are the level of their economic development, the nature of
their external economic relations, and the nature of the socioeconomic
structures prevailing in these countries (countries with a completely
free market economy, capitalist countries with an important public
sector, countries passing through a period of transition to socialism,
and countries with an already established socialist system, etc.). *This
differentiation is not likely to diminish. On the contrary, it is bound to
increase.* Unless it is fully taken into account, it is bound to reflect
itself in divergent positions, both vis-à-vis global relations of Third World
countries with the outside world, and vis-à-vis the various issues of direct
economic cooperation among Third World countries themselves.

The Possibility of Active Cooperation

It is our firm conviction that, in spite of the existing diversity of
conditions and interests among Third World countries, and despite the
certainty of increasing differentiation among them, there does exist a
sufficiently solid basis for fruitful cooperation—both in relations with
the outside world and of a direct, active nature. *That cooperation can
only materialize on any significant scale if two fundamental conditions
are satisfied at the same time:*

1. If such cooperation takes into account the various, possibly
even divergent, interests of Third World countries. Hence, it has ultimately to assume the nature of a package deal, in which the interests
of various groups of countries are balanced against each other, so as to
make it profitable for each country to accept the deal as a whole.

2. If such cooperation is so devised as to leave each country free
to pursue the path of socioeconomic development and to adopt the
economic policies consonant with the balance of social forces within
its own society. *Any attempt to put Third World countries in the
straitjacket of a single, predetermined path of socioeconomic development is bound to meet with failure.*

Seven Guidelines for a Charter of Economic Cooperation Among Third World Countries

These two conditions can be satisfied, and yet allow for an ample measure of fruitful economic cooperation among Third World countries, if a charter of cooperation is drawn which is based on some such guidelines as follows:

1. Trade between Third World countries should be direct. Imports from, as well as exports to, Third World countries which pass through the intermediacy of a third party should be prohibited.

2. A system of generalized preferences should be established between Third World countries. That system should cover transport and insurance as well.

3. Payments from one Third World country to another should not pass through non-Third World intermediaries.

4. Third World producers' associations which bring about rising prices should compensate other Third World countries for additional payments involved.

5. Technology devised in Third World countries should be made available free or at especially advantageous terms to other Third World countries.

6. Transnational Third World firms should have preferential treatment in Third World countries. In the sense of this article, no firm in which non-Third World capital participates can be considered a transnational Third World firm.

7. Taxes should be imposed on all exports from Third World countries to non-Third World countries and on imports from non-Third World countries. The receipts of the taxes should be devoted to development purposes. They should be operated by a special organization in which all developing countries are represented on the basis of equality.

Some brief explanatory comments might not be out of order here:

a) Changes in the present international economic order are essentially a function of power relationships. As the current North-South dialogue amply testifies, there is little hope for modification of that order unless Third World countries consolidate their own economic power base. That fundamental rule should not be forgotten because of the false dichotomy often drawn between "confrontation" and "cooperation." Cooperation, meaning solving issues by mutual agreement, is essentially a polite expression for the outcome of the relative positions of power attained by the respective negotiating parties. Nor is the talk about the increasing "interdependence of the world economy" very relevant in this respect, for the question must always be asked: for whose benefit and at whose expense? Besides, our proposed guidelines do not diminish lines of world interdependence. They merely change the direction of some of them, replacing North-South relations by South-South relations. What is really attempted by these guidelines, taken as a whole, is to reduce the vertical integration, and increase the horizontal integration; to make the Third World somewhat less directed toward the First World, and more directed toward itself. For the rest, these guidelines are so chosen as to close some of the channels through which surpluses are siphoned off from Third World countries to metropolitan centers.

b)   The above guidelines are so devised as to take account of the various interests of differently situated groups of Third World countries. In that sense they should be considered as an integrated program.

c)   It is a program to which all Third World countries can subscribe regardless of their level of economic development or of their socioeconomic structure. The one condition is that they believe in the objective reasons for and benefits from cooperation among Third World countries as an overriding factor to be taken into consideration in their own development. More specifically, free-market Third World countries, socialist Third World countries, Third World countries with a well-developed public sector, can all equally well subscribe to this program without prejudice to their chosen path of development.

d)   The above points are no more than guidelines. They need to be more scientifically studied, elaborated, and concretized. Special allowance must be made for periods of transition. This can be most profitably done under the auspices of such organizations as UNCTAD, the Third World Forum, and the Association of Third World Economists.

e)   The program is simple to operate. Mostly, it is composed of a series of injunctions and prohibitions which requires no complex machinery.

f)   An essential principle of this program is that *cooperation between Third World countries should not be the occasion or vehicle for reproducing between Third World countries the relations of hegemony and subordination which exist between metropolitan countries and Third World countries. Nor, of course, should it be the back door through which these latter relations are maintained or forced upon countries which attempt to liberate themselves from them.*

g)   Subscribing to this charter of cooperation need not necessarily run counter to existing international agreements to which various Third World countries are committed. It certainly does not preclude special regional arrangements.

Part V
The Developed World's Response to the Demands of the Developing Nations

Chapter 9

DEVELOPED COUNTRY REACTIONS TO CALLS FOR A NEW INTERNATIONAL ECONOMIC ORDER[1]

Richard N. Cooper

In recent years numerous groups, some governmental, some private have put forward appeals or claims or demands for changes in the workings of the world economy and in the decision-making machinery regarding how it is to work. While the claims differ in detail from forum to forum, they share several common themes. The first is that there should be larger transfers of resources and of technology from the rich industrial countries to the poor countries of the world. A second theme is that the poor and nonindustrialized countries should be subject to specially favorable treatment, and that in general they should be exempt from the prescriptions for government behavior with which the rich industrialized nations are (appropriately) charged. A third theme is that the decision-making machinery governing international economic questions should be revised to give greater participation and greater weight to the poor or nonindustrialized nations.

The rationale for these claims rests in part on the contention that all people have a right to satisfaction of certain basic human needs and that those who are able to do so already have a corresponding responsibility to satisfy that right for others in the name of the solidarity of humanity.[2] They rest in part also on the contention that at best the existing international economic order—meaning the set of institutions, formal rules, and information conventions that govern economic transactions among nations—disregards the special problems and concerns of developing nations, and at worst has fostered the exploitation of poor countries, so that some restitution for past and present injustices is in order.

The particular proposals that have stemmed from these claims are numerous and vary from group to group, but they include such items as:

1. establishing international commodity agreements on those commodities produced by developing countries, to assure that they receive equitable and remunerative prices (a variation of this involves indexing commodity prices to prices of manufactured goods, to assure that commodity prices rise no less rapidly than other prices in an inflationary world);

2. increasing official development assistance from the rich countries up to the United Nations target of seven-tenths of one percent of gross national product;

3. renegotiating the principles of allocation of Special Drawing Rights (SDRs) at the International Monetary Fund to give developing countries a larger share;

4. providing general debt relief in the form of forgiveness or postponement of the repayment obligations of developing countries on their external debt;

5. granting and enlarging preferential treatment for imports from developing countries into the developed countries;

6. increasing the flow of relevant technology to developing countries, at reduced cost to them;

7. asserting the right to all property within national boundaries, and hence, the right to take over foreign-owned property without regard to international legal conventions regarding compensation; and

8. changing the decision-making procedures in such institutions as the International Monetary Fund (IMF) and the International Bank for Reconstruction and Development (hereafter, the World Bank) to give greater weight to developing countries.

It is noteworthy that these claims have been directed almost exclusively at what in United Nations terminology are called the developed market economies, i.e., Western Europe, North America, and Japan, Australia and New Zealand. (These will be called the "western" countries hereafter.) In particular, they are not generally directed toward communist countries such as East Germany or the Soviet Union. The reasons for this are no doubt complex. The communist countries (Yugoslavia excepted) themselves do not participate in some of the important international forums, such as the World Bank, the IMF, and (with the further exceptions of Poland and Romania) the General Agreement on Tariffs and Trade (GATT). This would not restrict their contributions in other contexts, however, such as granting development assistance, participating in commodity agreements, or granting trade preferences. In general, the communist countries have lower per capita incomes than do the western countries, and this might seem to absolve them from being called upon to meet the claims. But some of the claims (such as those for rectification) are not especially related to income, and in any case some communist countries have per capita incomes that exceed those of the poorer western countries such as Italy and Ireland. Indeed, by 1976 the per capita income of East Germany exceeded that of the United Kingdom.[3] What is probably more important is the perception of leaders in developing countries that they are unlikely to alter the policies of communist countries much by making appeals in international forums, in part because of the nature of communist governments, in part because the communist countries cannot so easily be held hostage to them in terms of needed materials or vulnerable foreign investment. Their success with the western countries is likely to be substantially greater, largely because with appropriate arguments they can enlist important segments of public opinion in their cause.

PUBLIC RESPONSE TO CALLS FOR A NEW ECONOMIC ORDER

The initial response of the public in western countries to the stance adopted by developing countries was one of shock and astonishment: first, at the Arab oil embargo imposed in October 1973—the event that brought the public into general awareness that important changes were taking place—and then, by the four-fold increase in oil prices announced by the Organization for Petroleum Exporting Countries (OPEC) for January 1974. This assertion of market power emboldened the developing countries, under the leadership of Algeria, in 1974, to put forward a "program of action" in a special session of the United Nations for establishment of a new international economic order.[4] In November 1974, the United Nations General Assembly approved the Charter of Economic Rights and Duties of States, which among other (on the whole straightforward and widely accepted) provisions asserted (Article 5) "the right to associate in organizations of primary commodity producers in order to develop their national economies. . ." and the corresponding duty of all states to refrain from applying economic and political measures to limit that right—a provision that would legitimize OPEC's actions and those of other potential cartels among producing countries. The charter also asserted (Article 2) the right of any state to expropriate foreign-owned property within its borders, paying "appropriate compensation . . . provided that all relevant circumstances call for it." Resolution of any controversy regarding expropriation and compensation is to be determined under the domestic law of the nationalizing state. The charter also asserted (Article 28) the duty of all states to cooperate in adjusting the prices of their imports, i.e., to "index" the prices received by developing countries.

The Charter of Economic Rights and Duties of States had its origins long before the increase in oil prices, as did proposals for changing the international economic order. Many of the specific proposals that made up the content of the proposed new international economic order had been under consideration for some time. And the developing countries had increasingly used their majority in the United Nations General Assembly to push through resolutions over the objections of the western countries, as when, in 1969, they voted a moratorium on all attempts at mining the seabed until a new international regime for the seabed was worked out. But what astonished members of the western public was the new assertiveness with which these proposals were advanced, the extreme claims of some of the provisions, and the unwillingness of the majority of the General Assembly, made up of a cohesive group of developing countries, to compromise on many of the provisions. While many of the provisions of the charter were unexceptionable to all countries, a theme of extreme state sovereignty runs through the charter. The United States objected especially to the three provisions noted above.[5] The provision for settlement of disputes exclusively under domestic law, in particular, seemed to sweep aside a long (western) tradition regarding international settlement of disputes.

The initial reaction of astonishment was soon overtaken by a more differentiated reaction. Some Westerners applauded the new assertiveness of the developing countries and in their own writings supported them and contributed further to the claims for redressing past wrongs and for a moral obligation to make transfers from rich countries to poor countries. Others reacted with a sense of guilt, implicitly acknowledging the merit of the positions taken by the developing countries, and urged negotiation and a willingness to compromise on both sides in the emerging debate. They wanted some kind of accommodation. Still others reacted with anger at the seeming exploitation of newly found power—in votes in the General Assembly and in monopoly in the provision of oil—and urged stiff resolution against yielding to what was regarded as extortion. Numerous shadings, of course, exist within all of these groups, and to them must be added the diplomatic pragamatists, who are less concerned with the substantive merits of the particular proposals and the arguments for or against a new economic order than with the fact that a large number of countries are resolutely serious in their claims for a new order, and who urge diplomatic accommodation as necessary to restore a degree of harmony in relations among countries.

It must be observed that the idea of a new international economic order is, itself, a profoundly western idea. It has been advanced and rationalized by western-trained leaders in developing countries and even by a number of Westerners. Philosophically, the notion that conscious human action can change the "order" of things, even human things, and moreoever that mankind can attack world poverty in a systematic way with ultimate success are fundamentally western ideas, drawn from the idea of progress. They have no counterparts in the reflective philosophies of the East or in the doctrines of Islam concerning the execution of God's will.

The varied reactions to calls for a new economic order can be found to some extent in all western countries, and to some extent they correspond to the political spectrum from Left to Right. The radical-liberal-conservative political debate within countries has now become global.

GOVERNMENTAL RESPONSES TO CALLS FOR A NEW ECONOMIC ORDER

Governments of the western countries also differed in their responses to the new claims, but the variation was far less than it was among the literate public. The United States tended to be the most resistant to the various proposals to change, and the rhetoric that accompanied them.

Europe and Japan, much more dependent on imported materials, hence more vulnerable to serious deterioration in relations with primary producing countries, were verbally more accommodating in their responses. These differences can be found, for instance, in the response to the oil embargo and the increase in oil prices. The United States sponsored the formation of the International Energy Agency among the western countries, designed to deal with future embargoes should they arise; whereas France sponsored the Paris talks among oil-producing and oil-consuming countries, in order to establish a dialogue with the presumed objective of making future embargoes, or further large price increases, less probable. The United States initally resisted the idea of producer-consumer talks altogether, on the grounds that oil prices, in all likelihood, would be discussed and that such discussion would not be in the interests of the consuming countries. This resistance was based on the conviction that sooner or later the forces of competition would reduce oil prices. Immediately after imposition of the oil embargo (which formally was directed only at the Netherlands and the United States, because of their support of Israel), Japan, in an open effort to curry favor with the Arab oil producers, called on Israel to yield the occupied territories.

Even earlier, the United States (openly supported by Germany, but only silently supported by a number of other European countries) opposed changing the formula for the allocation of Special Drawing Rights (SDRs) to favor economic development, on the grounds that monetary management and resource transfers for development should not be commingled. And the United States had also opposed the extension of tariff preferences to less developed countries, whereas the European Community and Japan each made a symbolic nod toward developing countries by introducing a system of tariff preferences in mid-1971, although the systems then introduced were shamefully restrictive in the degree of preference actually provided. (The United States, bowing to international pressure, also introduced tariff preferences in 1975, with a scheme less restrictive than the European and Japanese ones, although it could hardly be called generous.) Resistance to price-raising commodity agreements has been more general among western countries, with the exceptions of Canada (which as a large exporter of primary products would stand to gain) and France.

The general picture, then, is one of western governments being skeptical of most of the proposals that have been put forward in the name of a new international economic order, but differing among themselves in their willingness to discuss the various proposals and even if necessary to implement them. The United States (often supported by West Germany) has tended to adopt a principled stand on the desirability of preserving relatively free markets, whereas other western countries have tended to adopt a more pragmatic approach aimed at mollifying the developing countries.

The calls for a new international order raise a host of questions—some concerning the philosophical foundations of claims for resource transfers between nations, or indeed between individuals; some concerning the system of governance at the global level; and some concerning the desirability and the feasibility of the particular proposals that have been advanced. It is not possible, even in a long chapter, to deal with all these questions satisfactorily, since a fair assessment must deal sometimes with profound philosophical questions and at other times with technical economic evaluation of the consequences of certain policies. Rather, the remainder of this chapter will raise a number of questions about the issues that have been posed by calls for a new economic order. Raising these questions itself represents a response, often a critical or skeptical response, concerning the nature of the claims and the character of the proposals that have been put forward.

AN OVERVIEW OF THE GROUNDS FOR TRANSFERS BETWEEN NATIONS

The developing countries have laid down a claim to certain economic rights. Who should confer those rights? Who incurs the *obligation* to honor those rights, especially if, as is claimed, transfers of resources from one community to another are required to honor the rights?[6] That one community or country should transfer goods and services to another community or country is not self-evident. Past conventions have held that a community is entitled to what it produces. Why should it give over some of its produce to others?

Three broad types of transfer should be distinguished: gifts, repayments, and purchases of some intangible. Discussions of transfer from developed countries have commingled the three types of transfer. What arguments can be brought for each?

Gifts

Gifts are given for a variety of reasons which can be captured in the words generosity, guilt, and duty. In each case, the *donor* is moved by some sentiment, or combination of sentiments, to transfer resources to others. Generosity is an act of grace, and can hardly be "demanded." Guilt stems either from having benefited by the commission of some wrong, or from uneasiness about disparities in circumstance. Gifts, in the former instance, bear some resemblance to repayments, discussed more extensively below. Guilt, in the latter instance, arises from feelings of undeservedness even if no specific past wrongs have been committed. Such feelings hardly form the basis for claims by others, so gifts arising therefrom also represent an act of grace rather than of atonement. Or they arise from a sense of duty, the duty of the well-off to aid those who are disadvantaged. Whence does such a duty arise?

There is a long tradition in western (as well as in non-western) thought, both religious thought and rationalistic thought, holding that those who are well-off should give to those who are not. Charity is a Christian virtue, although in Christian theology it falls short of being the duty it is in some other religious traditions. Rationalists, too, have favored redistribution toward the poor. The utilitarians tried (unsuccessfully) to prove rigorously that redistribution of wealth from rich to poor would make society as a whole better off, i.e., would enlarge total utility. More recently, the philosopher John Rawls has attempted (also unsuccessfully, in the view of his critics) to show on original contract grounds that a certain degree of redistribution toward the least well-off serves the aim of "justice."[7]

A less rigorous origin in rationalistic western thought for some degree of redistribution in society stems from an extension of the age-old notion of natural rights of individuals—to life, liberty, and the pursuit of happiness, as it was phrased by Jefferson in the American Declaration of Independence (an earlier draft used "property" rather than "the pursuit of happiness"). On the concept's traditional interpretation, these natural rights were aimed at justifying resistance to capricious acts by the ruling power, and to provide guidance to the ruling power on the moral limits to the exercise of that power. They were, implicitly, negative injunctions. No resource transfers were involved. In the late nineteenth century, the Fabian Socialists began to extend the notion of natural rights. The right to "life" entailed not merely the right not to have one's life taken arbitrarily by the ruling authority, for instance, but the right to sustenance and minimal health care. The corresponding obligation fell on the state, and hence, on other members of society, to provide the required sustenance and health care. Natural rights were transformed, in the view of these writers, from a negative restraint on the behavior of ruling authorities to a positive injunction to provide the minimum requirements of life.

Patrick Moynihan[8] has suggested that contemporary leaders in developing countries have been strongly influenced by the Fabian Socialists of early twentieth-century England, and Fabian thought provides the philosophical underpinning of their claims for transfers from relatively rich to relatively poor countries, on the grounds that such transfers will help—indeed, may be necessary for—those countries to realize their potential. In this line of argument these leaders are supported by what Robert Tucker[9] has called the "new political sensibility" in western countries, a sensibility that is also an outgrowth of Fabian and similar thinking.[10] The natural rights enunciated in this line of thinking apply to individuals, however, not to collectivities, and certainly not to nations. The extension of natural rights to nations without intervening argument (which so far as I am aware has not been forthcoming) represents an unwarranted "anthropomorphization" of nations—treating nations as though they are persons, and applying ethical principles that have been propounded for individuals.

The illegitimate extension of natural-rights principles to nations—despite their origin as setting limits on governmental action with respect to individuals—poses a difficulty for those who want to claim rights to transfers on these ethical grounds. The difficulties are further compounded by the often extreme claims to national sovereignty asserted by many developing countries. As Tucker has pointed out, the "new egalitarianism" asserted by the leaders of developing nations only begins at the water's edge, so to speak: it applies to nations, not to individuals within their borders. The convergence of view between leaders of developing countries and those Westerners subject to the new political sensibility is thus more apparent than real. There is, in fact, a deep tension between them, for the developing countries insist on the principle of total noninterference in their national affairs even while they are calling for transfers of resources in the name of fundamental rights of individuals. Their own indifference to the poorest members of their own populations—those on whose behalf these claimed rights are presumably advanced—is frequently egregious. And it threatens to undermine at least one basis for support—probably the most important basis of support—among Westerners for transfers of resources to the developing nations.[11]

The view that natural rights pertain to individuals rather than to nations has strong implications for a number of specific proposals put forward by developing countries toward implementation of a new international economic order. It rules out justifying on ethical grounds any proposal which simply transfers resources unconditionally to developing countries, without serious inquiry into whether the resources thus transferred are, in fact, serving the ethical purposes—support of the basic needs of life and self-improvement—that provide their rationale. In particular, it rules out such proposals as general relief on external debt, transfers through higher commodity prices, and rewriting the formula for SDR allocation to give greater distribution directly to developing countries.

The position could be salvaged by arguing that resource transfers to countries with low per capita incomes will somehow ultimately benefit the poorest members of those countries regardless of the policies that the governments are actually pursuing. Such a line of argument would represent a new version of trickle-down theory that is so much in disrepute among those who favor transfers to the poor. If trickle-down theories are admissible, however, other versions should be closely examined for their relative efficacy in raising incomes of the poorest members of society. Such an examination might well result in a finding that unrestricted transfers to governments are not the best way to accomplish the result.[12]

One way to reconcile the tension between the strong assertion of national sovereignty by developing countries and the use of "natural rights" arguments for transfers to poor peoples would be to focus resource transfers on those countries that have demonstrated their effectiveness in reaching the poorest members of their societies. Another would be to concentrate transfers on those programs, such as improved agricultural productivity or improved water supplies and public health, that in their nature are likely to help the poorest members of society (among others) by addressing basic human needs. Indeed, the United States foreign aid program was directed by Congress to move in the latter direction in the Foreign Assistance Act of 1973, a reflection of congressional distrust of unrestricted transfers between governments and of dissatisfaction with more "development-oriented" foreign aid. Such transfers would not be specifically linked to industrialization, but they would contribute to economic development in the agricultural sector directly and to other sectors insofar as improved nutrition and health enhanced the productiveness of the labor force.

Repayments

In the present context resource transfers that are repayments concern repayment of past debt only in the metaphorical sense: they are reparations or rectification payments for wrongs committed in the past. Once again, it is easier to pose questions than to provide answers, but even the posing of questions can illuminate the complexities involved in the notion of payments to rectify past wrongs. We must first ask what we mean by "wrongs" that might give rise to a claim for rectification payments, and then we must address the historical issue of whether such wrongs were in fact committed by those to whom the claims are presented.

In the economic context, wrongs are usually identified with economic exploitation. How can we define economic exploitation in a meaningful way?[13] Suppose that two communities A and B begin a series of economic transactions with one another that last for some time. We can then make some distinctions among possible outcomes of these transactions. First, A may gain from them while B loses. If B loses, however, we must ask why B engaged in them in the first place. If we have defined the transactions with sufficient care (to include any intangibles that might also be involved in them), B must have been ignorant or subject to coercion.

Second, both parties may gain from the transactions, but A may gain proportionately more. This result could arise from some special bargaining strength of A over B (such as the absence of alternative sources of A's products or the presence of implicit threats by A), or it could arise simply because B has a strong demand for A's products relative to A's demand for B's products, such that the terms of trade between them settle closer to B's initial (pretrade) prices than to A's.

Third, what sounds similar, but, in fact, is not the same: A may enjoy persistent profits above competitive levels in A's economy, whereas B may not enjoy above-normal profits on its transactions with A, relative to profits elsewhere in B's economy. (Note that it is logically possible for the terms of trade to favor B relative to the pretrade position, even while A, but not B, enjoys above-normal profits on the transactions.)

These distinctions permit us to offer one potentially useful definition of "exploitation," or rather the absence of exploitation, in economic transactions: they must be undertaken voluntarily and they must not involve persistent above-normal profits, normal profits being reckoned with respect to each of the trading economies.

Establishment of exploitation in this sense might be said to provide the basis for claims to rectification payments. But how far back does one go in history? And for distant past wrongs, who must make the payments, and who is entitled to receive them?

In the seventh to tenth centuries, the Muslim Arabs conquered and confiscated many Christian (and non-Christian) lands by sword, clearly a nonvoluntary or coercive transaction. Does that give rise to a current claim for reparations? (Note that rectification payments are to right past wrongs, and therefore, claims might as justifiably be made from the now rich to the now poor as the other way around.) Spain in the sixteenth century plundered the New World, and as a result, many Spaniards lived lavishly at home. Members of the same families settled in Central and South America, often being the ancestors of today's leading families there. Does that give rise to a legitimate claim by Latin American countries on contemporary Spain?

The west African slave trade flourished during the seventeenth and eighteenth centuries. While some of the slaves may have been kidnapped by European slave traders, most were purchased from powerful tribal chieftains, and competition among the European slave buyers was fierce.[14] Is there a basis for rectification claims by American blacks on contemporary west African countries, where the descendants of those chieftains who enslaved others and received payment for them still reside?

In the late eighteenth century the powerful Barbary State of Algiers captured American seamen and held them for ransom, clearly exploitative since it involved coercion. Should the United States lay a claim for reparations on Algeria?[15] Or is there a moral statute of limitation on claims for rectification, and if so, how far back does it go?

Other difficult questions arise. In 1853 the American Commodore Perry arrived with two frigates in Japanese ports that had until then been closed to international trade (except for occasional transactions through Dutch traders) and induced the Japanese to change their policies and to allow other Europeans to trade and to establish consulates. While Perry was restrained in his official communications, the threat of force was clearly there: his arrival in warships was an intimidating act.[16] No doubt American traders profited from the opening of Japan to international trade. But so did Japan. It could be argued that Japan would not have developed its high income of today if that early external intimidation had not been used. Query: does Japan have a claim today on the United States for having violated its preferences of 1854? Or should the claim be reversed because Japan ultimately gained disproportionately (assuming it did) from the sequence of transactions that followed?

To pose such a question, which is admittedly artificial, suggests two further questions: first, *whose* preferences were violated in 1854? Japan at that time was experiencing substantial internal dissension, with many rival feudal factions grouped loosely around the shogun and the emperor, and with competition between them for assertion of authority. Second, how appropriate is it to compensate for admitted wrongs to generations now long dead when their descendants are not obviously worse off because of the wrong? And who indeed are the relevant heirs—only those in direct lineage to those who were wronged, or all those resident in the same geographical area, somehow defined? In short, difficult intergenerational and internal distributional questions arise. If I have not been wronged, and my current position is not worse than it would otherwise be because of some wrong done someone in the past, what theory of justice or entitlement gives me a claim for reparations on anyone else? Particularly when those who perpetrated the wrong are also long since dead?

The argument for intergenerational, international rectification payments must rest on the assumption that wrongful acts by one group's forebears to another's left the former group better off and/or the latter group worse off than they otherwise would have been. To assess these conditions involves a counterfactual question ("What would things have been like if the wrong had not been done?") that even with a willingness to use rough and ready techniques is usually difficult to answer satisfactorily.

One line of thought seems to cut through these difficulties. The French writer Antoine has written that:

> . . . individuals, groups, and nations which, even by ethical means, have secured for themselves an advantageous, strong and prosperous position in the world, and by so doing have impeded (even if it is only indirectly because goods available on this planet are limited) the economic development or the social promotion of other individuals or other peoples, are responsible to the latter for the deprivation and they ought to remedy it, by making use of the very possibilities which their better position confers on them . . . an obligation rooted in justice can exist as a consequence of our acts even when no fault of injustice has been committed.[17]

Even if one were to accept this general principle of responsibility without guilt (note that it represents a compound rationale involving both reparations based on past deprivation and gifts based on duty), as no doubt many would, there remains the important assumption that those making the claim have in fact been "deprived" of something or that their progress has been "impeded." It is quite possible, however—indeed in many cases quite likely—that close contact with former colonial powers, and more generally economic contact with western countries, has left the former colonies and other dependencies economically *better* off than they would otherwise be. Existing poverty in Africa and Asia and Latin America should not blind us to the all but universal poverty that existed in these areas before the European powers established themselves overseas, which in much of Africa was less than a century ago. The introduction of modern legal and commercial systems, of capital, and of modern technology has helped a number of these countries to rise above the grinding poverty of the past. That much poverty remains is not a question. That that economic poverty exists, directly or indirectly, because of past colonial rule is highly doubtful.[18]

Moreover, in those instances in which living standards seem to have declined, it is usually due to rapid population growth that has worsened the land/man ratio to the point at which subsistence agriculture becomes more difficult. This population growth in turn was due in part to improved health, sanitation, and transportation systems introduced by or with the help of the European powers. The population on the island of Java, for instance, increased by a factor of nearly fourteen in the period 1815 to 1960, from four and one-half million persons to 63 million. (Great Britain's population increased five- to six-fold during the same period of time.) Actions taken by Europeans to improve health and food distribution were not at the time or generally today regarded as "wrongs" or injuries. Who is responsible for the poverty that results from a larger but healthier population? Is reparation called for? And when population growth is the culprit, will reparation help? Or will it paradoxically (on this line of support for reparation) only provide the basis for yet larger rectification payments in the future?

The foregoing discussion has raised some questions about the types of circumstances that might provide the basis for rectification payments. The discussion needs to be completed by addressing the historical question whether the wrongs that might provide such a basis were in fact committed. Did economic exploitation in the sense of the above-normal profits, as defined above, for instance, actually occur? We have many anecdotes, but relatively little systematic information. Such an examination is a major undertaking and one which is beyond the scope of the present chapter, however.

Purchases

When we speak of resource transfers involving a "purchase," we, of course, do not mean a direct purchase of goods or services, for that would involve an exchange rather than a transfer. Rather, we are referring to some less tangible quid pro quo in terms of the behavior of the countries receiving the transfer. Traditionally such transfers are designed to achieve safety or good will. The "demands" set forward in some of the rhetoric surrounding calls for a new international order suggest that "if you don't deliver . . . we'll injure you" in some way. This approach represents a kind of extortion; and implicit threat to punish involves coercion. On another view, transfers would involve bribery, an attempt to purchase good will and assistance in carrying out certain objectives. As James Scott[19] points out, the distinction between extortion and bribery is often difficult to make, as when requests to a government official for important approvals get "lost" in the absence of a bribe.

Extortion and bribery are words that are loaded with unfavorable connotations. It would perhaps be preferable to use more neutral words—such as *dash* or *bakshish*—drawn from countries where payments for bureaucratic services are common and generally accepted.

Whatever one calls the transfer, the motive for it is prudential in nature. It involves the purchase of desired behavior or some protection against undesired behavior or consequences. What is the behavior that might be thus "purchased" by governments of western countries through transfers to developing countries? It might involve a very generalized form of "good" behavior, such as less offensive rhetoric, fewer tendentious resolutions in the United Nations and elsewhere, more constructive negotiations on issues of common interest. It might involve cooperation in suppressing international terrorism or the drug traffic, avoidance of nuclear proliferation, willingness to allow "exploitation" of natural resources, cooperation in managing the world's commons by limiting pollution or agreeing to international management of ocean fisheries, and so on.

The discussion thus far implies that the recipient of the transfer in some sense controls or influences the results. This may not be the case. Of some events no group of persons, even governments, may be in control. The community making the transfer may however believe that by making the transfer it can influence the course of events so that undesired outcomes are less likely. It is, in effect, paying to reduce future

risks. Jan Tinbergen, chairman of a distinguished group sponsored by
the Club of Rome to review the international economic order, emphasized, for instance, the importance of reducing income inequality in
order to increase political stability.[20] This type of motive reflects a
view of how human collectivities evolve, whether or not under the guidance or direction of government.

Buying insurance against world political instability or other unwanted
developments represents a motive for transferring resources, but it does
not provide a basis for a claim to receive transfers, since that implies a
degree of control by the claimant.

Are transfers effective in achieving the desired ends? This question
cannot be answered in general, although it should always be asked when
a "purchase" motive lies behind the transfer. Sometimes yielding to
"demands" is taken as weakness of will and simply leads to more demands. It can also lead to resentment among the domestic public of the
transferring countries. "Millions for defense, but not one cent for
tribute," a sentiment expressed by Charles Pinckney during discussions
of the young United States with old-world France in the 1790s, is a
common reaction to any suggestion of extortion. On the other hand,
sometimes a gesture of good will demonstrated through a transfer may
indeed be reciprocated by good will. Some undesirable actions, such as
the development of nuclear weapons, are more likely to be governed by
a cool assessment of the necessity for national survival than by the presence of economic concessions. But in other areas cooperation may well
be "purchased," in the sense that is used here. Success depends on the
antecedent circumstances and the finesse of the transaction.

AN ECONOMIC ASSESSMENT OF
THE NIEO PROPOSALS

The foregoing discussion has focused on the bases on which various
claims to resource transfers among countries might be made. We turn
now to the substantive proposals that have been put forward to effect
these transfers, or otherwise to improve the condition of the developing
countries. As was noted at the outset, the disposition among Westerners
to respond favorably to the calls for increased resource transfer and
other changes shows great variation. Most of the actions fall in the economic arena, and it is probably fair to say that most economists are
more skeptical than others about the effectiveness of the proposals at

achieving the desired objectives.[21] This chapter cannot undertake a comprehensive and thorough analysis of even the leading proposals, but some flavor of the skepticism about the more prominent proposals can be indicated.

Commodity Agreements

Several rather different objectives fall under the rubric of commodity agreements, by which is meant some systematic attempt to influence the prices at which commodities are sold among countries, or an attempt to store certain commodities for emergency use. Some proposals are addressed to the aim of assuring "remunerative prices," which means higher prices than in the past. Others are addressed at stabilizing commodity prices over time. Still other proposals have involved "indexing" commodity prices to the prices of manufactured goods, that is, assuring unchanging terms of trade between the two classes of goods. Finally, some proposals have addressed the need to store certain commodities, especially foodstuffs, against the possibility of future shortages.[22]

Questions have been raised—especially, but not exclusively in developed countries—about both the feasibility and the desirability of commodity agreements of various types. Consider first the class of agreement aimed directly or indirectly at assuring commodity prices that are higher than they otherwise would be, that is, aimed at transferring resources to producers of those commodities via the medium of higher prices. There is, first of all, the question whether such an agreement can be made to work for any length of time. Unless existing sources of supply are limited and unique, higher prices will stimulate an expansion of output from existing sources and will encourage the development of new sources of supply. The history of commodity cartels is replete with instances in which an attempt to raise prices over a prolonged period has stimulated new sources of supply—sometimes within the consuming countries, sometimes in other producing countries—which in turn gradually undermined the attempt to hold prices up. To support the high prices, ever tighter controls have to be maintained on production—or, if the producers are willing to build up stocks indefinitely, on exports—including the production of would-be entrants to the markets. In short, it involves a high degree of control over the market, control that is unlikely to be possible except in a few cases. Moreover, even when expansion of production is not a decisive difficulty, substitution on the side of consumption away from the commodity whose price has been raised serves to thwart the purposes of the agreement. Few materials or foods are so crucial that they cannot be replaced with some other product.

Recently we have seen the example of a steep increase in oil prices by the fourteen members of the Organization of Petroleum Exporting Countries (OPEC). While some observers envision the generalization of OPEC to other commodities, others contend that oil really represents a special case, arising from the fact that *at the margin* only a few countries—and notably Saudi Arabia—could expand production at all rapidly, that oil is an essential commodity to industrial countries for which demand was growing rapidly, and that, therefore, the control over increases in production by a relatively few countries could effect a substantial increase in prices. Even then, it is doubted that the success of OPEC will last indefinitely, for while substitution possibilities in consumption are low, they are present and can take effect in time.

The second question concerns the desirability of price-raising commodity agreements even if they were to prove to be feasible. The notion that the less developed countries are the world's hewers of wood and drawers of water, while the developed countries are the skilled artisans making its manufactured products, is too simple. Most primary products are in fact produced in high-income countries. Such countries as the United States, Canada, Australia, Sweden, and France—not to mention South Africa and the Soviet Union—are substantial exporters of primary products. Even Japan, with few natural resources, is the world's largest exporter of one primary product, raw silk. At the same time, some developing countries are heavy importers of primary products, not only foodstuffs but increasingly also industrial raw materials. As a result of these patterns, price-raising commodity agreements would not offer a straightforward transfer of resources from developed to developing countries; they would, on the contrary, generate a quite arbitrary distribution of gains and losses among both developed and less developed countries. Moreover, the less developed countries that would benefit tend to be those that are better off; with minor exceptions, the poorest countries would not benefit, and often would lose, from raising commodity prices. Such an action would thus not contribute much to the alleviation of world poverty. Attempts to reduce substitutability by broadening coverage of commodity agreements (e.g., by covering both copper and aluminum, or all the vegetable oils) would only aggravate the problem of an arbitrary distribution of the gains.

There is another reason why commodity agreements might not contribute to the alleviation of poverty. Except in those primary producing countries with strong governments which are devoted seriously to the alleviation of poverty, the benefits of the increased prices would accrue to those who own the resources whose prices had been increased—for agricultural commodities, the land where the commodity is grown. Raising a country's export receipts is not the same as raising the incomes of its poorest members or even of its government. While some resource transfers in their nature pass through the hands of the government, this is not true of commodity prices. Powerful pressures would exist to pass them directly to the owners of the resource.

Among the industrialized countries, only France has supported the notion of "organizing world markets," presumably with a view to raising commodity prices. (This last motive is clear when French farm products are involved, but French officials have also spoken more generally of the need to assure fair and remunerative prices.) Because of the opposition of other western countries, notably the United States, France has been spared the difficult task of spelling out the details of a workable plan.[23] When the European Community came to make special arrangements for the former colonial territories of its members, however, it significantly adopted, in the Lome Agreement, an arrangement aimed at stabilizing export earnings, not—with the sole exception of sugar—commodity prices. When it got down to operating details, that seemed the preferable course of action.

The arguments against price-raising commodity agreements apply a fortiori to the indexing of commodity prices. But to them must be added the point that in periods of high demand, full indexing, if it were successful, would prevent the prices of raw materials from rising even though that would be desirable.

Proposals for commodity agreements aimed at stabilizing commodity prices, or at creating emergency stores, have been more favorably received. Some observers entertain strong doubts about the feasibility of such agreements (can buffer-stock managers really be expected to have greater wisdom than specialized commodity dealers, it is asked), and about the desirability of any government interference in markets that may not be perfect but are likely to be made worse rather than better by government intervention. Moreover, they point out that price fluctuations actually help to stabilize export earnings when the source of price movement is variation in supply; for financing development, it is earnings, not prices, that represents the crucial variable.

Others, however, point out that the objectives of buffer-stock management would differ from those of private speculators, who have no interest in reducing price variability as a social objective; and that appropriate government management could reduce price variability that goes beyond that required for sensible resource allocation. The experience of 1972-1975, when many commodity prices shot up three or four times, only to fall back precipitously, raised questions around the world about the desirability of such wild price movements, which are a source of discomfort to consumers as well as to producers.

It is also recognized that, in principle, emergency stocks of food grains should be kept against the contingency of sudden crop failures, and that the private sector will not generally carry stocks in anticipation of shortfalls in areas of the world with low income. Many practical questions remain about the modus operandi of either price-stabilizing buffer stocks or emergency stocks; but at least the idea is deemed worthy of discussion. Reluctance by industrial countries to discuss any kind of commodity agreement stems from their suspicion that what is created as a price-stabilizing agreement will be used to try to raise prices.

Trading Arrangements for Manufactured Goods

The principal proposal advanced by the developing countries regarding trade in manufactured products concerns the granting of tariff preferences by the industrial countries to products from developing countries. This proposal was pressed very hard in the second UNCTAD meeting in 1968, and in 1971. The European Community and Japan each introduced generalized tariff preferences, but in schemes so restrictive that they virtually assured little value to developing nations.[24] The United States finally introduced a somewhat different, but still not very generous, scheme of tariff preference for developing countries in 1975. Persuasion of the industrial countries to introduce preferences—and thereby to break in yet another way with the "most favored nation" principle of the GATT—represents a symbolic victory for the developing countries which may actually hurt them more than it helps, since a quid pro quo for introducing preferences has been a loosening of the restraints on "safeguard" action by industrial countries to protect domestic industries against injury from imports. Assurance of access to the markets of the industrial countries is far more important to the actual trading interests of developing countries than are tariff preferences even at their best, much less at their actual levels. Gaining tariff preferences from the United States clearly cost, in the legislative process on the

Trade Act of 1974, great relaxation of the standards under which "escape clause" action could be applied to limit imports. The same is likely to be true also of Japan and the European Community, although the relationship is not so clear because the formulation of trade policy is not so open in those two areas as it is in the United States.

Developing countries are now concentrating on the extension of tariff preferences to commodities not earlier covered, and to the preservation of preferences they have already won. The latter efforts are perhaps surprising in view of statements from leaders of developing countries in the late Sixties that the granting of tariff preferences would not be allowed to impede the general liberalization of world trade through later reductions in general tariff levels. In the current round of trading negotiations, however, several developing countries have proposed the "binding" of tariff preferences, i.e., an agreement by industrial countries not to lower tariffs among themselves on products of interest to developing countries.

A second issue in trade policy concerns the tariff structure of industrial countries, which is such that simple processing of raw materials tends to be located in industrial countries rather than near the source of the raw materials because of the tariff "escalation" according to state of processing. (Even low tariffs on processed materials can be sufficient to protect the processing activity if the raw material enters at still lower or zero duties.) In the current round of trade negotiations the United States has proposed the elimination of duties below five percent, with an equal percentage reduction of duties above that. In general, such a formula for tariff-cutting would aggravate the problem of tariff escalation, and might paradoxically increase protection for a number of processing activities. The European formula—percentage cuts proportional to the height of the tariff—would be a better approach in this regard, although it is motivated by quite different, and more doubtful, considerations.

A third issue in trade policy is the proliferation of "nontariff barriers" to trade, of which the most important for the developing countries is so-called voluntary export restraints, usually introduced under the threat of import quotas, as an escape clause action. This point was already touched on above.

The central issue in trade in manufactured goods is the willingness of the industrial countries to see their present industrial structure change in the face of growing imports from developing nations, and how rapidly. They can resist the change or they can facilitate it. Resistance will certainly come from those economic interests that are adversely affected by the imports—certain business firms (although the increasing conglomerateness of firms reduces their dependence on any one line of business) and especially relatively unskilled or semiskilled workers who engage in activities that can increasingly be undertaken by developing countries. Some observers speak both fearfully and contemptuously of "cheap foreign labor" which works under conditions far inferior to those obtaining in the United States or Europe. But, of course, the inferior working conditions and wages reflect the low levels of income and productivity in developing countries, and the way to raise wages and improve conditions is to provide for productive employment. Protectionist concerns in industrial countries are greatly aggravated by economic recession, when unemployment rates are high for reasons that have nothing to do with imports from developing countries.

Financial Arrangements

At the fourth UNCTAD meeting, in May 1976, and at meetings of the Conference on International Economic Cooperation (CIEC) the developing countries pressed strongly for a moratorium on payments on external debt, or at least on external debt to official organizations in the western countries, such as foreign aid agencies or export financing agencies. The industrial countries received this proposal coolly. The distribution both of the effort and of the relief would be highly capricious and unrelated both to capacity for financial support in the creditor countries and to financial need in the debtor countries. In particular, those countries that had already lent the most would, through a moratorium, be called upon to provide still more. And the debtor countries that had borrowed most freely would be given the greatest relief, regardless of need or of incentive to achieve satisfactory economic performance. Some developing countries acknowledged outside the formal discussions that they too would not welcome a general moratorium, for it might jeopardize their future access to borrowing from private sources (mainly banks) in the financial centers of the world, something which Mexico, Brazil, Korea, the Phillippines, and other countries had developed with great success in the early Seventies.

While some observers held that there was no serious debt "problem" in that standard sources of finance could be relied upon, many observers in industrial countries acknowledged that some formal action might have to be taken to deal with the heavy external debt. They felt, however, that it should be done on a country-by-country basis, since the volume and character of the debt varied widely and since the economic circumstances of each country differed greatly. The case-by-case approach would permit the specification of a financial plan that would gradually restore the financial soundness of the individual countries following the extraordinary circumstances of 1974 and 1975, when a combination of high grain prices, high oil prices, and world recession created serious financial disturbance to most countries around the world. It is, of course, precisely the prospect of debt relief being conditional on policy advice from the creditors that so offends some developing countries: they do not like being told what they must do by way of monetary or budgetary policy. The creditor nations are equally affronted by the notion that they should provide additional financial resources carte blanche. The issue of control remains central to much of the dispute between developed and developing countries.

A second financial issue concerns the creation of international liquidity and the distribution of benefits that flow from that creation. Concretely, the less developed countries have argued that the formula for distributing Special Drawing Rights (SDRs) created by the International Monetary Fund should be drastically revised to increase their share, which at present amounts to only about a third of the total, based on their quotas at the IMF.[25]

Creation of SDRs involves the creation of purchasing power, but it does not involve the creation of real resources: those would still have to be provided by the countries that ultimately receive the SDRs in payment for exports and then hold on to them. As a source of development assistance SDRs are not quite as attractive as they might seem at first glance, since a country must pay interest (currently at about five percent) on any difference between its allocation of SDRs and its holdings of them.

Apart from the numerous technical issues associated with creation of international reserve assets, the notion of direct distribution of purchasing power to all (IMF-member) countries, without any conditions or expectations attached, is offensive to many Westerners, particularly given the nature of the governmental regimes in a substantial number of developing countries today and their casual regard (by western standards) for human rights. This problem could be solved by channeling SDRs through some aid-giving intermediary, such as the International Development Association, which would select countries and activities to support on the basis of poverty or contribution to economic development—conditions that in their present mood, standing on an exaggerated principle of sovereign equality, developing countries are likely to resist.

Multinational Corporations

The principal issues arising from multinational corporations in their relations with developing countries concern recourse of the corporation to its home government, compensation on nationalization, transfer pricing (especially as a device for evading exchange control regulations or limits on profits), and interference in the domestic affairs of the host country, including bribery. The emotionalism and ignorance surrounding multinational corporations has impeded serious discussion of the issues. For many socialists, northern as well as southern, multinational corporations symbolize all the alleged evils of the capitalist system and are castigated no matter what their actual behavior. In partial response, many defenders of multinationals interpret any criticism of their behavior as an attack on the system of free enterprise—as it sometimes is, but need not be—and thus refuse to consider critical observations on their merits. This is not the place for an extended discussion of multinational corporations and their role in the contemporary world economy. Suffice it to say that there may be more common ground than is initially apparent between governmental critics in less developed countries and general opinion in the western countries, which is quite critical of some behavior of multinationals.

The question of the interference of a multinational corporation in the internal affairs of a host country, for instance, is linked to the issue of its resort to its home government. Is the foreign-owned corporation to be regarded as a local corporate citizen or not? If so, it should foreswear resort to the home government of its owners (except in case of violation of a treaty between governments). But it should also be free to "interfere," i.e., to participate, in local politics to the same extent as local enterprises do. The resort to the home government for assistance is sometimes the consequence of not having the political channels of redress that are routinely available to local enterprises.

When it comes to nationalization of foreign investment, the question hinges on the principles of compensation; the right (as opposed to wisdom) of a country to "nationalize" any economic activity within its borders is rarely questioned these days. The reluctance of many developing countries to allow compensation to be determined by third-party arbitration is seen by western corporate executives as prima facie evidence of their intention to confiscate, not merely to nationalize, foreign-owned property. Less developed countries resent the loss of "sovereignty" compulsory arbitration seems to imply. (If they really want to maintain full sovereignty in every sense, however, they should not enter any treaties with binding obligations; one of the important assertions of sovereignty is precisely to be able to commit oneself to future courses of action.) They also fear that awards will be made by standards with which they do not agree. Perhaps the problem could be eased by agreeing ahead of time on the standards to be applied. In particular, compensation might be made on the basis of historical costs plus a fair, even a generous, rate of return, rather than on some assessment of present value. The latter criterion, which business firms often espouse, arouses especially strong resentment when natural resources and extraction "rights" are involved.

Appropriated Foreign Assistance

Less developed countries are themselves ambivalent on the question of appropriated foreign assistance. On the one hand, they have expressed disappointment that the developed countries are not meeting the official development assistance target of 0.7 percent of gross national product in each donor country that was agreed in the United Nations General Assembly. On the other hand, they have a host of dissatisfactions with foreign assistance, both bilateral and multilateral, as it is actually administered. Too many conditions attach to such assistance—stipulations regarding economic policy on program loans, requirements to buy in the donor country giving bilateral assistance, limitations on the types of goods and services that can be purchased with project loans, and so on. The reactions, of course, vary from country to country, and in many instances the restrictions are not onerous, or may even be welcome. But the donor-recipient relationship is an intrinsically difficult one, and is likely to leave both parties dissatisfied.

The ambivalence in developing countries is met by increasing questioning in donor countries about whether foreign aid is worthwhile to the recipients and justifiable to themselves. The United Nations target of one percent of donor-nation gross national product to be transferred (through private as well as official channels, through official export credits as well as foreign aid grants) to developing countries was in fact achieved for the first time in 1975, for a total of $39 billion. It is a comment on the times that there was no rejoicing, only assertions that the amounts were not high enough and the terms were not easy enough. There is an intrinsic difficulty with direct resource transfers between countries based on distributive considerations: more is never enough, so targets are arbitrary and their attainment merely provides the occasion for setting a higher target.

With respect to conditions attaching to foreign assistance, it is worth noting that while intergovernmental transfers *within* countries are common, they usually carry with them strong implicit or explicit conditions. Totally unconditional transfers, such as the developing countries are calling for, are rare. In most countries (e.g., Great Britain, France) local governments are the legal creatures of the national government, so the recipient is directly accountable to the government which is making the grant. In federal countries such as the United States certain subnational governments (the states) have a constitutional existence and are not subordinate to the national government. But United States government grants to the separate states are all conditional. Either they are restricted to certain categories of expenditure, by program, such as highway construction, aid to families with dependent children, urban renewal, improvement of sewage systems, etc., with financial accountability to the federal government under each program. Or, in the case of "revenue sharing," they are not restricted as to program, but they are subject to general requirements on the behavior of the recipient state, notably on questions of civil rights and racial or sex discrimination, conditions of a type and stringency that would strongly offend developing countries if applied to them. Thus even within the United States, with its relatively high homogeneity of values and where governments are politically responsible to the same voting public, transfers are used to influence the pattern of expenditure and governmental behavior. Totally unconditional aid is not congenial.[26]

International Rules and Procedures

The foregoing discussion has focused on the major substantive proposals that have been made by developing countries toward a new international economic order. In addition, and perhaps more important in the long run, they have made a number of proposals concerning the determination of the international rules of economic behavior and the applicability of the international rules to developing countries. On the latter point, they have called for special treatment of developing countries wherever possible, including exemption from the rules governing behavior and even exemption from the procedures of discussion of complaints and resolution of disputes. Thus, the addition of a new Part IV of the General Agreement on Tariffs and Trade was necessary to encourage developing countries to adhere to GATT already in the early 1960s, and more recently, it has become routine to add the qualifying phrase "with due regard to the special circumstances of developing countries" to every new international agreement in the economic arena—even when, as in the case of the January 1976 Jamaica Agreement on international monetary reform, the agreement itself carries virtually no restrictions on national action, provided the International Monetary Fund is notified. There is a serious question about how long an international organization or a body of rules can function with respect from its adherents when a substantial portion of them are entitled to exemption. A corrosive effect is likely to set in, and remaining members will gradually feel less obligated by the agreement. The agreement may be formally scuttled (as the abortive International Trade Organization was, in large part because it had become a Christmas tree of exemptions and allowance for special circumstances) and/or serious discussions may be moved elsewhere, to more restricted forums.

Moreover, exemption from the rules and procedures of international agreement is not consistent with the "equality" part of the sovereign equality among nations to which developing countries attach so much importance. Continuing favorable treatment is likely to result in continuing perception of them as second-class nations. To command the respect they desire, they must adhere to at least some rules of the game.

In addition to special treatment, the developing countries have also called for changes in the rules as they apply to developed countries and in procedures for making the rules. They object to the kind of weighted voting system that exists in the International Monetary Fund and the World Bank (with the western countries holding about two-thirds of the votes), and they desire a stronger formal voice in making decisions. (This is somewhat different from presence in the key discussion. Nine of the formal seats of the Committee of 20 and 18 of the members of the 27-nation Conference on International Economic Cooperation are from developing countries.) In the Law of the Sea discussions the developing countries have so far insisted on unconditional authority being granted to a new authority to manage mining on the seabed, without constitutional restraints on the exercise of that authority—so it could stop mining altogether, for example—combined with an absolute majority to developing countries on the authority.

On such matters the American reaction is one of profound suspicion. This suspicion of a "tyranny of the majority" has been reinforced by recent Third World bloc voting in the United Nations on issues on which many individual developing countries had no direct interest (such as the "Zionism is racism" resolution of 1975) or even (as in the case of landlocked countries on the 200-mile economic zone in the Law of the Sea conference) when the proposed resolution is against their national interest, all in the name of Third World solidarity.

The American reaction in this dimension has deep roots in the constitutional and legal tradition of the United States. It was the first country that derived its government explicitly from the consent of the governed; it is the world's oldest "democracy" in that sense. But the drafters of the American constitution found themselves in a dilemma: on the one hand, they recognized that a democracy was the only viable and legitimate form of government; on the other hand, they feared misrule by majority. Their resolution of the dilemma was not to compromise democracy, but to limit the legitimate acts of government. Students of American government learn of the "checks and balances" built into the three great branches of the federal government, of the "separation of powers" between the federal government and the various state governments, of the "Bill of Rights" which protects individuals against certain kinds of government action, and of the complicated rules for selecting the legislature to assure both continuity and responsiveness to popular will. The American constitution is really aimed at protecting the rights of numerous and shifting minorities within the context of majority democratic rule.

This background is helpful in understanding the negative American reaction to sweeping General Assembly resolutions—although on earlier occasions the United States itself made use of majorities that it could muster in the General Assembly—or to attempts by the Third World to introduce one-nation, one-vote procedures into other forums. It is not a new reaction against majority rule now that the United States finds itself frequently in the minority, although that no doubt heightens sensitivities; rather, it reflects traditional mistrust of majority rule, built into the foundations of American government. One consequence of aggressive calls for a new international economic order (NIEO), backed by resolutions such as the Charter of Economic Rights and Duties that seem to be one-sided in their approach, is to undermine further American faith in the United Nations as an effective and even as a desirable international forum.

CONCLUDING COMMENTS

A clear impasse exists on the question of unrestricted transfers from developed to developing countries. The developing countries demand more in transfers, channeled in a variety of different ways: higher commodity prices, a larger share in the creation of international money, straight foreign aid, and so on. Given the current American suspicion of government in general, and of the governments of developing countries in particular, these proposals are not likely to be well received.

Proposals for a new international economic order involve a deep paradox: developing countries want maximum freedom of action and assert strongly their demands for sovereign equality, including lack of interference in their internal affairs. Yet many of the proposals they have put forward, if implemented, would require profound internal changes within the western countries, for example with respect to the functioning of markets, the generation and dissemination of technical knowledge, the enforcement of contracts, and tax-expenditure programs. The inconsistency in position has not been missed.

In reality, the proposition that countries should not be subject to outside-generated influence and change—developed and developing countries alike—is untenable in today's interdependent world. An extreme position of self-reliance, such as China and Burma each adopted, would be required. Collective self-reliance, now strongly supported by many leaders in developing countries, will not be sufficient to assure insulation from outside influence. In the context of resource transfers, donor countries will at least want enough influence to assure that the funds are used for their stated purposes, whether these be to foster economic development, to relieve poverty, or what have you. One way to provide some assurance that the transferred funds are in fact serving to satisfy basic human needs is to restrict their use, with appropriate auditing, to activities that in their nature will do that. Examples would be activities to increase the production of food, to improve water supplies and sanitation facilities, to extend local health care and family-planning clinics, and so on. Developing countries could be told that funds are available for incremental activities in the areas indicated, subject to periodic audit for effectiveness. Beyond that, the recipient country would be on its own.

More generally, however, "transfer of resources" is an unfortunate choice for emphasis in discussions of a new international economic order, for it suggests taking from one group and giving to another. Such a process is rarely harmonious and is especially unlikely to be so when the developing countries insist that the transfers be made with a minimum of scrutiny and guidance. That demand undermines the one basis on which transfers are likely to be agreeable to those making them, namely, satisfying general sentiments in favor of distributive justice.

The implicit assumption underlying the focus on resource transfers is that B's route to prosperity is by getting it from A. In game-theoretic terms, it involves a zero-sum game: B's gain is A's loss, and vice versa. This has been the dominant assumption throughout much of human history, and remains the dominant assumption within many developing countries today. A major contribution to material success in western countries was the ability to break out of that framework into "positive-sum" thinking: the eighteenth century doctrine of progress shifted the "game" from one of man against man to one of man against a parsimonious nature. By cooperating with one another, or by establishing political-economic regimes whereby men's actions were mutually reinforcing rather than mutually destructive, men could improve their collective condition and at least lay the groundwork for improving the condition of each one of them.

Possibilities for Mutual Gain

Human "solidarity" is not a sentiment in harmony with zero-sum thinking. If we want to achieve global solidarity rather than global discord, the emphasis must be shifted to the areas in which there are possibilities for mutual gain. Here is not the place to spell such areas out in detail, but five in the economic arena can be mentioned briefly.

First, the commercial policies of the developed countries should be geared more clearly toward accommodating the growth in exports of industrial products from developing countries. In particular, tariff structures that now distort the location of early-stage processing of raw materials in developed countries should be altered to permit economic location nearer to the raw materials. In the long run all countries would gain by such a change. In addition, the developed countries should avoid the use of trade restrictions on competitive manufactures from developing countries; problems of dislocation to domestic industries can be handled with adjustment assistance to the factors that are injured. The developing countries would do well to concentrate their negotiating efforts on limiting the resort to "safeguards" by developed countries rather than on gaining further preferences on paper. They would also gain by reducing their own sometimes absurdly high protection against imports, which increasingly will deny other developing countries important markets and inhibit mutually productive specialization among developing countries.

Second, the western countries should manage their own economies much better than they have in the past; that alone would go a long way toward stabilizing the export earnings of developing countries. To the extent that they fail to manage demand smoothly, they can rightly be called upon to provide foreign exchange assistance to developing countries through generous compensatory financing arrangements. Beyond this, both developed and developing countries have an interest in reducing the wild commodity price fluctuations such as have been experienced in the past decade. Reducing price variability is a task distinct from raising average prices, and has much greater chance for realization. Wide price swings, quite apart from their effects on earnings, are disturbing both to consumers and to producers, and commodity agreements based on buffer stocks could reduce the variation of prices.

Third, the high mobility of multinational corporations creates potential problems for all governments, home governments as well as host governments. At their best, multinational corporations can contribute greatly to the process of economic development (but those countries that do not accept this judgment, or for other reasons prefer not to rely on them, should not be pressured into doing so). But by skillful manipulation, they can also evade taxes and exchange control regulations, exert undue influence on national policies, and diminish world competition. Governments have a collective interest in providing an environment in which the social benefits from the activities of these great corporations can be enjoyed while minimizing the costs. In particular, closer cooperation on global antitrust policy and on disclosure of financial information should be undertaken.

Fourth, management of some of the global "commons" requires the joint efforts of many nations. This is especially true of the world's stocks of marine life and of the quality of the oceanic and atmospheric environments. Many of these are regional rather than global issues, and global solutions would often be inappropriate. But international cooperation on a regional basis is essential for effective management. Moreover the revenue potential of proper management of the world's fish stocks is substantial, but cooperation in installing the right kind of management regime is essential not only if the stocks are to be utilized for maximum human benefit but also to realize those potential revenues.[27]

Fifth, in the long run the relationship between the earth's food supply and its population will govern whether it can evolve into a humane, pluralistic global society or whether large masses of people are condemned to starvation and the populations of the relatively rich countries must inure themselves to the continuing presence of poverty, destitution, and starvation—with undesirable consequences for their own system of values. Sound long-term policy calls for whatever efforts can effectively be made by the developed countries—partly through financial assistance, partly through transfer of relevant technology—to improve food supplies, nutrition, family planning information, and general health care in the developing countries.

These suggestions are not meant to exclude resource transfers from developed to developing nations—indeed, proper management of the oceans would generate a useful source of revenue for such transfers—but rather to shift the focus of discussion away from those areas that are in their nature conflictual and potentially acrimonious, to those areas where all participants to a negotiation among sovereignly equal nations may hope for some gain. Such a shift in focus would improve substantially the prospects for a new international economic order.

Chapter 10

TOWARD A TRANSFORMATION OF THE INTERNATIONAL ECONOMIC ORDER? INDUSTRIAL WORLD RESPONSES[1]

Reginald Herbold Green

Change has often followed crises, some of which have arisen from the politicizing of international economic issues, which in turn reflects the politics of domestic economic affairs and the blurring of traditional distinctions between domestic and international concerns.

—Kermit Gordon[2]

Global politics are becoming egalitarian rather than libertarian with demands from more politically activated masses focusing predominantly on material equality rather than on spiritual or legal liberty. Moreover, the global distribution of power is beginning to favor political systems removed philosophically, culturally, ethnically and racially from American antecedents while the process of redistribution of that power is threatening new forms of violence.

—Zbigniew Brzezinski[3]

INTRODUCTION AND GROUND CLEARING

The response of the industrial (or developed or rich) world to the the demands for a structural transformation of the international economic order is complex. Significant variations exist by country, by ideology, by class, by interest group, by issue, by structural relationship with developing peripheral countries, by national economic structure and by time period. Models assuming unified industrial world interests can be constructed—whether Marxist,[4] laissez faire,[5] gunboat,[6] or "redistributed productive efficiency"[7]—but they oversimplify to the point of distortion. Varying interests, attitudes and perceptions result in varying dominant coalitions both within individual industrial countries[8] and in the industrial world as a whole.[9] This would be inexplicable were there a homogenous set of interests, constraints, and goals.[10] Such homogeneity might simplify negotiation but, on balance, would decrease the chances of positive results.

The first problem in explicating developed world responses is to select a time frame. A case can be made for a 1969-70 starting point, especially because of changing Third World and academic perceptions of development about that time. However, until 1973, industrial world response to Third World demands was largely confined within international organizations specifically concerned with center-periphery problems. For this there were two reasons. First, Third World leaders did not perceive themselves as having power to force structural changes in the international economic order. Second, when industrial world decision makers put international economic order issues high on their agendas they were concerned primarily with North-North interactions and conflicts, especially disintegration of the Bretton Woods monetary system.

Therefore, the historic frame of this paper is 1973-1977. The action which made international economic order (IEO) issues central in the industrial capitalist economies and which focused attention on North-South economic relations was the Organization of Petroleum Exporting States' (OPEC) unilateral quintupling of the price of oil in 1973. By sustaining its action OPEC has kept the new international economic order (NIEO) at the center of industrial economy concerns.

This statement should not be read to mean more than it says. The claim that OPEC created a radically unfair price ratio for oil is debatable—1977 oil/manufactures terms of trade are little better than 1937 or 1947. The fear that OPEC marked the beginning of a tidal wave of

Third World government-organized commodity cartels confronting First World private (but state-backed) manufactured goods cartels is either a delusion, a state of shock (partly explained by the general 1973-74 commodity price boom which had quite different causes) or an organizing slogan for a hard-line response.

It has been widely asserted that the oil-price increases caused and continued the 1974-? capitalist industrial world recession. This is an odd proposition. The increases cost about two percent of capitalist industrial economy gross domestic product (GDP). That is not enough to explain a cumulative loss of half a year's output over 1973-77. Indeed, industrial economies have exported much of their oil-import bill to poor countries—whose increased trade deficits are affected by manufactured goods inflation as much as by oil-price inflation. It is notable, however, that in the aggregate the rich countries have received OPEC investments and deposits which have outstripped their trade deficits.[11]

OPEC in itself is not a model for a NIEO. Higher oil prices do weaken many Third World economies. OPEC as an organization proposes neither a uniform national development strategy nor an integrated program for economic order reconstruction. OPEC did accomplish three things, nonetheless. It demonstrated that joint action by a group of peripheral-economy states on decisions critically affecting the international economic order was possible and could be profitable. It encouraged other Third World countries to act on the premises that in unity is strength and that negotiation backed with the threat of confrontation could be effective. It caused First World decision makers to fear that this approach (whatever its payoff to the Third World) could deal serious stochastic shocks to an already malfunctioning industrial world economy.

The Quest for NIEO: Armageddon, El Dorado or Global Industrial Relations?

Third World demands for structural international economic change have been summarized in the rubric New International Economic Order and the tactics in Cooperation against Poverty (CAP) and Trade Union of the Poor (TUP).[12] The former is endorsed and the latter pronounced respectable by the United Nations Charter of Economic Rights and Duties of States.[13] These terms and debates surrounding them have been obscured as much as clarified in the industrial capitalist world. This is partly because there is not total homogeneity on goals or tactics among Third World NIEO, CAP, and TUP advocates. Further, to date there have been only prenegotiations—not operational negotiations on first steps toward structural change. Therefore, NIEO, CAP, TUP do not constitute present realities. Instead, there are objectives for initiating change in a stated direction more than detailing its end results. Combined with the fact that OPEC is relatively unified, able to act unilaterally, and precise as to goals, these imprecisions lead to a widespread industrial world tendency to see NIEO as OPEC writ large.

In fact, Third World demands for change center on three global "distribution" issues:

1. production and therefore trade (including productions and trade in knowledge);

2. surplus allocation including terms of trade (broadly defined to include transfer pricing, terms of investment, the institutional structures of production, finance and commerce); and

3. power to make decisions in respect of production and surplus allocation nationally and to play an integral role in global decision making.

In each case the Third World demands more in an absolute sense. However, in the first two cases this does not constitute a demand for reductions in First or Second World absolute levels. Indeed, the focus on relative growth is not as strong in the NIEO context as it was in the "gapmanship" of the 1960s.[14] In the case of power, the demand is clearly for a reduction in industrial-world power to influence (or make) political economic decisions in peripheral economies and for a shift from industrial-world hegemony to mutual interest protection in global political economic decision making. The industrial world perception that the Third World has shifted from asking for concessions "cap in one hand and fetlock in the other" to demanding participation in decisions as a right is correct. The parallel perception of this as the politics of envy[15] is much less so. Most Third World decision makers are concerned with their own state's absolute level of development, not with literal "catching up." Gratuitous damage to industrial world economies is not an end propounded in NIEO demands. Confrontation is perceived as a last resort or a means to achieve negotiations, not as a goal.

Negotiations in any serious sense are just beginning. There are few detailed articulations of NIEO as a process of structural change. Fewer still go beyond a three- to five-year initial period. Because the building blocks of structural change are superficially similar to those of marginal tinkering, these articulations are deceptively similar to old agendas for refurbishing the old international economic order. These articulations also give a superficial impression of shopping lists. This results from their authors' belief that for starting a process of structural change some areas of action are essential but no single project, policy or institution is uniquely necessary or adequate. The size and thrust of the package is seen as more critical than its components.

Industrial world perceptions of NIEO are confused and confusing. The initial shock reactions are gone. However, there is a persistent perception of NIEO demands as a new form of mendicancy, a new way of requesting international welfare transfers. The rich world believed the 1945-70 international economic order was a golden age which served the world well and needed only a few marginal modifications to round off the rougher edges for losers.[16] This paternalistic view was consistent with considerable personal and some national concern for equity and welfare of the global "lower classes." It was no more simple hypocrisy than that of nineteenth-century industrialists and landowners reacting against early trade, cooperative and peasant union demands. Perception of the NIEO demands as an international analogue to initial radical social democratic demands on the national level is quite uneven—highest in Scandinavia, the Netherlands, and Canada, lowest in the United States, West Germany, Japan, and the United Kingdom. The perception may also be high in the Soviet Union but given the history of social democracy in Europe it hardly commends NIEO to Soviet decision makers.

As a result of the above perceptions, many counterproposals fall between peripheral relevance and diversionary tactics. For example, the sudden resurgence of a rhetoric of aid and trade concessions— rhetoric since to date performance in both fields is stagnant—misses the point of the NIEO demands. The latter are based on the premises that structural changes in production, e.g., à la the Lima Declaration goal of 25 percent of industrial output in less developed countries by the year 2000 versus seven to eight percent today;[17] in the ownership of production and trade—the transnational corporations (TNCs) and nationalization debates;[18] and in the procedures of international institutions are critical. Without such changes trade concessions are seen as a poultice on a gangrenous wound and aid flows as blood transfusions without applying tourniquets to severed arteries. Many other industrial world proposals are not unsound and might, in the context of a broader strategic approach, be perceived by Third World decision makers as relevant. Access to industrial economy markets for processed manufactured goods, to financial institutions for loans and to interim sources of expanded concessional transfers are also part of NIEO demands. However, they do not constitute the entirety of such demands and are now offered by the developed world as alternatives to substantial structural change.

Socialist Europe: The Voices of Silence

The positions of the main European industrial socialist (communist) states will not be treated in the same detail as that of the capitalist industrial states. They are excluded for three reasons. First, socialist industrial economies are not central to the international economic order, especially in relation to the Third World. Second, they are not a significantly divergent element, their economic relations with most Third World states are broadly similar to those of capitalist industrial states.[19] Finally, industrial socialist states have avoided taking a lead in responding to NIEO structural change demands.

The Soviet Union—as a net commodity (including fuel) exporter—has benefited from the OPEC initiatives; its bloc partners have been net losers. However, this hardly constitutes an adequate explanation of the Soviet opposition to NIEO. Other explanations seem more cogent. Self-reliance, collective self-reliance, and "trade union of the poor" tactics are directed at all dominant industrial economies including socialist ones. Unlike nationalization, these tactics are not selectively aimed at capitalist international economic forms. Changes in response to NIEO, furthermore, might strengthen transnational corporations globally and national bourgeois coalitions in some less poor countries. They might also draw a few ex-poor countries into the capitalist industrial center.

Therefore, the NIEO campaign is deeply disturbing Soviet decision makers. It creates cross-class coalitions which put the Soviet Union in the camp of the status quo-oriented exploiters.[20] Strong Soviet opposition to NIEO is not seen as politically practicable, however, since several socialist states closely linked to the Soviet Union (Rumania and Cuba, as well as Yugoslavia and China and other radical Third World states such as Algeria and Tanzania) are firm NIEO advocates: to denounce NIEO as too radical would be tactically disastrous; to term it a capitalist ploy would be unconvincing.[21]

Perspectives

In order to explain in more detail developed world responses to Third World demands, this survey will provide: a historical sketch of 1973-77; an attempted typology of hard-line, marginalist, moderate and structural change responses; and a review of possible patterns of dialogue and action over the next few years.

CRISIS MANAGEMENT, CONTAINMENT, COUNTERATTACK, CONCILIATION: A HISTORICAL SKETCH

The immediate reaction to 1973 OPEC price boosts and embargoes was stunned disbelief and aimless flurry. At that point—albeit not by January 1974—the major petroleum companies were in a state of shock;[22] their home governments were engaged in damage-containment exercises. By 1974 shock changed to anger and containment to counter-attacking.

Ignoring the rumored military dimension,[23] these counterattacks included:

1. reduction of dependence on OPEC oil and creation of a counter-vailing rich users cartel—the International Energy Association;

2. use of food supplies and world food shortages to reduce the burden of oil-import bills combined with threats to use food-supply dominance even more politically than in the past;

3. passing on oil-price increases via export prices to regain balance-of-trade stability at the expense of third parties;

4. creation of financial safety nets for industrial capitalist and—on a more limited scale—non-oil-exporting Third World economies;

5. rhetorical concern for, and modest aid to, "most affected" states (usually suppressing that drought and grain-price boosts hit many worse than oil prices over 1973-75);

6. rigid opposition to NIEO proposals at the 1974 United Nations Sixth Special Session and regular annual General Assembly session;

7. efforts to divide the Third World by claims that OPEC, far from blazing a trail, was the chief barrier to more aid and trade;

8. efforts to co-opt some OPEC countries into the center "clubs" as associates (not full members);

9. retooling environmental concerns of the Stockholm Conference into "limits to growth" in a "finite world"[24] leading to the *triage* and lifeboat arguments for selective genocide and to a "them or us" stance on resource use.

Except for the last, these were spearheaded by the United States and especially by Henry Kissinger. This was not a simple extrapolation of the leading United States position among capitalist industrial economies nor of past priority given to economic affairs by the Secretary of State. The OPEC challenge strengthened the United States vis-à-vis other industrial capitalist states because it was a net primary product exporter (the largest gainer from commodity price increases in 1973 and among the largest in 1974) and was less dependent on energy imports. The disparity in positions actually hampered United States attempts to organize a counterattack. Western European states were more alarmed at the risk of head-on confrontation and more prone to seek special trade and finance deals. Only the raising of industrial export prices was uniform. That hardly constituted a coherent strategy since its gross (if not net) impact was dominantly on other industrial capitalist states.

Dr. Kissinger's style of centering attention on crises gave him little prior involvement with North-South issues. Because the NIEO demands were not readily resolvable, co-optable or routable by a single set of concentrated negotiations they were not readily amenable to his favored approach—a point also true for later conciliatory (e.g., World Food Conference, Seventh Special Session) or sidetracking (e.g., UNCTAD raw materials bank proposal) responses.[25]

Toward Dialogue

The 1973-74 industrial nation movement toward counterattack was followed by a 1975 shift toward dialogue. The Paris Talks, the Commonwealth Group of 10, the initial Integrated Commodity Program discussions and the 1975 United Nations Special Session were its products. Divisions among the industrial nations made a holding operation (testing the possibility of negotiation while retaining the option to counterattack) the easiest approach upon which to agree.

By 1975 the oil-price impact had to a degree been accomodated; other aspects of the commodity boom (at least for developing country products) had faded; recycling of oil exporter financial surpluses was working moderately well. There was no urgent need to confront (perhaps, also, no urgent perceived need to negotiate). Domestic and North-North international economic problems remained serious. Buying time by North-South dialogue while attempting to create greater industrial economy buoyancy to give negotiating room or counterattacking leeway appeared sensible. Pessimism, fear of change, or cynicism also counseled talking even if no results were expected. In fact, developments occurred on a number of fronts in 1975 to further North-South dialogue.

Some decision makers and advisors, especially in Canada, Scandinavia, the Netherlands, felt a need to explore a package deal broadly acceptable to, and serving at least some mutual interests of, North and South. This stand was stronger in quasi-establishment academic organizations and in networks linking individuals from both North and South.[26] The EEC Secretariat and many EEC national decision makers were willing to experiment with this approach and were concerned that, if industrial capitalist economies recovered together over 1976-78 with no NIEO agreement, a new commodity prices explosion and possibly new "OPECs" would result.[27]

In this context the United Nations Conference on Trade and Development (UNCTAD) floated its initial integrated commodity proposals as a middle road between producers' associations and the status quo. The elements in the package were not new. The real initiative was an attempt to put price stabilization (explicitly including ceilings), marketing (explicitly including access), and processing together in one package and to cover a broad range of commodities so that a majority of economies crossing the North-South divide would benefit.[28] The proposals came at a time of uncertainty as to commodity prices, with Third World exporters fearing falls and industrial importers fearing rises.

The refusal of the United States to consider basic foods as candidates for the program made the proposals less attractive to the EEC, Japan and the Third World. Adding indexation and bolstering the Common Fund's proposed role beyond buffer stocks restored balance but weakened European support.[29] This trend toward deadlock became clear in 1976. In 1975 UNCTAD did appear to offer a forum for moving to an agreed process of change on commodity issues.

The International Labor Organization (ILO) stressed three main themes in the documentation and runup to the 1975 World Employment Conference:[30]

1. "basic needs" (defined at both the national and individual levels) as a goal on which there could be North-South agreement;

2. transformation programs (on the model of Sweden's active employment strategy) to combine international economic structural change with sustained or increased industrial-economy worker and community welfare;[31] and

3. combining transformation and basic needs to overcome the industrial economy recession through a changed international economic order—a packaging designed to create a basis of common goals and interests from which to develop programs and policies.

The ILO's problem lay not in generating plausible ideas or non-divisive dialogue, but in how few governments (or unions or TNCs) took it seriously, precisely because it was not and could hardly become a formal negotiating forum for NIEO.

The Kingston Conference of Commonwealth Heads of State in 1975 was marked by British initiatives for sustaining and stabilizing real export earnings. The United Kingdom, with an export bias toward the Third World and heavy dependence on commodity imports,[32] had reason to believe that North-South confrontation would be expensive and that moderately higher but more stable commodity prices and more buoyant Third World economies were in its interest.

From Kingston came the Commonwealth Group of 10 whose first interim report[33] just before the Seventh United Nations Special Session appeared to be a broad North-South sketch of a possible set of goals and processes. However, United Kingdom decision makers had already begun to rate the risks of such change as higher and the gains from a North-South settlement as lower and moved steadily toward a passive hard-line position.[34]

Three other developments demonstrated the trend toward dialogue in 1975. The first was at the Paris Talks. Originally these were conceived as major OECD member-major OPEC member energy talks. The OPEC side insisted that their scope be broadened to cover all major NIEO issues and that the Third World side be a "representative" group. The United States opposed this—it has consistently sought to avoid any appearance of OPEC winning concessions for the rest of the Third World. The EEC states took the opposite view—exploration of possible package agreements was desirable. To offer concessions on commodities or trade or aid or debt in return for lower oil-price rises might be a sound tactic either to get stability in North-South relations or to isolate OPEC. When the talks broke down over United States refusal to broaden participation and scope, the United States found itself isolated and agreed to broad front discussions. The Paris Talks made little headway, but it was not until late 1976 that failure to reach even partial agreement threatened breakdown.[35]

The second of these developments was that the Club of Rome— entrepreneurs of "limits to growth"—became concerned that confrontation would have high costs whoever won. As a result Professor Jan Tinbergen from the Netherlands was commissioned to create a North-South technical team to prepare a major report on "Reforming the International Order" (RIO).[36] RIO's goal was to identify an international economic reform package in the joint interests of North and South and, in particular, to respond to the desire (of TNCs as much as developing countries) to alter the distribution of world economic activity.

Finally, the high point of the trend to dialogue was the United Nations Seventh Special Session. Both North and South delegates stressed the need to negotiate and blocked out very broad goals and areas for negotiation. The atmosphere was quite different from the confrontation over the charter a year earlier. The northern delegates sought in 1975 to recover ground on three substantive issues as a quid pro quo for agreeing that talks could proceed on others. These three were nationalization and regulation of TNCs (which the charter had explicitly approved and stated to be subject to national laws, not voluntary codes or international arbitration) and commodity access.[37] On the first point the North position went on record; on the second, pre-existing talks on TNC conduct codes were shifted toward the consideration of international rules;[38] on the third there was acceptance of the concept of a "right of access to raw materials."

Many industrial economy decision makers and conference participants in 1975-76 were uncertain whether the South wanted to negotiate or to confront. On its face this doubt is inexplicable—radical South spokesmen were among the most articulate in spelling out detailed areas and goals to be reached by negotiation. In many cases they specified that, within broad parameters, initial and further packages were open for discussion and trade-off. Why then the doubt? The question is important because this open skepticism eroded Third World confidence in industrial economy willingness to negotiate in good faith. Furthermore, when prenegotiating efforts went badly in 1976, this situation contributed to a mutual retreat toward rigidity and confrontation.

The succeeding Third World shift from mendicancy to trade union-type demands was a shock to the industrial states. OPEC had taken its 1973-74 action unilaterally. Past negotiations had consisted of South's pleas and North's decisions; the northern participants now suspected the South sought not a balancing but a reversal of the relationship. The majority of those directly involved in the North perceived even the South's short-term minimum claims as unreasonable (a position almost literally the inverse of southern perceptions).

Toward a Breakthrough? Or a New Crisis?

The apparent logic of the 1975 dialogue was for broad-agreement negotiations in 1976 and detailed operational negotiations in 1976-78. Whatever else can be said, it is clear that no serious broad agreement has yet been reached while detailed negotiations (e.g., copper, tea, hard fibers) have been peripheral, unproductive or both. Four causes can be advanced: First, since 1975 had seen no agreement even on interim goals, negotiation was premature. Second, because international institutions have had limited and specialized economic regulatory roles,[39] the new infrastructural requirements for serious negotiation were underestimated. Third, while not eager to revert to confrontation, neither North nor South saw significant overlap of their own lowest demands and the other's highest offers, and thus each was locked into waiting for the other to move. Finally, on the northern side no sense of urgency prevailed; combined with hard-line goals of dividing the South, this made agreement of low priority.

In 1976 the Paris Talks continued but made no progress. In 1977 they were wound up by a de facto agreement to produce a list of joint decisions on minor matters, a few apparent "agreements to agree" (notably on the Common Fund), rather sad and irritated restatements of initial positions and calls to move negotiations to other fora.[40] The World Employment Conference also produced a potentially useful dialogue, but not in any context of ongoing national policy reformulation of international negotiation in which it could trigger action.

The Tokyo GATT deliberations in 1976 offered some concessions to poor countries—perhaps almost enough to offset the tightening of overt and "agreed" import restriction generated by unemployment and trade balance concerns in several industrial economies.[41] However, GATT is not a viable forum for basic North-South negotiation. Its complexity, the nature of its reciprocity rules and the dominance of North-North trade have always made for ineffective poor country participation. A forum other than GATT concentrating on broad agreements subject to simple execution on North-South trade would be more likely to achieve a trade breakthrough.

UNCTAD barely averted a major breakdown in 1976. No real agreement was reached on either debt relief or commodity trade structuring—the two central issues—through mid-1977. The London Summit[42] (of the North) and the Final Communiqué of the Paris Talks[43] suggest possible progress toward some type of commodity agreements and Common Fund. What this means in practice is as yet unclear; South and North perceptions are close to agreement on practicable mechanisms and goals but a real gap remains.

On the issue of debt, the industrial countries desired to minimize losses and avoid barriers to exports. Since the bulk of present resource flows to Third World countries is via commercial banks, most home nations of these banks perceived a broad write-off for debt relief as unacceptable.[44] A minority supported write-offs for the very poor to avert domestic instability in the borrowers leading to disorderly debt repudiation. Hopefully, this strategy would aid world trade and very poor country economic development, as well. The negotiations were complicated because the South position did not differentiate between high-volume, commercial borrowers (e.g., Brazil, Mexico) who feared write-off discussions could jeopardize their future borrowing and the very poor or very heavily indebted for whom serious debt relief even at the price of lower new inflows could be significantly positive.

On commodities—at least until mid-1977—the industrial world delegations split into three factions.[45] Hard liners opposed the Common Fund as an improper interference with market forces, as likely to raise costs, and as an unacceptable broadening of the OPEC-type cartel approach. The United States (until 1977), West Germany, Japan, and the United Kingdom composed this camp.[46] The Group of 16 (the smaller industrial countries led by Scandinavia and the Netherlands) advocated agreement in principle to a Common Fund with immediate detailed negotiations on the fund, individual commodity agreements, and other aspects of the integrated program. This group saw confrontation as a negative-sum game, stable and probably somewhat higher commodity prices as just and conducive to a healthier world economy and joint control over world commodity marketing as desirable. The United States moved toward a cautious variant of this position in 1977. Similarly, the European industrial socialist states vaguely endorsed the Common Fund but sought to substitute long-term bilateral contracts. Increasingly they moved toward opposition to the integrated program over 1976-77.

Lull Before What?

Late 1976 through 1977 was a period of suspended animation. In part this was because the Third World viewed as bad tactics a showdown with the United States before allowing for policy changes by the Carter Administration. However, more basic factors may be involved, as well.

The industrial capitalist countries perceived time as on their side. Many saw the pressure of payments deficits and the passage of time without results on NIEO as likely to force acceptance of marginal amelioration of the present system by individual countries. The result might be a splintering of Third World unity and, perhaps, of OPEC itself. Now that the initial shock of the 1973-74 period has abated there was, and is, a real doubt as to how serious a problem Third World power—partially excluding the special case of oil—really can pose.[47]

This lull is not likely to last. The Common Fund negotiations, the debt debate, and/or GATT-centered trade talks are likely to produce either a breakdown or a breakthrough.[48] If the former, the lull will end in a crisis of some type; if the latter, rather more serious negotiations will begin.

ELEMENTS OF REACTION AND RESPONSE

The nonhomogeneity of industrial economy responses to the NIEO demands and proposals is complex. Individuals have shifted stances, as have national decision-making coalitions. Coalition makeup has changed, leading to altered "national" positions. Overall industrial economy responses have reacted to changing contexts and evolved over time. There is, however, some value in identifying four strands of response:

a) hard-line demand rejection and counterattack;

b) minimalist negotiation of peripheral concessions;

c) serious substantive negotiation; and

d) search for common goals for major structural change responsive to NIEO demands.

However, for decision-making groups, states, institutions, and interstate bodies (and for most individual actors or advisors)[49] actual patterns of reaction and response have often included elements of two or more categories. That is the case for terming them strands rather than categories.

Contain, Counterattack, Restore: The Hard Line

The main elements in, and proponents of, the hard line have been sketched in the historical section. The key tactic has been divide and rule. Secretary Kissinger's theme song was that OPEC caused the 1971-76 stagnation of real income in the poorest countries. Industrial economy recession limited export-led growth for the less poor semi-manufactured- and manufactured-goods exporters. Inflation and the monetary crisis limited public transfers to poor countries. All these were OPEC's doing. In short, the old international economic order's failure to generalize economic development via trickle-down came because energy costs had risen. The parallel claim was that the OECD countries were true friends of the poor to be helped by them in repelling the OPEC challenge.

This set of assertions is unsound—the 1945-70 record and the whole 1970-75 crisis of development thinking underscore that—but presumably these claims have always been intended as political polemics, not analyses.[50] Even TNC spokesmen view them with reservation and regret that more is not offered to capitalize on those aspects of NIEO they support. The splitting tactics have to date largely failed as well. OPEC has not broken up. The Group of 77 and the nonaligned have shifted from broad rhetoric to broad draft goals to broad negotiating frames and some agreed negotiating stances. The trial run of actual group negotiations has shown, if anything, more splintering among developed than among developing countries. It also showed the Third World side willing to settle for significant but hardly revolutionary changes plus real but limited African, Caribbean, and Pacific countries' participation in some decisions. That result suggests the hard line as a barrier to chaos is unnecessary.

The domestic mobilization side of the hard line has been half ineffective and half an unguided missile. Except for the winter of 1973-74, it is doubtful whether mass perception of OPEC as a villain affecting day-to-day life was attained. The "limits to growth" turn to environmentalism led to the *triage* and lifeboat models of aseptic genocide, but these were neither usable by policy makers nor likely to rally as many persons in the street as they appalled. What did flourish from "limits to growth" was a dialogue on environment, participation, new lifestyles, and resource saving which was iconoclastic, anti-authoritarian, and a considerable nuisance from most decision makers' viewpoint. Its prime impact was not on North-South dialogue. To the extent it did relate to this dialogue, advocacy of structural changes more consistent with NIEO than with the hard line was dominant.[51]

A more subtle hard-line variant has been raising "technical" objections to major proposals without offering serious counterproposals. Any proposal for structural change is in part a leap in the dark. For example, the size of stockpiles necessary to stabilize commodity prices depends to a large degree on future institutional patterns and expectations. Past experience is a poor guide and technical supply/demand data only a rough one. Any broad proposal advanced for serious negotiation is unlikely to be fully detailed, especially in respect of operational procedures and institutions. To do so before negotiation is likely to be a waste of time or an impediment to negotiation. Finally, a large number of individual NIEO proposals—taken literally—are subject to very serious technical objections.

Technical criticisms can be in good faith and are a necessary part of the negotiating process. However, there are other aspects to a barrage of detailed technical criticisms directed at outline proposals. They are premature; the initial step in successful structural change is to agree on broadly acceptable interim objectives and directions of change,[52] then to evaluate major substantive constraints, and only thirdly, to go to technical issues. Since the first step is clearly not accomplished, concentration on the third is illogical if there is a desire for negotiated change and disingenuous if there is not. Many technical objections appear to be designed to halt change without the stigma of overt rejection. For example, 1973-76 United States technical objections to any government intervention in commodity markets looked a trifle inconsistent with its domestic agricultural, copper price and subsidy, or security stockpile operations.[53] Flat assertions that price indexation is unworkable ignore the facts that the proposals were not rigid as to form (the concept stressed was fair relative prices) and that there are many domestic schemes for de facto indexing which are less than optimal but still highly workable.

In the short run, such objections allow industrial economy decision makers to halt change without saying no.[54] They do not resolve issues or conflicts but do erode mutual trust—again very clear in terms of New Commonwealth decision-making perceptions of the United Kingdom during 1976.[55] These results are aggravated when no serious, substantive counterproposals are put. Again the trade union analogy is illuminating. An employer who raised technical feasibility objections to all pay, fringe benefits, working conditions and worker participation proposals from a union and made no serious counterproposals would be widely perceived as bargaining in bad faith. One who rejected some, agreed to others and made relevant counterproposals to the balance would not necessarily be seen as unreasonable and would allow serious negotiation.

Marginal Changes: Tidying up the Old Order

The marginal change strand is partly a hard-line variant perceiving costs of confrontation as relatively high and those of marginal change as quite low. In that sense the United States, West Germany, Japan and the United Kingdom have at times held marginal change-oriented positions. The United States combination of "carrot and stick"—money for food and nonpayment of ILO and UNESCO contributions—was not necessarily an ill-coordinated set. It had respectable intellectual and analytical proponents.[56]

Another source of marginalism is a perception that major change is impossible to achieve. Bureaucratic and technocratic points of view combined with short-term historical analysis do seem to support that perception.[57] So, too—especially in the case of the United Kingdom— does perception of weakness compounded by a history of inability to gain from change.

A positive basis for marginal reform is the perception that not very much is wrong with the international economic order. South output, for example, grew rapidly—by both comparative and absolute standards—over the period 1955-70. An external barrier to its growth now is the North recession. What is needed is fuller operation of free trade— with many barriers to that perceived to be in the South—and a somewhat more poverty-focused orientation of aid—with the barriers again largely in the South. This view often challenges aid (including commodity agreements) as likely to deter needed change in the South.[58]

The preceding view contains an internal and an external contradiction. Free trade in practice has usually meant the right of the economically strong to proceed without let or hindrance into the territory of the economically weak. It is hardly responsive to NIEO demands as a whole even if it has some relevance to market access. Free trade and perfect competition might be a positive response but only the romantic Right (e.g., P. T. Bauer) advocates that. Serious free traders either hesitantly and with safeguards (e.g., Harry Johnson)[59] or full-bloodedly (e.g., Milton Friedman) accept that free trade means concentration of economic power in large units based in industrial capitalist (or socialist) states.

In many instances an international analogue of the domestic "blame-the-victim" response seems to be present.[60] Many such criticisms are valid (for northern economies, too) but the view that the South is poor basically because it does not take advantage of the opportunities open to it and angry because it does not have the patience to wait is both open to analytical criticism and counter productive in dialogue. The international economic order—for whatever reason—does operate on the basis that "to him who hath shall be given" and often on the corollary "and from him who hath not, even that little which he hath shall be taken." The effective way to influence southern decision makers' reviews of domestic and international economic policies is not to deny that reality, much less to defend it as a natural law or a moral commandment.

Broad Front Reforming of the Old Order

The distinction between flexible advocates of marginal change and cautious advocates of major reform is a fuzzy one. Two common characteristics are: agreement with Third World NIEO advocates that major changes in trade, resource transfers and attention to problems of absolute poverty are needed; but disagreement with the system envisaged by NIEO either on the ground that marginal changes could meet Third World needs or because proposed changes (e.g., RIO) are based on neoclassical comparative advantage analysis which would transform world production and trade but not meet the surplus and power distribution issues raised in NIEO.

In 1975 this reformist stance appeared to be the dominant form of response. With the heavy inflow of Trilateral Commission-Brookings Institution[61] personnel into the new United States administration it may have regained that position. It has been the stance of the EEC Secretariat and the ground on which joint EEC stands have been possible. It is also the central position within most of the smaller industrial countries. Equally, it is the dominant staff stance of several international organizations, e.g., the World Bank, IMF, United Nations Secretariat and a significant strand in others including ILO and UNCTAD (e.g., the initial Common Fund).

The raison d'être of broad reformism is simple. Whatever the merits of the 1945-70 system, it cannot be recreated and the 1973-77 operation of the international economy has been unsatisfactory. Second, whatever the intrinsic merits of the NIEO demands, they are backed by enough power and flow from enough real grievances to require serious responses. Third, confrontation is an expensive way to achieve change especially if early negotiations can avert it. Fourth, negotiation can be used to gain vis-à-vis other North economies in relations with the South—a realistic stance and not cynical unless it presupposes lack of other North followers will obviate delivery.[62] Fifth, some changes in the structure of production and ownership could provide mutual benefits. Finally, absolute poverty (especially absolute hunger) threatens stability as do the remnants of colonialism; therefore, self-interest counsels elimination of absolute poverty (and negotiated majority rule as in southern Africa).

This position remains within the context of continued capitalist industrial economy leadership (dominance) of the global economic system. It advocates minimum safety nets, some redistribution out of growth, and marginal alteration in control over key institutions (e.g., IMF, GATT, IBRD). In the context of the 1960s' aid and trade debate these would have appeared to be major initiatives. Their problem is that of ideas whose time came and went before they were seen as serious candidates for implementation. On a negotiating list basis, this response can be hard to distinguish from initial step, coalition building, structural change presentations. In practice and in face-to-face discussion, the divergence is much wider because of the different premises as to where their proponents are attempting to go.

Structural Change Advocacy

While not dominant in terms of official North-South policy stances beyond the "like-minded" group (Norway, Sweden, Netherlands, Denmark, Finland, and Belgium) and not clearly or stably dominant in all of these, the response to NIEO demands seeking serious negotiation on structural change is one which has relatively wide advocacy among intellectual and advisory circles of quasi-establishment standing. This response—given the different vantage points, immediate concerns and critical perceptions of most of its authors—tends to be different from NIEO demands. It also diverges because it is responsive, not initiatory, and is more concerned with building First World coalitions and articulating first steps toward a process of change than in formulating points of arrival. This can result in additions to the Third World demands—such as transformation assistance, First World internal participation, environment and lifestyle issues—as well as attempts to isolate immediate practicable agendas.

There are three clusters among First World structural change advocates.[63] The first can be termed "Third World firsters" whose real concerns on North-South issues are Third World-focused. To a degree the Overseas Development Council in the United States and the Institute of Development Studies in the United Kingdom might be so categorized, albeit this is to oversimplify. Included, too, are voluntary pressure groups such as the World Development Movement in the United Kingdom and the International Coalition at UNCTAD. The latter have fairly radical postures, largely middle-class professional memberships, catchy polemics and limited ability to convince decision makers.

The second cluster is almost the inverse—its NIEO concerns arise out of its demands for domestic restructuring.[64] Some trade-union leaders and radical social scientists are in this grouping. From this perspective the need to make changes internationally is an opportunity to mobilize for changes already desired at home (e.g., control over TNCs,[65] using "limits to growth" and "basic needs" to argue for a less affluent lifestyle). Yet, this posture often gives no coherent response to NIEO demands and is not a convenient building block for a domestic coalition to back international structural change negotiations. Equally, calls for even modest lessening of consumption growth—let alone asceticism or severe restraint—tend to drive away more support than they gain.[66]

The last cluster perceives national and international economic, political and social order changes as necessary in the interests of the majority of First and Third World people. This cluster is largely radical, social democratic and/or unorthodox Marxist in ideological position. It is dominantly intellectual and, therefore, tends to stress reasoned discourse with decision makers and advisors and (contrary to most of its members' own avowed convictions on participation) rarely seeks direct mass support. The exceptions appear to be largely in the "like-minded" country group (where there is a higher proportion of political, permanent official and union involvement) and in the World Council of Churches which seeks (perhaps not very effectively) to interact with the communities of Christians within its membership.[67]

This last cluster's preference for negotiation as opposed to confrontation presumably flows from the intellectual bias and base of its members. They perceive confrontation as a highly expensive way of resolving clashes especially when unconditional victory is not a relevant goal. They do not perceive themselves as of much relevance to mapping confrontation strategy wherein their position as advocates of the "enemy" would be more difficult than in the context of negotiation. This approach is logically sound and potentially operational if its perception of broad common interests is correct or if the price of resisting change is very high. Neither of the latter points has been demonstrated to the satisfaction of a majority of First World actors.

PROBLEMS, POTENTIALS, SCENARIO PIECES

What can be said of the probable course of industrial economy response and the evolution of North-South dialogue-confrontation-negotiation-implementation over 1978-81? Can there be enough optimism to invest major effort in the process? Would it matter much to the industrial capitalist economies (more specifically to their dominant decision-making coalitions) if there was a breakdown? No definitive answers are available, of course. Scenarios which attempt them may be useful pedagogically but are forced either to operate at a long-term, abstract level or are based on such detailed and numerous assumptions that the assumptions determine the results. What follows is less formal and more process-oriented or, perhaps, merely more impressionistic. It is not a prescription nor an expression of the author's preference but an attempt to identify some critical trends, possibilities and difficulties as they relate to the short- to medium-term industrial economy response to Third World demands.

Do Responses Differ Significantly? How?

The question of whether there are substantively differing industrial economy responses to NIEO demands is one which many Third World analysts answer negatively (as does Nurul Islam in Chapter 7 of this volume). If that perception, rather than the more complex one of this chapter, is correct, then NIEO negotiations are nowhere near beginning and the medium-term forecast must be for a series of mutually damaging confrontations.

However, the differences do appear to be real. The "like-minded" are not shadow members of the Group of 77. It would be odd if they were, given their different histories, contexts, structures and objective requirements. The concrete achievements of these nations are limited because they are small; they are not taken all that seriously by larger industrial capitalist states, and they are fairly recent converts to the proposition that the old aid and trade debates are outdated. Their stance simply is not identical or even broadly similar to that of West Germany, for example.

Equally, the emerging stance of the Carter Administration is not seen as very responsive to date by many NIEO advocates. That may well prove to be the case but even in what has been proposed concretely on food, aid, commodities and (less clearly) debt default safety nets, the contrast with the previous administration is more than nominal.

The denial of differences between industrial economy responses should be of concern to the First World even if it is less than accurate. It represents clearly how wide the gulf in 1973-77 dialogue has been between dominant industrial economy spokesmen and Third World expectations; how nominal the results of four years of dialogue seem from the periphery; how real is the danger of a breakdown because of Third World perceptions that the First World is "negotiating" in bad faith. These are factors gravely prejudicial to achieving mutually agreeable change.

Looking ahead, the crucial differences on the First World side still appear to be in perceptions of NIEO. Hard liners and their fellow-traveling marginalists are excluded here as their path is toward confrontation. This chapter views the latter route as something to be avoided if at all possible.

One set of First World perceptions of NIEO seems to hamper even dialogue. In a highly intelligent form, from an analyst not unsympathetic to NIEO, these are well illustrated by Richard Cooper (Chapter 9) in this volume. This position can be summarized as "transfer payments," "national autonomy and international management," and "positive-sum games."

If transfer payments mean charity, that is not what the NIEO demands are about. If they are "reparations," that is a minor rhetorical but hardly a major operational theme. If one defines—as does Cooper—virtually all transactions as involving transfer payments, then NIEO is about the terms of transfer (which may be of trade, of access, of control). However, that is so far from the common understanding of transfer that it hardly seems to help clarify dialogue.

Third World demands for national autonomy and greater power in international institutions are not perceived by them as contradictory. First, they note that industrial economies have a far higher degree of autonomy—including from international agencies—and more control over such agencies. Second, they seek selective international management and control because (like the present United States administration) they believe that, on balance, there is too little intergovernmental economic management and control. Third, if they, too, are to transfer real power to international bodies they must have effective participation in those bodies. This is not a position radically divergent from that of most industrial economies, and dialogue could usefully be directed to identifying concrete areas of agreement and divergence.

By and large NIEO demands are seen by their proponents as positive sum (that is, as mutually beneficial to all participants). There is no preference for negative-sum ones. However, in the absence of serious counterproposals from the industrial economy actors over 1973-77, there has been a tendency to push on any front showing the least sign of give. Escape from this potential dead end lies in the hands of industrial economy leaders. They can state clearly what areas they view as mutually beneficial, and then make substantive proposals on these issues so that the mutual benefits can be clearly recognized.

It is the case, of course, that a greater share in power to the Third World would reduce the share of the First World. Camouflaging this fact is not helpful to reasoned dialogue. However, if joint management increases the real combined power of all parties, each can still gain absolutely. In that sense the United States proposals for more international management suggest that it does see "positive-sum games" on power but their nature and extent might usefully be articulated more clearly.

The second set of industrial economy perceptions of NIEO (which are closer to the Third World's and the author's) are probably most clearly represented by political leaders in Norway, Sweden and the Netherlands. The economic settings of these three nations are, on their face, quite divergent. Norway is about to become a major petroleum exporter and is already a net raw-material exporter. Sweden is a marginal net raw material exporter. Both have quite limited trade links with the South. The Netherlands is an ex-colonial metropole which has systematically altered the structure of its important North-South links and was initially very badly hit by the oil-price rise.

There do appear, however, to be relevant characteristics shared by these three nations. First a domestic social democratic tradition has begun to be applied to international as well as domestic affairs. Second, successful experience with institutions and policies for transformation assistance have made structural change at least an acceptable concept to treasuries, trade unions and communities in these nations. Third, domestic economic management has to date been able to tackle both inflation and unemployment with a degree of success which promotes confidence in the ability to cope with change. Fourth, none is, nor can aspire to be, a great power. Therefore, relative power shifts resulting from NIEO do not appear as threatening to these nations as to the United States, West Germany, Japan, the United Kingdom or France. Fifth, because each is small and heavily externally oriented in production and use patterns, decision makers here are much more given to analyzing domestic, international economic and political issues jointly than is the case in the United States (or the Soviet Union).

There is some indication that an accomodation between these two sets of developed country perceptions is imminent. This indication arises from recent statements by West German (Chancellor Schmidt) and American (Zbigniew Brzezinski) spokesmen which imply more sympathy for the second, more dialogue-oriented perspective. Both these leaders have recognized the need for major international changes and do not necessarily see them as being imposed by conflict rather than negotiation.

Toward Interim Goals

A start toward negotiation requires a First World coalition supporting major reformist and structural change. This is not impossible—on first steps they are not in vast disagreement. On subsequent developments the process, by its own momentum, might carry its own power of conviction.

A set of interim, medium-term goals need to be agreed upon between North and South. They cannot be either as broad as "mutually beneficial development" or as formalistic as "avoiding conflict." Because there is no present common ground between dominant North decision makers and their South parallels on *ultimate* goals, stress should be on immediate and medium-range objectives which might lead to specific initiatives and to continuing negotiations. Examples include:

1.   greater international economic predictability and stability sought via global management, parameter setting and regulation;
2.   less asymmetry in North-South, North-North, and South-South

relations, including more joint decisions and more responsibility for international consequences of domestic decisions;

3. more balanced and stable growth of industrial economy-Third World economic relations including avoiding drastic changes and providing support for transition following external shocks;

4. concentrated and coordinated efforts to end the 1973-? North recession and South depression by broader economic interaction, not by economic isolationism; and

5. recognition of common concerns of North and South—e.g., TNC regulation, knowledge transfer and pricing, and stability—as a basis for negotiated "solutions" to positive-sum games.

Operational Coalition Construction

To build North coalitions able to negotiate will present problems. Sector, enterprise, and class interests diverge and are clearly seen to diverge. Some rhetoric so stresses these divergences as to prevent coalition building. A free-enterprise, free-trade rhetoric will not do. Doubtless it could secure major backers, but even in the North alone it would exacerbate conflicts, e.g., harden labor opposition to NIEO as a TNC plot. A modified RIO model has more chance. Productive efficiency through structural change could have a cross-group, cross-class and cross-frontier appeal. The same can be said of the initial negotiating agenda lists of some structural change advocates.[68]

"Unequal exchange"[69] is not a possible coalition-building theme (especially if it is a correct analysis!). "Equality of opportunity" probably suffers from the same problem for opposite reasons—it is perceived by too many as either a minor step toward egalitarianism or a strategy for maximizing actual inequality. However, there are types of economic inequality which can serve as the basis for coalition organization especially if their national parallels are used to show that such inequality is neither necessary, contributive to economic progress nor beneficial to more than a few subclasses and enterprises.[70]

Emphasizing mutual interest—e.g., stability, balanced trade growth, and limiting consumer price increase—is critical to organizing coalitions able to pay a price in negotiations without breaking up. This is not to say moral concerns do not influence individuals and, indirectly at least, state decision makers. Moral arguments are most likely to be acted on when they can be linked in a cumulative way to parallel perceived self-interests.

Toward a Process of Coherent Negotiation

If northern countries desire to achieve through negotiation a less unstable, less conflictual "reformed" or "new" economic order, procedural as well as substantive changes need attention. Some negative ones include:

1.   Divide-and-rule tactics as a strategic instrument to splinter the South should cease.

2.   North bargaining positions should not be created on the basis of least common denominators, excluding anything to which one or two states object. The result is a very narrow and inflexible position which is really not negotiable but is a "negative shopping list."

3.   The rhetorical anti-OPEC crusades and individual OPEC-member co-optation campaigns should halt. The first envenoms North-South relations. The latter is unlikely to succeed.

Positive procedural points include:

1.   Coherence, articulation and diversity need to be built into the negotiating process. For example, the General Assembly can, at most, conduct dialogues leading to broad agreement on goals and areas for negotiation. UNCTAD can, at most, carry the dialogue into more detail and negotiate the parameters of major decisions. Beyond that point, more thinking is needed. A system is needed in which small working groups responsible to limited constituencies can turn the broad parameters into detailed draft texts.[71] The latter would be referred back to a final decision-making group (e.g., an annual session of UNCTAD) and thence to governments for approval or international bodies for action. Negotiating sessions with 150 delegations are unlikely to work at all. A constituency system plus referral could provide a more flexible approach able to consider an adequate number of topics. Each could be referred to a separate working group with coordination flowing from the initial parameters and from the final referral back to a global forum.

2.   Procedures of negotiating forums need to be designed so that all states can utilize them. If GATT is expected to deal with North-South trade issues it offends against this criterion. Either a rethinking of GATT procedures to allow effective South participation and influence or a new North-South trade-negotiating forum is needed.

3.   The purpose of the NIEO negotiating process is, and needs to be seen as, resolving problems on an agreed basis to achieve mutually beneficial change. This may seem a truism—but much of what passes

for North-South negotiation is now perceived as a substitute not simply for confrontation but for action.

Conditions for Continued Progress

A process of serious negotiation is most unlikely to emerge and to continue unless five conditions are met. First, there must be a sustained movement at the international level parallel to that toward social democracy nationally. To cite a "like-minded" country source:

> If we are ever to come any nearer to achieving a new and more equitable international order, we must try to create a mixed economy subject to regulation . . . in line with what many nations have in their national economy.[72]

This is not to imply a need for social democratic coalitions in all countries. At that level a good deal of "pluralism" or diversity is both possible and inevitable.

Second, Third World unity on North-South negotiation must not simply endure but must become more self-confident. In the absence of such unity, the "trade-union" pressure will break down and the industrial economy marginalists will "win"—for a time. OPEC is a minatory example. Northern nation refusal to negotiate seriously over 1960-1972 led to 1973-74 unilateral action. If 1947 and 1974 oil prices had been identical but the movement between had been a moderately smooth trend achieved via negotiation (not a fall followed by an explosion), industrial economy development would not have been radically more difficult up to 1973 and would have been radically easier since. More confident unity is needed to allow more diversified negotiations. Divide and rule by the North, and the resultant fear of desertion by the South, imposes artificial rigidity on both sides. This is not to imply that southern policies need be identical any more than should northern ones.

Third, more initiatives and influence from the "like-minded" states and those actors in other states with similar analytical and value premises are critical. The United States' past hegemony (and especially the intellectual arrogance with which it is often expressed) has not been contributory to successful negotiation.

The United States is often unique both in its rhetorical stance and in the particular interests its decision makers see as critical. This does not prevent its taking a constructive part in negotiation; its sheer size means that its role will be major. Indeed the 1977 United States shift toward exploring positive negotiation has made it perhaps the most constructive of the major industrial economies. The more typical United States role, however, suggests that initiatives from smaller states with more social democratic approaches (on whom international economic order affairs impinge more sharply) should play a markedly larger future role.

Fourth, some results of a tangible nature are required soon to build confidence that the process is worth the price and to sustain trust that the majority of actors are bargaining in good faith. In this context failure to reach agreed lines for negotiation at CIEC (Paris Talks) or real progress on commodites (including the Common Fund) is dangerous. Similarly, clear cases of massive perceived injustice—notably southern Africa and Palestine—must be faced by industrial capitalist states in ways demonstrating serious commitment to just resolutions.

Finally, the process must support North-North measures to overcome the North recession. This is not merely because North growth is probably a political precondition for significant progress on production and trade restructuring, but because Northern actors need clear gains to justify major negotiated changes domestically.

Costs of Breakdown

It is an open question whether these conditions can be met. Breakdown is not unlikely. This is not to say any confrontation is evidence of breakdown any more than one strike is evidence of insoluble worker-owner conflict. Specific, limited confrontations will be a part of any process of serious negotiation for significant changes. The critical issue is whether confrontation will become dominant over negotiation. If so, what will the price be for the industrial capitalist economies?

Armageddon will not follow—at least not swiftly, nor surely. The initial results for the North would probably be to prolong the 1973-? recession; to be faced with costly (to North and South) economic "guerilla warfare"; to be unable to create a stable set of North-South political or economic relationships. However, that combination of strains is likely to cause something structurally key to the North and to the international economic order to snap. It could be the financial system in the face of massive (willed or forced) defaults on bank credit; it could be the ability (and belief in their ability) of some northern decision-making coalitions to manage their domestic economies; it could be the collapse of the necessary faith in the viability of the polity by broad majorities in some industrial states.

At that point the scenario becomes darker and cloudier. One type of optimist would predict the final triumph of socialism—the least probable short-term result. The more pessimistic point to the consequences of collapsed policies, economies, polities and lives from 1925 to 1935 and what that meant from 1935 to 1945—not in the sense of predicting a simple rerun but of a warning of the likely type and order of consequences. Others quite literally foresee violence (up to nuclear level) by Third World individuals or states who perceive themselves as having nothing to lose.

ENVOI

To conclude on a note of slightly greater optimism of the will (if not necessarily of the intellect) one can look at how Thorvald Stoltenberg of Norway has posed issues of response and chances of progress:

We can obtain a picture of what the developing countries are pressing for if we look back on the political developments in many of the industrial countries over the past 50 years. We have just succeeded in getting away from a national economic order based on the free play of market forces, which first and foremost served to benefit certain privileged groups. . . . It should not be necessary to remind you of the fact that these market interventions only became possible after a long political struggle. There was no lack of opposition and dire warnings when the first trade unions were formed . . . plenty of conservative economists . . . could "prove" that regulating the agricultural markets would be technically impossible. . . . Today, this issue, which was the subject of so much vehement criticism is supported by all responsible political parties. Today the poor countries of the world demand a new international economic order . . . a system of . . . control of the international markets. We support these demands . . . believe they are just . . . the developing countries' needs are the same as we know from our own national development. . . . The parallel between the development process in some industrial countries and the development the developing countries now wish to promote under the auspices of the new international economic order . . . [we support] precisely because we wish to continue the development process internationally and nationally which we have hitherto experienced [only] at the national level. We are aware of the pitfalls. We recognize that it is not just a question of applying national models to the international scene . . . the organizations which do exist are far from being equipped with the necessary ways and means. We have now entered a phase where we must seek to translate the New International Economic Order from mere words into action. The raw materials fund and the writing off of debts have come to signify the first phase in this process. Continued discussion as to whether this is the right way to start seems pointless. The developing countries are united in their stand on their demands. The developed countries' ability and will to cooperate will be the test case which will decide whether we are now to advance into a period of cooperation or of confrontation between rich and poor countries.[73]

NOTES

INTRODUCTION

1. I am much indebted to my colleagues, Manfred Bienfeld and David Evans for criticisms which helped me avoid some serious errors, especially misrepresentations of Marxism. Some of the themes have been aired in seminars at Stanford University, California, and elsewhere. This has proved a hard chapter to write and I am particularly in the debt of my secretary, Madeline Rowe, who has coped with illegible handwriting and incomprehensible insertion signs in numerous drafts as I have struggled for logical structure and clarity.
2. This is widely believed to have been based on papers read to "The Apostles," an intellectually exclusive club at Cambridge University which still meets.
3. The chapter published here is in fact an extension and revision of the arguments in Warren's well-known article, "Imperialism and Capitalist Industrialization," *New Left Review* 81 (September-October, 1973).
4. There is one misunderstanding which I am sure that Warren would have corrected if it had been brought to his attention. Hans Singer did not make a "remarkable prophecy" that it was a "near certainty" that "by 1990 Third World overall employment rates will total anywhere between 50 and 73 percent." Singer showed that some rates could reach this *on certain assumptions* and using certain concepts of unemployment, both of which he went on to reject. Warren confused *prophecy* with *projection*.
5. The chapter by Richard Cooper deserves careful attention. He has not merely been a member of the Trilateral Commission; he has become, since writing the chapter, the Under-Secretary of State for

Economic Affairs in the Carter Administration. If I were a member of a government of some other country, especially a poor one, I would file his call for "closer cooperation . . . on disclosure of financial information" by multinational corporations; it might be useful one day.

6. What follows should not be considered a precise or exhaustive summary of Warren's position: that is not my object. Nor shall I try to summarize the often rich arguments of other authors in this book, although I shall cite their positions at relevant places.

7. East European trade negotiators, even for trade within the COMECON area, use world prices as a starting point.

8. Those who find this totally unbearable had better treat it as just leg-pulling.

9. Although Adam Smith had more excuse for being Eurocentric because he was writing at an earlier date, he was perhaps less so. The explanation may lie in the fact that his upbringing was in Britain, not Germany.

10. Since Marxism is historically relativist, stressing that ideologies reflect the needs of particular classes at a particular time, it logically demands that it should itself be changed as time passes, eventually beyond recognition.

11. Marx used the word in an even stranger way, meaning roughly some procedure that got to the heart of reality and dispelled myths.

12. "European" as used here includes countries of European settlement, especially the United States, Canada, Australia and New Zealand.

13. I do not wish to imply that any neoclassical theory is in fact appropriate for all European countries, especially now.

14. In the Marxist convention, "nonproductive services" are omitted. This makes little essential difference to the observed rate (although it may lead to a serious neglect of services in policy). It is curious, however, that Bill Warren used "bourgeois" national income concepts, derived from Keynesian economics, without apparent qualms.

15. It would be interesting to check whether there has been *any* increase in per capita income in Britain since the Middle Ages, pricing cathedral, monastery, castle and mansion construction at today's replacement cost, allowing, of course, for current wages of masons, carpenters, etc. This would, at current rates of interest, provide an estimate of imputed rents. One would also have to value personal services, such as running royal courts, at today's hourly wage rates (allowing for the decline in productivity), and paintings, sculptures, and artisanal products at current market prices. (One would have to take into account, of course, all the medieval buildings and works of art which have disappeared in the meantime.) One would also of course have to include all the do-

mestic outputs (such as baking bread, making clothes, teaching, etc.) that are now commercial. In strict neoclassical practice, one would value them all at prices which allowed not only for inflation but also for backward discounting, making the medieval income per head many millions of times that of today! The reader might well ask why one should attach any value at all to castles when people were hungry—but for a neoclassical economist even to pose that question would bring down the whole house of cards.

16. Statisticians were only driven to stretch their imaginations in this way because neoclassical economists persuaded politicians that economic growth would curb unemployment, poverty, etc.

17. This was not true, however, of Marx and Engels themselves, who frequently referred to ethnic influences, especially when as journalists they were actually analyzing reality.

18. Marxists generally ignore the composition of consumption, and (what is brought out explicitly in the work of Kalecki) assume that in a capitalist system only capitalists save.

19. I owe this point to Paul Streeten.

20. As Manfred Bienefeld has pointed out to me, Warren in one crucial respect departed from the Marxist approach, in that he failed to specify and analyze the contradictions of the capitalist system, and to discuss the conditions for their being resolved.

21. The ease with which Chicago School economists can be converted into Marxists is shown by a number of examples (e.g., John Gurley). As and when theoretical censorship is relaxed in Eastern Europe, we can expect to see conversions in the other direction (already foreshadowed by some of the cultural currents running in Prague's premature liberalization and by Soviet interest in "Western" mathematical economics).

22. Of course, the Soviet structure was not in fact as egalitarian as its ideology, especially if judged by the concentration of economic power, rather than simply of income.

23. On the extreme Right were the governments of Italy and later Nazi Germany, which used biological arguments to justify inequality.

24. Apart from propaganda, financial and military aid, technical assistance and educational scholarships, there are powerful multilateral means of influencing development strategies—e.g., the International Monetary Fund's conditions for financial support.

25. This is not to say that policies derived from Chicago School doctrines, such as the need to give up protectionist policies, would be against the national interest of the United States (or Japan or West Germany).

26. In the 1970s, it is being similarly neglected in Africa by both powers.

27. Much of this paragraph applies to trade union leaders too.
28. In many countries, even communist leaders are acceptable to capitalists: there may be nobody else willing and able to help a company avoid strikes.
29. "Nationalism" can also be considered a proxy for all motivations that are neither materialist nor individualist, e.g., traditionalism; antinationalism stands for "economism."
30. The use of two dimensions of ideology has been suggested before, e.g., Eysenck's dimension of "tough-mindedness," together with a Left-Right dimension. So the form of the diagram is not original. Many others have implicitly used the degree of "democracy" as a second dimension.
31. But of course not only these.
32. Some Marxist movements in southern Africa have even (very unsuccessfully) based their tactics on the supposed common interests of black and white workers (e.g., in the mines).
33. For this reason, the conventional dichotomy has not become completely irrevelant. Thus the attempt of the Allende government in Chile to achieve a major shift in the distribution of economic power provoked a basically Left-Right confrontation by welding together military fascists and liberals, exemplified by the presence of "Chicago boys" (such as Cauas, de Castro, and Bardon) in the Pinochet cabinet.

CHAPTER 1, pp. 21-52

1. I am grateful to Ajit Ghose and Jeffrey James for assistance in preparing this chapter, and to Albert O. Hirschman, Dudley Seers, Karsten Laursen and J. C. Voorhoeve for helpful comments.
2. Gunnar Myrdal, *Asian Drama*, vol. 1 (Harmondsworth: Penguin Press, 1968), p. 9.
3. Albert O. Hirschman, "A Generalized Linkage Approach to Development, with Special Reference to Staples," *Essays on Economic Development and Cultural Change in Honor of Bert F. Hoselitz*, vol. 25, Suppl., 1977, ed. Manning Nash. The two articles by Paul A. Samuelson were "International Trade and the Equalization of Factor Prices," *Economic Journal* 59 (June, 1948), pp. 163-84; and "International Factor-Price Equalization Once Again," *Economic Journal* 59 (June, 1949), pp. 181-97.
4. *Ibid.*, p. 68.
5. Paul Streeten, "A Critique of the 'Capital/Output Ratio' and Its Application to Development Planning," in *The Frontiers of Development Studies* (London: Macmillan, 1972), chapter 6.
6. Paul A. Baran, "On the Political Economy of Backwardness," *Manchester School of Economic and Social Studies* 20 (January, 1952), pp. 66-84.
7. Walter Galenson and Harvey Leibenstein, "Investment Criteria, Productivity and Economic Development," *Quarterly Journal of Economics* 69 (August, 1955), pp. 343-70.

8. Since W. W. Rostow's *The Stages of Economic Growth* (Cambridge: Cambridge University Press, 1960) veers between the tautologically trivial and the historically false, it could be said of the former that it was not even wrong. See also W. W. Rostow, "The Take-off into Self-Sustained Growth," *Economic Journal* 66 (March, 1956), pp. 25-48.

9. Colin Leys, "The Role of the University in an Underdeveloped Country," *Education News* (April, 1971), Department of Education and Science, Canberra. For a critique of the linear theory, see chapter 2 of *Development in a Divided World*, ed. Dudley Seers and Leonard Joy (Harmondsworth: Penguin, 1971).

10. André Gunder Frank, "The Development of Underdevelopment," *Monthly Review* (September, 1966), pp. 17-31; and *Capitalism and Underdevelopment in Latin America* (New York: Monthly Review Press, 1967).

11. It is paradoxical that the socialist or radical advocates of "delinking" propose something that was triggered off by capitalist hostility to the Soviet Union, the People's Republic of China, and Cuba. A similar paradox arises from the fact that the burning of wheat and the dumping into the sea of coffee in the Thirties brought home to many the irrationalities of capitalism, while similar restriction schemes are advocated in the Seventies by socialists.

12. Gunnar Myrdal, *Economic Theory and Under-developed Regions* (London: Duckworth, 1957).

13. Albert O. Hirschman, *The Strategy of Economic Development* (New Haven, Connecticut: Yale University Press, 1958), chapter 10.

14. See Harry G. Johnson, *Economics Policies Toward Less Developed Countries* (Washington, D.C.: Brookings Institution, 1967); and Ian Little, Tibor Scitovsky and Maurice Scott, *Industry and Trade in Some Developing Countries* (OECD) (Oxford: Oxford University Press, 1970). Some of the country studies on which this work was supposed to be based are considerably less critical of the policies criticized in the main report. See e.g., Joel Bergsman, *Brazil: Industrialization and Trade Policies* (OECD) (Oxford: Oxford University Press, 1970). Another important study in the same vein is Bela Balassa and Associates, *The Structure of Protection in Developing Countries* (Baltimore: Johns Hopkins University Press, 1971), sponsored by the World Bank and the Inter-American Development Bank.

15. A different kind of reconciliation has been proposed by Albert O. Hirschman as long ago as 1957, at a conference of the International Economic Association in Rio de Janerio, where he advocated that an alternation of close contact with the center and of enforced isolation from it may be the most effective way for the periphery to develop. More recently, he set down his reasons for this point of view in the following terms:

> A discussion has long been raging about whether close contact by means of trade and capital flows with the advanced

industrial countries is beneficial or harmful to the less developed countries. Some authors have been able to cite important static and dynamic, direct and indirect benefits that accrue to these countries from close contact. Others have shown that close contact had a number of exploitative, retarding, stunting, and corrupting effects on the underdeveloped countries and that spurts of development in the periphery have often been associated with periods of interruption of contact, such as world wars and depressions. To neither of these two warring parties has it apparently occurred that they may quite conceivably both be right. In order to maximize growth the developing countries could need an appropriate alternation of contact and insulation, of openness to the trade and capital of the developed countries, to be followed by a period of nationalism and withdrawnness. In the period of openness, crucial learning processes take place, but many are of the latent kind and remain unnoticed and misperceived. They come to fruition only once contact is interrupted or severely restricted: the previous misperceptions are then forcibly swept away. Thus both contact and insulation have essential roles to play, one after the other. (*A Bias for Hope: Essays on Development and Latin America* [New Haven, Connecticut: Yale University Press, 1971], pp. 25-26.)

As Albert O. Hirschman adds on another occasion, "Unfortunately it is not easy to spell out the correct phasing of such an alternation."

16. For a list of harmful impulses, see Paul Streeten, *op. cit.*, pp. 5-12.
17. For an analysis of the conflict between closing the "Communication Gap," due to lack of external contact, and closing the "Suitability Gap," due to excessive external contact, see chapter 22 of *The Frontiers of Development Studies*.
18. Hollis Chenery *et al.*, *Redistribution with Growth* (London: Oxford University Press, 1974), p. 228.
19. Here again, as in the evolution of thought on "delinking" discussed earlier, undercurrents and cross-currents present a more complex picture. The Indian planners from the beginning were concerned with the fate of the poor, with "basic" or "minimum human needs," and the much criticized community development program was directed at the welfare of the rural poor. The first World Bank mission, led by Lauchlin Currie, in its *Report* in 1950 also put primary emphasis on meeting basic needs in Colombia.
20. For an excellent survey of the change in objectives on which the above paragraphs have been drawn, see H. W. Singer, "Poverty, Income Distribution and Levels of Living: Thirty Years of Changing Thought on Development Problems," in *Essays in Honor of V. K. R. V. Rao* (forthcoming).
21. There were, of course, also pessimistic threads in the fabric of

thought of earlier years. The doctrine of the vicious circle of poverty can hardly be called optimistic. At the same time, the seeds of optimism were there: vicious circles could be transformed into virtuous circles, and the same forces that cumulatively prevent progress in one constellation can reinforce it in another. More specifically, the solution pointed to more foreign aid as a solvent of obstacles to progress. For a different view of cycles of optimism and pessimism see H. W. Singer, "Recent Trends in Economic Thought on Underdeveloped Countries," in *International Development Growth and Change* (New York: McGraw-Hill, 1968), chapter 1.

22. While a good deal of the debate on agriculture versus industry is a sham dispute, Michael Lipton has made a powerful case that "urban bias" has systematically caused the neglect or the exploitation of the rural sector for the benefit of the urban sector. See his *Why Poor People Stay Poor, Urban Bias in World Development* (London: Temple Smith, 1977).

23. R. Nurkse, *Problems of Capital Formation in Underdeveloped Countries* (London: Oxford University Press, 1953).

24. J. Adler and S. K. Krishnaswamy, "Comments on Professor Bye's Paper," in *Economic Development for Latin America*, ed. H. S. Ellis (New York: St. Martin's, 1961).

25. W. A. Lewis, "Economic Development with Unlimited Supplies of Labor," *The Manchester School of Economic and Social Studies* 22 (May, 1954), pp. 139-191.

26. M. Friedman, *A Theory of the Consumption Function* (New York: National Bureau of Research, 1955).

27. M. Abramovitz, "Resources and Output Trends in the United States since 1870," Papers and Proceedings of the American Economic Association (May, 1965); and R. Solow, "Technical Progress and Productivity Change," *Review of Economics and Statistics* (August, 1957); reprinted in Amartya Sen, ed., *Growth Economics* (Harmondsworth: Penguin, 1960).

28. A. K. Cairncross, *Factors in Economic Development* (New York: Praeger, 1962).

29. Albert O. Hirschman, *op. cit.*

30. T. W. Schultz, "Investment in Human Capital in Poor Countries," in *Foreign Trade and Human Capital*, ed. Paul D. Zook (Dallas: Southern Methodist University Press, 1962), pp. 7-14.

31. Robert E. Mabro, "Aspects of Economic Development in Iran," mimeographed for The Royal Institute of International Affairs, in *Iran, 1980-85: Problems and Challenges of Development*, Chatham House Conference, December 7, 1976.

32. James Meade, "Population Explosion, The Standard of Living and Social Conflict," *Economic Journal* 77 (June, 1967), pp. 233-255.

33. F. Dovring, "The Share of Agriculture in a Growing Population," *Monthly Bulletin of Agricultural Economics and Statistics* (September, 1959).

34. See Albert O. Hirschman, "Changing Tolerance for Inequality in Development," *World Development* 1 (December, 1973), pp. 29-36.
35. It would be quite erroneous to equate this trend toward authoritarianism with a turn away from what Myrdal has called "the soft state." Violence is not hardness, though some of the regimes come to power with the pretense to eradicate "softness," like corruption. See Gunnar Myrdal, *Asian Drama*, vol. 2 (Harmondsworth: Penguin Books, 1968).

CHAPTER 2, pp. 53-72

1. This paper would not have been written without the help of José Serra, who gave me advice on the selection of texts and carried out the research on bibliography which was indispensable to substantiate the analysis. He also suggested directions for the interpretation.
2. The central work of A. C. Mello e Souza is *Formação da Literatura Brasileira* (São Paulo: Livraria Martins, 1959), 2 vols. Among other things, Roberto Schwarz wrote "As Idéas fora do lugar" ["Ideas out of place"], *Estudios*, no. 3 (São Paulo: CEBRAP, January, 1973).
3. João Cruz Costa, *Contribuição a História das Idéas no Brasil* (Rio de Janeiro: Livraria José Olympio Editora, 1956), especially chapters 3 and 4.
4. Prebisch's article was "El desarrollo económico de la América Latina y algunos de sus principales problemas," United Nations, E/CN 12/89/rev. 1.
5. The following pages concerning the 1950s are based on documents from ECLA or by Raúl Prebisch. In the case of the former, the collaboration of such economists as Celso Furtado, Juan Noyola, Regino Botti, and others was of great importance. It is difficult to weigh individual contributions, since there is no research on this aspect. Prebisch's article has been called by Hirschman "the ECLA Manifesto." See, Albert O. Hirschman, "Ideologies of Economic Development in Latin America," in *A Bias for Hope: Essays on Development and Latin America* (New Haven, Connecticut: Yale University Press, 1971), pp. 280-281.
6. These data concerned the trade of the United Kingdom with the Third World. This statistical base was considered insufficient evidence by some of Prebisch's critics, as explained in more detail below. The basic argument was that the lack of competitiveness of the United Kingdom industrial commodities, in relation to those of Germany, Japan, the United States, and other developed economies, could have distorted the results.
7. ". . . it follows that the exchange values of manufactured articles, compared with the products of agriculture and of mines, have, as population and industry advance, a certain and decided tendency to fall . . ." J. S. Mill, *Principles of Political Economy*, Ashley, ed.

(New York: Longmans, Green and Company, 1909), p. 703.

8. Prebisch did not predict any law concerning the necessary worsening of terms of trade. He just tried to explain empirical findings by proposing an interpretive hypothesis and suggested some practical measures to ease a difficult economic situation in periphery countries. Haberler's critique is in "Los términos de intercambio y el desarrollo economico" in H. S. Ellis, *El desarrollo y América Latina* (Mexico: Fondo de Cultura Economico, 1957), pp. 325-351. Professor Haberler's basic argument is that the relation between prices of commodities is not an adequate indicator for measuring the terms of trade. It would be better to analyze the "single factoral terms of trade," by isolating the effects of alterations in productivity for one export commodity on the international price of the product. There would be a fall in the relative prices lower than the reduction of costs induced by a technological change.

9. *Ibid.*, p. 306.

10. In a sense, the "catastrophist" perspective, which later led to the formulation of theories of "the development of underdevelopment," was deeply incrusted in the ECLA theory. It would be incorrect, however, to suppose that the emphasis in ECLA's argument on the deficiencies of international market mechanisms led to mainly static or catastrophist formulations. Such formulations were contained in some of ECLA's positions, but only implicitly. The 1949 document did incorporate the idea of cycles: it asserted that the prices of manufactured products would fall less during a recession than those of primary products, while at the end of a boom the latter would rise faster. The overall results would be negative for primary products. It would be wrong, then, to say—as Haberler implied—that ECLA's diagnosis was based on a purely static conception of the relations between center and periphery.

11. On this point, see the series of lectures given in July-August, 1950 by Jacob Viner of Princeton University in Rio de Janeiro, under the auspices of the Fundação Getulio Vargas. They were published as *International Trade and Economic Development* (New York: Free Press, 1952).

12. *Ibid.*, p. 44.

13. Gunnar Myrdal, *The Political Element in the Development of Economic Theory* (London: Doubleday and Kegan Paul, 1953).

14. The most complete formulation of the theory of circular causation with cumulative effects can be found in Gunnar Myrdal, *Economic Theory and Under-Developed Regions* (London: Duckworth and Co., 1957); published in the United States under the title *Rich Lands and Poor* (New York: Harper and Row, 1958), especially chapters 2 and 11.

15. R. Nurkse, *Problemas de formación de capital* (Mexico: Fondo de Cultura Económico, 1955), chapter 1.

16. Several authors took the road of the theory of "balanced development." Rosenstein-Rodan, for example, had rejected the idea that

there were advantages in autarkic national development and proposed a style of development based on substantial international investments and loans. He also defended a growth strategy based on large-scale planning for different and complementary industries. Through this mechanism, the industrialization of the periphery would have the advantage of absorbing the rural populations, instead of leading them to emigrate and thereby add to the stream of capital flowing into the developed countries. See his article, "Problems of Industrialization of Eastern and South-Eastern Europe," in *The Economics of Underdevelopment*, ed. A. N. Agarwala and S. P. Singh (London: Oxford University Press, 1943), pp. 245-255. In another paper, he redefined this view and defined the advantages of concentrating efforts to give a "great initial thrust" to backward economies through investment on a large scale. See P.N. Rosenstein-Rodan, "Notas sobre la teoría del gran impulso", in Ellis, *op. cit.*, pp. 67-93.

17. Maurice Dobb, *Political Economy and Capitalism* (New York: International Publishers, 1945). Paul Singer points out the contradictory way in which Dobb develops his ideas when, having shown that there would be investment on the periphery to avoid the tendential fall of the profit rate, he says that *industrial production* in the colonies would be a complement and not a rival to that of the metropolis. Paul Singer, "The International Division of Labor and Multinational Companies" (São Paulo: CEBRAP, 1976), p. 16.

18. Paul Baran, "On the Political Economy of Backwardness," in Agarwala and Singh, *op. cit.*, p. 83.

19. *Ibid.*, p. 91.

20. Baran's book, *The Political Economy of Growth* (New York: Monthly Review Press, 1957) shows the curious position of the American neo-Marxist view of development. Baran systematically criticizes the solution proposed by Nurkse and, with limitations, accepts that of Prebisch, concerning the role of foreign investments. See chapters 6 and 7.

21. The best discussion of ECLA and its development policies is in Albert O. Hirschman, "Ideologies of Economic Development in Latin America," in *A Bias for Hope, op. cit.* This essay and another from the same book—"The Political Economy of Import-Substituting Industrialization in Latin America"—are fundamental to an understanding of the history of these ideas and of the process of development.

22. In this respect, Prebisch's lecture on "La Planificación Económico," *Panorama Económico* (Santiago), no. 231, is significant. In it he asserts: "Through planning we want to redistribute income, once having increased it, to the benefit of the masses of the people."

23. *Ibid.*, p. 3.

24. Prebisch, *op. cit.*, 1951, p. 51.

25. Prebisch, "Problemas teóricos y practicos del crescimiento económico," United Nations paper no. 52 II (New York: United Nations, September, 1952), p. 146 says:

Nowadays foreign investments are appealed to in preference to the development of internal activities.

In the essay on dependency written by Faletto and myself, in 1966-67, emphasis is laid precisely on the consequences of this process. Baran had only perceived it in a tangential way. Analyses of imperialism dwelt much more on the aspects related to colonialism and exploitation of the enclave type or of primary products, than on industrilization with a view to the internal market. Even in more recent times, several authors have continued to think of the relation between center and periphery in the light of the old imperialist-exporting relationships.

26. Prebisch, "Problemas teóricos . . .," *op. cit.,* p. 46. It should be noted, however, that in the same text Prebisch shows that the peripheral countries should make the effort to capitalize primary production in order to improve the standard of living of the population, and that "foreign investment, which used to be the principal element in the primary production sector, becomes a supplementary element, indeed of considerable significance."

27. For an anthology of the main texts, see CEPAL, *El Pensamiento de la CEPAL* (Santiago: Editorial Universitaria, 1969). To evaluate the way in which the "teachings of ECLA" were transmitted in the mid-Sixties, see the handouts of the Chair of Economic Development, written by Oswaldo Sunkel and collaborators. The book by Sunkel and Pedro Paz, *El subdesarrollo latino-americano y la teoría del desarrollo* (Mexico: Siglo XXI, 1970), brings together other developments in Latin American thinking on the subject.

28. I have written several papers on this change in the relation between center and periphery. A summary of this theme can be found in English in F. H. Cardoso, "Dependency Revisited, " Heckett Memorial Lecture, University of Texas at Austin, Texas, 1973; and "The Consumption of Dependency Theory in the U.S.A.," *Latin America Research Review* 80 (July-August, 1973); and "Current Theses on Latin American Development and Dependency: A Critique," Ibero-American Language and Area Center, *Occasional Papers,* no. 20 (New York: New York University, 1976).

29. Aníbal Pinto, "La concentración del progreso técnico y de sus fructos en el desarrollo latino-americano," *Trimestre Económico,* no. 25 (January-March, 1965), and "Heterogeneidade estrutural e modelo de desenvolvimento recente," in *América Latina, ensaios de interpretação económica,* coordinated by José Serra (Rio de Janeiro: Paz e Terra, 1976). The latter is a Brazilian translation of a collection previously published in Mexico. The introduction by Serra, "O Desenvolvimento da América Latina," is an excellent guide to the analysis of this period.

30. See Pedro Vuskovic, "Concentracion y marginalizacion en el de-

sarrollo latino-americano," 1969; and "A distribuição de renda e as opções de desenvolvimento," in Serra, *op. cit.*, originally published in 1970.

31. Vilmar Faria analyzes these developments well and in detail. See his "Occupational Marginality, Employment and Poverty in Urban Brazil" (Ph.D. diss., Harvard University, 1976), especially pp. 41-49. For a review of this stagnationist viewpoint in ECLA, see pp. 37-40 of this dissertation.

32. The first version of dependency studies in connection with development was a report that I presented at ILPES in 1965. Following this report Enzo Faletto and I published *Dependencia y desarrollo en América Latina*, whose first complete version was circulated in 1967, at ILPES.

33. F. H. Cardoso, *op. cit.*, 1977.

34. For the full development of these ideas, see F. H. Cardoso and E. Faletto, *Dependencia y Desarrollo en América Latina* (Mexico: Siglo XXI, 1969).

35. The most challenging critique seems to be Francisco de Oliveira's "A Economia brasileira: crítica á razão dualista," in *Estudos*, no. 2 (São Paulo: CEBRAP, October, 1972), pp. 3-82.

CHAPTER 3, pp. 75-96

1. I am grateful for helpful comments received from the participants at the conference, my Institute of Development Studies colleagues, Chris Colclough, Ron Dore and Hans Singer, and from Wouter Tims.

2. Commission on International Development (Pearson Commission), *Partners in Development* (New York: Praeger, 1969).

3. Dag Hammarskjöld Foundation, *What Now? Another Development* (Uppsala: 1975).

4. Max F. Millikan and Donald L. M. Blackmer, eds., *The Emerging Nations: Their Growth and United States Policy* (London: Asia Publishing House, 1961), pp. ix, x, 45, 60, and 98.

5. Francis Bator, Donald Blackmer, Richard Eckaus, Everett Hagen, Daniel Lerner, Max Millikan, Ithiel de Sola Pool, Lucian Pye, Rosenstein-Rodan, and Walt Rostow.

6. Marx seemed to hold a similar position nearly a century earlier when he said, "The industrial countries show the less developed countries the image of their own future."

7. *Partners in Development, op. cit.*, p. 3.

8. *Ibid.*, p. 4.

9. *Ibid.*

10. The authors of *The Emerging Nations, op. cit.*, had suggested a target of 0.60 percent for official United States assistance in 1961.
11. W. W. Rostow, *Politics and the Stages of Growth* (New York: Cambridge University Press, 1971), p. 238.
12. *Ibid.*, p. 251.
13. *Ibid.*, p. 263.
14. *Ibid.*, p. 265.
15. Perspective Planning Division, Government of India, *Perspective of Development—1961 to 1976: Implications of Planning for a Minimum Level of Living,* August 1962; reprinted in T. N. Srinivasan and P. K. Bardhan, eds., *Poverty and Income Distribution in India* (Calcutta: Statistical Publishing Society, 1974).
16. I remember a very large number of visiting experts, economists and planners, from the West as well as from East Europe, who came to ISI between 1962 and 1967 and were shown this paper. I fail to remember anybody who showed any interest in it.
17. For instance, see: B. S. Minhas, *Fourth Plan: Objectives and Policy Frame* (Bombay: Vova, 1969) (a summary of this small book was presented to the *Crisis in Planning Conference* held at Sussex in summer of 1969); "Rural Poverty, Land Redistribution and Development Strategy," *Indian Economic Review* 5 (April, 1970), pp. 97-123; "Mass Poverty and Strategy of Rural Development in India," Economic Development Institute, World Bank, Washington, D. C., September, 1970 (this paper was widely circulated in the World Bank and was also presented in a seminar at the World Bank). A number of latter-day enthusiasts of the poverty-focused development strategies in the World Bank considered this paper too normative and off-beat for their tastes: V. M. Dandekar and N. Rath, *Poverty in India* (Poona: Indian School of Political Economy, 1971); M. L. Dantwala, *Poverty in India: Now and Then* (India: Macmillan, 1973); T. N. Srinivasan and P. K. Bardhan, eds., *op. cit.*
18. An analysis of these political developments and their impact on planning and development policies in India may be seen in B. S. Minhas, *Whither Indian Planning?* (Dehradun, India: The Indian Renaissance Institute, 1974).
19. Planning Commission, Government of India, *Towards an Approach to the Fifth Five Year Plan* (June, 1972).
20. Perspective Planning Division, Government of India, *A Technical Note on the Approach to the Fifth Five Year Plan of India, 1974-1979,* April 1973; and Planning Commission, Government of India, *Draft Fifth Five Year Plan, 1974-79,* December 1973.
21. An excellent account is available in Fernando Cardoso, "The Originality of the Copy: ECLA and the Idea of Development," chapter 2 of this book.

22. For example, see Dudley Seers, "Challenges to Development Theories and Strategies," Presidential address, *Society for International Development World Conference*, New Delhi, November 1969; and also "What Are We Trying to Measure," *Journal of Development Studies*, 8 (April, 1972), pp. 21-36.

23. Albert O. Hirschman, "Changing Tolerance for Income Inequality in the Course of Economic Development," *The Quarterly Journal of Economics* 87 (November, 1973), pp. 544-566.

24. Hollis Chenery *et al.*, *Redistribution with Growth* (London: Oxford University Press, 1974), p. xiii.

25. *Ibid.*, p. xiii.

26. *Ibid.* p. xvi and xviii. For an early assessment of the rural development programs for specific poverty groups and areas in India, see my "Rural Development for Weaker Sections: Experience and Lessons," *Commerce* 125 (October 14, 1972). This paper has been reproduced in a number of places and also as Chapter II of my book, *Planning and the Poor* (New Delhi: S. Chand, 1974).

27. This analogy holds that the "lifeboat" earth can support only a limited number of people and that a small part of the mankind who are safely aboard must not jeopardize their ability to survive by extending a helping hand to the billions of others who would swamp the vessel. A modified version of this ethic is called *triage*, after the battlefield aid-station practice of categorizing the wounded in three groups: those likely to survive without immediate attention, those likely to die in any case, and those who can be saved if they get immediate attention. Under this rule, some countries would receive selective help and aid but other countries whose chances of survival are considered virtually nil would be abandoned by withholding from them food and technical and economic aid. For dissenting views on these theses, see W. David Hopper, "The Development of Agriculture in Developing Countries," *Scientific American* 235 (September, 1976), pp. 197-205; and also some other articles in the same issue.

28. *What Now: Another Development, op. cit.*

29. *Ibid.*, p. 26.

30. *Ibid.*, p. 63.

31. *Employment, Growth and Basic Needs: A One-World Problem* (Geneva: International Labor Office, 1976), p.31.

32. *Ibid.*, p. 32. India's *Draft Fifth Five Year Plan* (December, 1973) worked out all this in detail for 1974-1979. An earlier exercise, PPD-ISI, *Perspective of Development, op. cit.*, in 1962, had explored (in quantitative terms) the implications of planning for a minimum level of living for the period 1961 to 1976. Also it is of interest to note that the two-part definition of basic needs recommended

by ILO is similar to the one followed in these two documents of the Indian Planning Commission.

33. What self-reliance might mean for development strategy in India is discussed in my *Planning for Self-Reliance* (Bombay: Commerce Publication Division, 1975); and "Self-Reliance," *Seminar*, no. 198 (February, 1976).

CHAPTER 4, pp. 97-122

1. The search for substantive material on Mexico and Papua New Guinea, only a part of which is utilized in the present chapter, was assisted by a grant from the Menil Foundation, which also assisted a general library search for recent literature and statistics. Muriel Brookfield carried out the necessary inquiries in Canberra and in Papua New Guinea, and thanks are due to her friends and mine in both places for the aid given in interpreting the present situation in Papua New Guinea; a fuller report on this work will appear elsewhere. I am also grateful to Rodolfo Stavenhagen for assistance with access to the more recent Mexican material.

2. A. G. Gilbert, "Note on the Incidence of Development in the Vicinity of a Growth Center," *Regional Studies* 9 (1975), pp. 325-33.

3. M. Lipton, *Why Poor People Stay Poor: A Study of Urban Bias in World Development* (London: Temple Smith, 1977).

4. M. Castells, *The Urban Question—A Marxist Approach* [trans. from *La Question urbaine* (Paris: Maspero, 1972)] (London: Arnold, 1977), p. 447.

5. G. Myrdal, *Economic Theory and Underdeveloped Regions* (London: Duckworth, 1957).

6. A. O. Hirschman, *The Strategy of Economic Development* (New Haven, Connecticut: Yale University Press, 1958).

7. F. Perroux, "Note sur la notion de pole de croissance," *Economie Appliquée* 8 (1955), pp. 307-20.

8. For example, see J. R. Boudeville, *Problems of Regional Economic Planning* (Edinburgh: Edinburgh University Press, 1966).

9. J. Friedmann, *Regional Development Policy: A Case Study of Venezuela* (Cambridge: Massachusetts Institute of Technology Press, 1966).

10. T. Hermansen, *Growth Poles and Growth Centers in National and Regional Development—A Synthetic Approach* 69, no. 26 (Geneva: United National Research Institute for Social Development, 1969).

11. See E. A. J. Johnson, *The Organization of Space in Developing*

Countries (Cambridge: Massachusetts Institute of Technology Press, 1970), p. 71.

12. H. Brookfield, *Interdependent Development* (London: Methuen, 1975).

13. A. R. Porter and P. W. de Souza, "The Underdevelopment and Modernization of the Third World," *Commission on College Geography Resource Paper*, vol. 25 (Washington: Association of American Geographers, 1975).

14. A. G. Gilbert, *op. cit.*

15. J. G. Williamson, "Regional Inequality and the Process of National Development: A Description of the Patterns," *Economic Development and Cultural Change* 13 (1965), pp. 3-43.

16. A. G. Gilbert and D. E. Goodman, "Regional Income Disparities and Economic Development: A Critique," in *Development Planning and Spatial Structure*, ed. A. G. Gilbert (Chichester and New York: John Wiley, 1976), pp. 113-41.

17. Economic Council of Canada, *Second Annual Review: Toward Sustained and Balanced Economic Growth* (Ottawa: Queen's Printer, 1965), pp. 102-7.

18. A. G. Gilbert and D. E. Goodman, *op. cit.*

19. For example, see M. S. Ahluwalia in Hollis Chenery *et al.*, *Redistribution with Growth: Policies to Improve Income Distribution in Developing Countries in the Context of Economic Growth* (London: Oxford University Press, 1974).

20. OAS (Consejo Interamericano y social), *Lineamentos para Alcanzar el mayor Empleo y Crecimiento en América Latina* (Washington, D. C.: Organization of American States, 1973).

21. M. S. Ahluwalia, *op. cit.*, p. 19.

22. Among theoretical statements which have greatly improved the theory of unequal development as between regions in recent years, that of H. Siebert, *Regional Economic Growth: Theory and Policy* (Scranton, Pennsylvania: International Textbook Company, 1969), is outstanding.

23. R. Robinson, ed., *Developing the Third World: the Experience of the Nineteen-Sixties* (Cambridge: Cambridge University Press, 1971).

24. R. Robinson, *op. cit.*, pp. 85-94.

25. *Ibid.*

26. *Ibid.*

27. ECLA (United Nations Economic Commission for Latin America), *Economic Survey of Latin America for 1970* (New York: United Nations, 1972).

28. *Ibid.*, p. 64.

29. M. Castells, *op. cit.*

30. J. K. Galbraith, *The New Industrial State* (Boston: Houghton-Mifflin, 1967).

31. J. J. Puthucheary, *Ownership and Control in the Malaysian Economy* (Singapore: Eastern Universities Press, 1960).

32. For example, see K. Levitt, *Silent Surrender: the Multinational Corporation in Canada* (Toronto: Macmillan, 1970).

33. J. Weeks, " 'Review' of Nguyen Khac Vien, ed., *Agricultural Problems: Some Technical Aspects,"* in *Journal of Development Studies* 8 (1972), pp. 338-39.

34. R. Robinson, *op. cit.*, pp. 85-94.

35. Editors of *A Blueprint for Survival, The Ecologist* (Harmondsworth: Penguin, 1972).

36. D. H. Meadows, D. C. Meadows, J. Randers, and W. W. Behrens, *The Limits to Growth: A Report for the Club of Rome's Project on the Predicament of Mankind* (New York: Universe Books, 1972).

37. J. S. Steinhart and C. E. Steinhart, "Energy Use in the U.S. Food System," *Science* 184 (1974), pp. 307-15.

38. T. O'Riordan, "Environmental Ideologies," *Environment and Planning* 9 (1977), pp. 3-14.

39. For example, see N. Allaby, *Who Will Eat* (London: Thomas Stacey, 1972).

40. J. Darmstadter, with P. D. Teitelbaum and J. G. Polach, *Energy in the World Economy: A Statistical Review of Trends in Output, Trade and Consumption since 1925* (Baltimore and London: Johns Hopkins Press for Resources for the Future, 1971), p. 37.

41. J. Friedmann, "A General Theory of Polarized Development," in *Growth Centers in Regional Economic Development*, ed. N. M. Hansen (New York: Free Press, 1972), pp. 82-107.

42. *Ibid.*, pp. 100-01.

43. C. Furtado, *Diagnosis of the Brazilian Crisis* (Berkeley and Los Angeles: University of California Press, 1965).

44. M. Castells, *op. cit.*

45. Out of a large number of possible sources on the modern history of Mexico, three are of major significance from the present point of view. C. C. Cumberland, in *Mexico: The Struggle for Modernity* (New York: Oxford University Press, 1968), provides a comprehensive history. J. W. Wilkie, in *The Mexican Revolution: Federal Expenditure and Social Change since 1910* (Berkeley and Los Angeles: University of California Press, 1970), examines the financial policies of postrevolutionary Mexican governments, with special emphasis on the use of the "active state" among several accounts of the revolution itself. And J. Womack, Jr., in *Zapata and the Mexican Revolution* (New York: Random House, 1968), offers a particularly profound treatment of the role of peasantry. A comprehensive economic analysis is provided by C. W. Reynolds, in *The Mexican Economy: Twentieth Century Structure and*

Growth (New Haven, Connecticut: Yale University Press, 1970).

46. F. Chevalier, *Land and Society in Colonial Mexico: the Great Hacienda* (Berkeley and Los Angeles: University of California Press, 1963).

47. B. Higgins, *Economic Development: Problems, Principles and Policies* (New York: Norton, 1968).

48. For example, see W. L. Orozco, *Los Ejidos de los Pueblos,* reprint [originally *La organización de la república: los ejidos de los pueblos y exposición jurídica* (Guadalajara, Jal.)] (Mexico, D. F.: Ediciones el Caballito, 1975).

49. D. Barkin and T. King, *Regional Economic Development; the River Basin Approach in Mexico,* Cambridge Latin America Studies 7 (Cambridge: University Press, 1970), pp. 76-77.

50. ECLA, *op. cit.,* p. 68.

51. Flavia Derossi, *The Mexican Entrepreneur* (Paris: Development Center of the Organization for Economic Co-operation and Development, 1971).

52. P. G. Casanova, *Democracy in Mexico* [translated by D. Salti from *La democracia en Mexico* (Mexico, D. F.: Ediciones Era, 1965)] (New York: Oxford University Press, 1965).

53. See P. G. Casanova, *ibid.*; J. Wilkie, *op. cit.*; and Barkin and King, *op. cit.*

54. R. Stavenhagen, *Sept Thèses Erronées sur l'Amérique Latine: ou Comment décoloniser les sciences humaines* (Paris: Editions Anthropos, 1973).

55. R. Stavenhagen, *ibid.*; and F. I. Restrepo, "La transferencia de recursos a la agricultura," *El Economista Mexicano* 3 (1976), pp. 21-38.

56. E. J. Wellhausen, "The Agriculture of Mexico," *Scientific American* 235, no. 3 (1976), pp. 128-53.

57. F. I. Restrepo, *op. cit.*

58. Barkin and King, *op. cit.*

59. P. Hasluck, *A Time for Building: Australian Administration in Papua New Guinea, 1951-1963* (Melbourne: Melbourne University Press, 1976).

60. For example, PNG, Central Planning Office, 1974, p. 13.

61. Spread cited in H. Colebatch, "The Rural Improvement Program: Does It Improve Access," *IASER Discussion Paper 14* (Boroko: PNG, 1977), p. 12.

62. H. Colebatch, *op. cit.*

63. D. Conyers, "The Provincial Government Debate," *IASER Monograph 2* (Boroko: PNG, 1976).

64. J. Friedmann, *op. cit.* (1966).

65. A. G. Gilbert, *op. cit.*

66. H. C. Brookfield and M. Cohen, "Urban and Regional Subsystems in Peninsular Malaysia," *Internal Report RPO 297,* mimeographed (Washington, D.C.: IBRD, 1974).
67. M. H. Watkins, "A Staple Theory of Economic Growth," *Canadian Journal of Economic and Political Science* 29 (1963), pp. 141-58.
68. G. Myrdal, *op. cit.*
69. M. Lipton *op. cit.*
70. T. G. McGee, *The Urbanization Process in the Third World: Explorations in Search of a Theory* (London: Bell, 1971).
71. For example, see R. Stavenhagen, "El campesinado y las estrategios de desarrollo rural," *Cuadernos del Centro de Estudios Sociológicos* 19 (Mexico, D.F.: El Colegio de Mexico, 1977).

CHAPTER 5, pp. 125-143

1. See, e.g., Edwin Lieuwen, *Generals vs. Presidents: Neomilitarism in Latin America* (New York: Praeger, 1964); Morris Janowitz, *The Military in the Political Development of New Nations* (Chicago: University of Chicago Press, 1964).
2. For general discussions, see Edward Shils, "The Military in the Political Development of the New States," in *The Role of the Military in Underdeveloped Countries,* John J. Johnson, ed. (Princeton, New Jersey: Princeton University Press, 1962); and Samuel Huntington, *Political Order in Changing Societies* (New Haven, Connecticut: Yale University Press, 1968); and Gavin Kennedy, *The Military in the Third World* (London: Duckworth, 1973), to mention only a few samples of the extensive literature.
3. Samuel Decalo, *Coups and Army Rule in Africa: Studies in Military Style* (New Haven, Connecticut: Yale University Press, 1976), p. 243 ff.
4. John J. Johnson, "The Latin American Military as a Politically Competing Group in Transitional Society," in *The Role of the Military in Underdeveloped Countries,* John J. Johnson, ed., *op. cit.*
5. Stanislav Andreski, *Military Organization and Society* (London: Routledge and Kegan Paul, 1954), p. 162.
6. Manfred Halpern, "Middle Eastern Armies and the New Middle Class," in Johnson, ed., *op. cit.,* p. 281.
7. Decalo, *op. cit.,* p. 15.
8. See the useful survey article by Mary Kaldor, "The Military in Development," *World Development* 4, no. 6 (1976), with an extensive bibliography.

9. Emile Benoit, *Defense and Economic Growth in Developing Countries* (Lexington, Massachusetts: Lexington Books, 1973).

10. E.g., Alfred Stepan, *The Military in Politics: Changing Patterns in Brazil* (Princeton, New Jersey: Princeton University Press, 1971); and Anour Abdel Malek, *Egypt: Military Society, The Army Regime, the Left and Social Change Under Nasser* (New York: Vintage, 1968).

11. Frank Barnaby, "Arms and the Third World: A Background," *Development Dialogue* (1977), p. 22.

12. Barnaby, *op. cit.*, p. 24.

13. Anthony Sampson, *The Arms Bazaar* (New York: Viking, 1977), p. 316.

14. United Nations, *Developing Countries and Levels of Development*, stencil, E/AC.54/L.81 (October 15, 1975), p. 19. See, also, the more detailed comments by Bill Warren on this point in chapter 6 of this volume.

15. Ian M. D. Little, *Perspectives for the Second Half of the Second United Nations Development Decade*, paper for the Committee for Development Planning, p. 22.

16. Hollis Chenery *et al.*, *Redistribution with Growth: Policies to Improve Income Distribution in Developing Countries in the Context of Economic Growth* (London: Oxford University Press, 1974), p. xiii.

17. See, e.g., T. N. Srinivasan and P. K. Bardhan, eds., *Poverty and Income Distribution in India* (Calcutta: Statistical Publishing Society, 1974).

18. Montek S. Ahluwalia, "Rural Poverty and Agricultural Growth in India," paper at Bellagio Workshop, April, 1977.

19. Hollis B. Chenery, "Transitional Growth and World Industrialization," paper presented at the Nobel Symposium on the International Allocation of Economic Activity, Stockholm, 1976.

CHAPTER 6, pp. 144-168

1. This chapter represents a substantially edited version of a much longer paper which is extensively documented with empirical evidence. Space limitations in the present volume unfortunately restricted the amount of original material which could be presented. This discussion concerns the countries of the noncommunist Third World only. The author wishes to thank for their help and intellectual stimulus Dr. Shobana Madavan, Mike Safier, Peter Ayre, Dr. Richard Jeffries, Professor Dudley Seers, and Biplap das Gupta.

The United Nations Research Institute for Social Development (UNRISD) was particularly helpful in supplying me with materials from their data bank. The author is also indebted to his research assistant, Mrs. Shaziya Kazioglu, for her diligence, patience, and general helpfulness.

2. The fourth horseman of the Apocalypse is, of course, war. The other disasters, together with the rich world-poor world gap, may be confidently expected to bring this in their train.

3. Cf. Hans Singer, "Brief Note on Unemployment Rates in Developing Countries," *Manpower and Unemployment Research in Africa* (April, 1970), p. 2. The likely range for 1980 is given as between 34 percent and 52 percent.

4. On this point, see Bill Warren, "Imperialism and Capitalist Industrialization," *New Left Review* 81 (September-October, 1973).

5. Above all, it should be recollected that despite the heterogeneity referred to, all developing countries, without exception, have in the postwar period, been part of the great upsurge combining nationalism and the demand for a better life which is bringing the great majority of mankind, formerly quiescent, into the forefront of history and into the modern world.

6. As we shall see, they must be when the rich world-poor world polarization thesis is considered.

7. We shall argue (see below) that despite the undoubted defects of this measure as an indicator of material welfare, the cross-temporal picture it suggests is broadly accurate.

8. Other grounds may, of course, exist. We shall consider these below.

9. Simon Kuznets, *Economic Growth of Nations: Total Output and Production Structure* (Cambridge, Massachusetts: Harvard University Press, 1971), pp. 30-31.

10. United Nations, Department of Economic and Social Affairs, *Analyses and Projections of Economic Development: 1. An Introduction to the Technique of Programming* (New York, 1955), p. 10; and United Nations, Department of Economic and Social Affairs, *Economic Survey of Latin America 1955* (New York, 1956), p. 3, cited in P. T. Bauer, *Dissent on Development*, student ed. (London: 1976), p. 34.

11. P. Bairoch, *The Economic Development of the Third World Since 1900* (London: Methuen, 1975), p. 184.

12. P. T. Bauer, *op. cit.*, pp. 35-37, discusses some of the abundant but scattered evidence for this, especially in connection with west Africa and southeast Asia. This growth was, of course, patchy. It was only as the economic contact of the poor countries with the advanced capitalist world became generalized in the twentieth century and especially after World War II that Third World eco-

nomic growth too became generalized.

13. Kuznets, *op. cit.*, p. 22, gives the figures as growth rates per decade.

14. France, Belgium, Germany, Switzerland, Denmark, Norway, Italy, Canada, and Australia.

15. Kuznets, *op. cit.*, p. 41. Utilization of the long-term rates of increase of per capita product is appropriate since, for the periods after modern economic growth began, no significant acceleration or deceleration is found and, specifically, Kuznets' data provided no support for Rostow's "take-off" theory of an initial acceleration of the growth rate of per capita product followed by constant sustained growth at a high rate.

16. United Nations Commission for Trade and Development, *Handbook of International Trade and Development Statistics* (New York, 1976), p. 341.

17. United Nations, Department of Economic and Social Affairs, *1974 Report on the World Social Situation* (New York, 1975), p. 6.

18. On the other hand, the combination of a comparatively late start and extremely rapid growth of modern economic activities, often with a comparatively unsuitable cultural environment, may create tensions of a highly ambiguous character at once contributing to forward-looking change and simultaneously raising anew specters of irrationalism, especially of xenophobic nationalism, following Europe's own catastrophic example.

19. In particular it has been concluded that the Third World is becoming more and more economically subordinate to and dependent on the developed capitalist world and that politically the result is the growing importance of international economic polarization as the greatest single menace to world peace and harmonious international political relations generally. Of course, growing polarization is not the sole basis for these conclusions, but it is an important element.

20. United Nations, *Yearbook of National Accounts Statistics, 1975*, vol. III, *International Tables* (New York: Department of Economic and Social Affairs, 1976), pp. 2, 4-5.

21. *World Bank Atlas.*

22. The range of growth rates of GNP per capita for all market economies (developed and undeveloped together) was from +10.5 percent per annum to −2.1 percent per annum, i.e., 12.6 percentage points. Taking five equal percentage intervals between the lowest and highest growth rates and allotting the countries into their appropriate range, we get the crude results above. Weighting of the countries according to population would tend to suggest greater polarization owing to the relatively slow growth of some of the largest developing countries. On the other hand,

Israel and the southern European countries (Greece, Spain and Portugal) have been counted as DMEs, which rather minimizes the suggestion of depolarization. Turkey has been counted among the developing countries, Israel among the DMEs *(ibid.).*

23. The majority and the poorest x percent, are often treated as interchangeable. In fact, the majority may be getting better off relative to the upper-income classes while the poorest 20 percent may not— or vice versa. Moreover, policies to improve the relative position of the poorest 20 percent may conflict with policies to improve the relative and absolute position of the mass of the population (perhaps the poorest 60 percent).

    This is quite likely to be the case since poverty is highly correlated with location (especially in isolated, rural areas) and recent evidence supports the view that increasing urbanization is more economically efficient than a more even urban/rural allocation of resources, subject to the constraint that agricultural output growth is not neglected. A summary of the evidence on this point is given by Koichi Mera, "On the Urban Agglomeration and Economic Efficiency," *Economic Development and Cultural Change* 21, no. 2 (January, 1973), pp. 309-24. Further, the fact that the poorest quartile is getting statistically worse off may be no indication of the deterioration of a particular poor group ("underprivileged" suggests that those concerned ought to be privileged). The constituent individual or household membership or social composition of the lowest 20 percent may be changing significantly over a comparatively brief time period. This is likely to be the case in periods of rapid overall socioeconomic change and particularly when commercialization and industrialization are making an impact on predominantly agrarian societies where social demarcations are not rigid, and kinship and patron-client relationships are important, as in much of Asia and Africa. This obvious and indeed crucial aspect of modernization is generally overlooked in the literature of redistribution with growth.

24. M. S. Ahluwalia, "Income Inequality: Some Dimensions of the Problem," in H. Chenery *et al.*, *Redistribution with Growth* (London: Oxford University Press, 1974), p. 13. Thirteen of the countries are underdeveloped countries, i.e., Taiwan, South Korea, Sri Lanka, Mexico, Brazil, India, Venezuela, Peru, Panama, El Salvador, Colombia, Iran, and the Philippines. The exclusion of five non-Third World countries does not affect the validity of Ahluwalia's conclusions. Ahluwalia's work is, to date, the most comprehensive reliable summary of the evidence on the relationship of postwar redistribution to growth. Its general findings may be taken as definitive of the current state of knowledge on the sub-

ject. Individual time-series studies of income distribution also show
no clear pattern. Tanzania appears to have reduced income inequality
between 1967 and 1972, but the sources of data and methods of
estimation are unclear. (Reginald H. Green, "Tanzania," *ibid.*,
pp. 268-75.) Sri Lanka witnessed substantial equalizing redistribution between 1953 and 1973. (Lal Jayawardane, "Sri Lanka,"
ibid., pp. 273-280.) South Korea witnessed apparently a substantial
decline in income inequality throughout the postwar period as a
whole, although the data are fragmentary. (Irma Adelman, "South
Korea," *ibid.*, pp. 280-285.) There appears to have been a substantial reduction in inequality in Taiwan between 1960 and 1970,
although, here again, the evidence is shaky. It does appear fairly
certain, however, that, whether substantial or not, some sort of
decline in inequality did take place. (Gustav Ranis, "Taiwan,"
ibid., pp. 285-90.) Between 1960 and 1970, e.g. in Mexico, income
distribution became increasingly unequal over time as measured by
the Gini coefficient for the years 1950, 1958, 1963, 1968 and
1969, according to Gunter van Ginneken. (*Mexican Income Distribution within and between Rural and Urban Areas*, World Employment Programme Research Working Papers [Geneva: ILO, 1974],
pp. 98-99.) On the other hand, Richard Weiskoff's study ("Income
Distribution and Economic Growth in Puerto Rico, Argentina and
Mexico," in Alejandro Foxley, ed., *Income Distribution in Latin
America* [Cambridge: Cambridge University Press, 1976]), of
changes in Mexico based on the years 1950, 1957 and 1963 shows
the Gini coefficient *declining* from 1950 to 1957 and rising only
from 1957 to 1963. Almost exactly the same picture holds for
Puerto Rico between 1953 and 1963 where the different measures
show contradictory results. The picture for Argentina for the years
1953, 1959 and 1961 is of rising inequality between 1953 and
1959 with a decline between 1959 and 1961, leaving, according to
all measures except the coefficient of variation, income more unevenly distributed in 1961 than in 1953. In Brazil income inequality
has risen between 1960 and 1970 as measured by the Gini coefficient. (Albert Fishlow, "Brazilian Size Distribution of Income," in
Income Distribution in Latin America, Alejandro Foxley, ed.
[Cambridge: Cambridge University Press, 1976].) In Peru, the
redistributive effect of the reforms between 1968 and 1972 appears
to have been minimal, about three percent or four percent of
national income ("The Impact of Current Reforms on Income
Distribution in Peru," *ibid.*) In western Malaysia between 1957 and
1970 (with observations also for 1960 and 1967) the Gini coefficient rises from 1957 to 1960, falling thereafter through 1967
to 1970 but with income still more unequal in 1970 than in 1957.

(Lim Lin Lean, *The Pattern of Income Distribution in West Malaysia 1957-70*, World Employment Programme Research [Geneva: ILO, 1976]). For Ghana between 1956 and 1968 all measures of change in inequality of monetary income distribution agree, showing growing inequality. (Kodwo Ewusi, *The Distribution of Monetary Income in Ghana*, Technical Publication series no. 18, Institute of Statistical, Social and Economic Research, University of Ghana [Legon: 1971].) In India the size distribution of income appears to have widened over the period 1951-60. (Subramanian Swamy, "Structural Changes and the Distribution of Income by Size: The Case of India," *Review of Income and Wealth*, series 13, no. 2 [June, 1967], pp. 155-174.) If we exclude the countries for which the different measures give conflicting results (Puerto Rico, Mexico, and Argentina), and which in fact by cross-national comparisons with other developing countries already have relatively equal income distribution, no obvious general predominance of decreasing or increasing inequality is discernible.

25. Ahluwalia, *op cit.*, p. 17. These findings are regarded by Ahluwalia as providing some confirmation for the following scenario. "On the one hand, the process of development gives economic impetus to the modern high-income sectors and dislocates traditional low-income sectors, thus promoting relative inequality and perhaps even absolute impoverishment. On the other hand, development also promotes the demand for skilled labor, raising real wages and employment levels in the modern sector, thus enabling low-income groups to share in the benefits of growth. Under some optimistic assumptions about the trend in wage share, this may lead to a reduction in relative inequality. These conflicting influences are usually reconciled by treating them as sequential, i.e., income inequality increases in the early stages of development but then declines as development continues."

26. *Ibid.*, p. 13.

27. H. T. Oshima, "The International Comparison of Size Distribution of Family Incomes with Special Reference to Asia," *Review of Economics and Statistics* 44, no. 4 (1962), pp. 439-445; and S. Kuznets, "Economic Growth and Income Inequality," *American Economic Review* (March, 1955).

28. Felix Paukert, "Income Distribution at Different Levels of Development: A Survey of Evidence," *International Labor Review* (August-September, 1973), p. 115.

29. The 26 developing countries with GNP above the $500 level compares with nearly half that number only four years before (*Finance and Development*, no. 1 [1972], p. 1), a difference which cannot be accounted for solely by inflation.

30. Ahluwalia, *op. cit.*, p. 17.

31. In the case of Taiwan, account must be taken of the pre-1945 development. Nevertheless, this neither invalidates the principle nor the illustrative relevance of the example. It should be emphasized that the writer does not himself propose a new Utopian picture of a situation of continuously improving distribution once the turning point has been passed, without limit and without reversals. In a market economy there are limits to such a trend (indeed in a socialist economy too, but here the limits are set further out) and a secular trend is consistent with significant and even prolonged reverse shifts in distribution, as some of the evidence cited in note 24 above suggests, as well as with cases not conforming to the trend.

32. The fact that as growth proceeds, institutional factors play a part in improving income distribution implies that changing policies can and ought to be a relevant part of the process.

33. It is only too easy, of course, to envisage policies of substantial egalitarian redistribution which lower the potential or actual welfare of the poorest groups (as compared to alternative policies and outcomes). In conditions of great poverty we consider this an immoral approach, and cannot agree therefore with Dudley Seers ("What Are We Trying to Measure," in *Measuring Development*, N. Baster, ed., [London, 1972], p. 23), that in the context of severe underdevelopment equality should be regarded as an aim in itself.

34. *Report of the Director-General to the Tripartite World Conference on Employment, Income Distribution and Social Progress and the International Division of Labor* (Geneva, 1976).

35. Outstanding postwar examples are Taiwan, South Korea and Singapore. There are, of course, equally outstanding exceptions to this statement, e.g., Sri Lanka.

36. The establishment of a railway system in the Sudan created a relatively well-paid group of railway workers and benefited well-off contractors and traders while increasing absolute rewards to poor, former subsistence farmers now able to sell food to the towns, and to low-paid casual labor in cotton picking (by increasing their mobility).

37. Locational differences, combined with the inefficiency of allocating scarce complementary resources (to human labor) too thinly, inevitably mean that the spread of opportunities is an uneven process.

38. Hirschman noted the relevance of this point for developing countries years ago (*The Strategy of Economic Development*, 1?th printing [New Haven, Connecticut: Yale University Press, 1958],

p. 32 ff.), but its crucial implications have been largely ignored in both the development literature and in development planning.

39. Eventually, of course, this institutionalization becomes more and more "socialized" and creates the basis for an advance to socialism. But that is another story.

40. It should not be forgotten that several decades of civil war were necessary for the establishment of an egalitarian regime in China with all that implied in terms of economic loss. This implies no suggestion that the Chinese communist struggle was unjust or its outcome undesirable, but it does call attention to the glibness of those who call for similar egalitarian results in breathlessly short time periods and without experienced and realistic communist political leaderships available.

41. Thus Charles Elliott looks with disfavor on the market selection and allocation of resources to Zambian farmers on the basis of their economic efficiency as an unfortunate case of increasing inequality (see Baster, *op. cit.*, p. 43), while C. L. G. Bell and John H. Dulay solemnly discuss how to restrict (!) the spillover benefits of rural feeder roads so that they do not also benefit richer farmers, traders and contractors, but only the poor farmers (in Chenery, et al., *Redistribution with Growth, op. cit.*).

42. There is a relevant discussion relating to this point in W. G. Runciman, *Relative Deprivation and Social Justice* (Harmondsworth: Penguin Books, 1973), Part One. Of course, the fact that a policy of income equality may not be generally accepted is no reason not to attempt to gain its acceptance. But it is unrealistic to assume that it is widely accepted.

43. *Report of the Director-General, op. cit.*

44. For example, J. Krishnamurty found an open unemployment rate, from National Sample Survey data of only 1.6 percent for all India for 1966-67 ("Some Aspects of Unemployment in Urban India," in *Journal of Development Studies* [January, 1975], p. 13), while Adolfo Figueroa notes that in Peru the 1961 census gave a national open unemployment percentage of only 2.8 percent while the 1967 survey of Lima's labor market gave a figure of 4.2 percent. ("Income Distribution, Demand Structure and Employment: The Case of Peru," *The Journal of Development Studies* [January, 1975], p. 21.)

45. ILO, *Yearbook of Statistics*, 1975.

46. *Report of the Director-General, op. cit.*, p. 133.

47. Although this does appear to have happened in individual cases at certain times, e.g., in Egypt and India. (United Nations Department of Economic and Social Affairs, *The Determinants and Consequences of Population Trends*, vol. I [1973], pp. 309-310.)

48. *Ibid.*, pp. 195-96, p. 315.
49. David Turnham and Ingelies Jaeger, *The Employment Problem in Less Developed Countries: A Review of Evidence* (Paris: OECD, 1971), p. 59.
50. *Ibid.*, p. 60. Unfortunately, Turnham then fudges his point by advocating the poverty approach to underemployment.
51. For example, *Employment and Equality: A Strategy for Increasing Productive Employment in Kenya* (Geneva: ILO, 1972), chapter 13; and C. J. Fapohunda, *Development of Urban Infrastructure in Greater Lagos,* World Employment Programme Research (Geneva: ILO, 1974), p. 54; and J. Weeks, "Introduction," *Manpower and Unemployment Research in Africa* (November, 1973), p. 5 (on Ghana); and Kalmann Schaefer and Cheywa R. Spindel, *Urban Development and Employment in Sao Paulo,* World Employment Programme Research (Geneva: ILO, 1974), pp. 4-5; S. V. Sethuraman, *Urbanization and Employment in Jakarta,* World Programme Research (Geneva: ILO, 1974), Chapter 7; Heather Joshi, Harold Lubell, and Jean Mouly, *Urban Development and Employment in Abidjan,* World Employment Programme Research (Geneva: ILO, 1974), chapter 4; Dr. A. N. Bose, *The Informal Sector in the Calcutta Metropolitan Economy,* World Employment Programme Research (Geneva: ILO, 1974).
52. Prostitutes are often classified with beggars and thieves but their occupation must be regarded as socially beneficial in cities with large single male immigrant populations.
53. Biplap das Gupta's analysis of the informal sector in Calcutta constitutes an exception. He concludes that the Calcutta urban informal sector makes little contribution to the national economy and creates innumerable economic and social problems which cannot be easily solved. "Calcutta's Informal Sector," *Institute of Development Studies Bulletin* (October, 1973), pp. 72-3.
54. One observer has argued that "the majority of the urban population in black Africa obtains its housing, transport, services, fuel, food and clothing through the non-enumerated sector." (John Weeks, "An Exploration into the Nature of the Problem of Urban Imbalance in Africa," *Manpower and Unemployment Research in Africa* [November, 1973], p. 17.)
55. Cf., Louis Emmerij, "A New Look at Some Strategies for Increasing Productive Employment in Africa," *International Labor Review* (September, 1974).
56. Particularly positive verdicts on the economic contribution of the informal sector are given in ILO, *Employment and Equality, op. cit.*; in Fapolunda, *op. cit.*; in Weeks's *op. cit.*, "Introduction"; in Shaefer and Spindel, *op. cit.*; and in Joshi, Lubell and Mouly, *op. cit.*,

p. 418, for Kenya, Lagos (Nigeria), Ghana, São Paulo (Brazil) and Abidjan (Ivory Coast), respectively. See also K. C. Zachariah, "Bombay Migration Study: A Pilot Analysis of Migration to an Asian Metropolis," in *Demography* (1966).

57. All the studies cited in note 51 except the ILO Kenya study give evidence of the importance of wage labor in the informal sector, with in addition many transitional forms between self-employment and wage employment. The ILO Kenya report's characterization of the informal sector as consisting primarily of self-employed has been strongly contested.

58. It is estimated, for example, that jobs in the production services subsector of São Paulo account for about 50 percent of total services jobs. The growth of such activities is a direct function of the economic development of the area and covers such activities as merchandising, wholesale and retail trade, transport, communications, real estate and banking services. Productivity levels are probably comparable with those in the secondary sector. Schaefer and Spindel, *op. cit.*, p. 4.

59. Due to the economies of breaking bulk arising from the character of the market, consisting as it does of large numbers of very low-income purchasers, and from the credit economies thereby attained; cf. P. T. Bauer, *West African Trade*, 1963 ed. (London: 1963) chapter 2; and Barry Lamont Isaac, "Traders in Pendembu, Sierra Leone, a Case Study in Entrepreneurship" (Ph.D. diss., University of Oregon, 1969), cited in Weeks, "Exploration into Urban Imbalance," *op. cit.*, p. 17.

60. Weeks's path-breaking discussion ("Urban Imbalance," *op. cit.*) is excellent on this point but tends to overemphasize self-employment and the competitive as opposed to the complementary relationship of the formal and informal sectors. A good description of their complementary characteristics on the supply side is given in Kenneth King, "Skill Acquisition in the Informal Sector of an African Economy: The Kenya Case," *Journal of Development Studies* (January, 1975). Complementarity on the demand side needs no argument for the informal sector in general but competitive relations may be more important in specific cases.

61. See references cited in Weeks, "Exploration into Urban Imbalance," *op. cit.*, p. 17.

62. E.g., see for Ghana, Planungsgruppe Ritter (Koenigstein, F. R. of Germany), *Project on Urbanization, Employment and Development in Ghana, Report on Two Surveys*, World Employment Programme Research (Geneva: ILO, 1974), pp. 52 ff.; and for Kenya, Kenneth King, *op. cit.* Examples could be multiplied.

63. E.g., W. J. Steel, "Empirical Measurement of the Relative Size and

Productivity of Intermediate Sector Employment: Some Estimates from Ghana," *MURA* (April, 1976), pp. 23-31. Stuart W. Sinclair draws attention to the dynamic implications of these studies for processes of capital accumulation in the informal sector in "The Intermediate Sector in the Economy," *MURA* (November, 1976).

64. United Nations, *1974 Report, op. cit.*, p. 40, footnote 29.

65. See, for example, for Sao Paulo: Schaefer and Spindel, *op. cit.*, pp. 4-5; for Jakarta: Sethuraman, *op. cit.*, pp. 6.31 and 6.39; for Abidjan: Joshi, Lubell and Mouly, *op. cit.*, p. 4.15; for Kenya: ILO, *Employment Incomes and Equality*, p. 5.

66. Bairoch, *op. cit.*, p. 160 for labor force figures; *United Nations Report on the World Social Situation, 1974* (New York, 1975), p. 290 for growth of agricultural and food output per capita for the 1950s and 1960s. See also the estimates for 36 countries during the 1960s by the FAO which also suggest, on the basis of indirect data, a slow rise in average rural productivity (FAO, *State of Food and Agriculture*, 1970, p. 135).

67. Turnham, *op. cit.*, p. 62.

68. This point is brought out in most of the World Employment Programme Research Studies.

69. For example, Sethuraman of Jakarta, *op. cit.*, p. 6.31.

70. J. Robinson, *Essays on the Theory of Employment*, 1937, p. 84.

71. Analogous to "dependence" and "underemployment," not to mention "underdevelopment" itself.

72. Although there are also, of course, slums of the traditional type in the Third World, i.e., decayed urban areas. The United Nations *1974 World Social Situation Report* distinguishes between slums and squatter settlements and notes that comparisons between rural and urban areas almost always show more overcrowding in the former than the latter (see pp. 235-36).

73. *Ibid.*, p. 233.

74. Cf., Zachariah, *op. cit.*; also J. C. Caldwell, *African Rural Urban Migration*, 1969.

75. UNRISD, *The Level of Living Index*, by Jan Drewnowski and Wolf Scott (Geneva: United Nations, 1966), p. 59. The nations in the study were Ghana, Mauritius, Morocco, United Arab Republic, Uganda, Argentina, Chile, Ecuador, Jamaica, United States, India, Israel, Japan, Thailand, Belgium, Denmark, Greece, Spain and Yugoslavia.

76. UNRISD, *Contents and Measurement of Socio-Economic Development: An Empirical Enquiry*, prepared by D. McGranahan, C. Richard-Proust, N. V. Sovani, M. Subramamian, Report no. 70.10 (Geneva, 1970).

77. I.e., expectation of life at birth; population in localities of 20,000

persons and over as a proportion of the total population; consumption of animal proteins per capita per day; combined primary and secondary enrollment as a percentage of the 5-19 age group; vocational enrollment as a percentage of the 15-19 age group; average number of persons per room; circulation of daily newspapers of general interest per 1,000 of the population; telephones per 1,000 of the population; radio receivers per 1,000 of the population; percentage of the economically active population in electricity, gas, water, sanitary services, transport, storage and communication; production per male agricultural worker in 1960 United States dollars; adult male labor in agriculture as a percentage of the total male labor force; electricity consumption in kwh per capita; steel consumption in kg per capita; energy consumption in kg of coal per capita; GDP derived from manufacturing as a percentage of total GDP; foreign trade (sum of imports and exports) per capita in 1960 United States dollars; and salaried and wage-earners as a percentage of the total economically active population.

78. Dudley Seers, *op. cit.*, pp. 22-24.
79. Seers remarks that "Egalitarians like myself face a theoretical paradox. If we argue that the national income is an inappropriate measure of a nation's development, we weaken the significance of a growing per capita income 'gap' between rich nations and poor." (*Ibid.*, p. 34.) Actually, we have here not a theoretical paradox but a classic example of wishing to have one's cake and eat it.
80. FAO, *The State of Food and Agriculture 1975* (Rome: FAO, 1976), p. 76.
81. *The State of Food and Agriculture 1970*, fig. III. 3.
82. UNRISD, Report no. 73.3, *Research Bank of Development Indicators*, vol. III, 1960-70, comparisons 11.8 and 12.50-55.
83. Donald McGranahan, "Development Indicators and Development Models," in Baster, *op. cit.*, p. 94. The correlations are 0.72 for the infant mortality rate and 0.77 for expectation of life at birth.
84. FAO, *State of Food and Agriculture 1974*, pp. 100, 101, 105.
85. Cf., Samir Amin, *Accumulation on a World Scale* (New York: Monthly Review Press, 1974).
86. I.e., the higher range of durable consumer goods. (Amin simply equates luxury goods with *all* durable consumer goods.) This is notably the case for West Africa and North Africa, the two regions in which Amin specializes. Cf., for West Africa, Anthony Hopkins, *An Economic History of West Africa*, and IMF, *Surveys of African Economies*, vol. VI (Washington, D.C.: IMF, 1975).
87. J. R. Wells, *Consumption, Market Size and Expenditure Patterns in Brazil*, Centre of Latin American Studies, University of Cambridge, Working Papers, no. 24 (1976).

88. Including sewing machines, refrigerators, televisions, gas and electric stoves, electric irons, table radios, portable radios, gramophones, fans, liquifiers, cake-mixers, floor-polishers, vacuum cleaners, washing machines, air-conditioners, motor cars, bicycles and motorcycles (*ibid.*, p. 13).
89. *Ibid.*, pp. 51-53.
90. The much-despised trickle-down theory has something to it after all. Newton was right.
91. Wilfred Beckerman has made this point in connection with the propaganda about pollution in *In Defense of Economic Growth* (London: J. Cape, 1974).
92. For example, see K. N. Raj, "Trends in Rural Unemployment," *Economic and Political Weekly*, Special Number (August, 1976); S. Hiroshima, ed., *Hired Labor in Rural Areas* (Tokyo: Institute of Development Economics, 1970).
93. It is significant that an explicitly procapitalist development economist, P. T. Bauer, early on was able to identify precisely this fundamental weakness in Indian planning. He emphasized not only the neglect of agriculture in resource allocation but also other crucial obstacles to the spread of commercialization, such as excessive neglect of road building and elementary education as well as restricted internal mobility. P. T. Bauer, *Indian Economic Policy and Development* (London: Allen and Unwin, 1961).

CHAPTER 7, pp. 171-197

1. Cheryl Page, ed., *Commodity Trade of the Third World* (London: Macmillan and Co., 1975).
2. The stockpiles of agricultural commodities held by the developed countries have not been used by them for stabilizing the prices or earnings of the developing countries; on the contrary, the purchases by and sales from such stockpiles have accentuated rather than mitigated the fluctuations in commodity prices. R. N. Cooper and R. Z. Lawrence, "The 72-75 Commodity Boom," Center Paper no. 235, Yale University Economic Growth Center, 1976.
3. Out of the 650 largest multinational companies, 638 originate in the United States and Japan with total sales amounting to $700 billion in 1971. By 1980, 300 large corporations are expected to control 75 percent of the world's total manufacturing output. Jan Tinbergen, coordinator, *Reshaping the International Order—A Report to the Club of Rome* (New York: E. P. Dutton & Co., 1976), pp. 23-24.

4. UNCTAD, *Transfer of Technology*, TD/190, December 31, 1975.

5. Between 1970-1974 the share of the developing countries was no more than three percent of the total incremental international liquidity provided from all sources. Jan Tinbergen, *op. cit.*, pp. 197-209.

6. In terms of the present debate on international economic issues, the Developed World basically comprises North America, the EEC, and Japan; the rest of the nonsocialist world in Latin America, Africa, and Asia are treated as part of the Third World. The socialist world, except Yugoslavia which considers itself a part of the Third World, keeps itself outside the stage of confrontation even though in the eyes of the majority of the developing countries, they are increasingly identified with the capitalist Developed World.

7. "The paramount objective of the anti-colonialist amalgam is the eradication of all the conditions and insignia of inequality and humiliation associated in the minds of the southern elites in the epoch of European domination. This objective guides southern positions across a broad spectrum of contemporary issues. . . anti-colonialism is an elite's [southern] deeply emotional response to a sense of humiliation." T. J. Farer, "The United States and the Third World: A Basis for Accommodation," *Foreign Affairs* 54 (1975), pp. 78-81.

8. The efforts at economic coordination and integration amongst the developed countries have been considerably facilitated by the coordination of political and security issues. The solidarity and the need for common action on the part of the developed capitalized countries received its greatest impetus on account of their confrontation with and perception of threat from the communist bloc, led by the Soviet Union, during the 1950s.

9. G. H. Jansen, *Non-Alignment and the Afro-Asian States* (New York: F. A. Praeger, 1966). "It is important that the developing countries should use their sovereignty and their independence at the political level as a lever for the attainment of their sovereignty and independence at the economic level. It is the economic issues in international negotiations that will now be the major concern of international politics." (*Economic Declaration*, Fifth Conference of Heads of State or Government of Non-Aligned Countries, Colombo, 1976.)

10. "The Group of 77 soon developed into a permanent instrument to systematically articulate the demands of the developing countries and to improve their negotiating capacity; its utility was cemented by the intransigence of the developed countries at the Geneva Conference." B. Gosovic, *UNCTAD: Conflict and Compromise* (Holland: A. W. Sigthoff-Leiden, 1972), p. 272.

11. "In this context, I submit it is somewhat naive for those engaged
    in world affairs to complain—as they often do with some indigna-
    tion—about how the representatives of the Third World have intro-
    duced 'politics' into the meetings of United Nations specialized
    agencies and the international fora. All such bodies are concerned
    with economic and social affairs. We will condemn negotiations to
    immobility if we go on expecting discussion to center only on
    technicalities." United Kingdom Ministry of Overseas Development,
    Challenges of the Rich-Poor Relationships, Overseas Development
    Paper no. 6 (Address to Congressional Group for Peace through
    Law, by F. Judd, Minister for Overseas Development, Washington,
    D. C., January 1977), p. 2.

12. D. L. Meadows *et al.*, *Limits to Growth* (Washington, D. C.:
    Potomac Associates, 1972); and M. Mesarovic and E. Pestal,
    Mankind at the Turning Point (London: Hutchinson, 1975).

13. The per capita production of minerals in the developed countries
    was 2.5 times the per capita production in the Third World, but the
    consumption of the developed countries was 16 times greater. The
    developed countries were obliged to import about half of their
    requirements, primarily from the Third World, whereas the latter
    consumed only one-quarter of their production and the centrally
    planned economies were virtually self-sufficient. (The United
    States and Canada imported only 25 percent of their requirements;
    Western Europe, 75 percent; and Japan, 94 percent. [J. Tinbergen,
    op. cit., p. 258.])

14. Military intervention might, in fact, further destabilize the supplies
    of raw materials or markets for exports by inflicting losses in the
    economies of the Third World and be counterproductive.

15. *UN Declaration and Action Program on the Establishment of a
    New International Economic Order*, UN General Assembly Resolu-
    tions 3201 (5-VI) and 3202 (5-VI), May 1, 1974. *Charter of
    Economic Rights and Duties of States*, United Nations General
    Assembly Resolution 3281, December 12, 1974.

16. Most of the oil-rich countries in the Middle East are in a category
    by themselves; they have barely emerged from a state of monarchy
    and feudalism. The only modern sector is the oil industry and its
    associated activities. The middle class, coming between the royal
    families and feudal estates, on the one hand, and the masses on the
    other, has yet to develop a significant strength of its own.

17. S. Webb and B. Webb described how in the eighteenth century
    "industrial society was still divided vertically trade by trade, in-
    stead of horizontally between employers and wage earners. This
    latter cleavage is what has transformed the trade unionism of the
    petty groups of skilled workmen into the modern trade union

movement." S. Webb and B. Webb, *The History of Trade Unionism* (London: Longmans, Green,1920), p. 6.

18. "It is to be expected that in the next two or three decades we will witness an intensified crisis in the developing world brought about by the twin impacts of demographic growth and the spread of education. Both will make global inequality even more intolerable at a time when equality is becoming the most powerful moral imperative of our time, thus paralleling the appeal of the concept of liberty during the nineteenth century." Z. Brzezinski, "U.S. Foreign Policy: Search for Focus," *Foreign Affairs* 51, no. 4 (July, 1973), p. 725. Also, G. Myrdal, "The Equality Issue in World Development," *Institute of International Economic Studies, Stockholm Reprint Series*, no. 47 (1975).

19. Paul Streeten, "It Is a Moral Issue," *Institute of Commonwealth Studies, Reprint Series*, no. 83E (*Crucible*, July/September, 1976).
   An additional aspect of the moral argument is that the developed countries owe reparation payments for their past colonial exploitation of the Third World. However, very few in the Developed World, especially among the ruling elite, feel any sense of guilt for the colonial exploitation of the Third World in the past. A number of developed countries did not have colonial empires in the past. Moreover, the present generations are unwilling to accept moral obligation to undo injustices perpetrated in the past by their forefathers.

20. The high percentage of the total primary imports originating from the Third World was due primarily to preponderance of the imports of fuel. For many tropical agricultural products, the developed regions are totally dependent on the Third World. This applies to such commodities as jute, sisal, copra, coconut oil, palm oil, coffee, cocoa, rubber, tea, and bananas; only in the case of sugar is dependence not very great and it varies from 17 percent to 54 percent. GATT, *International Trade 1973-76* (various annual issues); UNCTAD, *Handbook of International Trade and Development Statistics, 1973 and 1976.*

21. Uzi Arad, "National Resource Scarcity and Armed Conflict in 1980s," unpublished paper, Council of Foreign Relations, 1976; J. Tinbergen, *op. cit.*; and A. Edwards, *The Potential for New Commodity Cartel* (London: Economic Intelligence Unit, 1975).

22. J. Kay and J. Mirrless, "The Desirability of Natural Resource Depletion," in *The Economics of Natural Resource Depletion*, D. W. Pearce, ed. (New York: Macmillan, 1975), pp. 156-57.

23. Lester Brown, *World Without Borders* (New York: Random House, 1972), p. 194. The continuation of past trends leads to the following projections about the future of United States dependence:

"Of the thirteen basic industrial raw materials required by a modern economy, the U.S.A. was dependent on imports for more than one-half of its supplies of four of these in 1950, i.e., aluminum, manganese, nickel, and tin. By 1970, this list had increased to six, as zinc and chromium were added. Projections indicate that by 1985 the United States will depend on imports of more than one-half of its supplies of nine basic raw materials, as iron, lead, and tungsten are added. By the end of the century, it will be dependent primarily on foreign sources for its supply of each of the thirteen raw materials except phosphate."

24. There are many other commodities for which the developing countries control a share of internationally traded supplies comparable to the case of oil (i.e., more than 70 percent of world trade) but for most of them the value of trade is small so that the effort to control supplies, even if effective, would yield little benefit as compared to their organizational and administrative costs and effects. The fewer the number of countries which control supplies, the greater is the chance of success of collusive action. The number of the largest suppliers in the developing world, controlling 70 percent of the total trade of a few commodities which may be the likely candidates of cartel-type action, is given below.

Commodity	Number of Largest Suppliers
Coffee	10
Rubber	2
Cocoa	4
Tea	6
Tin	4
Bananas	9

Moreover, three developing countries control 56 percent of the world trade in bauxite; four countries control 48 percent of the world trade in copper; and two countries control 25 percent of the world trade in manganese. E. Stern and W. Tims, "The Relative Bargaining Strengths of Developing Countries," *The American Journal of Agricultural Economics* 57 (May, 1975), pp. 225-36.

25. The Trilateral Commission, *Seeking a New Accomodation in World Commodity Markets* (New York: The Trilateral Commission, 1976).

26. More important, the ability to sustain losses depends on the nature of the governments in the various countries. The ability of the governments to motivate the masses and to suffer sacrifices in the name of a national cause, however interpreted, varies widely amongst the different countries. An authoritarian regime is more

likely than a democratic government to be able to impose a cut-back in levels of living consequent on the disruption of supplies. The western capitalist democracies, which are subject to considerable popular pressure, may be particularly vulnerable to threats of disruption by the Third World in trade and investment flows.

27. R. J. Barnett and R. E. Muller, *Global Reach: The Power of Multinational Corporations* (London: John Kape, 1975), pp. 16, 123-47. Forty percent of the total profits of 298 multinational corporations in the United States is derived from their overseas operations. Thirty-two percent of the total foreign investment of all United States multinationals is located in the Third World. Applying the same percentage to the profits, it would appear that about twelve percent of the total profits of these corporations is derived from the Third World.

28. "It is in the sphere of human environment that the interdependencies between nations are perhaps most clearly evident. Third World countries acknowledge that, far from being an exclusive problem of the industrialized world, environmental degradation and overtaxing of nature are very much a part of their own predicament. The industrialized countries are increasingly recognizing that patterns of resources use and maldistribution are an important aspect of the environmental crisis. Both sides subscribe to the concept of spaceship earth. The sad fact is that very few practical steps have yet been taken to translate the implied awareness with a genuine blueprint for ecological survival." J. Tinbergen, *op cit.*, p. 33.

29. "By the end of the decade there are expected to be 500 reactors operating in 52 countries. Any country with reprocessing facilities for spent nuclear fuel is capable of producing nuclear weapons." J. Tinbergen, *op. cit.*, p. 25.

30. "Is it unrealistic to imagine a small group of MIT-trained sons and daughters of Indian, Japanese and American middle-class parents threatening to detonate a crude plutonium bomb in Boston unless American aid to Asia is immediately increased? Rather than the pacific image of a global village, the growth of transnational communication in a world of enormous inequality may merely bring in the Patty Hearst case with a global dimension." J. S. Nye, Jr., "Independence and Interdependence," *Foreign Policy*, no. 22 (Spring, 1976), p. 142.

31. J. Corbett and R. Garnaut, *Japan and Resource-Rich Developing Countries* (Canberra: Australian National University, 1976); and U. S. Council on International Economic Policy, Office of the President, *Special Report: Critical Imported Materials* (Washington, D. C.: December, 1974), pp. 5, 45, 46.

32. Recent negotiations on North-South issues have underlined the

attempts of the developed countries to unite in their response to the Third World demands. For example, the EEC tends to act as a bloc and seeks to coordinate its policies vis-à-vis the Third World with the United States and Japan within the framework of the OECD as well as by means of summit meetings of the big industrialized nations.

33. W. Diebold, "The Communist Countries in the World Economy of the 1980s," unpublished, Council of Foreign Relations, Inc., New York, 1976.

34. R. D. Hansen, "The Political Economy of North-South Relations: How Much Change?" *International Organization* 29, no. 4 (Summer, 1974), pp. 921-43.

35. R. S. McNamara, President, World Bank Group, *Address to the Board of Governors*, delivered at Manila, Philippines, October 4, 1974, p. 3.

36. W. R. Bohning, "Migration from Developing to High Income Countries," in *Tripartite World Conference on Employment, Income Distribution and Social Progress and Their International Division of Labour* (Geneva: International Labor Office, 1976), pp. 119-138.

37. Suggestions have already been made that Iran, Brazil, and Mexico should be invited to join the OECD and Saudi Arabia should be invited to meetings of the Group of 10, which makes major decisions on world monetary policy, because Saudi Arabia is one of the largest holders of foreign exchange reserves. The Trilateral Commission, *The Reform of International Institutions* (New York: The Trilateral Commission, 1976).

38. R. D. Hansen, "Major U. S. Options on North-South Relations: A Letter to President Carter," in *The U.S. and World Development: An Agenda for Action* (Washington, D.C.: Overseas Development Council, 1977), chapter II.

CHAPTER 8, pp. 198-240

1. Due to space limitations this chapter represents a significantly abridged version of the original colloquium paper. Certain points in sections four and five draw heavily on two earlier articles by the author, "Le Nouveau Syndicat du Tiers Mond," *Le Monde Diplomatique* (June, 1975); and "Economic Cooperation among Third World Countries," *International Development Review* 18 (1976), pp. 2-5.

The views expressed in this paper should not be attributed to the

United Nations Institute for Economic Development and Planning.
2. Keith Griffin, *The Green Revolution: An Economic Analysis* (Geneva: United Nations Research Institute for Social Development, 1972), pp. 56, 69, 70.

CHAPTER 9, pp. 243-274

1. I am grateful to Carolyn Cooper, Carlos Diaz-Alejandro, Roger Hansen, Ann Hollick, and Joseph S. Nye, Jr., for helpful comments.
2. E.g., Dennis Goulet, "World Interdependence: Verbal Smokescreen or New Ethic?" ODC Development Paper no. 21, March, 1976.
3. All intentional comparisons of per capita income must however be taken with extreme caution, since they are highly sensitive to the choice of exchange rate for conversion into common units, and they do not allow for substantial variation in the domestic purchasing power of a "dollar" or other standard unit of measurement. Standards of living among countries do not vary among countries as much as "per capita income" does.
4. Algeria is a member of OPEC. It has been suggested that calls for a new international economic order represented a tactic to divert the attention of those developing countries that do not produce oil away from the great hardships imposed on them by the sharp increase in oil prices. Responsibility for redressing the situation was thereby passed from the OPEC countries to the western countries. The OPEC price increases may have given greater impetus to the calls for action, but they were in train before the late-1973 price increases.
5. U.S. Department of State, *The United States and the Third World* (Washington, D.C.: Government Printing Office, July, 1976).
6. Note that in the list of particular proposals above, the first four clearly involve transfers of resources between nations, and the next three implicity do.
7. In *A Theory of Justice* (Cambridge, Massachusetts: Harvard University Press, 1972), Rawls argues that each community should choose that mode of organizing its affairs—including taxation and government expenditure—so as to leave the worst-off member of society in the best position that is possible. How much *re*distribution this would require is an *empirical* question that depends inter alia on techniques of production and the behavioral responses of productive members of the society to material rewards. Substantial disparities of income may be quite consistent with Rawls's view of justice. For three devastating critiques of Rawls's theory from three quite different perspectives, see Kenneth Arrow, "Some Ordinalist-Utilitarian Notes on Rawls' Theory of Justice," *Journal of Philos-*

ophy LXX (May 10, 1973), pp. 245-263; Allan Bloom, "Justice: John Rawls vs. the Tradition of Political Philosophy," *American Political Science Review* LXIX (June, 1975), pp. 648-662; and Robert Nozick, *Anarchy, State, and Utopia* (New York: Basic Books, 1974), chapter 7.

8. Daniel Patrick Moynihan, "The United States in Opposition," *Commentary* (March, 1974).

9. Robert W. Tucker, "Egalitarianism and International Politics," *Commentary* 60, no. 3 (September, 1975), pp. 27-40.

10. Moynihan's experience as United States Ambassador to India may have led him to overgeneralize; however, Fabian influence is much less pronounced in Latin America. It is noteworthy that the social minima called for by Sidney Webb, one of the original Fabians, involved subsistence, health, education, and *leisure*. This contrasts interestingly with the current emphasis on nutrition, health, education, and employment. In Edwardian England, long hours rather than shortage of work was seen to be the problem. On this point, see Sidney Webb, *Labor and the New Social Order* (London: The Labour Party, 1918).

11. Two recent indications of this effect can be mentioned. As a presidential candidate Jimmy Carter suggested in early 1974 that Americans were tired of taxing the poor of the rich countries in order to support the rich of the poor countries. And Clifton Wharton, former president of the Agricultural Development Council and long an advocate (with respect to foreign aid programs) of noninterference in the affairs of recipient nations, recently asked whether, with respect to food policy, we must not confront directly the political positions and policies of other nations.

12. For example, the neoclassical theory of trade suggests that in a country with a large population and few natural resources the relatively unskilled members of the labor force should benefit strongly from a policy of free trade. As a trickle-down approach to benefiting the poorest members of such countries, free trade may be far more potent than unrestricted transfers to governments. Of course, the two approaches—and others—are not necessarily mutually exclusive.

13. Like Lewis Carroll's Humpty Dumpty, we are, of course, free to define words the way we choose. Marx defined "exploitation" as the excess, if any, of market value over labor value embodied in a good. On this standard, virtually all economic transactions involve exploitation, and in particular the seller of foodstuffs or raw materials is always engaging in exploitation. The difficulty with this definition is twofold: it uses a word that has pejorative connotations to describe a universal phenomenon, and it fails to make

distinctions among different types of "exploitation" so defined that may be crucial in dealing with the question of rectification.

14. K. G. Davies, *The Royal African Company* (New York: Longmans, Green, 1957); D. P. Mannix with M. Cowley, *Black Cargoes* (New York: Viking, 1962); P. D. Curtin, *The Atlantic Slave Trade* (Madison: University of Wisconsin Press, 1969).

15. Over protest, the young United States paid Algiers $624,500 in 1796 to ransom over one hundred American seamen that had been captured in the open Atlantic in what was a clearly predatory manner. At a compound rate of interest of six percent, which is what the United States had to pay on foreign loans at that time—including one to help pay the ransom—that sum would amount to $23 billion in 1976. At the lower rate of three percent that prevailed through much of the nineteenth century, the potential claim would still be $131 million in 1976, or about $1.2 billion if it were adjusted from 1796 to 1976 dollars. On the early history of United States relations with the Barbary States, see Ray W. Irwin, *The Diplomatic Relations of the United States with the Barbary Powers, 1796-1816* (Chapel Hill: University of North Carolina Press, 1931), especially p. 72.

16. To underline the seriousness with which he took his mission, Perry returned early the next year for a response, this time with eight ships. See W. G. Beasely, *The Modern History of Japan* (New York: Praeger, 1966).

17. Pierre Antoine, "Qui est coupable? *Revue de l'action populaire* (November, 1959); also quoted in Goulet, *op. cit.*

18. The quotation from Antoine refers to competition for the earth's scarce goods, and the argument is frequently heard that the developed countries are using up the low-cost sources of raw materials around the world, thereby making development more difficult for the latecomers. Whatever the merits of this argument for the future, it cannot provide the basis for rectification payments to the extent that technology in the past has reduced costs at least as rapidly as the "natural" resource has deteriorated in availability. Whales are much scarcer now than 100 years ago, partly because improved technology has made them easier to catch. Available copper ores are lower in quality than they were 100 years ago, but, due to technological advance, copper costs less to produce today, relative to other goods. Indeed, most "resources" are not resources at all until the technology is available to extract and/or make use of them. Both petroleum and bauxite were economically worthless before crucial technological advances in the mid-nineteenth century.

19. James C. Scott, *Comparative Political Corruption* (Englewood

Cliffs, New Jersey: Prentice-Hall, 1972), p. 67.

20. Jan Tinbergen, "A New International Order," *NATO Review* (December, 1975), p. 9.

21. See, e.g., Nathaniel H. Leff, "The New Economic Order—Bad Economics, Worse Politics," *Foreign Policy*, no. 24 (Fall, 1976), pp. 202-215; and H. G. Johnson, "Commodities: Less Developed Countries' Demands and Developed Countries' Response," in J. Bhagwati, ed., *Proposals for a New International Economic Order* (Cambridge: The Massachusetts Institute of Technology Press, 1977).

22. These proposals arise in the context of North-South discussions. In addition, some proposals aim at creating security stocks, e.g., of oil or copper, by the industrialized consuming nations against the possibility of future embargo by less developed primary producing countries.

23. It is noteworthy, however, that in the early Sixties the United States supported the International Coffee Agreement, one purpose of which was to raise coffee prices.

24. For a critique of the European scheme—the Japanese one was similar in concept—see Richard N. Cooper, "The European Community's System of Generalized Tariff Preferences: A Critique," *Journal of Development Studies* 8, no. 4 (July, 1972), pp. 379-94. Both schemes were based on tariff quotas set in such a way that a successful developing country would soon pay the full tariff. But that prospect in turn would undermine any encouragement to investment in developing countries to take advantage of the preferences.

25. SDRs are a form of man-made international money to be used for financial settlements between central banks. They were journalistically labeled "paper gold" when they first came out, and that is more descriptive than their proper name, since they were designed to play the same role in international settlement as monetary gold played in the period 1935-1965. About $11 billion in SDRs were created and distributed during 1970-1972.

26. The same is true with respect to individuals, as the unsuccessful struggle over the "negative income tax" testifies. These proposals would have entitled individuals to grants that depended only on income and a few other factors, such as family size, and they would have replaced the current complicated system of welfare payments, which in principle involve a variety of conditions on the behavior of the welfare recipient, including periodic investigations by welfare workers. But American concern with "free riders" has so far proved too great to permit substitution of the simpler system for the more complex—and demeaning—system of welfare. Some

western countries, however, impose fewer conditions on their recipients of welfare.

27. See Richard N. Cooper, "An Economist's View of the Oceans," *Journal of World Trade Law* 9, no.4 (July, 1975), pp. 356-377. Potential revenues are estimated at over $2 billion a year at today's levels of harvest from the oceans.

CHAPTER 10, pp. 275-304

1. Professor Green wishes to thank Ken Laidlaw and Roy Laishley of the World Development Movement who assisted with the research for this paper, and inter alia Hans Singer, Oswaldo Sunkel, Enrique Oteiza, Richard Jolly, Guy Erb, William Cline, Louis Emmerij, Dharam Ghai, Juan Somavia and the participants in the February 1977 Rothko Chapel Colloquium for their comments on earlier versions of this paper and predecessors to some of its sections.

   Analysis of issues as complex and value laden as structural change in the international economic order cannot but be influenced by the values of the analyst. It is, therefore, desirable that these be made fairly explicit to avoid the need for detective work and the danger of misperception by readers. The present analyst views the present international economic order as structurally unjust and considers radical change as a necessary condition for new national economic orders in a majority of states. He also views building more symmetrical and balanced (including South-South) political economic relations as critical to achieving structural change. He is committed to a basic human needs-oriented, rather than a growth- and modernization-oriented process of development (in industrial as well as Third World countries), on libertarian as well as egalitarian grounds. He tends to view issues of international economic order primarily from a periphery not a center perspective. Yet, he believes that there are both substantial common interests in structural change for workers and consumers in the central and peripheral states as well as significant areas of conflicts of interest especially in respect to early transitional stages.

2. Kermit Gordon, "Foreword," in *World Politics and International Economies,* ed. C. F. Bergsten and L. B. Krause (Washington, D.C.: The Brookings Institution, 1975), p. vii.

3. Zbigniew Brzezinski, "Specter of an Isolated US in a Hostile World," *Foreign Policy* (1975), excerpted from *International Herald Tribune,* January 3, 1977.

4. Cf., e.g., C. A. Udry, "A New Economic Order?" *Imprecor,* no.

61/62 (November 11, 1976), p. 40 ff.
5. E.g., early (1973-74) Kissinger speeches and assurances that the old order had served mankind well.
6. E.g., "contingency planning" to seize physical control of Middle East oil or, more precisely, the leaking of such "planning."
7. E.g., J. Tinbergen, *RIO: Reshaping the International Order* (New York: Dutton, 1976).   (Report to the Club of Rome-RIO Project)
8. E.g., the United Kingdom's post-September, 1975 retreat from initiatives taken at and following Kingston Commonwealth Heads of State Conference.
9. E.g., confrontation at United Nations Sixth Special Session, conciliation at Seventh Special Session, disorder at UNCTAD Nairobi. (For fuller discussion see following section on crisis management.)
10. Those analysts supporting conspiratorial or far-Left Trotskyite Marxist positions would disagree.
11. The intent is not to suggest a grand conspiratorial design—certainly not a collusion to raise oil prices. However, industrial economy re-export of oil price increases (the 1973-76 variant of 1930s "exporting unemployment") and amassing petrodollars pursued as defensive policies have radically worsened poor country external balance positions while building in more inflation (and thus more unemployment) in the industrial economies.
12. The term "Cooperation against Poverty" is taken from a 1970 Tanzania paper for the 1971 (Lusaka) Non-Aligned Summit and "Trade Union of the Poor" from President J. K. Nyerere's September 1974, Georgetown (Guyana) speech.
13. United Nations, *Charter of Economic Rights and Duties of States* (OPI/542-75-38308), February, 1975; also United Nations *Monthly Chronicle*.
14. United Nations, *Toward a New Trade Policy for Development* (1964).
15. Cf., e.g., Dag Hammarskjold Foundation, *What Now? Another Development* (Uppsala, 1975); and H. W. Singer and R. H. Green, "Toward a Rational and Equitable New International Economic Order: A Case for Negotiated Structural Changes," *World Development* 3 (June, 1975), pp. 427-444.
16. Kissinger affirmed this view at the Sixth Special Session. Jan Pronk of the Netherlands has specifically criticized it in several speeches, inter alia that to December 1976 Society for International Development World Congress in Amsterdam.
17. "Declaration of Lima," UNIDO 1975 Conference Final Declaration.
18. Cf., e.g., *Charter of Economic Rights and Duties of States, op. cit.*
19. In a basically capitalist world, socialist states have little option but

to arrange trade with capitalist states on capitalist principles. At least in most cases the Soviet Union takes the same operational stance with developing economies. The addition of aid and arms in selected cases only broadens the similarity. Institutions are different—socialist state corporations do not normally use physical asset ownership overseas as a way to control activity and amass surplus (an approach putting them in the vanguard of a TNC trend to sell knowledge and control trade, with the "host" owning the physical assets and borrowing abroad to do so). The Soviet Union, needless to say, does not accept this interpretation; capitalist industrial economy radical analysts are divided on it.

20. Cf., e.g., Udry, *op. cit.*; C. Barker, M. Bhagavan, P. von Mitschke-Collande, and D. Wield, *Industrial Production and Transfer of Technology*, mimeographed (University of Dar es Salaam, Institute of Development Studies, 1976).

21. The western "new Left" does so denounce it; e.g., *ibid.*

22. The confusion and alarm in July-September, 1973 (not January, 1975) was clear in dealing with major oil company executives. That the oil companies had indeed planned price increases is fairly convincingly demonstrable, but OPEC preempted that action and in a form different from company planning.

23. Technically the difficulties of seizing the oil fields in working order—and keeping them in working order—are immense. Politically the price (in the North as well as the South) would be very high with an unpredictable ceiling. That United States contingency plans for such action existed and were allowed to leak to cause uncertainty is likely; that their implementation was actually seriously canvassed is less so.

24. This form of the debate and its use in the North-South relation context is presumably not what the authors of *Limits to Growth*, Meadows and Forrester (New York: E. P. Dutton and Sons, 1973) or its sponsors (the Club of Rome) intended. In the form used in North-South debate, the "limits" model is not technically sound unless one assumes NIEO requires near absolute equality of national GDP per capita at present North levels by the year 2000.

25. Indeed the differences underlay the rather odd combination of threats and vague promises far in excess of actual (or probably any intended) action and of dogged inaction rather than even step-by-step negotiation.

26. Brookings and the Overseas Development Council in the United States and the Institute of Development Studies in the United Kingdom were far more negotiation-oriented than the majority of dominant decision makers. The Dag Hammarskjold Foundation network in Sweden was more initiative-oriented (at that point)

than the future "like-minded" country group's decision makers.

27. Bauxite producers meanwhile had organized a modestly effective association, the copper producers' Intergovernmental Committee of Copper Exporting Countries (CIPEC) had shown itself at most marginal, and the initial banana-exporting country union efforts had been smashed (and/or literally bought off) by the relevant TNCs.

28. Subsequent studies—e.g., J. Behrman, *International Commodity Agreements,* Overseas Development Council, NIEO Series (New York: 1977); and R. H. Green, *The Common Fund: Prolegomena to Cost/Benefit Estimates,* Vienna Institute for Development, Occasional Paper 77/3—suggest that the buffer-stock stabilization proposals were a positive-sum game and one which would divide the gains in a manner giving both First and Third Worlds (but especially First) net advantages.

29. EEC member state support also weakened for internal reasons including the shift in United Kingdom stance.

30. See ILO, *Employment, Growth and Basic Needs,* World Employment Conference basic paper (Geneva, 1976), chapters 5 and 7.

31. Several ILO studies on increasing LDC exports (e.g., Luttrell and Herman) appear to postulate a factor intensity determined world production order of a rather rigid kind and without serious reference to surplus allocation and decision-making power issues, but this was not typical of the total World Employment Programme.

32. Over 1972-74 the commodity price explosion dominated the inflation/money supply/payments evolution which destroyed the Heath-Barber economic policy.

33. Commonwealth Expert Group, *Towards a New International Economic Order* (London: Commonwealth Secretariat, 1975).

34. The official United Kingdom position is that there has been no change. However, this is widely doubted by political as well as analytical observers. Cf., "British Responses to Proposals by Developing Countries Concerning an Integrated Commodity Programme and Common Fund," testimony to House of Commons Select Committee on Overseas Development by A. R. Jolly, H. W. Singer, R. H. Green, January 1977; and more important, the March 1977 *Report* of the Select Committee.

35. Cf., e.g., speech by CIEC (Paris Talks) Co-Chairman Perez Guerero to Society for International Development Fifteenth World Congress, December 1976.

36. J. Tinbergen, *op. cit.*; in addition there is the complementary 1976 Leontieff Report to United Nations, W. Leontieff, et al., *The Future of the World Economy: A United Nations Study* (New York: Oxford University Press, 1977).

37. There are clear ironies here. The United States had banned or

limited access to its food supplies, the United Kingdom was acting to block foreign government access to records of its TNCs, but also mounting an assault on Hoffmann-La Roche on grounds echoing South critics of TNCs.

38. Cf., divergences on this issue in *What Now, op. cit.*, and J. Tinbergen, RIO Report, *op. cit.*

39. E.g., the IMF's five percent share in 1945-75 liquidity creation and marginal weight vis-à-vis either the Group of 10 or the United States decisions leading to the Smithsonian meeting.

40. The last-minute attempts to wind up with a small gain giving way to last-second moves to wind down without a blowup can be traced in the successive *Financial Times* articles of May 30-June 6, 1977; most of the Final Communiqué and the "supporting" statements of the 7 and 19 (North and South) appear in June 6, 1977, *International Herald Tribune.*

41. E.g., attempts to renew the Multi-Fiber Textile Agreement broke down in July, 1977. EEC states—especially France—saw import restrictions amounting to freezes or rollbacks as a way to patch up their admittedly ailing textile industries. A United States attempt to provide a middle way by a technically new convention would, in effect, allow EEC to impose restrictions bilaterally with each Third World exporter.

42. The April 1977 United States-United Kingdom-Federal Germany-Japan-France-Italy-Canada-EEC Heads of Government meeting on world economics held in London.

43. The final documents in fact consist largely of annexes on earlier positions and points of disagreement plus a statement of regret over the failure to reach serious NIEO agreement by the Third World side.

44. This view is not unsound if it is centered on the need to distribute (limited) concessional resources to those least able to meet the external costs of debt service. General debt cancellation would not meet that test and could hinder use of commercial borrowing by those for whom that is an effective source.

45. Cf., speeches to Nairobi UNCTAD (UNCTAD, *Proceedings,* in preparation). For a summary see "Commodities in Nairobi" by D. Avramovic (Chief Technical Architect of UNCTAD Formulation of Common Fund) in *The New International Economic Order, Commodity Markets and the Common Fund* (forthcoming).

46. Note the "Statements of Reservation" by the first three (in which the United Kingdom reportedly almost joined) and the opposite "Statement of Inadequacy" of the Group of 16.

47. Cf., (from the minority side) "Memorandum of the Netherlands Government on the Development Policy of the EEC," *Information* (September, 1976), p. 1 ff.; "The New International Economic

Order," talk to Oslo Workers Society, Prime Minister Nordli, November, 1976.

48. Prophecies of breakdown in the short run may again prove too facile. The collapse of negotiation can come "not with a bang but with a whimper."

49. This is a perfectly rational pattern. Even for an individual operating other than as an inspired prophet some shifts in emphasis from context to context are inevitable quite apart from the possibility of changing views from dialogue or analysis of new data and concepts.

50. Perhaps this is too charitable a reading intellectually and too harsh a criticism ethically.

51. E.g., J. Galtung, "Alternative Life Styles in Rich Countries," *Development Dialogue* (1976), p. 83 ff.; *New Internationalist, passim*, various issues.

52. Cf., Singer and Green, *op. cit.*

53. Cf., U. S. National Commission on Supplies and Shortages, *Report*, 1977. The United States stance has since changed; cf., Secretary of Agriculture Bergland's speech to World Food Council meeting in June, 1977.

54. As an occasional tactic a victory by nitpicking to death to avoid confrontation may be useful; as a strategy it is likely to be counterproductive because it leads to challenge to the bona fides of all detailed criticisms.

55. This image is a cause for concern to a number of British politicians who accept that there has been a change in perception even if they are less agreed on its causes.

56. E.g., Testimony of "Ad Hoc Group on a United States Policy toward the United Nations" (inter alia R. Gardner, N. Cousins, C. Maynes) to Senate Foreign Relations Committee, April 1976.

57. S. Okita and W. D. Hopper speeches at Society for International Development Congress.

58. Cf., e.g., R. McKinnon, *Money and Capital in Economic Development* (Washington, D.C.: The Brookings Institution, 1973), especially p. 170 ff.

59. Johnson's stance flowed not from trust to TNCs but from distrust of government and intergovernmental body capacity and competence; cf., e.g., "Higher Oil Prices and the International Monetary System," in T. Rybezynski, *The Economies of the Oil Crisis* (London: Macmillan, 1976).

60. For a broad analysis of the concept, see W. Ryan, *Blame the Victim* (London: Orbach and Chambers, 1971); for an application to the North-South context see J. Lissner, "The Politics of Charity," *New Internationalist*, no. 45 (November, 1976), p. 12 ff.

61. Cf., Brzezinski, *op. cit.*; for a comprehensive analytical perspective from a broadly Trilateralist viewpoint, see Bergsten and Krause, *op. cit.*; for a critical review of the commission, see D. Johnstone, "Une Strategie 'Trilaterale,'" *Monde Diplomatique*, no. 272-23 (November, 1976), pp. 1, 13-17.

62. French proposals—with some reason—are often cited as examples as is Edward Heath's 1972 address to the Santiago UNCTAD.

63. Individuals may appear in more than one; e.g., the author in some contexts is in the first, and in others (like this chapter, or in Singer and Green, *op. cit.*) in the third.

64. Cf., e.g., J. Galtung, "Appraisal" in *Report of a Symposium on a New International Economic Order* (The Hague: Institute of Social Studies, 1975).

65. Cf., e.g., R. Barnett and R. Muller, *Global Reach* (New York: Simon and Schuster, 1974). For a discussion of the same issue organized to avoid the trap, cf., F. Bienefeld and M. Godfrey, "Labour and the Export of Jobs," *IDS Bulletin* 8, no. 3 (1977), p. 33 ff.

66. Cf., Swedish response to "How Much is Enough? Another Sweden," in *What Now*, presented in S. Lindholm, "'Another Sweden,' How the Swedish Press Reacted," *Development Dialogue*, no. 1 (1976), p. 68 ff.

67. See e.g., *Self-Reliance and Solidarity in the Quest for International Justice*, Report of a Consultation, Ecumenical Institute (of WCC) (Celigny, 1976); and the July 1977 Central Committee decisions in respect to a TNC-focused program.

68. Cf., e.g., *What Now, op. cit.*; Singer and Green, *op. cit.*

69. See e.g., UNCTAD, *Long-Term Problems of the World Economy and Their Implications for the Developing Countries*, Seminar Report Series 1, November, 1976, pp. 6-8.

70. Cf., e.g., Cooper, chapter 9, this volume.

71. This approach was used in the IMF's Morse Committee on International Monetary System Reform which had ten capitalist industrial and nine Third World members plus Australia. The technique worked and has been continued in the World Bank-IMF Interim Committee; the Committee's report was swept away in the 1973-74 financial order crisis.

72. Thorvald Stoltenberg, "The Demands of the Developing Countries as Seen by Norway," Quaker International Conference, Ivoire, September, 1976 (Oslo: Peace Research Institute), p. 20.

73. *Ibid.*, pp. 14-16, 35.

INDEX

ABOUT THE CONTRIBUTORS

HAROLD BROOKFIELD is professor of geography and chairman of the Geography Department at the University of Melbourne. He has done research on Southern Africa, Mauritius, Papua New Guinea, the Caribbean, Fiji, and Mexico. His publications include *Pacific Market Places: A Collection of Essays*, edited by H. Brookfield (Australian National University Press, 1969); *The Pacific in Transition* (London: Arnold, 1973); and *Independent Development* (University of Pittsburgh Press, 1975).

RICHARD N. COOPER is currently under secretary of state for economic affairs of the United States. He is on leave from Yale University where he holds the Frank Altschul Chair in International Economics. His recent publications include: *A Reordered World: Emerging International Economic Problems* (editor and contributor) (Potomac Associates, 1973); "Towards a Renovated International Monetary System" (with Motoo Kaji and Claudio Segre), *The Triangle Papers*, no. 1 (1973); and *Economic Mobility and National Economic Policy* (Almquist and Wicksell, 1974).

FERNANDO HENRIQUE CARDOSO is director of the Department of Sociology at the Brazilian Center for Analysis and Planning (CEBRAP). He has published widely on development-related themes, many pertinent to growth struggles in Latin America. Professor Cardoso's publications include *Dependencia y Desarrollo en America Latina* (Dependency and Development in Latin America) with E. Faletto (Siglo XXI, Mexico, 1969); *Politics y Desarrollo en Paises Dependentes* (Politics and Development in Dependent Countries) (Siglo XXI, Mexico, 1971); and *O Modelo Politico Brasileiro* (Brazilian Political Model) (Sao Paulo: DIFEL, 1972).

REGINALD HERBOLD GREEN is a fellow at the Institute of Development Studies, University of Sussex. Much of his published research reflects an interest in African economic development. His more recent publications include *Toward Ujamaa and Kujitegemea: Income Distribution and Absolute Poverty Eradication Aspects Tanzania Transition to Socialism* (IDS, 1974); "Political Independence and the National Economy," in *African Perspectives* (Cambridge, 1975); and *Productive Employment in Africa: An Overview of the Problem* (IDS, 1975).

ALBERT O. HIRSCHMAN is professor of the School of Social Science at the Institute for Advanced Study, Princeton, New Jersey. Many of his writings address the process of economic development in Latin America. Among his publications are *Studies of Economic Policy Making in Latin America* (New Haven: Yale University Press, 1971); and *Latin American Issues,* editor and co-author (Twentieth Century Fund, 1961).

NURUL ISLAM is presently assistant director-general of the Economic and Social Policy Department of the Food and Agriculture Organization of the United Nations (FAO). He has written on a number of development topics, many concerning the economic growth of Bangladesh. Some of his most recent publications are "North-South Economic Cooperation," *Growth and Change* (The Hague: Institute of Social Studies, 1976), *Development Planning in Bangladesh: A Study in Political Economy* (London: C. Hurst and Company, 1977), and *Development Strategy of Bangladesh* (Oxford: Pergamon Press, forthcoming).

FAWZY MANSOUR is coordinator of research at the U. N. African Institute for Economic Development and Planning (IDEP), Dakar, Senegal. He has a background in law as well as in economic development.

Among his most recent books are *International Economic Relations* (in Arabic), *Principles of Political Economy for Developing Countries* (in Arabic), and *The Theory of Price* (in Arabic).

BAGICHA SINGH MINHAS is a development research consultant at the International Bank for Reconstruction and Development. He is on leave from the Indian Statistical Institute, where he holds a position as research professor. Professor Minhas's published writings largely reflect his experience with economic growth and development in India. His most recent books include *An International Comparison of Factor Costs and Factor Use* (North Holland Publishing Company, 1963); *Fourth Plan: Objectives and Policy Frame* (Vara and Company, 1969); and *Planning and the Poor* (S. Chand and Company, 1974).

GORAN OHLIN is executive secretary of the Brandt Commission, the Independent Commission on International Development Issues in Geneva, Switzerland. He taught previously at Uppsala University and has served on the staff of the International Bank for Reconstruction and Development.

DUDLEY SEERS is director of the Institute of Development Studies at the University of Sussex in Falmer, England. He has published widely on subjects basic to economic development. Some of his better known publications are "Why Visiting Economists Fail," *Journal of Political Economy* (1962); "A Theory of Inflation and Growth," *Oxford Economic Papers* (1962); and *Crisis in Planning* (University of Sussex Press, 1972), ed. with Michael Faber.

PAUL STREETEN, presently on leave at the World Bank, is warden of Queen Elizabeth House and director of the Institute for Commonwealth Studies at Oxford University. Professor Streeten's published writings span a wide range of development related topics. His most recent books include *The Frontiers of Development*, and *Transnational Corporations and Developing Countries* (MacMillan, 1976).

The late BILL WARREN was lecturer in Economics at the School of Oriental and African Studies, University of London. His writings include "Biafra—Les Causes de la Guerre," *Les Temps Modernes* (February, 1970); "The State and Capitalist Planning," *New Left Review*, no. 72 (1972), and "Imperialism and Capitalist Industrialization," *New Left Review*, no. 81 (1973).

DATE DUE